D1180192

THE LITERARY HISTORY OF THE AMERICAN REVOLUTION 1763-1783

MOSES COIT TYLER

VOLUME II
1776-1783

REDERICK UNGAR PUBLISHING CO.
NEW YORK

TO

JEANNETTE GILBERT TYLER

THIS BOOK

IS

LOVINGLY DEDICATED

BY

HER HUSBAND

New Printing 1957

Library of Congress Catalog Card Number 57-6634

Printed in the United States of America

Second Printing 1963

in the American Classics series

PREFACE.

FOR the two volumes composing the present work, the most natural point of separation has seemed to be the year 1776,—a fact properly enough recorded in the secondary dates placed on the title-page of each. Thus, the chief aim of the first volume is to trace the development of political discontent in the Anglo-American colonies from about the year 1763 until the year when that discontent culminated in the resolve for American Independence; while the chief aim of the second volume is to trace the development of the Revolutionary struggle under the altered conditions produced by this change in its object and in its character, and to go on with the tale until the year when American Independence was formally acknowledged by the British government.

Such, then, being the broad distinction between the two volumes, I have carefully adhered to it in the presentation of the great features needful to the consecutive story which I had to tell. Nevertheless, though the most of my materials have adjusted themselves readily to this scheme of historic bisection, the same is not the case with them all; and it has not surprised me to find that in the treatment of a few great topics, I needed to give myself larger room and freer movement than would be possible under a rigorous conformity to the time-limits imposed by my general plan. Of course, the differentiation by dates between the first volume and the second, was intended merely for convenience; and whenever a subject could be presented more justly by being presented continuously and without any break in its connection with the Revolution, I have not hesitated to present it in that way. Accordingly, in the first volume, which really ends with 1776, I have permitted myself occasionally to move forward into the years following; even as in the second volume, which really begins with 1776, I have permitted myself still more frequently to move back into the years preceding, in order to gather up at once and to have before us in a single view all the parts of any subject which may so belong to the entire period of the Revolution as to refuse to be cut in two by a mere date in the middle of it.

M. C. T.

CORNELL UNIVERSITY,
19 July, 1897.

CONTENTS.

THE SECOND VOLUME: 1776–1783.

CHAPTER XXIV.

SAMUEL ADAMS AND WILLIAM LIVINGSTON: THEIR LITERARY SERVICES TO THE REVOLUTION.

CHAPTER XXV.

JOHN DICKINSON AS PENMAN OF THE AMERICAN REVOLUTION.

CHAPTER XXVI.

THOMAS PAINE AS LITERARY FREELANCE IN THE WAR FOR INDEPENDENCE: 1776–1783.

CHAPTER XXVII.

THE LITERARY WARFARE AGAINST AMERICAN INDEPENDENCE: LOYALIST WRITERS IN PROSE AND VERSE: 1776–1783.

CHAPTER XXVIII.

THE LITERARY WARFARE OF THE LOYALISTS AGAINST INDEPENDENCE: JOSEPH STANSBURY, TORY SONG-WRITER AND SATIRIST.

CHAPTER XXIX.

THE LITERARY WARFARE OF THE LOYALISTS AGAINST AMERICAN INDEPENDENCE: JONATHAN ODELL, THEIR CHIEF SATIRIST.

CHAPTER XXX.

FRANCIS HOPKINSON AS HUMOROUS CHAMPION OF AMERICAN INDEPENDENCE: 1776–1781.

CHAPTER XXXI.

SATIRES, SONGS, AND BALLADS FOR AMERICAN INDEPENDENCE.

CHAPTER XXXII.

THE DRAMATIC LITERATURE OF THE REVOLUTION.

CHAPTER XXXIII.

PRISON LITERATURE.

CHAPTER XXXIV.

PHILIP FRENEAU AS POET AND SATIRIST IN THE WAR FOR INDEPENDENCE: 1778–1783.

CHAPTER XXXV.

PULPIT-CHAMPIONS OF THE AMERICAN REVOLUTION.

CHAPTER XXXVI.

THREE ACADEMIC PREACHERS AND PUBLICISTS.

CHAPTER XXXVII.

TWO APOSTLES OF QUIETNESS AND GOODWILL: JOHN WOOLMAN AND ST. JOHN CREVECŒUR.

PAGE

CHAPTER XXXVIII.

FRANKLIN IN THE LITERATURE OF THE REVOLUTION.

CHAPTER XXXIX.

THE WRITERS OF HISTORY.

CHAPTER XXIV.

SAMUEL ADAMS AND WILLIAM LIVINGSTON: THEIR LITERARY SERVICES TO THE REVOLUTION.

I.—The decline of the reputation of Samuel Adams since the Revolution—His literary work always for a practical end—Greatness of his influence as a writer during the Revolution.

II.—Adams's early career—His early absorption in the politics of his town and colony—His chief function that of opposition—The great variety of public business in which he was employed—In 1765 becomes the real director of the policy of the opposition in the eastern colonies.

III.—The disinterestedness and simplicity of Adams's life—His democratic ways—His great contemporary renown in England for political astuteness and for control over events—His priority in the championship of the more important Revolutionary measures.

IV.—Adams's use of the political essay as an instrument of immediate influence—Had the instinct of a great journalist—His willingness to produce results and to keep himself out of sight—The great number of his literary disguises—His extraordinary diligence as a political writer.

V.—Outline of Adams's literary labors—His method in work—His traits as a writer and as a controversialist.

VI.—The consistency of Adams's public career—His controlling principle was individualism—His application of that principle to the doctrines of liberty, loyalty, civic duty, and domestic life.

VII.—Adams insists upon the due subordination of the military power in a free community—His early predictions of Independence.

VIII.—William Livingston, Revolutionary agitator and first governor of the State of New Jersey—His activity as a political writer—The great variety of his literary services to the Revolution—The effectiveness of his assaults upon the enemy as shown by their extraordinary hatred of him—His own hearty reciprocation of the sentiment.

I.

WHEN George Bancroft first set forth before the world, about the middle of the nineteenth century, the story of the great part taken by Samuel Adams in the American Revolution, it seemed to be an attempt to raise a mighty reputation from the dead; for it had been the fate of this man to atone for the prodigious hold he had upon his contemporaries, by losing for awhile and almost altogether his hold upon posterity. Not even yet has the time come, when an adequate account of the significance of his career, whether as a man of affairs or as a man of letters, can be read without some suspicion of paradox and extravagance.

Samuel Adams was, indeed, a man of letters, but he was so only because he was above all things a man of affairs. Of literary art, in certain forms, he was no mean master: of literary art for art's sake, he was entirely regardless. He was perhaps the most voluminous political writer of his time in America, and the most influential political writer of his time in New England; but everything that he wrote was meant for a definite practical purpose, and nothing that he wrote seemed to have had any interest for him aside from that purpose. Accordingly, as has been said by his latest biographer, " like cannon balls which sink the ship, and then are lost in the sea, so the bolts of Samuel Adams, after riddling British authority in America, must be sought by diving beneath the oblivion that has rolled over them." [1]

Deep as is the obscurity which has fallen upon his literary services in the cause of the Revolution, the fame of those services was, at the time of them, almost unrivaled by that of any other writer, at least in the colonies east of the Hudson River. So early as the year 1765, John Adams spoke of him, among a group of brilliant and accomplished men, as having " the most correct, genteel, and artful pen " of any of them.[2] In the year 1774, he again pointed out Samuel Adams as " the most elegant writer " who had figured

[1] James Kendall Hosmer, " Samuel Adams," 360. This is one of the volumes in the " American Statesmen " series, and for thoroughness, fairness, and suggestiveness, one of the best. It is especially remarkable for a certain delicate insight into character, and for its candor and justice toward both parties in the American Revolution,—thus heralding the new age of American historical writing.

[2] " The Works of John Adams," ii. 163.

in America in his time.[1] In the year 1768, James Otis, with his usual amplitude of assertion, publicly declared "that there was not a person in England capable of composing so elegant, so pure, and so nervous a writing," as a certain state paper by Samuel Adams then recently given to the public.[2] The one man among his contemporaries who had the most occasion to know and to dread the literary skill of Samuel Adams, bore witness to the fact that, though he was at first but an indifferent writer, yet "long practice caused him to arrive at great perfection, and to acquire a talent of artfully and fallaciously insinuating into the minds of his readers a prejudice against the character of all whom he attacked, beyond any other man I ever knew."[3] "Damn that Adams," groaned Governor Bernard; "every dip of his pen stings like a horned snake."[4] A Loyalist writer in the year 1775 spoke facetiously of Samuel Adams as "a sachem of vast elocution," and then added with more seriousness,—"what proceeds from the mouth of Adams, is sufficient to fill the mouths of millions in America."[5]

II.

Born in Boston in 1722, graduated at Harvard in 1740, he early showed an invincible passion and aptitude for politics. Though both orthodox and devout, he was disinclined to the ministry. Though fond of the discussion of politico-legal questions, he was easily dissuaded from the study of the law. Enrolled as a merchant's clerk in his native town, he had no difficulty, after a brief apprenticeship, in securing

[1] William Vincent Wells, "The Life and Public Services of Samuel Adams," i. 446.

[2] "Letters to the Ministry from Governor Bernard," 40. The state paper here referred to, is the petition to the king passed by the Massachusetts House of Representatives in 1768.

[3] Thomas Hutchinson, "The History of the Colony of Massachusetts Bay," iii. 295.

[4] "The Works of John Adams," ii. 425–426.

[5] Thomas Bolton, "Oration," Boston, March 15, 1775. Cited in Wells, "The Life and Public Services of Samuel Adams," ii. 410 n.

a release from his employer, who naïvely explained that young Adams "would never do for a merchant," as "his whole soul was engrossed by politics."[1] Having been by his father set up in trade, with a capital of a thousand pounds, he proved himself to be so much more apt at parting with his goods than at getting pay for them, that he soon had nothing left of what his father had given him. Being then taken as a partner into his father's business—that of a brewer—and being upon his father's death in 1758 made his successor in the business, he continued to concern himself so much with the affairs of the state house and so little with those of the malt house, that even the petty revenue to be derived from the office of tax collector for the town of Boston,—an office which he held from 1756 to 1764,—became a matter of convenience to him.[2]

In the meantime, the man whom his enemies had already nicknamed "Samuel the Maltster," and "Samuel the Publican," was far advanced in that line of activity which subsequently earned for him the additional titles of "Arch-Manager," "Man of the Town Meeting," "Father of Democracy," "Grand Incendiary," "Cromwell of New England," and "Man of the Revolution." The one title, however, which perhaps best describes him, as being free alike from sarcasm and from panegyric, is one which seems never to have been given to him—that of Citizen. It was simply as a citizen—it was in the exercise of the rights and duties of the free and fearless civic character—that he found his true vocation. Moreover, under the peculiar conditions of his time, the most important function of citizenship seemed to him to be that of criticism, opposition, destruction. For precisely that function he was supremely endowed,—he was the incomparable leader of his fellow-citizens in the development of astute, far-reaching, and masterly measures of destructive statesmanship. At the

[1] Wells, "Life of S. Adams," i. 12.

[2] The old and oft-repeated charge that Adams was a peculator in this office, has been disproved by A. C. Goodell, "Proc. of Mass. Hist. Soc.," xx. 213–223.

moment when the business of constructive statesmanship became the chief function in the emancipated commonwealth, the work of Samuel Adams was done.[1]

Even his thrifty fellow-townsmen, who perhaps nodded their heads at his thriftless ways in all matters pertaining to his own business, could not fail to note his singular appetence for the business of the public—his readiness to think and write and speak and plot and otherwise to toil, in order that the interests of the public should receive no harm. And nothing that affected the public interests was too inconsiderable for him to engage in—if the public so desired. In the records of the town of Boston—as we are told by a writer[2] who has turned them over with this subject in view—one finds the name of Samuel Adams so early as 1753 as a patient plodder in town business; and "scarcely a year passes from that date until the town meetings cease, crushed out by the battalions of Gage, when his name does not appear in connections becoming constantly more honorable," —from membership of committees to see that chimneys are properly inspected, and that precautions are taken against the spread of small-pox, to membership of committees to instruct the town's representatives in the assembly. Finally, in September, 1765, in the fever-heat of opposition to the Stamp Act, he himself became one of the town's representatives in the assembly; and from about that time, until 1774, when he was sent to represent Massachusetts in the Continental Congress, he was the real director of the policy of opposition in the eastern colonies.[3] In the assembly of Massachusetts no other member could rival him in minute knowledge of the rules and business of the house, in laborious devotion to its work, in steadiness, endurance, tact, shrewdness, persuasiveness, and in the not very noble art of manipulating committees and caucuses; and while some other men—notably James Otis and John Adams—were far

---

[1] Wells, "Life of S. Adams," ii. 466.

[2] Hosmer, "Samuel Adams," 36.

[3] Wells, "Life of S. Adams," i. 98.

more brilliant in debate, not even their dashing and dazzling speeches could win votes as did the brief, unadorned, informing, and convincing talks of Samuel Adams.

III.

It is easy to see, also, that his political influence was vastly increased by the evident purity of his character, his disinterestedness as to pecuniary gain, and his unassuming ways. He began to illustrate democratic simplicity and democratic friendliness, long before Jefferson was old enough to know the meaning of those words. Seated on a log by the side of some caulker in the shipyard, or pausing on a street corner for leisurely and confidential discourse with any cobbler or hod carrier who should care to spend his time in that way, he won extraordinary affection from his fellow-townsmen by his evident willingness to impart to the humblest of them the political fears, and hopes, and aims, which possessed his own soul respecting the commonwealth. In his concern for the interests of the public, he was "forgetful of the ordinary pursuits which occupy the minds of men. . . . He was truly and really contented with poverty"[1]; so that, in his old age, he could say, proudly, that "a guinea had never glistened in his eyes."[2] Abstemious, untiring, unswerving, he seemed never to care who had the credit of his measures—if only his measures had success. "He eats little," wrote his chief antagonist in the Congress of 1774, "drinks little, sleeps little, thinks much, and is most decisive and indefatigable in the pursuit of his objects."[3] So great became his ascendency over the people, that, as one of his biographers declares, "in the stormiest days preceding the outbreak of the war, it was common among the vulgar and uneducated to assert that he was actually gifted with prophecy, and not a few believed that he held peace or war in his keeping."[4] In 1771,

[1] Wells, "Life of S. Adams," i. 272.
[2] Ibid. ii. 195.
[3] Galloway, "Historical and Political Reflections," etc., 67.
[4] Wells, "Life of S. Adams," ii. 241.

Hutchinson reprobated this Boston politician as "an incendiary equal to any at present in London."[1] Two years afterward, in a private letter to Lord Dartmouth, Hutchinson explained at length the methods by which Samuel Adams had made himself so powerful and so dangerous: "Whenever there appears a disposition to any conciliatory measures, this person, by his art and skill, prevents any effect; sometimes by exercising his talents in the newspapers; . . . at other times by an open opposition, and this sometimes in the house, where he has defeated every attempt as often as any has been made. But his chief dependence is upon a Boston town meeting, where he originates his measures, which are followed of course by the rest of the towns, and of course are adopted or justified by the assembly."[2] By the year 1774, his reputation had become so great in England that, according to Josiah Quincy, many people there considered him "the first politician in the world."[3] It was not without reason that in the royal offers of amnesty to the American rebels in case of their repentance, no place for repentance was left for one who was probably the first to avow the doctrine of American Independence, and who, next to the British ministry itself, was probably the most influential in securing its adoption. Even though a disinterested student may abate somewhat from the extreme assertions made on his behalf by recent eulogists of Samuel Adams, it is a clear token of the immense influence he had upon political and military events in America, especially between 1765 and 1776, that it is now possible for reasonable men to claim for him that he was the first to deny all legislative authority of parliament over the colonies, as well as the first to suggest the leading measures made necessary by such denial,—intercolonial union, committees of correspondence, circular letters, the league for non-importation, and the establishment of an incipient

[1] Wells, "Life of S. Adams," i. 398.

[2] Quoted in Wells, "Life of S. Adams," ii. 100.

[3] Josiah Quincy, "Memoir of the Life of Josiah Quincy, Junior," 258.

national government under the title of the Continental Congress. Surely, of one who had an initial and a necessary part in the creation of a series of political devices so thorough-going and so epoch-making as were these, it is not altogether an extravagance to say—as has been said in our day by a masterly critic of those times—that, "in the history of the American Revolution," Samuel Adams "is second only to Washington."[1]

IV.

It comports with the particular purpose of this book, to direct attention to the fact that one principal instrument by means of which Samuel Adams so greatly molded public opinion, and shaped political and even military procedure, was the pen. Of modern politicians, he was among the first to recognize the power of public opinion in directing public events, and likewise the power of the newspaper in directing public opinion. It was, therefore, an essential part of his method as a politician to acquire and to exercise the art of literary statement in a form suited to that particular end. He had the instinct of a great journalist, and of a great journalist willing to screen his individuality behind his journal. In this service, it was not Samuel Adams that Samuel Adams cared to put and to keep before the public, —it was the ideas of Samuel Adams. Accordingly, of all American writers for the newspapers between the years 1754 and 1776, he was perhaps the most vigilant, the most industrious, the most effective, and also the least identified. Ever ready to efface himself in what he did, he realized that the innumerable productions of his pen would make their way to a far wider range of readers, and would be all the more influential, if they seemed to be the work, not of one writer, but of many. Therefore, he almost never published anything under his own name; but, under a multitude of

[1] John Fiske, quoted by Hosmer in "Samuel Adams," as one of the mottoes on the obverse side of the leaf containing the dedication.

titular disguises which no man has yet been able to number, —as "Alfred," "An American," "A Bostonian," "A Tory," "A Chatterer," "A Son of Liberty," "An Imperialist," "An Elector in 1771," "Valerius Poplicola," "A.," "A. B.," "E. A.," "Z.," "T. Z.," "Candidus," "Determinatus," "Sincerus," "Populus," "Cedant Arma Togæ," "Principiis Obsta," "A Religious Politician," "A Layman," "Observation," "Shippen,"—this sleepless, crafty, protean politician, for nearly a third of a century, kept flooding the community with his ideas, chiefly in the form of essays in the newspapers,—thereby constantly baffling the enemies of the Revolutionary movement, and conducting his followers victoriously through those battles of argument which preceded and then for a time accompanied the battles of arms. "Some of his essays over one signature extend, in consecutive series, through several years,—the argument being maintained right and left with his various Loyalist assailants,—while, with different names, he kept up contests simultaneously with others of the crown writers on distinct subjects. All this time his pen was employed on the state papers of the legislature and other public bodies, and in his extensive correspondence with patriots in the other colonies and with gentlemen in England. . . . If published entire, together with the arguments of his antagonists, they would present a formidable array of controversial papers, embracing all the issues between Great Britain and the colonies, and showing the gradual progress of events which culminated in American Independence." [1]

V.

In the long line of his state papers—the official utterances of the several public bodies with which he was connected and which so long trusted him as their most deft and unerring penman—one may now trace, almost without a break, the development of the ideas and the measures which formed

[1] Wells, "Life of S. Adams," i. 445 n.

the Revolution. It was he who drafted, both in 1764 and in 1765, the instructions of the town of Boston to its representatives in the assembly[1]; and in October, 1775, the assembly's answer to the governor's speech[2]; and in 1768, the assembly's petition to the king, the assembly's letters to the chief members of the British ministry,[3] the assembly's letter of instructions to its agent in London,[4] and the assembly's circular letter to the legislatures of the other colonies[5]; in 1769, the remonstrance of the house of representatives to the governor,[6] and the "Appeal to the World," sent forth by the town-meeting of Boston[7]; in 1772, Boston's statement of the "Natural Rights of the Colonists as Men"[8]; in 1773, the two answers of the house of representatives to the governor's speech on the authority of parliament,[9] and the circular letter of the town of Boston to all its sister towns in Massachusetts[10]; in 1774, the circular letter of the town of Boston and of its nearest neighbors to the committees of correspondence throughout all the colonies[11]; in 1775, the address of the Continental Congress to the Mohawk Indians[12]; in 1776, the resolves of Congress for the disarmament of the Tories[13]; in 1778, the manifesto of congress against the barbarities practised by their enemies in the conduct of the war[14]; in 1779, an important portion of the new constitution of the State of Massachusetts, particularly the bill of rights,[15] together with the address of the constitutional convention to the people of Massachusetts.[16]

---

[1] Wells, "Life of S. Adams," i. 46 and 65. [2] Ibid. 71 n.

[3] These letters, together with the petition to the king, were printed the same year in London, by Almon, under a title which became celebrated—"The True Sentiments of America."

[4] Wells, "Life of S. Adams," i. 152–158. [5] Ibid. 170. [6] Ibid. 255–256.
[7] Ibid. 282. [8] Ibid. 502–504. [9] Ibid., ii. 29, 31 n. [10] Ibid. 108–109.
[11] Ibid. 157–158. [12] Ibid. 282–284. [13] Ibid. 364–366.
[14] Idid. iii. 46–47.

[15] Ibid. 80–89. Where it is argued that too much has been claimed for John Adams and too little for Samuel Adams as to the authorship of this important document. [16] Ibid. 90–96.

If we take into account the strain of thought and of emotional energy involved in all these years of fierce political controversy and of most perilous political leadership, we shall hardly fear to overestimate the resources of Samuel Adams in his true career of agitator and iconoclast;—especially the elasticity, the toughness, the persistence of a nature which could, in addition to all this, undertake and carry through, during the same long period, all the work he did in literary polemics,—work which alone might seem enough to employ and tire the strength even of a strong man who had nothing else to do. Some glimpse of the secret of his strength, and of his actual method while engaged in the forging of his politico-literary thunderbolts, is given us through a vivid picture of him as drawn by his great-grandson: "Frugal and temperate in his habits, his wants were few, and his powers of endurance fitted him for ceaseless industry. Most of his public papers were written in a study or library adjoining his bedroom; and his wife, after his death, related how, in the stillness of the night, she used, in the Revolutionary times, to listen to the incessant motion of the pen in the next room, whence the solitary lamp, which lighted the patriot in his labors, was dimly visible. Mr. Joseph Pierce, who personally knew Samuel Adams, and whose business obliged him for a long time to pass after midnight by the house, related, early in the present century, that he seldom failed to see the study lighted, no matter how far the night had gone, 'and he knew that Sam Adams was hard at work writing against the Tories.'"[1]

The traits of Samuel Adams the writer are easily defined —for they are likewise the traits of Samuel Adams the politician, and of Samuel Adams the man. His fundamental rule for literary warfare was this—"Keep your enemy in the wrong."[2] His style, then, was the expression of his intellectual wariness,—a wariness like that of the scout or the bush-whacker, who knows that behind any tree

[1] Wells, "Life of S. Adams," i. 202–203. [2] Ibid. 447.

may lurk his deadly foe, that a false step may be his ruin, that a badly-aimed shot may make it impossible for him ever to shoot again. Jefferson, who first became aware of the intellectual quality of Samuel Adams as it came out in the debates of Congress, long afterward described him as "truly a great man, wise in council, fertile in resources, immovable in his purposes. . . . As a speaker he could not be compared with his living colleague and namesake, whose deep conceptions, nervous style, and undaunted firmness, made him truly our bulwark in debate. But Mr. Samuel Adams, although not of fluent elocution, was so rigorously logical, so clear in his views, abundant in good sense, and master always of his subject, that he commanded the most profound attention whenever he rose in an assembly by which the froth of declamation was heard with the most sovereign contempt."[1]

Whether in oral or in written speech, his characteristics were the same,—simplicity, acuteness, logical power, and strict adaptation of means to the practical end in view. Nothing was for effect—everything was for effectiveness. He wrote pure English, and in a style severe, felicitous, pointed, epigrammatic. Careful as to facts, disdainful of rhetorical excesses, especially conscious of the strategic folly involved in mere overstatement, an adept at implication and at the insinuating light stroke, he had never anything to take back or to apologize for. In the wearisome fondness of his century for Greek and Roman analogies, he shared to the full; and in a less degree, in its passion for the tags and gew-gaws of classical quotation. Of course, his style bears the noble impress of his ceaseless and reverent reading of the English Bible. To a mere poet, he seldom alludes. Among secular writers of modern times, his days and nights were given, as occasion served, to Hooker, Coke, Grotius, Locke, Sidney, Vattel, Montesquieu, Blackstone, and Hume.

---

[1] "The Writings of Thomas Jefferson," H. A. Washington ed., vii. 126.

VI.

Perhaps no long public career was ever more perfectly self-consistent than his. From boyhood to old age, his master principle was individualism. As an undergraduate in college, having occasion to choose a subject for a public discussion, he revealed the bent of his mind by taking that of "Liberty."[1] In 1743, for his master's degree at Harvard, he wrote a Latin thesis on the affirmative side of the question,—"Whether it be lawful to resist the Supreme Magistrate, if the Commonwealth cannot be otherwise preserved,"[2]—a mettlesome doctrine, which, as his latest biographer has graphically said, "he proceeded to discuss in the presence, not only of the college dignitaries, but of the new governor, Shirley, and the crown officials, who sat in state near the young speakers at commencement, as do their successors to-day. . . . No one knew that as the young man spoke, then, for the first time, one of the great Revolutionary group was asserting the right of resistance by the people to arbitrary oppressors. Shirley was perhaps lost in some far-away dream of how he might get at the French; and when thirty years after, in his retirement at Dorchester, he asked who the Sam Adams could be that was such a thorn in the side to his successors Bernard and Hutchinson, he was quite unconscious of the fact that he himself had had the benefit, close at hand, of the first scratch."[3]

From the day of his graduation till his work as a political writer was done, he did but play variations on this robust doctrine and its corollaries. Men shall be talking much of liberty—no one more than he; but what is liberty? Broadly, it is a something which distinguishes "a society of wise and reasonable creatures from the brutal herd, where the strong-

[1] Wells, "Life of S. Adams," i. 6.

[2] Ibid. 10. "An supremo Magistratui resistere liceat, si aliter servari Respublica nequit? Affirmat respondens Samuel Adams."

[3] Hosmer, "Samuel Adams," 17–18.

est horns are the strongest laws."[1] "The perfection of liberty, . . . in a state of nature, is for every man to be free from any external force, and to perform such actions as in his own mind and conscience he judges to be rightest; which liberty no man can truly possess whose mind is enthralled by irregular and inordinate passions,—since it is no great privilege to be free from external violence, if the dictates of the mind are controlled by a force within which exerts itself above reason."[2] As "no man's life is his own in such a sense as that he may wantonly destroy it at his own pleasure, or submit it to the wanton pleasure of another, so neither is his liberty."[3] "But, alas! in this exalted sense, liberty is rather admired in the world than truly enjoyed. What multitudes of persons are there who have not so much as the shadow of it; who hold their property and even their lives by no other tenure than the sovereign will of a tyrant, and he often the worst and most detestable of men, who, to gratify the least humor or passion in his nature, does not scruple to massacre them by thousands!"[4]

So, too, in his time, men shall be talking much of loyalty—others, perhaps, much more than he. But what is loyalty? According to Samuel Adams, it is "the beauty and perfection of a well-constituted state. It cannot, indeed, subsist in an arbitrary government, because it is founded in the love and possession of liberty. It includes in it a thorough knowledge of our constitution, its conveniences and defects as well as its real advantages; a becoming jealousy of our immunities, and a steadfast resolution to maintain them. It delights in the quiet and thankful enjoyment of a good administration, and it is the scourge of the griping oppressor and haughty invader of our liberties."[5] "Whoever, therefore, insinuates notions of government contrary to the constitution, or in any way winks at any measures to suppress or even to weaken it, is not a loyal man."[6]

---

[1] Wells, "Life of S. Adams," i. 19. This book is the best repository we have of the writings of Samuel Adams.

[2] Ibid. [3] Ibid. [4] Ibid. 20. [5] Ibid. 16. [6] Ibid. 17.

"Whoever acquaints us that we have no right to examine into the conduct of those who, though they derive their power from us to serve the common interests, make use of it to impoverish and ruin us, is, in a degree, a rebel—to the undoubted rights and liberties of the people."[1]

These definitions, put forth by Samuel Adams when he was but twenty-six years of age—seventeen years before the Stamp Act, twenty-eight years before the Declaration of Independence—mark the solidity and the clarity of the foundation which he thus early laid for that system of stalwart political philosophy which he was to continue to teach during all those years of storm and stress wherein he served as the inspirer and leader of his people. Moreover, while keeping full in view that side both of liberty and of loyalty which points toward rights, he did not forget that for both there was a side which points toward duties. "It is not unfrequent," said he, "to hear men declaim loudly upon liberty, who, if we may judge by the whole tenor of their actions, mean nothing else by it but their own liberty, — to oppress, without control or the restraint of laws, all who are poorer or weaker than themselves."[2] "He that despises his neighbor's happiness because he wears a worsted cap or leather apron, he that struts immeasurably above the lower size of people, and pretends to adjust the rights of men by the distinctions of fortune, is not over loyal."[3] Nor did Samuel Adams, like some other speculative democrats of that age, content himself with being a democrat chiefly in theory: his theory of democracy was also the gentle and faithful practice of his life. Not only were the lowliest and most helpless people made to feel in his presence that they were his brethren, but no man, no woman, however lowly and helpless, could be his slave. When one day, a full decade before the Declaration of Independence, his wife told him of the valuable present of a slave-girl she had just received, he said to her:

---

[1] Wells, "Life of S. Adams," i. 17. [2] Ibid. 22. [3] Ibid. 17.

" A slave cannot live in my house: if she comes, she must be free."[1] And free she was.

VII.

On no other topic of the Revolution was his writing more trenchant or more characteristic, than on that of the due subordination of the military power,—a topic which to Americans became peculiarly interesting about the time of the entrance of the British regiments into the town of Boston in 1768. " Military power," said he at that time, " is by no means calculated to convince the understandings of men. It may in another part of the world affright women and children, and perhaps some weak men, out of their senses, but will never awe a sensible American tamely to surrender his liberty."[2] " Are we a garrisoned town, or are we not? If we are, let us know by whose authority and by whose influence we are made so. If not—and I take it for granted we are not—let us then assert and maintain the honor, the dignity, of free citizens, and place the military where all other men are, and where they ought always and will be placed in every free country,—at the foot of the common law of the land! To submit to the civil magistrate in the legal exercise of power, is forever the part of a good subject; and to answer the watchmen of the town in the night, may be the part of a good citizen, as well as to afford them all necessary countenance and support. But to be called to account by a common soldier, or any soldier, is a badge of slavery which none but a slave will wear."[3]

In 1773, in view of the colossal blunders in statesmanship presented by the farcical and galling policy of the British king and ministry, he wrote: " That Great Britain should continue to insult and alienate the growing millions who inhabit this country, on whom she greatly depends, and on whose alliance in future time her existence as a nation may be suspended, is perhaps as glaring an instance of human

---

[1] Wells, "Life of S. Adams," i. 138. [2] Ibid. 233. [3] Ibid. 231.

folly as ever disgraced politicians or put common sense to the blush." [1] In 1774, in the midst of the labors of the first Continental Congress, he published these words of stern meaning: "If the British administration and government do not return to the principles of moderation and equity, the evil which they profess to aim at preventing by their rigorous measures, will the sooner be brought to pass, namely, the entire separation and independence of the colonies." [2] "I wish for a permanent union with the mother country, but only on the terms of liberty and truth. No advantage that can accrue to America from such an union, can compensate for the loss of liberty." [3] In February, 1776, when, in his opinion, no choice was left to Americans but that between servitude under Great Britain and separation from her, he wrote: "I account a state a moral person, having an interest and will of its own; and I think that state a monster whose prime mover has an interest and will in direct opposition to its prosperity and security." [4]

VIII.

Another example of the American statesman who, while weighted with the responsibilities of political leadership, had also the aptitude and the inclination for much work as a writer in the political journals, was William Livingston, a member of the Continental Congress from 1774 to 1776, for a short time in the latter year a brigadier-general in command of the militia of New Jersey, and from August, 1776, until his death in July, 1790, governor of that State by repeated choice of its people. [5] A positive, aggressive, rugged man, with Scottish fire and Scottish tenacity, a good lover, a good hater, the robustness of his temper streaked with veins of humor, imagination, and tender-

[1] Wells, "Life of S. Adams," ii. 91.
[2] Ibid. 149.
[3] Ibid.
[4] Ibid. 363.
[5] Of the character of William Livingston, I have treated more fully in my "History of American Literature during the Colonial Time," ii. 218–223, where also will be found an account of his literary work prior to the Revolution.

ness, a considerable student of books, a poet, an orator,[1] an essayist, a satirist, he was noted throughout the last seven years of the Revolutionary period for the gusty vigor with which he governed his little commonwealth, organized, sustained, and spurred on her soldiers, and to the military warfare against the enemy added a most vivacious literary warfare—bombarding them through the newspapers with intermittent showers of shot and shell in the form of arguments, anathemas, jokes, and jeers. To have a rough and ready part in that species of warfare, was indeed an old habit and passion of his life; and after many a noisy and smoky word-battle with his antagonists in the later colonial days, it was quite impossible for him to refrain from entering, in a similar manner, into the more deadly disputes of the Revolution.

Undoubtedly, a considerable number of his contributions to the Revolutionary newspapers are now wholly beyond identification. In "The Pennsylvania Packet" for February 18, 1777, is to be seen a well-certified and a most typical specimen of his work, entitled "The Impartial Chronicle, or the Infallible Intelligencer: upon the Plan and after the Manner of the New York Mercury,"[2]—the same being a droll and an effective burlesque on the alleged imaginativeness and mendacity of the Loyalist, Hugh Gaine, as a purveyor of political and military news. In December, 1777, being then in need of a literary organ within his own dominions, he gave his powerful aid to the establishment of "The New Jersey Gazette," conducted by Isaac Collins; and under his favorite pseudonym of "Hortensius," Livingston wrote for this paper, especially during the first year of its existence, some of the most telling articles it contained,[3]—such as the fol-

[1] In 1776, as governor of New Jersey, Livingston addressed the legislature of that State in a speech, which was declared by John Adams to be "the most elegant and masterly ever made in America." "Letters of John Adams, Addressed to His Wife," i. 168.

[2] Reprinted in 1789 by Mathew Carey in "The American Museum," v. 295-298; 371-374.

[3] T. Sedgwick, "Life of Livingston," 247-248.

lowing: "On the Exchange of Burgoyne,"[1] "On the Conquest of America,"[2] "A Satire on Sir William Howe,"[3] "To his Majesty of Great Britain,"[4] "Annotations on his most gracious Majesty's . . . most gracious Speech,"[5] "On Lord North's Speech,"[6] "On Reunion with Great Britain,"[7] and "On the British Commissioners."[8] No modern reader of these essays is likely to regard Theodore Sedgwick's praise of them as excessive when he declares that, "combining eloquent appeals to the patriotism of the colonists, with the most scoffing ridicule of the menaces and denunciations of the British, they by turns enlisted every feeling which can arm the breasts of individuals or nations against vacillation and fear."[9] During a part of the year 1779, this tireless disputant lent the help of his slashing pen to the columns of "The United States Magazine," published at Philadelphia under the editorship of Hugh Henry Brackenridge.[10]

It is a somewhat droll fact that, in the very midst of these versatile and quickening efforts for the great cause, he was suddenly persuaded to desist from them altogether, in consequence, it is said, of open objections made by members of the New Jersey legislature,—they deeming it an indecorum for their chief-magistrate to be a partisan scribbler in the newspapers.[11] At any rate, his literary services to the Revolution had such vindication as could be furnished by the superabounding hatred of himself with which they inspired the enemy. "My good friends in New York," he said in 1778 in a letter to Henry Laurens, "have faithfully promised to cut my throat for writing—which they seem to resent more than fighting."[12] In the meantime, however, and until his good friends in New York should find it convenient to accomplish their design upon him, they partially appeased their impatience by applying to him such flatter-

[1] Dec. 17, 1777. [2] Dec. 24, 1777. [3] Jan. 7, 1778. [4] Jan. 21, 1778.
[5] Feb. 11, 1778. [6] May 6, 1778. [7] Sept. 9, 1778. [8] Sept. 21, 1778.
[9] T. Sedgwick, "Life of Livingston," 249. [10] Ibid. 327.
[11] Ibid. 327–328. [12] Ibid. 280–281.

ing terms as "Spurious Governor," "Don Quixote of the Jerseys," "Despot-in-Chief in and over the rising State of New Jersey," "Itinerant Dey of New Jersey," "Knight of the most honorable Order of Starvation, and Chief of the Independents."[1] For a man like Livingston to be seriously disturbed by such missiles, was hardly probable: he himself in his day had fabricated and flung too many of them. As to the hope, so frankly avowed by the Loyalists, of wreaking physical vengeance upon him, it was not in Livingston's nature to refuse to them a reciprocation of the same cordial sentiment; for, at a time when the affairs of the Loyalists in New York seemed tumbling to ruin, he indicated his point of view respecting the chief of them, by saying in a letter to Gouverneur Morris: "If Rivington is taken, I must have one of his ears; Governor Clinton is entitled to the other; and General Washington, if he pleases, may take his head."[2]

[1] Sedgwick, "Life of Livingston," 247. [2] Ibid.

CHAPTER XXV.

JOHN DICKINSON AS PENMAN OF THE AMERICAN REVOLUTION.

I.—John Dickinson's ancestry and education—His early entrance into politics in Delaware and Pennsylvania—In the Stamp Act Congress—In the Continental Congress—Odium incurred in 1776 by his opposition to American Independence—His military services—Is driven into retirement—His return to Congress in 1779—Governor of Delaware in 1781, and of Pennsylvania in 1782.

II.—The brilliant talents and services which won for him the title of "Penman of the American Revolution"—As a writer of state papers—As a writer of political essays for the newspapers and of pamphlets, from 1762 to 1775.

III.—Having in Congress opposed the resolution for Independence, he joins the army to fight against the British—Both these acts entirely consistent with his avowed principles—By nature and training a conservative and a peace-maker—His hatred of violence and war—Believes that all difficulties between the colonies and the mother-country could be settled in a peaceful way—His characteristic method in controversy—He uses English principles with which to fight against English aggressions—His claim that the American opponents of the ministry are the true champions of English constitutional liberty—His efforts to avert war and revolution.

IV.—The blending of his influence as a political writer during the Revolution, with his influence as a politician—In 1767 he succeeds James Otis as our predominant political writer, as in 1776 he is succeeded by Thomas Paine —The great decline of Dickinson's influence in 1776—Fitted to lead in a constitutional controversy, but not in a revolutionary one—His method, also, too gentle for the later stage of the Revolution—He is regarded with contempt by more robust politicians—The injustice then done to his talents and character.

I.

THE year 1765, which is marked by the first contributions of John Dickinson to the literature of the American Revolution, presents him to us as an accomplished young barrister of Philadelphia, already noted for his large reading in history and politics,[1] already noted for the purity and brilliance of his English style. He was born in 1732, on the eastern shore of Maryland, at Crosia-Doré,—an estate which even then for nearly a century had been the seat of the Dickinson family, as it still is after the lapse of a second century and more than the half of a third. Having been carefully educated by private tutors at home, he read law for three years in the office of John Moland of Philadelphia. In 1753, he was entered of the Middle Temple, London, where he resided for three years, having for fellow-students Edward Thurlowe, Lloyd Kenyon, and William Cowper. In 1760, he began his political career by taking a seat as member of the assembly of Delaware. In 1762, according to a usage then not uncommon, he was transferred to the assembly of Pennsylvania; and in that body he served with great distinction until 1765, and again from 1770 until the expiration of the colonial government in 1776. Moreover, in 1765 he represented Pennsylvania in the Stamp Act Congress, as he did also in the several sessions of the Continental Congress from 1774 until some time in July, 1776. Having, by his opposition to the proposal for American Independence, incurred the deep dislike and distrust of the more radical members of the party to which he belonged, he left his seat in Congress in order to take command of a brigade of Pennsylvania troops called out to aid in resisting the threatened attack of the British upon New York; and on the tenth of August, from his camp at Elizabethtown, New Jersey, he thus wrote to his friend, Charles Thomson, secretary of Congress: "The enemy are moving, and an attack on New York is quickly expected. As for myself, I can form no idea of a more noble fate than, after being the constant advocate for and promoter of every measure that could possibly lead to peace or prevent her

[1] William Rawle, the elder, wrote of Dickinson: "His law knowledge was respectable, although not remarkably extensive, for his attention was directed to historical and political studies." Charles Janeway Stillé, "The Life and Times of John Dickinson," 37.

return from being barred up; after cheerfully and deliberately sacrificing my popularity and all the emoluments I might certainly have derived from it, to principle; after suffering all the indignities that my countrymen now bearing rule are inclined, if they could, so plentifully to shower down upon my innocent head,—than willingly to resign my life, if Divine Providence shall please so to dispose of me, for the defense and happiness of those unkind countrymen whom I cannot forbear to esteem as fellow-citizens, amidst their fury against me."[1]

Notwithstanding the lofty principle upon which he thus acted, and the nobility of his devotion to the safety of his imperiled countrymen, he was pursued, even into the field of battle, by the enmity of his late associates, unable, as is apt to be the case with all revolutionary associates, to pardon the man who, having gone with them a part of the way, hesitated to go with them the whole of it. "I had not been ten days in camp at Elizabethtown," he wrote, "when I was by my persecutors turned out of Congress. While I was exposing my person to every hazard, and lodging every night within half a mile of the enemy, the members of the convention at Philadelphia, resting in quiet and safety, ignominiously voted me, as unworthy of my seat, out of the national senate."[2] By a studied insult, likewise, he was driven soon afterward to resign his commission in the army.[3] Upon his return to Pennsylvania, he served for a short time in its legislature, and then withdrew to an estate of his in Delaware, resolved to retire for awhile from all participation in politics, but to volunteer as a private soldier at the next call for troops.[4] In this capacity he carried a musket in the battle of Brandywine.[5] In May, 1779, he appeared once more in Congress, but as a member from Delaware, serving, however, only until the autumn of that year. In 1781, he was made governor of Delaware. In 1782, he was made governor of Pennsylvania, and as such

[1] Stillé, "Life of Dickinson," 202–203. [2] Ibid. 206.
[3] Ibid. [4] Ibid. 209. [5] Ibid. 214.

was serving the commonwealth at the close of the Revolution.[1]

II.

This is the man who, being thus occupied during all those years by great practical employments in peace and war, yet had such productiveness in literary labor and so exquisite a genius as to win for himself the title of "Penman of the American Revolution." By the author of a recent sketch of his life, he has been described as "the great colonial essayist."[2] By the editor of the latest edition of his writings, it has been claimed for him that, in the literature of the Revolution, he is "as preëminent as Washington in war, Franklin in diplomacy, and Morris in finance."[3]

No other man in those days had a finer gift for putting into form—into luminous, urbane, and stately form—the constitutional and political principles on which, in his opinion, the American opposition to the British ministry was to be conducted; and, prior to the middle of 1776, no other man was so much employed by the several public bodies with which he was connected, in giving expression to those principles in the great state papers of the time. It was he who, in 1765, drafted the "Resolutions in relation to the Stamp Act," adopted by the assembly of Pennsylvania, as well as the "Declaration of Rights," and the "Petition to the King," adopted by the Stamp Act Congress. It was he who, in July, 1774, wrote the "Resolves" promulgated by the convention of Pennsylvania; also, their "Instructions to the Representatives in Assembly," and their elaborate "Essay on the Constitutional Power of Great Britain over the Colonies in America." It was he who, in Octo-

---

[1] Both in Delaware and in Pennsylvania, the governor was then entitled president of the supreme executive council.

[2] Wharton Dickinson, in "The Magazine of American History," x. 223.

[3] Paul Leicester Ford, "The Writings of John Dickinson," i. Preface ix. This edition, which is to be included among the issues of the Historical Society of Pennsylvania, is still in process of publication.

ber, 1774, wrote the "Address of Congress to the Inhabitants of the Province of Quebec" and the first "Petition of Congress to the King's Most Excellent Majesty." It was he who, in the early summer of 1775, wrote the second "Petition of Congress to the King's Most Excellent Majesty," as well as "The Declaration by the Representatives of the United Colonies of North America, now met in Congress at Philadelphia, setting forth the Causes and Necessity of their taking up Arms."[1] It was he who, in November, 1775, and again in June, 1776, wrote the "Instructions" of Pennsylvania to its representatives in Congress; who, in July, 1776, wrote the "Revision of the Bill of Rights" for the State of Pennsylvania; who, at about the same time, wrote the first draft of the "Articles of Confederation," as then submitted to Congress; who, finally, in May, 1779, wrote the "Address of Congress to the Several States on the Present Situation of Affairs."

But besides these imposing official expressions of the argument and sentiment of the American Revolution, John Dickinson likewise gave a more personal utterance to them, in almost innumerable ways, through the public press. During a period reaching back to at least three years prior to the Stamp Act, and reaching forward to at least one year subsequent to the Declaration of Independence, he was an almost constant writer of political essays for the newspapers, of broadsides, and of other fugitive productions,[2] the most of which, as he probably intended they

---

[1] The authorship of this powerful and noble paper has been somewhat in doubt, partly in consequence of the conflicting claims of Jefferson and Dickinson. The claim of Dickinson has, however, in recent years, been placed beyond question by George Henry Moore, an abstract of whose paper on the subject may be found in "The Magazine of American History," viii. 514–516. More adequate quotations from it are given by Stillé, "Life of Dickinson," Appendix iv. 353–364. The paper itself was printed in New York, 1890, and is entitled "John Dickinson, The Author of the Declaration on taking up arms in 1775." Also, "Jefferson's Writings," P. L. Ford ed., i. Introd. xxiv.; and 462–482.

[2] This, in substance, seems to be the opinion of the one man who, by his

should be, are now quite beyond the possibility of recognition. A mere glance at the list of his miscellaneous writings upon Revolutionary topics—so far as those writings are known to us—can hardly fail to give the reader a lively impression of the literary energy and versatility of the man, and of the vastness of the work he did during those tremendous years, in molding the opinions of his countrymen, and in conveying impulse and direction to events which have since acquired a world-wide celebrity and influence. Thus, in November,[1] 1765, he issued, as a broadside, a stirring "Address to Friends and Countrymen on the Stamp Act"; and this he reënforced by publishing in the following month a plausible and strong pamphlet, entitled "The Late Regulations respecting the British Colonies Considered." In 1766, under the signature of "A North American," he published "An Address to the Committee of Correspondence in Barbadoes,"—a paper bearing upon its title-page a sarcastic motto adapted, rather than precisely quoted, from Shakespeare[2]:

> "This word rebellion hath froze them up,
> Like fish in a pond."

On the second of December, 1767, in "The Pennsylvania Chronicle," he began the publication of a series of essays, which soon attained to a greater reputation, on both sides of the Atlantic, than had been reached by any previous production in American literature,—the "Letters from a Farmer in Pennsylvania," twelve in number, the last one appearing on the fifteenth of February, 1768.[3] In April of

---

special studies, is the most competent to give an opinion on the subject,—Mr. Paul Leicester Ford, to whose industry in research and to whose critical acumen we are indebted for the identification of a number of John Dickinson's writings hitherto unknown. "The Writings of John Dickinson," i. Pref. xi.

[1] The exact date is somewhat in doubt: the one here given is approximately correct.

[2] Second Part of King Henry IV., i. 1. This use among us of the word rebellion so early as the year 1766, is notable.

[3] A somewhat extended account of the "Farmer's Letters" and of their important effects, is given in chapter X. of this work.

that year, he published at Philadelphia "An Address read at a Meeting of Merchants to consider Non-Importation," —an appeal which three months later he supplemented by a "Letter" to the same merchants on the same subject. In July, 1768, he published "A Song for American Freedom," —a rather clumsy hymn of patriotic duty and enthusiasm, which, however, so perfectly fitted the needs and the moods of the friends of the Revolution that, in spite of its lack of poetic merit, it became, in all parts of the land, and down to the outbreak of hostilities, the most popular lyric produced among us during that period. In November, 1773, he published "Two Letters on the Tea-Tax." In May, 1774, he published "Letters to the Inhabitants of the British Colonies"—these letters being four in number. In December, 1775, he published a "Speech to the Assembly of New Jersey." In July, 1776, he published "An Essay for a Frame of Government in Pennsylvania." [1]

III.

To him who now reads that John Dickinson, having opposed in Congress the resolution for American Independence, immediately thereafter left that body in order to lead a brigade of American troops against the British, it will probably seem either that he had somewhat too suddenly repented of his opposition to Independence, or else that he was guilty of conduct inconsistent with his principles. Neither inference would be correct. In truth, his conduct throughout that particular emergency was in perfect accord with all his political teachings, which involved, especially, these two principles:—first, that it was the ancient and manly method of loyal Englishmen, in cases of extreme danger, to make demand for political rights with arms in

[1] In 1801, at Wilmington, Delaware, was published in two volumes, "The Political Writings of John Dickinson, Esq."

their hands, and even embodied in military array against the king's troops; and, secondly, that every citizen, having said and done his best to secure the prevalence of his own view, was bound to submit himself to the decision of the community to which he belonged, and help to carry it out. Indeed, no other American who finally supported the American Revolution in its ultimate issue—that of secession from the empire—exhibited, from first to last, a more perfect familiarity, or a more perfect sympathy, with the great historic precedents set by the English people in the management of fundamental controversies between subjects and their sovereign.

Both by nature and by culture, John Dickinson was a conservative, having an uncommon horror of all changes that violated the sequences of established law. His philosophy of politics was practical, rather than merely speculative: it was the product of an orderly and peace-loving mind, revering the dignity of human nature, familiar with political history, trained to the solution of legal problems by the maxims and methods of English law, and convinced that every dispute between man and man could better be settled by reason and by good humor, than by brute fury and brute force. In the alarming differences which had arisen between the American portion of the British empire and the sovereign power, he saw no difficulties which could not under such treatment be happily adjusted, if, indeed, both parties to the controversy sincerely desired them to be so adjusted. Accordingly, in all his writings, whether official or personal, his endeavor was to place the American claim on historic constitutional grounds—such as Englishmen at home must respect; to persuade all Americans, in the assertion of their rights, to be fearless and firm, as their English ancestors had always been under similar circumstances; to persuade both Americans and Englishmen that they were alike interested in a wise, just, and lasting settlement of this great dispute, and that, in its discussion, the exercise of amenity and of good humor would be of the greatest use. Always he prefers to fight English oppression by English principles against oppression; to shew to the people of England, that it was their own rulers, and not the Americans, who were violating the constitution; and that the demands of the Americans, so far from being the spawn of a factious or revolutionary temper, were derived immediately from "the records, statutes, law-books, and most approved writers of our mother-country—those 'dead but most faithful counselors' (as Sir Edward Coke calls them) 'who cannot be daunted by fear, nor muzzled by affection, reward, or hope of preferment, and therefore may safely be believed.'"[1] "We well know," he wrote in 1774, "that the colonists are charged by many persons in Great Britain, with attempting to obtain . . . a total Independence on her. As well we know the accusation to be utterly false. . . . NOLUMBUS LEGES ANGLIÆ MUTARI. This is the rebellion with which we are stigmatized. We have committed the like offense, that was objected by the polite and humane Fimbria against a rude senator of his time: we have 'disrespectfully refused to receive the whole weapon into our body.' We could not do it, and—live; but that must be acknowledged to be a poor excuse, equally inconsistent with good breeding and the supreme legislature of Great Britain. For these ten years past, we have been incessantly attacked. Hard is our fate, when, to escape the character of rebels, we must be degraded into that of slaves; as if there was no medium between the two extremes of anarchy and despotism, where innocence and freedom could find repose and safety. Why should we be exhibited to mankind as a people adjudged by parliament unworthy of freedom? The thought alone is insupportable. Even those unhappy persons, who have had the misfortune of being born under the yoke of bondage . . . no sooner breathe the air of England, though they touch her shore only by accident, than they instantly

[1] "The Political Writings of John Dickinson," P. L. Ford ed., ii. 41.

become freemen. Strange contradiction! The same kingdom, at the same time, the asylum and the bane of liberty!

"To return to the charge against us, we can safely appeal to that Being, from whom no thought can be concealed, that our warmest wish and utmost ambition is, that we and our posterity may ever remain subordinate to, and dependent upon, our parent state.[1] This submission our reason approves, our affection dictates, our duty commands, and our interest enforces. If this submission, indeed, implies a dissolution of our constitution, and a renunciation of our liberty, we should be unworthy of our relation to her, if we should not frankly declare, that we regard it with horror; and every true Englishman will applaud this just distinction, and candid declaration. Our defense necessarily touches chords in unison with the fibres of his honest heart. They must vibrate in sympathetic tones. If we, his kindred, should be base enough to promise the humiliating subjection, he could not believe us. We should suffer all the infamy of the engagement, without finding the benefit expected from being thought as contemptible as we should undertake to be.

"But this submission implies not such insupportable evils; and our amazement is inexpressible, when we consider the gradual increase of these colonies from their small beginnings in the last century to their late flourishing condition, and how prodigiously, since their settlement, our parent state has advanced in wealth, force, and influence, till she has become the first power on the sea, and the envy of the world,—that these our better days should not strike conviction into every mind, that the freedom and happiness of the colonists are not inconsistent with her authority and prosperity. . . . What unknown offenses have we committed against her within these ten years, to provoke such an unexampled change in her conduct towards us? In the last war, she acknowledged us repeatedly to be faith-

[1] This avowal was made by Dickinson, and officially promulgated by the Convention of Pennsylvania, in July, 1774.

ful, dutiful, zealous, and useful in her cause. Is it criminal in us that our numbers, by the favor of Divine Providence, have greatly increased ? That the poor choose to fly from their native countries in Europe to this continent ? Or, that we have so much improved these woods, that if we can be forced into an unsuccessful resistance, avarice itself might be satiated with our forfeitures ?

"It cannot with truth be urged that projects of innovation have commenced with us. Facts and their dates prove the contrary. Not a disturbance has happened on any part of this continent, but in consequence of some immediately preceding provocation. . . . Our highest pride and glory has been, with humble and unsuspecting duty to labor in contributing to elevate her to that exalted station she holds among the nations of the earth, and which, we still ardently desire and pray, she may hold, with fresh accessions of fame and prosperity, till time shall be no more.

"These being our sentiments, and, we are fully convinced, the sentiments of our brethren throughout the colonies, with unspeakable affliction we find ourselves obliged to oppose that system of dominion over us, arising from counsels pernicious both to our parent and to her children; to strive, if it be possible, to close the breaches made in our former concord, and stop the sources of future animosities. And may God Almighty, who delights in the titles of just and meciful, incline the hearts of all parties to that equitable and benevolent temper, which is necessary solidly to establish peace and harmony, in the place of confusion and dissension."[1]

IV.

If we attempt to estimate the practical effects of John Dickinson's work as a political writer during the American Revolution, we shall find it not easy to disentangle and to separate them from the practical effects of his work as a

[1] "The Political Writings of John Dickinson," P. L. Ford ed., ii. 48–57.

politician. The two lines of power were closely interwoven: each, in the main, helped the other, as each was liable, in its turn, to be hindered by the other. At any rate, just as the politico-literary influence of James Otis was, upon the whole, predominant in America from 1764 until 1767, so, from the latter date until some months after the outbreak of hostilities in 1775, was the politico-literary influence of John Dickinson predominant here. Moreover, as he succeeded to James Otis in the development of Revolutionary thought, so was he, at last, succeeded by Thomas Paine, who held sway among us, as the chief writer of political essays, from the early part of 1776 until the close of the Revolution itself.

The prodigious decline in the influence of John Dickinson, at the approach of the issue of Independence, is a thing not hard to explain: it was due in part to his personal characteristics, in part to the nature of his opinions. From the beginning of the troubles until some months after the first shedding of blood, in 1775, public opinion in America had set strongly in favor of making demand—even armed demand—for our political rights, but without any rupture of the colonial tie. It was, therefore, a period calling for clear and resolute statements of our claims, but with loyalty, urbanity, and tact. To be the chief literary exponent of such a period, John Dickinson was in every way fitted by talent, by temperament, by training. A man of wealth, cultivation, and elegant surroundings, practically versed in the law and in politics, considerate, cautious, disinclined to violent measures and to stormy scenes, actuated by a passion for the unity and greatness of the English race and for peace among all men, it was his sincere desire that the dispute with the mother country should be so conducted as to end, at last, in the perfect establishment of American constitutional rights within the empire, but without any hurt or dishonor to England, and without any permanent failure in respect and kindness between her and ourselves.

Nevertheless, in 1775, events occurred which gave a different aspect to the whole dispute, and swept an apparent majority of the American people quite beyond the sphere of such ideas and methods. John Dickinson's concession to parliament of a legislative authority over us, even to a limited extent, was roughly discarded; instead of which was enthroned among us the unhistoric and makeshift doctrine that American allegiance was due not at all to parliament, but to the crown only. Moreover, the moderation of tone, the urbane speech, the civility in conduct, exemplified by Dickinson in all this dispute with England, then became an anachronism and an offense. We were plunged at last into civil war—we had actually reached the stage of revolution; and the robust men who then ruled the scene, being of opinion that revolutions are apt to take place in some disregard of urbanity, and that civil wars have a peculiar tendency to give prominence to whatever is uncivil, were disposed, with no little contempt, to brush aside the moderate, conservative, and courteous Dickinson, who, either for advice or for conduct, seemed to them to have no further function to perform in the American world. His "Farmer's Letters" were declared by Jefferson to have been "really an 'ignis fatuus,' misleading us from true principles." [1] Even Edward Rutledge, who, in June, 1776, agreed with Dickinson in his opposition to the plan for Independence, nevertheless expressed some impatience with his intellectual fastidiousness and nicety,—declaring that the "vice of all his productions, to a considerable degree," was "the vice of refining too much." [2] Of course, to an impetuous and blustering man of affairs like John Adams, such a political theorist as John Dickinson, with his qualms and his scruples and his splitting of hairs, could have seemed but a "piddling

---

[1] "The Writings of Thomas Jefferson," H. A. Washington ed., vi. 486. Though the words cited in the text were written by Jefferson a late as in 1815, they evidently represent the opinions held by him in 1776.

[2] "The Correspondence and Public Papers of John Jay," H. P. Johnston ed., i. 67.

genius," who, for a whole year before the proclamation of American Independence, had been giving "a silly cast to our whole doings."[1] This celebrated sneer of John Adams's, which occurs in a letter of his written from Philadelphia in July, 1775, was followed, in April, 1777, by an allusion to the same person, by the same letter-writer, implying that, as he thought, the public had in the meantime come over to his contemptuous opinion of Dickinson: "The Farmer turns out to be the man that I have seen him to be these two years. He is in total neglect and disgrace here. I am sorry for it, because of the forward part he took in the beginning of the controversy. But there is certainly such a thing as falling away in politics, if there is none in grace."[2]

In the close quarters and heated air of the actual conflict, John Dickinson, it may be, could hardly have expected to receive appreciation, forbearance, or even simple justice, from his angry political associates, then playing a desperate game which, for many of them, meant either success or the scaffold. It will be the privilege of Time through her mouthpiece, History, to temper somewhat the harsh estimates which prevailed during the later portion of his life, respecting this able, brilliant, and noble-minded man.

---

[1] "Letters of John Adams, Addressed to his Wife," i. 268, Appendix. This letter was addressed to James Warren of Plymouth; was intercepted and published by the enemy; and for a time brought considerable disrepute and ill will upon the writer of it.

[2] Ibid. 207–208. In the original, the word "Farmer" is indicated by the first letter only.

CHAPTER XXVI.

THOMAS PAINE AS LITERARY FREELANCE IN THE WAR FOR INDEPENDENCE: 1776–1783.

I.—Paine's literary work between January and July, 1776—He then joins the Pennsylvania troops, and serves under General Roberdeau—Also, as aid-de-camp to General Greene at Fort Lee—Participates in Washington's retreat across New Jersey.

II.—In the midst of this retreat, he begins at Newark the writing of "The Crisis," which he continues at the subsequent stopping places—He publishes the first number at Philadelphia, December 19, 1776—Electrical effect of this paper—Its appeal to the emotions and the needs of the hour.

III.—His part in the labors and sacrifices of the war for Independence—His several employments by Congress—He serves under General Greene at the Battle of Brandywine—He stands by Washington at Valley Forge—In February, 1781, he accompanies John Laurens on a special mission to France—Their return at end of six months—His chief service after 1776 as a writer of "The Crisis"—The last number of "The Crisis" in December, 1783—His poverty during those years.

IV.—The secret of Paine's power over men and events—A great journalist—His aptness in expressing from day to day the real thought of the people—The range of his discussions during the war—He represents the faith of the American people in themselves and in a Higher Power helping them—His scornful addresses to Lord Howe and his brother—His predictions of British discomfiture—His inspiring appeals to the American people after defeat and amid discouragement.

V.—At the approach of peace, Paine turns from a prose song of congratulation, to explain the new dangers and new duties then confronting the people—Financial dishonor and disunion—His last literary services in the Revolution are on behalf of American honesty, and of American nationality.

I.

In the interval between the publication of his pamphlet, "Common Sense," in January, 1776, and the final determination of Congress, six months later, to take the very course recommended in that pamphlet, Thomas Paine followed up the lines of argument and appeal on which he had thus wrought, by writing for a Philadelphia journal a series of at least four articles over the signature of "The Forester."[1] During this interval, also, appeared in Philadelphia a brochure which in our time has been confidently attributed to Paine, bearing the whimsical title,—"A Dialogue between the Ghost of General Montgomery just arrived from the Elysian Fields, and an American Delegate, in a Wood near Philadelphia,"—a well-managed political colloquy, in which the argument for Independence is developed with much of Paine's vigor, but perhaps with rather more accuracy, delicacy, and polish, than one expects to find in him.

But the man who had so brilliantly served the American cause by the pen, seems to have been eager to serve it by the sword also. Accordingly, in the summer of 1776, soon after the Declaration of Independence, he joined as a volunteer General Roberdeau's division of the Pennsylvania troops, called "the flying camp." With these troops he served at Perth Amboy, and at Bergen; and when, after a few weeks, their time expired and they returned home, Paine, unwilling at such a time to avail himself of such an excuse for leaving the field, "went to Fort Lee and served as aid-de-camp to General Greene, . . . and was with him during the whole of the black times of that trying campaign."[2] Benjamin Rush mentions that during that period, Paine lived a good deal with officers of the first rank in the army, at whose tables his 'Common Sense' always made him a welcome guest."[3] General Greene himself, in a let-

[1] Dunlap's "Pa. Packet, or the General Advertiser," for April 1, April 15, April 22, and May 20, 1776. No other number appeared in that paper down to July 1. I think the fourth number was the last of the series. I found the first three numbers in "The Pa. Gazette," for April 3, April 10, and April 24; but the fourth number I failed to find in that paper. Rush speaks, Cheetham, 38, of these essays as appearing "in Mr. Bradford's paper," *i. e.*, "The Pa. Journal," where Conway, "Life," i. 73, seems to have read them.

[2] Paine's own words. "Political Writings," ii. 493.

[3] Cheetham, 38.

ter written at Fort Lee to his wife, on the second of November, gives a glimpse of the daily life of his military family, especially mentioning the curious fact that in that time of appalling distress, Paine was "perpetually wrangling about mathematical problems"[1] with a certain other officer of the army.

Whoever served in the American army, in any capacity, in the autumn of 1776, had an employment full of discomfort and peril. On the twenty-seventh of August, Washington had suffered a shattering defeat in the battle of Long Island. Then had followed, in awful rapidity, a gloomy succession of disasters,—the abandonment of New York on the fifteenth of September, the defeat at White Plains on the twenty-eighth of October, the surrender of Fort Washington on the sixteenth of November, the stampede from Fort Lee on the eighteenth of November, finally, Washington's harassed retreat through New Jersey, and, on the eighth of December, his escape across the Delaware. In all these calamitous and distressing experiences,—defeats, retreats, marchings, and countermarchings, before a victorious and scornful foe,—Paine seems to have participated. A letter-writer in the British army, describing the capture of Fort Lee, connects Paine with the event in a somewhat grotesque manner: he relates that on the appearance of the British troops before that fortress, "the rebels fled like scared rabbits," leaving in their intrenchments "some poor pork, a few greasy proclamations, and some of that scoundrel 'Common Sense' man's letters, which we can read at our leisure, now that we have got one of the 'impregnable redoubts' of Mr. Washington's to quarter in."[2]

II.

It was in the midst of the dismay and disorder of this retreat across New Jersey, that Paine was inspired to begin that series of impassioned and invigorating pamphlets

[1] G. W. Greene, "The Life of Nathaniel Greene," i. 253.

[2] Markoe, in Moore, "Diary of the Am. Rev.," i. 350.

which at once became famous under the title of "The Crisis," and which continued to appear intermittently down to the close of the war. He has himself related how, on the scrambling retreat from Fort Lee, he began at Newark the first number of "The Crisis," "and continued writing it," as he says, "at every place we stopt at,"[1] until it was finished, and issued from the press at Philadelphia on the nineteenth of December,[2]—just four days before that on which Washington announced to some of his officers his purpose to recross the Delaware and to strike the enemy at Trenton. Those were perhaps the darkest days of the Revolution. Even Washington had then written: "If every nerve is not strained to recruit the new army with all possible expedition, I think the game is pretty nearly up."[3]

It was under such circumstances that the first number of "The Crisis,"[4] bearing the resounding signature of "Common Sense," greeted the American people with words that were electrical, and that soon became classic: "These are the times that try men's souls. The summer soldier and the sunshine patriot will, in this crisis, shrink from the service of his country; but he that stands it now, deserves the love and thanks of man and woman. Tyranny, like hell, is not easily conquered; yet we have this consolation with us, that the harder the conflict, the more glorious the triumph."[5]

As he passes on from paragraph to paragraph of this tremendous harangue, he touches with unfailing skill, with matchless power, the springs of anxiety, anger, contempt,

---

[1] "Political Writings," ii. 493.

[2] First in "The Pennsylvania Journal" on the date above mentioned. Conway, "Life," i. 85. It was then issued in pamphlet form, dated Dec. 23, 1776.

[3] "Writings," Sparks ed., iv. 231.

[4] This title, which of course was an obvious one for a pamphlet written under such circumstances, had been several times used before Paine made it famous; by Samuel Cooper for a pamphlet against the excise, published in Boston in 1754; and by a writer in London in 1766 for a pamphlet in defense of the colonies against the policy of the Stamp Act. According to Lossing, "Cycl. U. S. Hist., i. 347, the title was also used in London, in 1775–1776, for a series of papers "to be continued weekly during the present bloody civil war in America."

[5] "Political Writlngs," i. 75.

love of home, love of country, fortitude, cool deliberation, and passionate resolve; and he closes with such a battle-call as might almost have startled slain patriots from their new graves under the frozen clods: "Up and help us; lay your shoulders to the wheel; better have too much force than too little, when so great an object is at stake. Let it be told to the future world, that in the depth of winter, when nothing but hope and virtue could survive,[1] the city and country, alarmed at one common danger, came forth to meet and repulse it. . . . It matters not where you live, or what rank of life you hold, the evil or the blessing will reach you all. . . . The heart that feels not now, is dead. The blood of his children will curse his cowardice, who shrinks back at a time when a little might have saved the whole, and made them happy. I love the man that can smile in trouble, that can gather strength from distress, and grow brave by reflection. 'T is the business of little minds to shrink; but he whose heart is firm, and whose conscience approves his conduct, will pursue his principles unto death. . . . It is the madness of folly to expect mercy from those who have refused to do justice. . . . By perseverance and fortitude, we have the prospect of a glorious issue; by cowardice and submission, the sad choice of a variety of evils,—a ravaged country, a depopulated city, habitations without safety, and slavery without hope, our homes turned into barracks and bawdy-houses for Hessians, and a future race to provide for, whose fathers we shall doubt of. Look on this picture and weep over it; and if there yet remains one thoughtless wretch who believes it not, let him suffer it unlamented."[2]

III.

From the day on which he finished this pamphlet onward to the very close of the war, Paine seems to have had his

[1] In the text occurs here a supernumerary "that," which may have been due to a mere slip of the pen, but more likely indicates the actual state of Paine's grammatical development at that time.

[2] "Political Writings," ii. 80–82.

personal share in nearly every form of service or of privation which befell the American people. During the greater portion of this period, he gained his livelihood either by acting as secretary to the committee of Congress on foreign affairs, or as clerk in the commercial house of Owen Biddle, or as clerk to the general assembly of Pennsylvania. In September, 1777, while preparing at Philadelphia the dispatches of Congress for Franklin in Paris, he was interrupted by the booming of the cannon at Brandywine. Instantly dashing off a fresh number of "The Crisis," for the purpose of giving check to a popular panic, he threw aside his pen and by personal entreaty endeavored to induce the authorities to adopt some practicable plan for a volunteer defense of the city. Failing in this, he hurried away to the army, and as aid-de-camp to General Greene, and perhaps in other capacities as well, he partook to the full of the toils and perils of the troops during the remainder of that autumn, even standing by Washington's side in the grim retirement of Valley Forge.[1] In February, 1781, at a time when further American resistance was in danger of collapsing through sheer lack of the means to carry on the war, Paine sailed out of Boston harbor on the frigate "Alliance," in the company of Colonel John Laurens,—the latter going as minister extraordinary to France for the purpose of securing for Congress a special loan from the king. Just six months afterward, Paine and Laurens again appeared in Boston harbor, having with them, as the fruits of their expedition, 2,500,000 livres in silver, and in convoy a ship laden with clothing, ammunition, arms,—a most opportune supply, which had perhaps an essential part in the train of events which led, two months later, to the surrender of Cornwallis.[2]

Noble-minded and important as were these various ser-

---

[1] Paine gave a graphic sketch of his military experiences at that time, in a long letter to Franklin, which is printed in Conway, "Life," i. 104–113.

[2] "Secret Journals of Cong.," i. 351, 368–375; Hildreth, iii. 363. "Writings of Geo. Washington," Ford ed., ix. 355 n.

vices rendered by Paine to the American cause, on sea and land, in office and field, they could in no way be compared, as contributions to the success of the Revolution, with the work which he did during those same imperiled years merely as a writer, and especially as the writer of "The Crisis." Between December, 1776, when the first pamphlet of that series was published, down to December, 1783, when the last one left the printer's hands, this indomitable man produced no less than sixteen pamphlets under the same general title, adapting his message in each case to the supreme need of the hour, and accomplishing all this literary labor in a condition of actual poverty,—poverty so great that on one occasion, shortly after his return from France, he was obliged to apologize to his friend Laurens, then at the siege of Yorktown, for some delay in forwarding to headquarters a pair of new boots which that gallant officer had ordered in Philadelphia, by the naïve confession that he had not then in hand money enough to pay the bootmaker.[1]

IV.

The marvelous power which this untitled and impecunious penman wielded over the minds of men and over the course of events, during the entire period of our Revolution, was essentially the power of a great journalist. He had to the full the journalistic temperament,—its tastes, capacities, limitations. He had no interest in the past except so far as the past had a direct message for the present. His life was the life of to-day. He rose from his bed every morning to ask what was the uppermost thought, the keenest necessity, the most notable event, of that particular day. Books to him were of no vital account: his only library was a heap of pamphlets, and a pocket stuffed full of newspapers. All that he wrote was suggested by an occasion, and was meant for one. By some process of his own he knew just what the

---

[1] Paine's letter to Laurens, in Conway, "Life," i. 173–174.

people thought, feared, wished, loved, and hated: he knew it better than they knew it themselves. The secret of his strength lay in his infallible instinct for interpreting to the public its own conscience and its own consciousness, and for doing this in language which, at times, was articulate thunder and lightning. The history of the long war may be read in the blazing light of these mighty pamphlets, in which with the confident look, with the unhesitating voice, of a leader born to lead, he rallied the people in many an hour of disaster and fright, pleaded with them, rebuked them, inspired them, and pointed out to them the path of duty and of victory, or, standing in front of them, on their behalf flung his jests, taunts, and maledictions at the foe. Thus, he addresses, on one occasion, the leading British officer just then in America, in order, as he says to him, "to expose the folly of your pretended authority as a commissioner, the wickedness of your cause in general, and the impossibility of your conquering us at any rate." As regards the American people, he says, "my intention is to shew them their true and solid interest; to encourage them to their own good; to remove the fears and falsities which bad men have spread, and weak men have encouraged; and to excite in all men a love for union, and a cheerfulness for duty."[1]

In those days, certainly, Thomas Paine represented, not only the faith of the people in themselves, but their faith in God and in God's guidance and mastery of the affairs of this world, and in the ultimate victory of God's cause against every possible league of men and of devils. Speaking always in the character of an avowed Christian, and to a nation of Christians, Paine declares: "God Almighty will not give up a people to military destruction, or leave them unsupportedly to perish, who have so earnestly and so repeatedly sought to avoid the calamities of war, by every decent method which wisdom could invent. Neither have

---

[1] "Political Writings," i. 94.

I so much of the infidel in me as to suppose that He has relinquished the government of the world, and given us up to the care of devils." "If we believe the power of hell to be limited, we must likewise believe that their agents are under some providential control."[1] "There has been such a chain of extraordinary events in the discovery of this country at first, in the peopling and planting it afterwards, in the rearing and nursing it to its present state, and in the protection of it through the present war, that no man can doubt but Providence hath some nobler end to accomplish than the gratification of the petty elector of Hanover, or the ignorant and insignificant king of Britain." We dare to believe that ours is the cause to which Providence will give the victory, because "we fight not to enslave, but to set a country free, and to make room upon the earth for honest men to live in."[2]

And who is it, at this late day, who can any longer doubt the wisdom of our resolve to cast aside the colonial character, and to set up a national establishment for ourselves? "To know whether it be the interest of this continent to be Independent, we need only ask this easy, simple question: Is it the interest of a man to be a boy all his life?"[3]

And you, my Lord Howe, in your so-called proclamation,—a preposterous compound of assumptions, promises, and threats,—you have the audacity to speak of our claim to Independence as something "extravagant and inadmissible." "Why, God bless me, what have you to do with our Independence? We ask no leave of yours to set it up; we ask no money of yours to support it; we can do better without your fleets and armies than with them; you may soon have enough to do to protect yourselves without being burdened with us. We are very willing to be at peace with you, to buy of you and sell to you, and, like young beginners in the world, to work for our living. Therefore, why

---

[1] "Political Writings," i. 76, 77.
[2] Ibid. 146–147, 131.
[3] Ibid. 105.

do you put yourselves out of cash, when we know you cannot spare it, and we do not desire you to run into debt?"[1]

And, moreover, what a ridiculous thing it is for a man in your circumstances to issue a proclamation at all! "Your authority in the Jerseys is now reduced to the small circle which your army occupies, and your proclamation is nowhere else seen, unless it be to be laughed at. The mighty subduers of the continent have retreated into a nut-shell; and the proud forgivers of our sins are fled from those they came to pardon. . . . In short, you have managed your Jersey expedition so very dexterously, that the dead only are conquerors, because none will dispute the ground with them."[2]

As to those troops of yours, with which you have tried to overawe us, and from which the world has been taught to expect so much, what is their real condition? "Like a wounded, disabled whale, they want only time and room to die in; and though in the agony of their exit, it may be unsafe to live within the flapping of their tail, yet every hour shortens their date, and lessens their power of mischief."[3] "Their condition is both despicable and deplorable: out of cash, out of heart, out of hope. A country furnished with arms and ammunition, as America now is, with three millions of inhabitants, and three thousand miles distant from the nearest enemy that can approach her, is able to look and laugh them in the face."[4]

"Your cargo of pardons," he says contemptuously to the three British commissioners who came out in 1778, "will have no market. It is unfashionable to look at them—even speculation is at an end. They have become a perfect drug, and no way calculated for the climate."[5] "You may plan and execute little mischiefs; but are they worth the expense they cost you, or will such partial evils have any

---

[1] "Political Writings," i. 86. [2] Ibid. 92.
[3] Ibid. 101. [4] Ibid. 122. [5] Ibid. 157.

effect on the general cause? Your expedition to Egg-Harbor will be felt at a distance like an attack upon a hen-roost, and expose you in Europe with a sort of childish phrenzy. Is it worth while to keep an army to protect you in writing proclamations, or to get once a year into winter-quarters?"[1]

As he had bestowed much frankness on Lord Howe, he is disposed to treat his brother, Sir William, with equal distinction: "Indolence and inability have too large a share in your composition, ever to suffer you to be anything more than the hero of little villanies and unfinished adventures."[2]

"Let me ask, sir, what great exploits have you performed? Through all the variety of changes and opportunities which the war has produced, I know no one action of yours that can be styled masterly: You have moved in and out, backward and forward, round and round, as if valor consisted in a military jig. The history and figure of your movements would be truly ridiculous could they be justly delineated. They resemble the labors of a puppy pursuing his tail; the end is still at the same distance, and all the turnings round must be done over again."[3] "The time, sir, will come when you, in a melancholy hour, shall reckon up your miseries, by your murders in America. Life with you begins to wear a clouded aspect. The vision of pleasurable delusion is wearing away, and changing to the barren wild of age and sorrow. The poor reflection of having served your king will yield you no consolation in your parting moments. He will crumble to the same undistinguishable ashes with yourself, and have sins enough of his own to answer for. It is not the farcical benedictions of a bishop, nor the cringing hypocrisy of a court of chaplains, nor the formality of an act of parliament, that can change guilt into innocence, or make the punishment one pang the less. You may, perhaps, be unwilling to be serious; but this destruction of the goods of Providence, this havoc of the human

---

[1] "Political Writings," i. 165. [2] Ibid. 134. [3] Ibid. 140–141.

race, and this sowing the world with mischief, must be accounted for to Him who made and governs it. To us they are only present sufferings, but to Him they are deep rebellions." [1]

Turning to his fellow-countrymen on the day after a harrowing defeat, his words go forth as a trumpet call to reassurance and to a renewal of the conflict: "Those who expect to reap the blessings of freedom, must like men undergo the fatigues of supporting it. The event of yesterday was one of those kind alarms which are [2] just sufficient to rouse us to duty, without being of consequence enough to depress our fortitude. It is not a field of a few acres of ground, but a cause, that we are defending; and whether we defeat the enemy in one battle, or by degrees, the consequence will be the same. . . . We have always been masters at the last push, and always shall be while we do our duty. . . . Shall a band of ten or twelve thousand robbers, who are this day fifteen hundred or two thousand men less in strength than they were yesterday, conquer America, or subdue even a single State? The thing cannot be done, unless we sit down and suffer them to do it. Another such a brush, notwithstanding we lost the ground, would, by still reducing the enemy, put them in a condition to be afterwards totally defeated. . . . It is distressing to see an enemy advancing into a country, but it is the only place in which we can beat them, and in which we have always beaten them, whenever they have made the attempt. . . . You have too much at stake to hesitate. You ought not to think an hour upon the matter, but to spring to action at once. Other States have been invaded; have likewise driven off the invaders. Now our time and turn is come, and perhaps the finishing stroke is reserved for us. When we look back on the dangers we have been saved from, and reflect on the

---

[1] "Political Writings," i. 145–146.

[2] The text reads "is." On the day after an unfortunate battle, most men, especially most men whose efforts to be grammatical have been postponed until middle life, are liable to some embarrassment from their nominatives.

success we have been blessed with, it would be sinful either to be idle or to despair." [1]

Near the close of the first three years of the war, he sums up the results in a single sentence: "It is now nearly three years since the tyranny of Britain received its first repulse by the arms of America,—a period which has given birth to a new world, and erected a monument to the folly of the old." [2]

V.

And when, at last, the final victory is come and actual peace draws on, this unfatigued prophet consents to pause long enough to chant, in sinewy prose, a virile song of congratulation; but almost before its close he begins to beckon his fellow-countrymen away from mere exultation, and from past success, to point toward the new dangers and the new duties which that very success is about to lay upon them: "The times that tried men's souls are over—and the greatest and completest Revolution the world ever knew, gloriously and happily accomplished. But to pass from the extremes of danger to safety—from the tumult of war to the tranquillity of peace—though sweet in contemplation, requires a gradual composure of the senses to receive it. Even calmness has the power of stunning, when it opens too instantly upon us. . . . In the present case, the mighty magnitude of the object, the various uncertainties of fate which it has undergone, the numerous and complicated dangers we have suffered or escaped, the eminence we now stand on, and the vast prospect before us, must all conspire to impress us with contemplation. To see it in our power to make a world happy, to teach mankind the art of being so, to exhibit on the theatre of the universe a character hitherto unknown, and to have, as it were, a new creation intrusted to our hands, are honors that command reflection, and can neither be too highly estimated, nor too gratefully received. In this pause, then, of reflection, while the storm

---

[1] "Political Writings," i. 128–130. [2] Ibid. 149.

is ceasing, and the long-agitated mind vibrating to a rest, let us look back on the scenes we have passed, and learn from experience what is yet to be done." [1]

But just before us lie two immense dangers: the first, financial dishonor, the second, disunion. To guard against, to avert, these two dangers—this is the new duty which now summons us: "The debt which America has contracted, compared with the cause she has gained, and the advantages to flow from it, ought scarcely to be mentioned. . . . Character is much easier kept than recovered; and that man, if any such there be, who, from sinister views, or littleness of soul, lends unseen his hand to injure it, contrives a wound it will never be in his power to heal. As we have established an inheritance for posterity, let that inheritance descend, with every mark of an honorable conveyance. The little it will cost compared with the worth of the States, the greatness of the object, and the value of national character, will be a profitable exchange." [2]

"But that which must more forcibly strike a thoughtful, penetrating mind, and which includes and renders easy all inferior concerns, is the union of the States. On this, our great national character depends. It is this which must give us importance abroad and security at home. . . . In short, we have no other national sovereignty than as United States. . . . Individuals, or individual States, may call themselves what they please; but the world, and especially the world of enemies, is not to be held in awe by the whistling of a name. Sovereignty must have power to protect all the parts that compose and constitute it; and as the United States, we are equal to the importance of the title, but otherwise we are not. Our union, well and wisely regulated and cemented, is the cheapest way of being great —the easiest way of being powerful, and the happiest invention in government which the circumstances of America can admit of . . . . I ever feel myself hurt when I hear

[1] "Political Writings," i. 256–257. [2] Ibid. 258–259.

the union, that great palladium of our liberty and safety, the least irreverently spoken of. It is the most sacred thing in the constitution of America, and that which every man should be most proud and tender of. Our citizenship in the United States is our national character. Our citizenship in any particular State is only our local distinction. By the latter we are known at home, by the former to the world. Our great title is AMERICANS." [1]

---

[1] "Political Writings," i. 259–260.

CHAPTER XXVII.

THE LITERARY WARFARE AGAINST AMERICAN INDEPENDENCE: LOYALIST WRITERS IN PROSE AND VERSE: 1776–1783.

I.—The writings of the Loyalists during this stage of the Revolution inferior in amount to those of the Revolutionists—Their decline in the use of serious discussion—Three peculiarities in the attitude of the Loyalists—Their confidence in the soundness of their own opinions; their contempt for the Revolutionists as vulgar and unprincipled; their perfect expectation of the success of the British arms.

II.—The Loyalist sarcasm on the practical denial of liberty by the pretended American champions of it—Many colonists forced into support of the Revolutionary measures—"The Pausing American Loyalist"—"The Rebels"—"A Familiar Epistle."

III.—The Loyalist taunt concerning the plebeian origin and occupations of the Revolutionary leaders—"A Modern Catechism"—List of American officers as published in Germany—The "brace of Adamses"—A Charleston satire.

IV.—The attacks of the Tory satirists concentrated on Congress, as a body representing the vulgarity and profligacy of the Revolutionary movement.

V.—The exploits of Congress in the field of finance a theme for Tory derision—The depreciation of American paper-money—Jests thereon from the Tory newspapers—Satire on the tattered condition of the American army.

VI.—Tory jests upon individual leaders of the Revolution—Especial attention paid to Thomas Paine.

VII.—Tory mirth over the military and naval disappointments of the French alliance—Failure of the allied campaign of 1778—"The Epilogue," as sung by Congress at the conclusion of the Farce "Independence"—Failure of the allied campaign of 1779—The mirthful ballad "About Savannah"—"A New Ballad."

VIII.—Some serious Loyalist discussion of the state of affairs consequent on the American alliance with France—"Letters of Papinian"—The unnaturalness of the French alliance, and its disastrous effects, set forth in "A Letter to the People of America."

IX.—The possible calamities to overtake the Americans at the hands of their French allies, exhibited by many Tory writers—Outline of their opinions on the subject—"The Prophecy," on French and Papal despotism in America, after its separation from England by the help of Roman Catholic France.

X.—Distrust as to the wisdom of the French alliance, even among Revolutionary statesmen—The letters of Silas Deane, in 1781.

I.

In the effort to obtain a just view of the part actually taken by the Loyalist writers, especially in the final and supreme stage of the Revolution when Independence had become its avowed object, we find ourselves confronting, at the outset, two notable facts: first, the marked inferiority of Loyalist literature, as regards mere amount, by comparison with the literature produced during the same time by the Revolutionists; secondly, the lessened confidence of the Loyalist writers in serious argumentative discussion, together with a corresponding increase in their employment of mere emotional appeal—that is, of rapturous assertions of the nobility, strength, and assured success of their own cause, and derisive assertions of the baseness and the weakness of the cause of their countrymen in rebellion.

That the writings of the Loyalists, from 1776 to 1783, were in number inferior to those of the opposite party, can now surprise no one who considers the circumstances of that time, when all active Loyalists had been ruthlessly harried out of the country or harried into the enemy's lines, and when in all the length and breadth of the land, from New Hampshire to Georgia, not a newspaper, not a printing-press, was left at their service, excepting, of course, in the city of New York and in such other large towns as might chance to be for any part of the time under British occupation. Moreover, it will not be forgotten that such execrable things as Tory writings, even if they got into print, could hardly get into circulation; they could come in only as they were smuggled in, and they could pass from hand to hand only by that sort of stealth which is itself a confession of crime.

As regards mere vivacity, the literature of the Loyalists is in no respect a loser by its increasing disuse of serious debate, any more than it is a loser thereby as regards its importance for historic interpretation—for its use to us in our effort to enter into the inward life of that period. On both sides, men took part in the struggle, not merely with their brains and their hands, but with their hearts; they waged the war in the sphere of sentiment and passion, as well as in that of reason and physical force; they hurled at one another not only facts and arguments, but sarcasms and taunts and curses; they fought one another, as with logic, so also with wit and humor and scoff and scorn. Of course, the spiritual history of such a controversy is left half told, so long as the emotional side of it is left untold.

Finally, if we would do justice to this branch of Loyalist literature—if we would even understand it—we must have in mind certain peculiarities in the attitude of the Loyalists toward the Revolution, and especially toward their own countrymen who were pushing it on. In the first place, as to the constitutional and political questions involved in the controversy, the Loyalists had an unclouded conviction that they themselves were right. In the second place, belonging as they did, in many cases, to the oldest, wealthiest, most dignified families in the country, and accustomed always to take the lead in the affairs of their several colonies, they, of course, looked down with contempt and disgust upon the whole Revolution as a thoroughly plebeian movement,—propelled from the beginning, as they thought, by upstarts and adventurers,—obscure attorneys, blacksmiths, shopkeepers, and ploughmen, who were thus presuming to flout at their betters, and to turn the world upside down in the hope of being themselves at last on top. In the third place, the Loyalists fully expected to be on the winning side. They had the most perfect assurance of the ultimate and utter failure of the rebellion; they could not conceive it as possible, that these colonial rebels, with their lack of money, their lack of military supplies, their lack of military training and experience, could hold out very long, even though they should at last have foreign help, as against the most stupendous military and naval power in the modern world.

These three peculiarities in the attitude of the Loyalists

resulted in such a condition of mind as made it natural for them to apply to the rebellion, and especially to the rebels, whatever words they could command from the vocabulary of derision and hate, all the more so when they finally lost faith in any good to be got by arguing with these extremely determined criminals. Then, indeed, with whatever gifts they had for prose or verse, they set themselves to the task of keeping up their own spirits and of keeping down the spirits of their opponents, by lyric celebrations of the nobility and invincible might of their own cause, and by the most scornful vituperation of the cause which they so hated and despised. Since they could not reason down the rebellion, they meant, not only to fight it down, but to laugh it down, to sneer it down, and to make it seem to all the world as ridiculous as, to themselves, it already seemed sordid and vulgar and weak.

II.

From the very beginning of any sharp division between the two parties, a favorite sarcasm on the part of the Tories had been one aimed at the gross inconsistency of the Whigs in conducting what they called the cause of liberty by methods which simply crushed and stifled liberty,—the only liberty allowed to anybody by the Whigs being the liberty to think just as they thought. Consequently, not a few persons, it was said, were included in the Whig ranks because of their own timidity; they had been dragooned and terrorized into an apparent support of the Revolution; their Whiggism was but a mask assumed for personal safety against intolerable social pressure and mob-violence. Thus, the most practical measure of the Congress of 1774 was its so-called "association," which had been carried into every community and had been offered for the individual assent of every colonist. From that moment, fidelity to the "association" had become a test of every man's political rectitude. He who should hesitate, above all, he who should refuse, to sign the "association," became the object of public suspicion and detestation; and if at all prominent in the community, he was liable to gross personal indignities—to be tarred and feathered, to have his house mobbed, to be ruined in business and in property. Many a man, said the Loyalists, had signed the "association," not because he desired to do so, but because he did not dare to refuse. There remain to us from that time some capital verses in the form of a parody on Hamlet's soliloquy, illustrating the moral ignominy of this situation, wherein, according to the Tories, multitudes of loyal Americans were compelled to become trimmers and hypocrites and rebels, or else to flee from home and country and their established means of livelihood, and to find in England only exile, the cold pity of strangers, and in many cases hunger and rags and a miserable death. This little poem, written by some unknown Tory of that period, is called "The Pausing American Loyalist"; and it represents such a person as communing with himself over the horrid situation, and balancing in his mind the contrasted claims of that frightful alternative which was thus presented to him:

"To sign, or not to sign!—That is the question:
Whether 't were better for an honest man
To sign—and so be safe; or to resolve,
Betide what will, against 'associations,'
And, by retreating, shun them. To fly—I reck
Not where—and, by that flight, t' escape
Feathers and tar, and thousand other ills
That Loyalty is heir to: 't is a consummation
Devoutly to be wished. To fly—to want—
To want?—perchance to starve! Ay, there 's the rub!
For, in that chance of want, what ills may come
To patriot rage, when I have left my all,
Must give me pause! There 's the respect
That makes us trim, and bow to men we hate.
For, who would bear th' indignities o' th' times,
Congress decrees, and wild Convention plans,
The laws controll'd, and inj'ries unredressed,

The insolence of knaves, and thousand wrongs
Which patient liege men from vile rebels take,
When he, sans doubt, might certain safety find,
Only by flying? Who would bend to fools,
And truckle thus to mad, mob-chosen upstarts,
But that the dread of something after flight
(In that blest country, where, yet, no moneyless
Poor wight can live) puzzles the will,
And makes ten thousands rather sign—and eat,
Than fly—to starve on Loyalty!
Thus, dread of want makes cowards of us all;
And, thus, the native hue of Loyalty
Is sicklied o'er with a pale cast of trimming;
And enterprises of great pith and virtue,
But unsupported, turn their streams away,
And never come to action." [1]

If, while the two parties were thus beginning to take sides upon the issue thus formed, such tyranny was exercised over the opinions and actions of men, to what monstrous size might not this tyranny be expected to grow after the issue had become settled, and seasoned, in blood? At no later period of the Revolution, therefore, was there any failure on the part of the Tory writers to call attention to this shocking aspect of the much-vaunted movement for liberty: as, in 1778, in a ballad called "The Rebels,"—

"For one lawful ruler, many tyrants we've got,
Who force young and old to their wars, to be shot" [2];

or, as in "A Familiar Epistle," addressed to Robert Wills, the printer of the "Carolina Gazette," by a young Loyalist

[1] This parody, which clearly belongs to the period between the first and second Congresses, is given by F. Moore, "Diary of the Am. Rev.," i. 169, as from the "Middlesex Journal" for Jan. 30, 1776, where, if that date be correctly given, it was probably reproduced from some copy printed at least a year earlier.

[2] The whole ballad is given in F. Moore, "Songs and Ballads of the Rev.," 198.

of Charleston, who was seized and thrown into jail for the crime of having written it:

"Excuse me, dear Robert, I can't think it true,
Though Solomon says it, that nothing is new.
Had he lived in these times, we had rather been told
Our West World 's so new, it has nothing that 's old.
But should he insist in his own way to have it,
I would beg leave to ask of this wise son of David
A few simple questions: as, where he e'er saw
Men legally punished for not breaking the law?
Tarr'd, feather'd, and carted for drinking Bohea?—
And by force and oppression compell'd to be free?—
The same men maintaining that all human kind
Are, have been, and shall be, as free as the wind,
Yet impaling and burning their slaves for believing
The truth of the lessons they 're constantly giving?"[1]

III.

Closely connected with this taunt that the pretended champions of liberty were actual perpetrators of despotism, and, indeed, often woven with it into the same passage of satire, was the added taunt as to their low origin and vulgar occupations and characters:

"With loud peals of laughter, your sides, sirs, would crack,
To see General Convict, and Colonel Shoe-black,
With their hunting-shirts and rifle-guns;
See cobblers and quacks, rebel priests and the like,
Pettifoggers and barbers, with sword and with pike,
All strutting, the standard of Satan beside,
And honest names using, their black deeds to hide."[2]

---

[1] The whole poem is given in "The Loyalist Poetry of the Rev.," 58–60. Its exact date is not ascertained. Though it appeared in "The Pennsylvania Ledger" for February 14, 1778, it had probably been printed before.

[2] Part of the ballad called "The Rebels," by the Loyalist officer, John Ferdinand Smyth, in F. Moore, "Songs and Ballads of the Rev.," 197–198.

The keynote of a great deal of Loyalist sarcasm is given in this charge that the Revolutionist party is a party of upstarts and nobodies, while the Loyalist leaders, from their superior wealth, cultivation, social position, and from their habits of political prominence, claimed to be and seemed to be the old nobility, who, standing by the law and the right, were being displaced and hustled aside by proletariats—by political parvenus and nondescripts. The Revolution was brought about, they said, not by the true men of the country—the men who had the most stake in it—but by needy young lawyers, by bankrupts and defaulters, by uneasy adventurers, by word-spouting cobblers and tinkers who found mending the state an easier and a more lucrative job than that of mending kettles and patching shoes. Thus, in "The New York Gazette" for May 23, 1778, was printed "A Modern Catechism," consisting, in part, of the following questions and answers:

"Q. Who have been the principal advocates for, and instigators of, the American Revolution?

"A. An unprincipled and a disappointed faction in the mother country, and an infernal, dark-designing group of men in America audaciously styling themselves a Congress. . . .

"Q. What kind of men compose the Congress?

"A. It consists of obscure, pettifogging attorneys, bankrupt shopkeepers, outlawed smugglers, etc., etc.

"Q. Of what complexion are their mobs and leaders?

"A The wretched banditti . . . are the refuse and dregs of mankind; their generals are men of rank and honor nearly on a par with those of the Congress."

Even in Europe was spread this opinion as to the low-born origin and vulgar characters of many of the Revolutionist party, as may partly be seen from a list of them drawn up by Professor August Schlözer, of Göttingen, probably from information furnished him by some of the German auxiliaries in America. According to this list, General McDougall was originally a sailor, Arnold a horse-dealer,

Putnam an inn-keeper, Sullivan a breeches-maker, Knox a blacksmith, Greene an advocate, disbarred, Wayne a tanner-boy, Irvine a hatter, Maxwell a swineherd, Nagle a cowherd, and Glover a tailor; while others are named as of broken and disreputable business antecedents.[1] It was no uncommon thing, in the earlier years of the Revolution, for Samuel Adams to be described as a mere tax-collector embarrassed by official dishonesty, as a vulgar and an unscrupulous village politician; and John Adams, as a reckless political adventurer, with nothing to lose and everything to win by tumult, as spurred on to desperate measures by poverty, by disappointment, and by a passion for notoriety; and when, in 1770, Governor Shirley spoke contemptuously of their lack of standing, describing them as that "brace of Adamses," the younger of them replied in language which seemed proudly to concede the point of social inferiority: "Is it not a pity that a brace of so obscure a breed should be the only ones to defend the household, when the generous mastiffs and best-blooded hounds are all hushed to silence by the bones and crumbs that are thrown to them? Even Cerberus himself is bought off with a sop."[2]

In a different form the same classic sneer of the Tories is embalmed in these lines, written by an unknown versifier in South Carolina:

"Not only our money from nothing appears,
From nothing our hopes, and from nothing our fears,
From nothing our statesmen, our army, our fleet,—
From nothing they came, and to nought they 'll retreat,
And no arms they handle so well as their feet.
Down at night a bricklayer or carpenter lies,
With next sun a Lycurgus or Solon doth rise;
. . . .
Priests, tailors, and cobblers fill with heroes the camp,
And sailors, like crawfish, crawl out of each swamp."[3]

[1] Aug. L. Schlözer, "Correspondence," viii. 3.
[2] "The Works of John Adams," ii. 233, 295.
[3] "The Loyalist Poetry of the Rev.," 59–60.

IV.

Moreover, it is habitual with the Loyalist writers to speak of the men who brought on and conducted the Revolution, not only as upstarts, as mere nobodies tossed into prominence by social commotion, but as positively bad men, as insincere and selfish men, as political hypocrites and knaves, who were knowingly misleading the people into crime and ruin. No doubt the Tories truly thought that the Revolutionary leaders were as a class what they uniformly called them, great scoundrels; and finding the choicest representatives of these scoundrels brought together in Congress, very naturally they poured out upon that particular body by name their choicest execration. A sufficiently vigorous example of this pleasant habit of theirs is furnished to our hands by a Tory ballad called "The Congress," which was written in the spring of 1776, and which at once endeared itself to the whole Tory party by the comprehensiveness and alacrity of its curses upon every man and hat and shoestring in that detestable sham-legislature:

"These hardy knaves and stupid fools,
Some apish and pragmatic mules,
Some servile acquiescing tools,—
These, these compose the Congress!

"When Jove resolved to send a curse,
And all the woes of life rehearse,
Not plague, not famine, but much worse—
He cursed us with a Congress.

"Then peace forsook this hapless shore,
Then cannons blazed with horrid roar;
We hear of blood, death, wounds, and gore,
The offspring of the Congress.

"Imperial Rome from scoundrels rose,
Her grandeur 's hailed in verse and prose;

Venice the dregs of sea compose ;
So sprung the mighty Congress.

" When insects vile emerge to light,
They take their short inglorious flight,
Then sink again to native night,
An emblem of the Congress.

" With freemen's rights they wanton play ;
At their command, we fast and pray ;
With worthless paper they us pay,
A fine device of Congress.

" With poverty and dire distress,
With standing armies us oppress,
Whole troops to Pluto swiftly press,
As victims to the Congress.

. . . . . .

" Good Lord ! disperse this venal tribe ;
Their doctrine let no fools imbibe—
Let Balaam no more asses ride,
Nor burdens bear to Congress.

" With puffs, and flams, and gasconade,
With stupid jargon they bravade ;
We transports take—Quebec invade—
With laurels crown the Congress.

" Our mushroom champions they dragoon,
We cry out hero, not poltroon,
The next campaign we 'll storm the moon,
And there proclaim the Congress.

" Old Catiline, and Cromwell too,
Jack Cade, and his seditious crew,
Hail brother-rebel at first view,
And hope to meet the Congress.

"The world 's amazed to see the pest
The tranquil land with wars infest;
Britannia puts them to the test,
And tries the strength of Congress.

"O goddess, hear our hearty prayers;
Confound the villains by the ears;
Disperse the plebeians—try the peers,
And execute the Congress.

"See, see, our hope begins to dawn!
Bold Carleton scours the Northern lawn,
The sons of faction sigh forlorn,
Dejected is the Congress.

"Clinton, Burgoyne and gallant Howe,
Will soon reward our conduct true,
And to each traitor give his due,
Perdition waits the Congress.

. . . . . .

"Prepare, prepare, my friends, prepare
For scenes of blood, the field of war;
To royal standard we 'll repair,
And curse the haughty Congress.

"Huzza! huzza! we thrice huzza!
Return peace, harmony, and law!
Restore such times as once we saw,
And bid adieu to Congress."[1]

V.

Besides the vulgarity and the political profligacy of the men who composed the American Congress, the amazing exploits of that body in the field of public finance were a

[1] "The Loyalist Poetry of the Rev.," 70–74.

theme for inextinguishable laughter on the part of the Tories. It must be admitted that, to an unfriendly observer, there was no slight inducement to satire in the fiscal policy of this famous legislature, obliged, as it was, to provide for the expenses of a great war, and yet being itself destitute of the power to raise a dollar by any form of taxation. No doubt, also, there were in Congress some members with very magnificent conceptions of the ability even of such a legislature to create money merely by setting in motion a printing press; like that delegate who, in a debate on the necessity of a tax as a means of getting money for the public debt, is said to have exclaimed—"Do you think, gentlemen, that I will consent to load my constituents with taxes, when we can send to our printer and get a wagon-load of money, one quire of which will pay for the whole?"[1]

Whatever may have been its justification, Congress did attempt to create money by its own fiat as applied to certain oblong bits of paper, and with results among the most ghastly in the history of finance; its issues of such money amounting to six millions of dollars in 1775, to nineteen millions in 1776, to thirteen millions in 1777, to over sixty-three millions in 1778, and to one hundred and forty millions in 1779.[2] Although, at first, this paper circulated at par, yet shortly after the Declaration of Independence the process of depreciation began and then went on with terrific speed. At the end of the year 1777, one Congress-dollar was worth only thirty-three cents, at the beginning of the year 1779 only twelve cents, and at the beginning of 1780 less than two cents.[3] A correspondent of General Gates, writing from Virginia in the latter year, mentions the payment of eleven dollars for a pound of brown sugar, of seventy-five dollars for a yard of linen, and

---

[1] Pelatiah Webster, "Political Essays," 7–8 n.

[2] Charles J. Bullock, "The Finances of the U. S. from 1775 to 1789, with Especial Reference to the Budget," 130.

[3] Ibid. 126, 129, 130, 136.

of one hundred dollars for a pound of tea.[1] When, in the year 1780, Gates was ordered by Congress to proceed from his home in Virginia to the army in South Carolina,—not a long journey—he was allowed thirty-thousand dollars in continental money for his traveling expenses. On arriving at his destination, he found it necessary to build a hundred yards of picketing as an enclosure for some British prisoners in his custody, and was somewhat startled to find that it cost him $500,000.[2] In 1781, Jefferson records the fee of his physician for two calls as $3000, and the price of three quarts of brandy as $355.50. Thomas Paine mentions the purchase of a pair of woolen stockings, for which he paid $300.[3]

This grotesque depreciation in the currency provided by the Revolutionary government seemed to be ominous of its inevitable and speedy failure in the attempt to keep up the war with only such sinews of war; and doubtless, it was for its tremendous effect in deepening and extending public expectation of the speedy collapse of the Revolution, that the comedy of Congressional financiering received so much attention from the Tory humorists. Within three months after the Declaration of Independence, the "New York Gazette" contained a satirical advertisement calling for a quantity of Congress-dollars as a particularly cheap form of papering for the walls of a house; and, at about the same time, a lampoon insinuating that this money was then commonly used for kindling fires, lighting pipes, shaving, and still more ignoble uses; and a year or two later, the account of a "Dream," wherein was seen a vision of the "hall of justice" in the nether world, and the arrival there of the members of the American Congress. These mighty senators "were so fond of their usurped dignity as to have brought their chairs along with them at the expense of paying double ferriage" in crossing the Styx. This additional

[1] I take these items from the Gates Papers, still unpublished, belonging to the N. Y. Historical Society.

[2] Gates Papers.

[3] Conway, "Life of Paine," i. 161.

charge, however, had made little difference to them, "as they had all taken in Charon, who was such a simpleton as to take Congress-dollars in payment, which he is now offering at the rate of thirty-seven for one, swearing at the same time that" these American Congressmen "and their lumber were the most disagreeable load he ever carried; for every one in his turn attempted to take the helm, and one Putnam was finding fault with the constitution of his boat."[1] Even among the friends of the Revolution, the disgust of the people with the currency provided by Congress became so great that in 1781, according to a lively narrative given in the same repository of Loyalist humor, there was in Philadelphia a boisterous parade composed of citizens of that town wearing paper dollars in their hats for cockades, and carrying in front of them a dog besmeared with tar but having paper dollars stuck on instead of feathers, this dog being followed by a jailor in the act of refusing the paper money which a poor prisoner had offered him for a glass of rum, and by a group of tradesmen who had shut up their shops and would sell no more goods for such money.[2] All this was exhibited in front of the state house, with Congress inside and invited to witness the spectacle without any charge.

Of course, in such a condition of the public finances, the officers and men of the Revolutionary army were reduced to the greatest distress, and often presented a tattered appearance perhaps unrivaled in military history, except by Falstaff's men,—since the paper dollars in which they received their pay, instead of relieving them, only added to the rags of which they already had an abundance. After the arrival of the French allies, many American officers were unable, for lack of decent clothes and decent food, to reciprocate social courtesies with these elegant foreign friends. Not from inhumanity, surely, but on account of its pertinence to the question as to how long a rebellion supported

[1] "The New York Gazette," Jan. 30, 1779. [2] Ibid. May 12, 1781.

in such a way might be expected to hold out, this impoverished condition of the American army was constantly held up to ridicule. A single specimen of such Tory ridicule may suffice us: it is an entry in the diary of a British officer in New York for March 1, 1777. "A deserter from the rebel army at Westchester, who came into New York this morning, says that the Congress troops are suffering extremely for food and rum; that there is not a whole pair of breeches in the army; and that the last news from Mr. Washington's camp was, that he had to tie up his with strings, having parted with the buttons to buy the necessaries of life. There is great plenty of rag money, but since old Franklin went to France, there is no one left to argue it into the favor of the Jerseymen, who, though justly called Republicans, are not willing to give even bad provisions for Congress notes, or mere rebel promises to pay." [1]

VI.

The Tory humorists were by no means content with ridicule of the rebellion in general, or even of certain great groups of rebels embodied in the shape of a congress or of an army; they perhaps found their keenest sport in pointing their shafts at individual rebels, as Washington, Charles Lee, Putnam, William Livingston, Robert Morris, Franklin, the Adamses, and, especially, at their own erring brother of the quill, Mr. Thomas Paine. Thus, in their chief newspaper, for January 30, 1779, are reported, by the favorite means of a prophetic vision, certain transactions soon to take place in the infernal regions, involving the doom to be meted out to the leading rebels, as fast as they shall present themselves before that ultimate tribunal. Among them, in due course, arrived Paine, who, having "a huge bundle of papers on his back, openly accused Mr. Robert Morris of negligence and dishonesty in his dealings with the public.

[1] Smythe's Diary, cited in F. Moore, "Diary of the Am. Rev.," i. 399–400.

Morris arose in great rage to reply, or knock him down," whereupon the papers on Paine's shoulders, "expanding themselves, assumed the form of wings; and his body, suddenly diminishing, exhibited the form of a mosquito, which immediately flew away into Tartarus, where he found the climate agreeable to his constitution."

Some months afterward, in the same newspaper, the same troublesome rebel penman is made the object of a salutation so ardent as to require the aid of verse:

"Hail mighty Thomas! in whose works are seen
A mangled Morris and distorted Deane;
Whose splendid periods flash for Lee's defense,—
Replete with everything but Common Sense.
You, by whose labors no man e'er was wiser,
You, of invective great monopolizer;
You, who, unfeeling as a Jew or Turk,
Attack a Jay, a Paca, and a Burke;
You, who, in fervor of satiric vein,
Maul and abuse the mild and meek Duane,
And eager to traduce the worthiest men,
Despite the energy of Drayton's pen,—
O say, what name shall dignify the lays
Which now I consecrate to sing thy praise!
In pity tell by what exalted name
Thou would'st be damned to an eternal fame:
Shall Common Sense, or Comus greet thine ear,
A piddling poet, or puffed pamphleteer?
. . . .
But sure no mortal mother did thee bear;—
Rather a colic in the prince of air,
On dusky pinions borne o'er Æther's plain,
Expelled thee from him in a griping pain.
. . . .
Such was thy origin: such be thy fate—
To war 'gainst virtue with a deadly hate;
By daily slanders earn thy daily food,
Exalt the wicked, and depress the good;

And, having spent a lengthy life in evil
Return again unto thy parent devil!"[1]

VII.

A tremendous opportunity for the Tory satirists was furnished by what proved to be the military and naval anticlimax of the French alliance,—that grotesque and yet imposing combination of the autocrat of France with these fierce democrats of America whose political principles contained nothing which was not detestable to him. As to the Americans themselves, the immediate effects of the French alliance were to relax their own energies in the war, and to deepen still further that torpor, that supineness, that reluctance to make any more sacrifices for the Revolution, which had already grieved the heart and paralyzed the arm of Washington. That the king of France had resolved to pay off sundry old scores against his good brother, the king of England, by putting his own fleets and armies at the service of the American insurgents, was an announcement received in America by the most gleeful predictions of immediate and vast successes against the British arms on land and sea. For several years, however, these predictions failed to come true.

Thus, the first campaign, that of 1778, brought with it only such humiliations as the defeat at Monmouth, the failure of the French fleet to appear at the right time at the mouth of the Delaware, its failure to overcome the difficulty of an allied attack on New York, its failure, also, in the allied attack on Newport. In short, the first year of the French alliance had been a fiasco. In view of these facts, the Loyalists raised the cry of victory,—claiming that the

---

[1] "The New York Gazette," for August 11, 1779. This newspaper, printed by James Rivington, is the great reservoir for Loyalist humor and sarcasm during the Revolution. The files of that paper most used by me in these researches are those in the library of the N. Y. Historical Society, although I have also turned over copies to be seen elsewhere, as at Boston, Worcester, and Philadelphia.

rebel cause was ruined and was about to be abandoned. An example of this is furnished by a sprightly and good-humored song, to the tune of "Derry Down," which was printed in broadside, and was posted up in the streets of New York, and even of Philadelphia, in October, 1778. It is entitled "The Epilogue," and is supposed to be sung by the members of the Continental Congress at the conclusion of the farce "Independence," which they had been for several years so ingloriously playing:

"Our farce is now finished, your sport 's at an end!
But ere you depart, let the voice of a friend,
By way of a chorus, the evening crown
With a song to the tune of a hey derry down,
Derry down, down, hey derry down.

"Old Shakespeare, a poet who should not be spit on,
Although he was born in an island called Britain,
Hath said that mankind are all players at best—
A truth we 'll admit of, for sake of the jest.

"On this puny stage we 've strutted our hour,
And have acted our parts to the best of our power;
That the farce hath concluded—not perfectly well—
Was surely the fault of the Devil in Hell!

"This Devil you know, out of spleen to the Church,
Will oftentimes leave his best friends in the lurch,
And turn them adrift in the midst of their joy,—
'T is a difficult matter to cheat the Old Boy.

"Since this is the case, we must e'en make the best
Of a game that is lost: let us turn it to jest!
We 'll smile, nay, we 'll laugh, we 'll carouse, and we 'll sing,
And cheerfully drink life and health to the king.

"Let Washington now from his mountains descend—
Who knows but in George he may still find a friend?

A Briton, although he loves bottle and wench,
Is an honester fellow than parlé vous French.

"Our great 'Independence' we give to the wind,
And pray that Great Britain may once more be kind:
In this jovial song all hostility ends,
And Britons and we will forever be friends.

"Boys, fill me a bumper! now join in the chorus!
There is happiness still in the prospect before us.
In this sparkling glass, all hostility ends,
And Britons and we will for ever be friends!"[1]

As to the second campaign under the French alliance, that of 1779, its only successes—like those at Stony Point and Paulus Hook—were in slight actions from which the French were absent; its greatest disaster was in the only action of the year at which the French were present. For, after the affair off Newport in the preceding year, D'Estaing, having first gone into Boston harbor and there repaired his fleet, had flitted away to the West Indies, and thenceforward, for many months, was seen no more. In September of 1779, in response to American solicitations, he sailed for the coast of Georgia "with a fleet consisting of twenty sail of the line, two of fifty guns, and eleven frigates. As soon as his arrival was known, General Lincoln with the army under his command marched for Savannah. . . . Before the arrival of General Lincoln, Count D'Estaing demanded a surrender of the town to the arms of France. Prevost asked a suspension of hostilities twenty-four hours for preparing terms, and the request was incautiously granted. Before the stipulated time had elapsed, Lieutenant-Colonel Maitland, with about 800 men, after struggling with great difficulties, arrived from Beaufort, and joined the royal army at Savannah. . . . On the morning of the 4th of October, the batteries of the besiegers were opened with 9 mortars, 37 pieces of cannon from the

[1] The entire song is given in F. Moore, "Songs and Ballads," etc., 220–223.

land side, and 15 from the water. . . . It was determined to make an assault. . . . On the 9th of October, while two feints were made with the militia, a real attack was made on Spring Hill battery just as daylight appeared, with two columns consisting of 3500 French, 600 Continentals, and 350 of the inhabitants of Charleston. The principal of these columns, commanded by Count D'Estaing and General Lincoln, marched up boldly to the lines; but a heavy and well directed fire from the galleys threw the front of the column into confusion. The places of those who fell being instantly supplied by others, it still moved on until it reached a redoubt, where the contest became more fierce and desperate. . . . A French and an American standard were for an instant planted on the parapet; but the assailants, after sustaining the enemy's fire for fifty-five minutes, were ordered to retreat. Of the French, 637, and of the Continentals and militia, 241 were killed or wounded. Immediately after this unsuccessful assault, the militia almost universally went to their homes, and Count D'Estaing, reëmbarking his troops and artillery, left the continent."[1]

Such was the end of the second year of the French alliance; and at the festival of mirth which this event gave to the Loyalists, one of the dishes with which they regaled themselves was this jocular street-ballad telling the story of the allied attack on Savannah:

"With warlike parade,
And his Irish brigade,
His ships and his spruce Gallic host, sir,
As proud as an elf,
D'Estaing came himself,
And landed on Georgia's coast, sir.

"There joining a band,
Under Lincoln's command,

[1] A. Holmes, "Annals," etc., ii., 297–298.

Of rebels and traitors and Whigs, sir,
'Gainst the town of Savannah
He planted his banner,
And then he felt wondrous big, sir.

"With thund'ring of guns,
And bursting of bombs,
He thought to have frightened our boys, sir;
But amidst all their din,
Brave Maitland pushed in,
And Moncrieffe cried, 'A fig for your noise, sir!'

"Chagrined at delay,
As he meant not to stay,
The Count formed his troops in the morn, sir;
Van, centre, and rear
Marched up without fear,
Cocksure of success, by a storm, sir.

"Though rude was the shock,
Unmoved as a rock
Stood our firm British bands to their works, sir;
While the brave German corps
And Americans bore
Their parts as intrepid as Turks, sir.

"Then muskets did rattle,
Fierce raged the battle,
Grapeshot, it flew thicker than hail, sir;
The ditch filled with slain,
Blood dyed all the plain,
When rebels and French turned tail, sir.

. . . .

"There Pulaski fell,
That imp of old Bell,
Who attempted to murder his king, sir;
But now he is gone—

Whence he 'll never return,
But will make Hell with treason to ring, sir.

" To Charleston with fear,
The rebels repair ;
D'Estaing scampers back to his boats, sir ;
Each blaming the other,
Each cursing his brother,
And—may they cut each other's throats, sir." [1]

Upon the whole, the military events of the year 1779 bore so unfavorable an aspect for the Revolutionary cause as to give some ground for the enemy's claim that the rebels, cursed by the outstretched hand of France, had at last reached the penitential stage of the business; as is exemplified by this stanza from " A New Ballad," which made its first appearance in England that year:

" Our brethren so frantic,
Across the Atlantic,
Who quit their old friends in a huff,
In spite of their airs,
Are at last at their prayers,
And of fighting have had quantum suff." [2]

VIII.

It has been already mentioned that, after the Declaration of Independence, there was among the Loyalist writers a very general disuse of serious argument in their discussion of any part of the Anglo-American controversy. To this statement at least one exception must be made—having reference to a most solemn phase of the situation brought about by the open alliance of France with the insurgent Americans. Upon the entrance of their ancient and dreaded enemy as an ally of one branch of the English race then at war with the other branch of it, there seemed, indeed, not

[1] Given in full in F. Moore, " Songs and Ballads," etc., 269–273.
[2] Ibid., 263.

only the opportunity but the necessity both for serious argument and for brotherly and even pathetic expostulation on the part of the few Loyalist writers who were then available for the purpose. These writers, accordingly, then came forward with some very able and impressive papers appealing to their brethren in rebellion to stop and reconsider the whole subject of their duty and of their safety; especially, trying to make them see the unnaturalness of such a combination with France, and the fatal consequences which must ensue whether it should result in defeat or in victory.

Perhaps no better example of this class of writings can be given than the "Letters of Papinian," addressed severally to John Jay and to the people of North America, and setting forth "the conduct, present state, and prospects of the American Congress." The writer of these letters is commonly supposed to have been the Reverend Charles Inglis, then rector of Trinity Church, New York, who had already taken a vigorous part in the literary discussion of the proposal for American Independence. With no little cleverness, he here sets forth the tremendous assumptions of power made by the Revolutionary leaders, the gross tyrannies practised by them upon the common people, the fallacious hopes with which they had fed their credulous followers, and the delusions which they had spread through the land respecting the character and purpose of the so-called movement for American rights and liberties. "You find these pretended enemies of oppression the most unrelenting oppressors, and their little finger heavier than the king's loins." [1] "There is more liberty in Turkey than in the dominions of the Congress." [2] The rebellion, begun by unprincipled and selfish men, has been without justification in any public necessity; it is therefore wicked; it is without prospect of success; it is destined to bring disaster upon all who continue to support it.

---

[1] "Letters of Papinian," 6. [2] Ibid. 21.

Another of the grave Loyalist pamphlets of that period bears the title of "A Letter to the People of America." The chief force of this paper is spent upon the effort to call back into life the old feeling of American confidence in the essential fairness and good will of the English, and the old American distrust and hatred of the French; and thus to induce the mass of the American people, fatally misled by Congress, to rise in their might, to overthrow that body of usurpers, and to restore the country to its natural and safe relations with the people of Great Britain.

IX.

The awful possibilities involved in the French alliance, as seriously portrayed by several Loyalist pamphleteers, were also exploited in livelier or more lurid colors by numberless minor writers for the Tory press. "Of course," said they, in substance, to their hostile brethren, "the determination of Great Britain to put down this rebellion of yours is strengthened a thousandfold by the interference of France in the quarrel. Let it be granted, however, for the sake of the argument, that by the help of France, you do succeed! What then? You will be worse off than if you had failed! Instead of England, a faithful and loving mother, even though at times a severe one, you will have France, a treacherous and cruel stepmother; instead of the usages of the English constitutional monarchy, you will be subject to the simplicity of French absolutism; instead of a ruling power kindred to you in blood, in language, in religion, you will be under a ruling power alien from you in all these particulars; and within ten years from the time that you shall have gained, by the aid of France, your release from England, you will be wrapped in the terrific embrace of a despotism that will know no limit and no pity. An absolute dominion over you will be set up by your late protectors; an American Bastille will be erected; the Romish religion will be established; the English language will be forbidden; the French language will be made the language of the country; and the maxims and proceedings of the French monarchy, of the French civil code, and of the Romish inquisition will be your reward for your infinite ingratitude and folly in casting off the enlightened, humane, and equitable authority of you rightful sovereign."

The most striking elements of this Loyalist appeal to race sympathies, to religious prejudices, even to not unreasonable fears, may now be seen by us as they were set forth in most realistic fashion, in 1779, in the form of a pretended forecast of what was to be written down by some literal and fact-loving diarist in America just ten years after that date:

"Boston, November 10, 1789.—His Excellency, Count Tyran, has this day published, by authority from his majesty, a proclamation for the suppression of heresy and establishment of the inquisition in this town, which has already begun its functions in many other places of the continent under his majesty's dominion.

"The use of the Bible in the vulgar tongue is strictly prohibited, on pain of being punished by discretion of the inquisition.

"November 11.—The Catholic religion is not only outwardly professed, but has made the utmost progress among all ranks of people here, owing, in a great measure, to the unwearied labors of the Dominican and Franciscan friars, who omit no opportunity of scattering the seeds of religion, and converting the wives and daughters of heretics. We hear that the building formerly called the Old South Meeting, is fitting up for a cathedral, and that several other old meeting-houses are soon to be repaired for converts.

"November 12.—This day being Sunday, the famous Samuel Adams read his recantation of heresy, after which he was present at mass, and we hear he will soon receive priest's orders to qualify him for a member of the American Sorbonne. . . .

"The king has been pleased to order that five thousand of

the inhabitants of Massachusetts Bay should be drafted to supply his garrisons in the West Indies; the officers for them are already arrived from France.

. . . .

"New York, November 15.—The edict for prohibiting the use of the English language, and establishing that of the French in all law proceedings, will take place on the 20th instant. At the same time, the ordinance for abolishing trials by juries, and introducing the imperial law, will begin to take effect. . . .

"November 17.—A criminal of importance, who has been long imprisoned in the New Bastille, was this day privately beheaded. He commanded the American forces against Great Britain for a considerable time, but was confined by order of government on suspicion of possessing a dangerous influence in a country newly conquered, and not thoroughly settled. . . .

"The king has been pleased to parcel out a great part of the lands in America to noblemen of distinction, who will grant them again to the peasantry upon leases at will, with the reservation of proper rents and services.

"His majesty has been graciously pleased to order that none of the natives of America shall keep any firearms in their possession, upon pain of being sentenced to the galleys. . . .

"November 22.—We hear from Williamsburg, in Virginia, that some commotions took place there when the new capitation tax was first executed. But the regiment of Bretagne, being stationed in that neighborhood, speedily suppressed them by firing upon the populace, and killing fifty on the spot. It is hoped that this example will prevent any future insurrection in that part of the country.

"November 23.—His majesty has directed his viceroy to send five hundred sons of the principal inhabitants of America, to be educated in France, where the utmost care will be taken to imbue them with a regard for the Catholic faith, and a due sense of subordination to government.

"It is ordered that all the trade of America shall be carried on in French bottoms, navigated by French seamen.

"Such is the glorious specimen of happiness to be enjoyed by America, in case the interposition of France shall enable her to shake off her dependence on Great Britain. 'Di talem avertite casum.'"[1]

Certainly, it is not easy for us Americans, more than a hundred years after that dreadful prophecy was uttered, and after every atom of its dire burden has been falsified by the facts of actual experience, to realize how awful, in 1779, was the possibility that it might be exactly fulfilled, and with what an ineffable anxiety, with what a sinking of the heart, with how horrible a dread, it must have been read by many thousands of Americans at a time when no mortal man could know whether or not it would come true. Nevertheless, it is through such a writing as this, that we may be enabled to enter more truly into the very history of our Revolution—to know something more of that history than what lies on the surface, than what was enacted in physical battles,—even the invisible, the spiritual, battles of the men and women who favored or who opposed the Revolution, the agony that was year by year in their souls, the grim campaigns they had to wage against imposing arguments, against towering scorn, against the most appalling threats, and the chances of a doom that carried with it almost every conceivable calamity.

X.

The impolicy of the French alliance was taken up in the gravest spirit, in 1781, by an eminent American politician who has never been classed among the American Loyalists. By the spring of that year, the record of American experience under the French alliance had remained still unbroken by a single example of success, on land or sea, in any way due

[1] "The New York Gazette," March 17, 1779, reprinted in F. Moore, "Diary of the Am. Rev.," ii., 148–150.

to the help of French battalions or of French ships. Then it was that Silas Deane, a graduate of Yale College, a member of the first and of the second Continental Congress, and from 1776 to 1778 employed by Congress as its diplomatic and commercial agent in France, wrote a series of nine or ten letters to as many different men in America, with the view of convincing them that the whole project for American Independence had been a mistake, that the alliance with France was a disaster, and that a speedy reconciliation with England on terms acceptable to both was the only means left by which America could escape from the doom to which she was then hurrying. These letters are well-written, plausible, powerful; and had it not been for the favorable turn given to American affairs by the capture of Cornwallis's army a few months after they were written, they might have had serious effects. They were, however, collected and published in 1782 [1]; but as, by that time, the success of the Revolution was assured, their prophecies of its failure, and their lamentations over the fatal blunder of having ever undertaken it, sounded very much like the ravings of a madman bewailing calamities which existed only in his own diseased brain.

---

[1] "Paris Papers, or, Mr. Silas Deane's late intercepted Letters." The most important of the private papers of Deane, edited by Mr. Charles Isham, have been published by the N. Y. Historical Society, forming three volumes of its "Collections," for 1886, 1887, and 1888.

CHAPTER XXVIII.

THE LITERARY WARFARE OF THE LOYALISTS AGAINST INDEPENDENCE: JOSEPH STANSBURY, TORY SONG-WRITER AND SATIRIST.

I.—The special difficulty of identifying the writers of Tory productions, whether serious or jocose—The preëminence of Joseph Stansbury as a writer of political songs and of playful political satires—His personal history—A favorite in the society of Philadelphia.

II.—Like all other Loyalists, he disapproved of the colonial policy of the home-government—His verses, about 1774, "On the Present Troubles"—His effort to keep alive the feeling of American kinship with England—His songs for the banquet of the Sons of St. George, 1771, and 1774.

III.—Stansbury draws back from the policy of carrying resistance to the point of separation—His epigram on a fiery Whig preacher, 1776—Takes refuge with the British army in New York, where he remains from 1778 till 1783—His activity as a writer of convivial political verse during those years—His war song, "The Lords of the Main," 1780.

IV.—His "New Song," on the inconsistencies of the champions of freedom in America—His song for "A Venison Dinner," 1781—His effort to keep up confidence in the suppression of the rebellion—Loyalist criticisms on the inactivity of the British generals—His satire on Sir Henry Clinton.

V.—Stansbury's optimism survives all the misfortunes of the war—"A Poetical Epistle to His Wife," 1780—"Liberty"—"Let Us be Happy as Long as We Can," 1782—Loyalist devotion to principle, even under defeat and ruin—Stansbury's lines in 1783, "God Save the King"—His inability to keep up the resentments of the war—His poetic irenicon—Homesick in Nova Scotia—His return to his old home as a reconstructed American Loyalist.

I.

AMONG writers on both sides of the Revolutionary controversy, the habit of anonymous publication was the prevailing one; but for obvious reasons of prudence, this habit was adhered to with peculiar strictness among writers on the Loyalist side—more especially among writers of lampoons and of other humorous and caustic pieces against the champions of the Revolution. The mass of such productions, so far as they have survived to our time in broadsides, in pamphlets, and in the files of a few newspapers, still defy all attempts to assign them to their several authors. Indeed, it is chiefly by means of the bitter allusions made by the Revolutionist writers to some of these facetious Tory penmen, that we now know even of the existence, in those days, of such masters of political sarcasm as Will Molineux, Dr. Young, Joseph Greenleaf, Sam Waterhouse, Vardell, and Isaac Hunt, the father of Leigh Hunt.

Of all the Loyalist verse-writers whose work can now in some measure be identified are two of chief eminence,—Joseph Stansbury and Jonathan Odell. As a satirist, no one on that side of the controversy approaches Odell, either in passionate energy of thought or in pungency and polish of style; while Stansbury is equally without a rival among his brethren as a writer of festive political songs, and of satire in verse characterized by playful humor rather than by hatred.

Born in 1740 in London, and for several years a very brilliant pupil in St. Paul's School, Joseph Stansbury[1] was early taken from the career of letters—for which he had quite unusual gifts—and was put into trade. In 1767, he came to America, and established himself in business in Philadelphia. Into the life of that cultivated and genial city he entered with instant sympathy. Being a young man of high character and of many literary and social accomplishments, he had not long to wait for acquaintance. He had great facility in the writing of songs, which he sang with a melodious voice and with much vivacity of expres-

[1] For materials relating to Stansbury, my principal sources are, the rare volume, admirably edited by Winthrop Sargent, and entitled "The Loyal Verses of Joseph Stansbury and Dr. Jonathan Odell"; also an unpublished biographical sketch of Stansbury written by his son, Arthur Joseph Stansbury, and copied "with but slight alteration" by Mr. Fred H. Wines of Springfield, Illinois, a grandson of the poet. For this manuscript I am indebted to Mrs. Jeanne Stansbury Holden of Detroit, who is one of the poet's granddaughters.

sion; and wherever he went, he was welcomed not only for his intelligence and his fine manners, but for the kindling zest and good cheer which he brought with him into all companies.

II.

Like the most of those Americans who refused to join in the final measures of opposition, he seems to have regarded the colonial policy of the home-government as very impolitic—a policy which was persisted in just long enough to spoil the old good humor of the colonists, and to ripen irritation into revolution. For example, there remains among his papers the fragment of a serious and rather stately song, "On the Present Troubles," written apparently after the ministry had pushed their colonial policy to the extremity of blood-shedding, but before the colonists had pushed their opposition to the extremity of Independence. Evidently, in that stage of the business, Stansbury's sympathies were strongly with the colonists. This song begins with a picture of Great Britain in the height and splendor of her wide lordship over the earth:

"On crystal throne, uplifted high,
  Imperial Britain sate;
Her lofty forehead reached the sky,
  Her awful nod was fate.
. . . .
Bright science made her name adored;
  Her robes the arts impearled;
Wide in her lap fair commerce poured
  The riches of the world."

But suddenly, according to the poet, a change is visible in the aspect of this superb creature,—a change due to the birth in her heart, first, of jealousy toward her own American children, and then of the dreadful purpose to treat them with harshness and even with cruelty:

"Her cheeks the rose in haste forsook,
By jealous fears pursued;
Her voice the earth's firm basement shook,
And turned the air to blood.
Her vengeance o'er the liquid wave
Explores these western climes:
Just Heaven! a people deign to save—
Whose wrongs are all their crimes."[1]

If, indeed, things have come to such a pass with the colonists that their "wrongs are all their crimes," what shall hinder this poet who says so from going on with his high-spirited companions who will presently insist that for these wrongs the only remedy is in Independence? Only this shall hinder: that Stansbury does not see that Independence is the only remedy for those wrongs, or even the best remedy! Another remedy, and a better one, as he thinks, lies in firm but constitutional opposition, that is, opposition inside the empire and not outside of it: in opposition, then, and not in secession. Therefore, that his fellow-colonists may not forget all this, nor commit the irreparable mistake, he would stir in their hearts, not only their love of liberty, but likewise their old sense of affectionate kinship to the mother land, and of pride in the splendid historic achievements of their race. Thus, it is not hard to imagine with what élan he must have sung, at the banquet of the American "Sons of St. George" in New York, in April, 1771, this song of his, to the tune of the "Black Sloven":

"Though placed at a distance from Britain's bold shore,
From thence either we or our fathers came o'er;
And in will, word, and deed we are Englishmen all,—
Still true to her cause, and awake to her call.

"Let Crécy, Poictiers, and let Agincourt show
How our ancestors acted some ages ago;

[1] "The Loyal Verses," etc., 3.

While Minden's red field, and Quebec, shall proclaim
That their sons are unchanged, or in nature or name.

. . . .

"Though party contentions awhile may run high,
When danger advances, they 'll vanish and die;
While all with one heart, hand, and spirit unite,
Like Englishmen think, and like Englishmen fight.

"Then here 's to our king—and oh, long may he reign,
The lord of those men who are lords of the main!
While all the contention among us shall be,
To make him as happy, as we are made free." [1]

This song, praying as it does, that the happiness of the king may be proportioned to the extent of his willingness to grant true British freedom to his American colonists, contains not a word which, in that year 1771, could not have been sung with all heartiness by Jefferson or Franklin, by John Adams or John Jay.

Three years afterward, in the midst of the political exasperation connected with the tea-business, Stansbury wrote another song, apparently for an occasion similar to the one just mentioned, and this time to that stirring tune, "Hearts of Oak," then in use wherever over the earth the English race had wandered. Here, also, by an appeal to the thrilling memories of race-kinship and of race-glory, he tries to sing his brother-colonists out of the slough of angry contention into which this miserable affair has plunged them, and to induce them, if possible, to deal with the difficulty in the larger and happier moods of patriotic Englishmen, especially in those robust days when their nourishment was beef and beer, and not such effeminate concoctions as are in his time offered to them for food and drink. If we care to fancy to ourselves this manly and gracious singer as he

[1] "The Loyal Verses," etc., 1–2, where the entire song is given.

stood up among the "Sons of St. George" at their banquet in 1774, and with full-throated voice poured out the leading lines of this song, it will not be hard for us, also, to hear the very roar of old-fashioned enthusiasm with which its chorus was caught up and repeated by his fellow-patriots around him:

"When good Queen Elizabeth governed the realm,
And Burleigh's sage counsels directed the helm,
In vain Spain and France our conquests opposed,—
For valor conducted what wisdom proposed.
Beef and beer was their food;
Love and truth armed their band;
Their courage was ready—
Steady, boys, steady—
To fight and to conquer by sea and by land.

"But since tea and coffee, so much to our grief,
Have taken the place of strong beer and roast beef,
Our laurels have withered, our trophies been torn,
And the lions of England French triumphs adorn.
Tea and slops are their food—
Which [1] unnerve every hand;
Their courage unsteady
And not always ready—
They often are conquered by sea and by land.

"St. George views with transport our generous flame:—
'My sons, rise to glory, and rival my fame;
Ancient manners again in my sons I behold,
And this age must eclipse all the ages of gold.'

. . . .

"While thus we regale, as our fathers of old,—
Our manners as simple, our courage as bold,—
May vigor and prudence our freedom secure,
Long as rivers, or ocean, or stars shall endure.

---

[1] The text reads "They."

Beef and beer are our food ;
Love and truth arm our band ;
Our courage is steady,
And always is ready
To fight and to conquer by sea and by land." [1]

III.

Stansbury's aspiration, that " vigor and prudence " may " our freedom secure," is one which could have been uttered equally well by both parties in the dispute; but for him, throughout the entire song, the note of race-unity seems to have drowned that of political suspicion. Accordingly, we are prepared to find two years later, when the plan for race-separation becomes the master-purpose of American politics, that Stansbury shrinks back from a project so shocking both to his affections and to his judgment. Even then, however, in his denunciations of this ultimate heresy of Independence, he is true to the mirthful mood which was habitual to him; as may be seen, for example, in an epigram written by him probably in May or June, 1776, on a fierce political sermon preached just then by a rebel friend of his, the Reverend William Piercy, to a battalion of the Philadelphia militia. The day, as it happened, was excessively hot; and while the preacher was delivering his discourse, there stood behind him in the pulpit a negro servant, remarkably black and remarkably ugly, who fanned the preacher with a vehemence well proportioned to the inflammatory energy of the harangue. Four lines were enough for Stansbury's comment upon the spectacle:

" To preach up, friend Piercy, at this critical season,
Resistance to Britain, is not very civil ;
Yet what can we look for but faction and treason,
From a flaming enthusiast—fanned by the devil ? " [2]

---

[1] " The Loyal Verses," etc., 4-5.

[2] Ibid. 6.

Notwithstanding the sharp discriminations caused by the famous procedure of July 4, 1776, Stansbury seems to have maintained both his residence and his business in Philadelphia during the whole of that year and of the year following. Of course, upon the occupation of the city by the British army in the autumn of 1777, he was in high favor. On the retirement of the British army from Philadelphia in the spring of 1778, Stansbury prudently went with it; and thenceforward, until the close of the war, his quarters were within the British lines at New York.

Just how he was employed during those years, is not certainly known. At any rate, whatever else he may have been doing, there is good reason for the statement that his clever and jovial pen was constantly at the service of the cause to which he had given himself with a devotion none the less sincere because altogether free from bitterness. It is probable that much of his printed work during this period is now quite beyond identification. Moreover, at the close of the Revolution, he burned a large number of his private papers relating to that period, and, by this act, put it out of our power to trace more perfectly just what he did in those days as a satirist and a song-writer. Nevertheless, enough remains of his ascertained work to enable us to feel sure that few aspects of the ever-changing situation between 1776 and 1783, could have escaped his keen and humorous attention, or could have failed to receive treatment at his hands either in some stirring lyric of patriotic enthusiasm, or in some form of bantering verse. Thus, fair examples of his range may be seen in the "Welcome to Howe,"[1] June, 1776; in the "Tradesmen's Song,"[2] for the king's birthday, 1777; in the "Song for the Times,"[3] and in "The Church and King Club,"[4] in 1778; in the rather caustic ballad of "The Town Meeting,"[5] 1779; in "Liberty,"[6] and "A Poetical Epistle,"[7] in 1780; in "A Song for St.

---

[1] "The Loyal Verses," etc., 10–11. [2] Ibid. 13–14. [3] Ibid. 34–35.
[4] Ibid. 36. [5] Ibid. 39–44. [6] Ibid. 63–64. [7] Ibid. 69–70.

George's Day,"[1] and in "The Royal Oak,"[2] 1781; and in "A Christmas Song,"[3] 1782.

Probably the strongest example of Stansbury's work as a writer of war-lyrics, is his spirit-stirring song called "The Lords of the Main," published in February, 1780, and intended for the use of the British sailors then engaged in fighting their ancient foes, the French and the Spaniards, at that time in alliance for the help of the American Congress—here alluded to under its derisive nickname of "Congo":

"When Faction, in league with the treacherous Gaul,
Began to look big, and paraded in state,
A meeting was held at Credulity Hall,[4]
And Echo proclaimed their ally good and great.
By sea and by land
Such wonders are planned—
No less than the bold British lion to chain!
'Well hove!' says Jack Lanyard,
'French, Congo, and Spaniard,
Have at you!—remember, we 're Lords of the Main.
Lords of the Main, aye, Lords of the Main;
The Tars of Old England are Lords of the Main.'

"Though party-contention awhile may perplex,
And lenity hold us in doubtful suspense,
If perfidy rouse, or ingratitude vex,
In defiance of hell we 'll chastise the offense.
When danger alarms,
'T is then that in arms
United we rush on the foe with disdain;
And when the storm rages,
It only presages
Fresh triumphs to Britons as Lords of the Main!
Lords of the Main, aye, Lords of the Main—
Let thunder proclaim it, we 're Lords of the Main!'

---

[1] "The Loyal Verses," etc., 76–77.
[2] Ibid. 81–82.
[3] Ibid. 84–85.
[4] Independence Hall, Philadelphia.

"Then, Britons, strike home—make sure of your blow:
The chase is in view—never mind a lea shore.
With vengeance o'ertake the confederate foe:
'T is now we may rival our heroes of yore!
Brave Anson, and Drake,
Hawke, Russell, and Blake,
With ardor like yours, we defy France and Spain!
Combining with treason,
They 're deaf to all reason;
Once more let them feel we are Lords of the Main.
Lords of the Main, aye, Lords of the Main—
The first-born of Neptune are Lords of the Main!" [1]

IV.

A frequent taunt of the Loyalists had reference to the arbitrary and even despotic measures often resorted to by the Revolutionary leaders in pushing forward their cause—which yet called itself the cause of freedom; and in some verses which he entitled a "New Song," Stansbury gave those Americans who resented such inconsistency the words wherein to confess the political disenchantment through which they were then passing. This is one stanza of the song:

"We fondly imagined that all future story
Should tell of our justice, our freedom, and glory;
We laughed at oppression—not dreaming or fearing
That men should be banished without charge or hearing.
For freedom, indeed, we supposed we were fighting—
But this sort of freedom 's not very inviting." [2]

Nothing that we now have of Stansbury's verse, presents him to us in a vein more characteristic or more attractive than a sparkling convivial song which he wrote for "A Venison Dinner at Mr. Bunyan's," in New York, in 1781,

---

[1] "The Loyal Verses," etc., 61–62, where is given a fourth stanza.

[2] "The Loyal Verses," etc., 16–17.

at a time of the year when Washington's headquarters were still in the highlands of the Hudson, and before that impenitent rebel had developed to the enemy his purpose of marching toward Virginia for an interview with Cornwallis:

"Friends, push round the bottle, and let us be drinking,
While Washington up in his mountains is slinking:
Good faith, if he 's wise he 'll not leave them behind him,
For he knows he 's safe nowheres where Britons can find him.
When he and Fayette talk of taking this city,
Their vaunting moves only our mirth and our pity.

"But, though near our lines they 're too cautious to tarry,
What courage they shew when a hen-roost they harry!
Who can wonder that poultry and oxen and swine
Seek shelter in York from such valor divine,—
While Washington's jaws and the Frenchman's are aching
The spoil they have lost, to be boiling and baking.

"Let Clinton and Arnold bring both to subjection,
And send us more geese here to seek our protection.
Their flesh and their feathers shall meet a kind greeting;
A fat rebel turkey is excellent eating,
A lamb fat as butter, and white as a chicken—
These sorts of tame rebels are excellent pickin'.

"To-day a wild rebel has smoked on the table;
You 've cut him and sliced him as long as you 're able.
He bounded like Congo,[1] and bade you defiance,
And placed on his running his greatest reliance;
But fate overtook him and brought him before ye,
To shew how rebellion will wind up her story.

"Then cheer up, my lads! if the prospect grows rougher,
Remember from whence and for whom 't is you suffer:—

---

[1] The common Tory nickname for the Continental Congress, whose agility in flight at the approach of the British is likened to that of this deer when pursued by the hunters.

From men whom mild laws and too happy condition
Have puffed up with pride and inflamed with sedition;
For George, whose reluctance to punish offenders
Has strengthened the hands of these upstart pretenders." [1]

This confident and jubilant tone on the part of the Loyalists within the British lines, belonged to a mood which was attained by them now and then, upon casual flashes of good fortune in the field, or upon occasions of special hilarity—as a venison dinner or the like; but their spirits were not commonly or without effort at so high a level. There is now something of the aspect of tragedy upon the words which they kept uttering to one another, in so many forms, day after day, and from year to year,—wherein they tried to make it appear to themselves that their affairs were going on prosperously, that the British generals were masters of the situation, that the French alliance and the Spanish conjunction were to be for the rebel Congress but futile copartnerships, and that soon—yes, very soon—this enormous and ghastly farce of American Independence would dissolve into its natural nothingness. Thus, in 1778, after the French had become avowed participants in the fight, Joseph Stansbury exclaims,—

"What though the Frenchman crowns the scene,
And we miscall him 'mankind's friend,'
Not all his power can rebels screen—
Rebellion 's drawing near her end.
Shot like a meteor through the skies,
It spread awhile a baleful train;
But now, by Jove's command, it dies,
And melts to common air again." [2]

Nevertheless, as we have now the means of knowing, these people were not really at ease. As the war dragged on, as one campaign of military shiftlessness and blundering succeeded to another, as the rebellion of their late brethren remained still uncrushed, and the end they hoped for kept

[1] "The Loyal Verses," etc., 79-80.
[2] Ibid. 34-35.

receding further and still further into the distance, the unhappy Loyalists became but too well acquainted with that form of heart-sickness which is born of hope deferred. For the immediate and complete suppression of the rebellion, no British general had a zeal that could match with their fiery impatience, or that did not seem listless by comparison with the flame and the wrath and the rancor of their devotion to it. In their demand for prompt and conclusive action, in their eagerness to have something done—to have the day seized, the occasion used, to have the rebels pushed and routed and crushed—they often turned in bitterness even upon the British generals themselves, muttering sullenly and helplessly at their procrastination, their self-indulgence, their lack of enterprise, their spiritless and fruitless methods. To the Loyalists, the war, as thus conducted, seemed to be not a war, but only a hypocritical and distressing pretense of one.

It is not likely that Joseph Stansbury, who was himself within the lines at New York and a member of the innermost circle of Loyalist counselors, failed to see and to feel all these defects in British military leadership; and yet, in giving vent to his criticism thereupon, he but obeyed the law of his own mind by doing so with good humor and with the light play of badinage rather than the fury of railing accusations. A capital instance of his way of applying sarcasms to the delinquencies of his own chiefs, is furnished by an occurrence of the year 1780. Just then, the rebels in the vicinity of New York seem to have become so perfectly assured of the preference of the British army for the contemplative over the active life, that they sometimes pushed their foraging expeditions even within the British lines, on one occasion carrrying off sundry quantities of hay from the very outskirts of the city and setting fire to some houses which were so near that the flames could be seen from Sir Henry Clinton's quarters. Of course, such exploits of brilliant and unwhipt audacity, and Sir Henry's apparent indifference to them, were inexpressibly galling to the Loyalists who stood looking on. Of course, each one gave vent to his disgust in his own way; and Joseph Stansbury's way was to write and post up in the streets of the town this pasquinade:

"'Has the Marquis La Fayette
Taken off all our hay yet?'
Says Clinton to the wise heads around him:
'Yes, faith, Sir Harry,
Each stack he did carry,
And likewise the cattle—confound him!

"'Besides, he now goes,
Just under your nose,
To burn all the houses to cinder.'
'If that be his project,
It is not an object
Worth a great man's attempting to hinder.

"'For forage and house
I care not a louse;
For revenge, let the Loyalists bellow:
I swear I 'll not do more
To keep them in humor,
Than play on my violoncello.

"'Since Charleston is taken,
'T will sure save my bacon,—
I can live a whole year on that same, sir;
Ride about all the day,
At night, concert or play;
So a fig for the men that dare blame, sir;

"'If growlers complain,
I inactive remain—
Will do nothing, nor let any others!
'T is sure no new thing
To serve thus our king—
Witness Burgoyne, and two famous Brothers!'"[1]

---

[1] "The Loyal Verses," etc., 67–68.

V.

The optimism of Stansbury seems to have been more than equal to the disasters which thickened about him and about the doomed political party with whose fortunes he had allied his own; and it was perhaps not the least of the services to which his life was put during those years, that he could be a messenger of indomitable hope and cheerfulness to many noble-minded and sensitive people who were associated with him in misfortune, but who lacked his genius for confronting it. Thus, late in the year 1780, in "A Poetical Epistle . . . to His Wife," he compresses into five lines of verse a large part of his secret for meeting the ills of this mortal state:

> "But prudence suggests we should never despair;
> And reason points out that good humor and patience
> Are better companions than half our relations,—
> Take off the rough edge of ill-nature and malice,
> And make our dark prison as gay as a palace."[1]

Somewhat more of his secret he had also revealed, a few months earlier, in a little poem called "Liberty," wherein he thus gives us to understand what, in his opinion, were the things in this world worth living for:

> "Splendid honors I disdain;
> Crowns of kings are lined with pain;
> Friendship only gives to me
> Social joys and liberty.
> Let me in my humble sphere,
> Free from envy, free from care,
> Spend the days allotted me
> Blest with peace and liberty."[2]

Of course all his fortitude was brought to the supreme test by the surrender of Cornwallis in 1781, whereby it was

---

[1] "The Loyal Verses," etc., 69.

[2] Ibid. 64.

made apparent to the rest of the world that the stake for which he and his friends had been playing was lost,—that nothing was in store for them but to be banished from the land and the homes they loved as dearly as did the men who were victorious over them. It was amid such calamities that Stansbury wrote, apparently for some assemblage of Loyalists in New York, this song, in which his optimism, driven to its last refuge, still refuses to yield:

"I 've heard in old times that a sage used to say,
The seasons were nothing, December, or May;
The heat, or the cold never entered his plan—
That all should be happy whenever they can.

"No matter what power directed the state,
He looked upon such things as ordered by fate:
Whether governed by many, or ruled by one man,
His rule was—be happy whenever you can.

"He happened to enter this world the same day
With the supple, complying, famed Vicar of Bray:
Through both of their lives the same principle ran—
My boys, we 'll be happy as long as we can.

"Time-serving I hate, yet I see no good reason
A leaf from their book should be thought out of season:
When kicked like a football from Sheba to Dan—
Egad, let 's be happy as long as we can.

"Since no man can tell what to-morrow may bring,
Or which side shall triumph, the Congress or King,
Since fate must o'errule us and carry her plan—
Why, let us be happy as long as we can.

"To-night, let 's enjoy this good wine and a song,
And relish the hour which we cannot prolong:
If evil will come, we 'll adhere to our plan—
And baffle misfortune as long as we can." [1]

[1] "Loyal Verses," etc., 86–87.

And when at last the English ministry, to the bitter grief of the king, made peace with the victorious rebels—conceding to them all that they had ever demanded—even then Stansbury and his fellow-Loyalists, having lost everything in the world but their loyalty, seemed to cling with a stern and a proud happiness to that ultimate and inextinguishable possession:

> "Though ruined so deeply no angel can save,
> The empire dismembered, our king made a slave,
> Still loving, revering, we shout forth honestly—
> God save the king!
> Though fated to banishment, poverty, death,
> Our hearts are unaltered, and with our last breath
> Loyal to George, we 'll pray most fervently—
> Glory and joy crown the king!"[1]

After the war was really ended, however, the party of the Loyalists gradually fell into two groups,—those who were willing to become reconciled to the result of the war, and those who forever refused. It was inevitable that Stansbury should take his place in the former group. In his heart was no lodging-place for the resentments of the old controversy. Upon the back of the very sheet on which he had written his "God Save the King," he wrote these lines of his irenicon:

> "Now this war at length is o'er,
> Let us think of it no more;
> Every party lie or name,
> Cancel as our mutual shame;
> Bid each wound of faction close—
> Blushing we were ever foes."[2]

Then it was, that whatever of his political verses he could lay his hands upon, he destroyed. "He even seemed to forget who had hated, and who had injured him."[3] Sup-

[1] "Loyal Verses," etc., 89. [2] Ibid. 89. [3] Ibid. 102.

posing that as between himself and his former political antagonists, this forgetfulness would be mutual, he removed with his family to a small village in New Jersey, a few miles to the east of Philadelphia; but before he had been there a week, he was seized and thrown into Burlington jail. From this he was soon released on giving his promise to leave the State within nine days.[1] Accordingly, in August, 1783, he set sail from New York for Nova Scotia, where thousands of his exiled political brethren were then beginning to make for themselves a new home and a new country. But Stansbury was not happy there. To his wife he wrote:

> "Believe me, love, this vagrant life,
> O'er Nova Scotia's wilds to roam,
> While far from children, friends, or wife,
> Or place that I can call a home,
> Delights not me;—another way
> My treasures, pleasures, wishes lay."[2]

In the autumn of 1785, he returned once more to Philadelphia, intending to resume his old business there; but into a house where he was supposed to lodge was thrown a letter, intimating that it would not be possible for him to live in Philadelphia, although, as was also hinted, it might be possible for him to die there.[3] After some years of insecurity, he found at last in 1793,[4] in the cosmopolitan largeness of New York, the home he had longed for; and there in serenity, and amid hosts of friends, he passed the remainder of his days, an altogether pleasant specimen of a reconstructed American Loyalist.

---

[1] MS. sketch by Arthur Joseph Stansbury.
[2] "The Loyal Verses," 90.
[3] Ibid. 101.
[4] MS. sketch by A. J. Stansbury.

CHAPTER XXIX.

THE LITERARY WARFARE OF THE LOYALISTS AGAINST AMERICAN INDEPENDENCE: JONATHAN ODELL, THEIR CHIEF SATIRIST.

I.—Odell's position among the Loyalist writers—His relentless spirit in satire described by himself—His New England ancestry—Surgeon in the British army before the Revolution—In 1767, he takes holy orders in London—His settlement as rector of Burlington, New Jersey.

II.—Odell disapproves of the American policy of the ministry, but would meet it by constitutional opposition only—Takes no public part in the controversy till after the beginning of hostilities — Outrage upon his private correspondence—His ode for the king's birthday, June 4, 1776—His parole to remain within his parish—Having given fresh offense, he is hunted from his hiding-places—His flight within the British lines, late in December, 1776.

III.—Odell received into confidence at the British headquarters—Remains in New York till the close of the war—Chaplain to a corps of Loyalist troops —His conception of the proper use of satire in controversy, after serious argument has been exhausted—His chief satires, "The Word of Congress," September, 1779; "The Congratulation," and "The Feu de Joie," November, 1779; and "The American Times," 1780.

IV.—Odell follows the models of English classical satire—He is the great exponent of Loyalist conscience and emotion in the last years of the war—The basis of their political system of politics and of patriotic duty—Odell denounces both the ministerial policy and American violence in resisting it —The Revolution not a case of justifiable rebellion—A popular phrensy produced by political sorcery—The sorcerers discovered by the poet in the very act of compounding the hell-broth of rebellion—Its ingredients.

V.—The futile efforts of sane men to stop the spread of Revolutionary madness —The perpetual renewal of error, even when discomfited—The inexhaustible supply of rebel chiefs—American society given over to the rule of the worst—Description of the Continental Congress—That body the centre of all political mischief, a nest of robbers and tyrants.

VI.—His arraignment of Congress for its duplicity—It is a political Proteus—He satirizes its servants, as Thomas Paine, and General John Sullivan—He arraigns the chiefs of the rebellion, as William Livingston, John Jay, Samuel Chase, Robert Morris, and Gouverneur Morris.

VII.—His attacks on Lord Sterling, Pulaski, and President Witherspoon—Comprehensiveness of his attacks—A partial relenting toward Henry Laurens—His solemn indictment of Washington.

VIII.—Odell's perfect confidence in the ultimate defeat of the rebellion—His song for the king's birthday, 1777—His prediction, in the autumn of 1778, of the speedy discomfiture of the rebels and of their French allies—"The Old Year and the New—a Prophecy"—The two sections of the Loyalist party at the close of the Revolution—The implacable section represented by Odell—His later career in Nova Scotia.

I.

WE now come to the most powerful and most unrelenting of the Tory satirists,—to Jonathan Odell, who, though closely allied to Joseph Stansbury in the objects for which he wrote, yet greatly differed from his associate both in the spirit and in the method of his writing. Being of a nature far deeper, sterner, and more virile than Stansbury's, less lovable, less mobile, less capable of any sort of moral concession for the sake of amenity, Odell reprobated so profoundly the later movement of the Revolution that it was seldom possible for him to relax into any sort of playfulness in speaking of it, or to admit it to the honors of even a semi-sarcastic dalliance, or to attack it with any species of satire other than that which was grim, scathing, absolutely implacable. He was faithful to his own ideal, when to a brother writer he said:

> "Thou, to the bottom, probe the dangerous sore,
> And in the wound the friendly balsam pour;
> Enough for me the caustic to apply,
> Twinge the proud flesh, and draw the face awry."[1]

And when he had occasion to implore the goddess of satire to aid him in his chosen task, it was with a true consciousness of his peculiar function as a satirist, that he prayed this prayer:

---

[1] "The Loyalist Poetry," etc., 24.

> "then grant me for a time
> Some deleterious powers of acrid rhyme ;
> Some ars'nic verse, to poison with the pen
> These rats, who nestle in the lion's den." [1]

In short, Odell's place among the Tory satirists corresponds pretty closely to that of Philip Freneau among the satirists on the side of the Whigs. Certainly, to him, of all the American verse-writers who opposed the Revolution, may best be applied the title which Sir Walter Scott invented for the purpose of doing honor to a certain Bishop of Llandaff —that of Toryissimus.[2]

Odell was born at Newark, New Jersey, on the 25th of September, 1737. His earliest American ancestor, William Odell, was among the founders of the colony of Massachusetts, and was living at Concord in 1639. Thus, the most inappeasable satirist of the American Revolution — the stanchest and fiercest champion of the principle of authority in church and state—came of the stock of the primal puritans of New England,—an ancestry rejoicing in a somewhat pronounced record of insubordination in both spheres of activity. After his graduation at the College of New Jersey[3] in 1754, he was educated for the medical profession,

---

[1] "The Loyalist Poetry," etc., 55.

[2] "The Journal of Sir Walter Scott," ii., 181.

[3] S. D. Alexander, "Princeton College During the Eighteenth Century," 31. This book, which was published in 1872, gives Odell's name in the list of the class of 1754, but has only this to say of him : "A grandson of President Dickinson ; was from Connecticut Farms, New Jersey. After graduating, he entered the ministry, but I can discover no facts as to his place of settlement, or of his after life." This amazing statement was published fifteen years after the sketch of Odell by Wintrop Sargent in his "Loyalist Poetry," and eight years after the similar sketch by Sabine in his "Loyalists of the American Revolution"; and when, also, references to Odell had long been lying about in such familiar works as Force's "American Archives," in Sparks's edition of the "Writings of Washington," and in William B. Reed's "Life and Correspondence of Joseph Reed." Can it be that Odell's career was thus blotted out, and refused remembrance, by his Alma Mater, as a tribute of satisfaction to good old President Witherspoon, whose mortal plumes were so mercilessly ruffled by this satirist in the later years of the Revolution ?

becoming a surgeon in the British army, and serving with his regiment in the West Indies. From this employment he withdrew after a few years, and, proceeding to England, prepared himself for the sacred ministry. On the 4th of January, 1767, at the Chapel Royal, St. James's, he received priest's orders at the hands of the Bishop of Norwich; and fifteen days afterward he received from the Bishop of London his license as a minister of the Church in New Jersey. On his arrival in that province, he was inducted by Governor William Franklin into the rectorship of St. Mary's parish, Burlington; and thenceforward, until his labors were stopped by the war, he gave himself with the utmost devotion to his duties as parish priest, as missionary, and as physician.

II.

Thus, Jonathan Odell began his career as a clergyman in America in the very year in which the English ministry, by the renewal of its project for colonial taxation, called back into life that ill-boding controversy that had seemed to die a happy death on the repeal of the Stamp Act only a twelvemonth before. This action of the ministry was deeply lamented by Odell, who clearly saw the need of a fresh consideration of the whole subject of the rights of the colonies within the empire, together with a clearer definition and a more stable defense of those rights. All this, however, he was confident, could be obtained in due time, and in the usual English way of robust political agitation—without sedition, privy conspiracy, or rebellion. It was a part of his temperament, as it also was of his profession, to look with utter disapproval upon every project for violent resistance to constituted authority—still more so upon every project tending toward a dismemberment of the empire. Moreover, during the eight years of passionate debate, from the Townshend Act in June, 1767, until after the battle of Bunker Hill in June, 1775, he abstained from all public participation in political affairs, feeling it to be his duty as a clergyman to promote " a spirit of peace and good order," and amid all those " perplexing and alarming troubles " to assist " by prudence and integrity of conduct " in the permanent establishment " of that harmony and peace, upon just and practicable grounds, which is essential to the happiness and glory of the whole empire." [1]

But after the battle of Bunker Hill, the dispute reached a stage at which such reserve was no longer possible on either side of the question. Nevertheless, even after that event, Odell still hoped to be permitted to pursue his calling in peace. " I told them," he said respecting the local committeemen who, in October, 1775, had arrested him for expressions used in two private letters which they had seized and broken open, "that I did not mean to dissemble my sentiments concerning the measures of Congress, but that I had made it a rule to myself from the beginning of our troubles, not to interfere directly or indirectly in public affairs; and though I neither could nor would make any sacrifice of my principles or duty, either as a loyal subject or a minister of the Church of England, yet my political conduct should be inoffensive, if they would allow a passive conduct to be so; and in short, that I presumed it reasonable in me to expect I should be indulged in the unmolested enjoyment of my private sentiments so long as I did not attempt to influence the sentiments or conduct of other men, and that private sentiments ought not to be made matter of public notice, much less of public censure." [2]

But with every month that passed, the flame of excitement kept rising; the year of the great decision soon came; and, of course, Odell's position was too conspicuous and his character too outspoken for him to remain unmolested in such an emergency. On the 4th of June, 1776, the birthday of King George, a number of British officers, who had been captured by General Montgomery in Canada sev-

---

[1] Odell's letter to the secretary of the S. P. G., July 7, 1775, given in Hills, " Hist. of the Ch. in Burlington," 307–308.

[2] Letter of Odell, Ibid. 314.

eral months before and were then held as prisoners at Burlington, celebrated the day by a dinner under the trees on a little island in the Delaware. It was but a few miles above the spot where the Continental Congress was in session. It was but three days before the resolution for Independence was presented to Congress by Richard Henry Lee. It was but one month before Independence itself was declared. Although at that very moment the air was all ablaze with the fiery demand for a total and final rejection of the authority of the king, Jonathan Odell wrote on behalf of these captive friends of his, a glowing ode for the royal birthday,[1] in which he sets forth, first, the enthusiasm with which throughout all other portions of the British empire the day was then being celebrated; next, the deplorable lack of enthusiasm for the king's birthday characterizing, at that time, a considerable party among his American subjects; and finally, their own undying devotion to the glorious monarch whose throne, it is here recorded, was to stand as long as the sun and the moon shall endure.

No doubt the gallant young fellows—young John André being one of them—who to the clashing accompaniment of their regimental music roared forth that proud and defiant song, felt an honest pity for the small provincial politicians who, just below them in Philadelphia, were even then chattering about Independence, and were dreaming their absurd dream of resistance to the invincible might of Britain. Meantime, the noise of their loyal merry-making, and particularly of Odell's song, made itself heard beyond the rim of the little island where they had held their celebration; and on the 20th of the following month, the provincial convention of New Jersey ordered that Jonathan Odell, as "a person suspected of being inimical to American liberty," be required to give his parole, pledging himself to remain "on the east side of Delaware river, within a circle of eight miles from the court-house of the city of Burling-

---

[1] "The Loyal Verses," etc., 7–9.

ton."[1] The course of Odell's life during the remainder of that year of mighty commotion, and until his final flight within the British lines, is best described in his own words, written in New York early in January, 1777: "After giving this parole, I remained unmolested at home till about the middle of last month, when a body of Hessians under the command of Count Donop came to Burlington intending to take post with us for the winter. Some of my neighbors thought it advisable to meet the commandant on his approach to the town, and to request him to spare the inhabitants from insult and their property from pillage. They requested me to go with them and assist in this charitable address, as an interpreter. I did so, and had the pleasure to find that I had a pretty good prospect of being of real service to my peaceable neighbors. But five gondolas, lying in the river, began to cannonade the town in order to prevent the troops taking quarter with us. Many houses were damaged but nobody hurt. The Hessian commandant, however, having with him no heavy cannon, thought proper to retire that night to Bordentown, intending to return with artillery sufficient to make good his quarters. In the meantime . . . as soon as it was known on board the gondolas that the troops had left us, the town was cruelly insulted and from day to day kept in alarm by those river tyrants. Mr. Lawrence, young Mr. Hawlings, and myself were in particular pursued by two captains and a number of armed men. We made our escapes, and were under the necessity of taking refuge among the king's troops. . . . I have been obliged to leave my wife and three children (the youngest not five weeks old) and to ramble as a refugee—God knows when to return."[2] During those days and nights of peril, in which the rector of Burlington was hunted like a felon from one hiding-place to another, he received most important aid from a shrewd and merry Quakeress, Margaret Morris, who then owned the

---

[1] "American Archives," 4 Ser., vol. vi. 1651.

[2] The whole letter is given in Hills, "Hist. of the Ch. in Burlington," 315.

great house upon the river bank, near Burlington, which had formerly belonged to Governor Franklin. Within this house was a secret chamber, of the greatest convenience in those troubled days, and named by its facetious proprietor the "augur hole." It was "a dark but quite roomy apartment, which had no window or aperture for light"; was just under the roof of one wing of the house, and could be reached only by entering a linen closet in the adjoining room, "drawing out the shelves," "prying up the movable back,"[1] and then stooping low and creeping in through the opening which would thus be revealed. It was to the shelter of this Quaker mansion, and especially of that very secluded portion of it, that Odell had fled; and a part of what happened to him then and shortly afterward, is thus told by the lively Quakeress, in her diary for December, 1776: "From the 13th to the 16th, . . . parties of armed men rudely entered the town, and diligent search was made for Tories. . . . A loud knocking at my door brought me to it. I was a little fluttered, and kept locking and unlocking that I might get my ruffled face a little composed; at last I opened it, and half a dozen men, all armed, demanded the key of the empty house.[2] I asked what they wanted there; they said, to search for a Tory. The name of a Tory, so near my own door, seriously alarmed me; for a poor refugee . . . was at that very time concealed, like a thief, in an augur hole. I rung the bell violently,—the signal agreed on if they came to search; and when I thought he had crept into the hole, I put on a very simple look, and cried out, 'Bless me, I hope you are not Hessians . . . but I 'll go with you into Colonel Cox's house' . . . So I marched at the head of them, opened the door, and searched every place, but we could not find the Tory. Strange where he could be! We returned—they greatly disappointed—I, pleased to think my house was not

[1] "Hist. of the Ch. in Burlington," 321 n.

[2] A neighboring house, belonging to a Colonel Cox. The key had been left with her.

suspected. . . . They left us, and searched J. V.'s and the two next houses, but no Tory could they find. . . . In the evening, I went to town with my refugee, and placed him in other lodgings. . . . Dec. 18th. . . . Our refugee gone off to-day out of the reach of gondolas and Tory-hunters." On the 12th of January, 1777, after this capable lady had heard of Odell's safe arrival in New York, she thus records her ideas as to his possible destiny: "We have some hopes that our refugee will be presented with a pair of lawn sleeves, when dignities become cheap; and suppose he will then think himself too big to creep into his old augur hole; but I shall remind him of the place, if I live to see him created first bishop of Burlington."[1]

III.

Upon his arrival in New York, Odell was received into high favor, which was increased rather than diminished under the test of time and trial. Being himself an old army man, he found among the officers about headquarters some ancient comrades and acquaintances; and into the habits and moods of military life he could, of course, enter with quick sympathy and adaptation. On the other hand, he was an American, of solid character and unusual intelligence: he knew the country, its people, its chief men, the currents and eddies of its agitated life. Moreover, he was a clergyman, a physician, a gentleman, cultivated by travel, by society, and by books. He was a fluent and keen prose writer, a poet, and a wit. With all these resources for effective service in many directions, and with every reason for self-restraint at last removed, he threw himself into the contest with the whole strength of his strong nature; he stood ready to lend a hand for any good measure that was in progress. He was "active in every way."[2] He served as chaplain of a corps of Loyalist American troops.[3]

---

[1] Hills, "Hist. of Ch. in Burlington," 321 n.

[2] W. B. Reed, "Life and Correspondence of Joseph Reed," ii. 170 n.

[3] Sabine, "Loyalists of the Am. Rev.," ii. 122.

From the first, he seems to have been confided in by men high in authority in the army, and to have been the recipient of some delicate trusts; and at least one sinister reminiscence attaches to him, namely, as an organ of communication between Major André and the traitor Arnold. A most criminal letter of Arnold's is still in existence, addressed to André under the name of "Mr. John Anderson," and "to be left at the Rev. Mr. Odell's, New York."[1] But by far the most memorable work wrought by Jonathan Odell during the Revolution, was what he did in his capacity as satirist.

A man of so much earnestness and forbearance as he, and so competent, likewise, to deal seriously with the issues around which the controversy was waged, would not be likely to resort to satire as a principal weapon of conflict, until all other methods of intellectual warfare had been tried. At least this conception of the place and function of satire appears to have been held by him; for in the preface to the most elaborate of his satirical poems, he says: "The masters of reason have decided, that when doctrines and practices have been fairly examined, and proved to be contrary to truth, and injurious to society, then and not before may ridicule be lawfully employed in the service of virtue. This is exactly the case of the grand American rebellion: it has been weighed in the balance, and found wanting; able writers have exposed its principles, its conduct, and its final aim. Reason has done her part, and therefore this is the legitimate moment for satire."[2]

This may, in a measure, explain the fact that although Odell was within the British lines from about the beginning of the year 1777, and was an alert and impassioned observer of the struggle, he seems not to have entered the field as a satirist until so late as the year 1778. Moreover, all his work in that field, so far as can now be ascertained, is embraced in these four poems: "The Word of Congress,"[3]

---

[1] "Writings of Washington," Sparks's ed., vii. 521.

[2] "The Loyalist Poetry," etc., 151–152.

[3] Ibid. 38–55.

published September 18, 1779; "The Congratulation,"[1] published November 6, 1779; "The Feu de Joie,"[2] published November 24, 1779; and "The American Times,"[3] written in 1779, and first published, perhaps, early in 1780.

IV.

All of these poems are framed after the models of English classical satire as presented by Dryden, Pope, and Churchill. Each has some slight plot by which the several topics are bound together; and each, plunging abruptly into its theme, dashes forward with fearless step, and a bitter, mocking, trenchant energy. Prefixed to the last of these poems is a motto from Juvenal,[4]—

"Facit indignatio versum"—

a motto that might with equal propriety be placed before them all. Throbbing along these verses is an indignation hot enough for the needs of any satirist; while the verses themselves, though tremulous and heaving with wrath, yet seem to leap toward their victims with a fury that is self-controlled, and to wield a blade polished and edged for the most scientific emotional surgery. Certainly, no student of the American Revolution who would now qualify himself to enter into the very thought and passion of those Americans who honestly opposed that great procedure, can refuse to himself a careful reading of these four satires of Jonathan Odell.

From these poems, to begin with, may one gather the

---

[1] "The Loyal Verses," etc., 45–50. From internal evidence this poem appears to have been written late in the year 1778; and though published in Rivington's "Gazette" at the date above named, it had probably been in print in some form before that time.

[2] Ibid. 51–58. [3] "The Loyalist Poetry," etc., 1–37.

[4] Sat. I. 79. His motto would have been more effective, had he quoted the whole line: "Si natura negat, facit indignatio versum."

principal ideas which formed the basis of the political system of the American Loyalists: first, that the colonial policy of the English ministry, in the matter of taxation, was a blunder; secondly, that in view of the political sympathies and tendencies of the English people, and especially of the great liberal leaders in parliament, the colonies could without doubt defeat this policy simply by persevering in their opposition within constitutional limits; and, thirdly, that the act of the radical chiefs in America in pushing their opposition beyond those limits, into open rebellion, into treason, into the attempt at national dismemberment, was not at all necessary to the political safety of America, and was therefore both a blunder and a crime,—the awful consequences of which must surely come in ruin and in suffering, not only to themselves who were guilty, but to millions of men and women who were not guilty. Thus, in his latest satire, reviewing the whole contest, Odell passes this deliberate judgment upon the causes of it:

"Stand forth, Taxation! kindler of the flame—
Inexplicable question, doubtful claim:
Suppose the right in Britain to be clear,
Britain was mad to exercise it here.
Call it unjust, or, if you please, unwise,
The colonists were mad in arms to rise.

"Impolitic, and open to abuse,[1]
How could it answer? what could it produce?
No need for furious demagogues to chafe,
America was jealous, and was safe;
Secure she stood in national alarms,
And Madness only would have flown to arms.
Arms could not help the tribute, nor confound:
Self-slain it must have tumbled to the ground."[2]

Here, then, is a vast enterprise of folly and crime into which a multitude of worthy people have been seduced, to

[1] This obviously refers to "Taxation."

[2] "The Loyalist Poetry," etc., 30.

their ineffable injury and sorrow, by the arts of a few ambitious chiefs. Without at all denying that there is such a thing as justifiable rebellion, here, certainly, as the satirist holds, is rebellion which is not justifiable. That a people so sound and orderly as the American people, should have been drawn, in such vast numbers, into a rebellion of this character, can be explained, he thinks, only upon the theory of a widespread delusion or phrensy produced by some powerful potion—some maddening cup of sorcery—some horrid

> ". . . draught designed
> To cheat the crowd, and fascinate mankind."

And the satirist is so fortunate as to have surprised the makers of this fatal draught while in the very act of compounding it:

> "What group of wizards next salutes my eyes—
> United comrades, quadruple allies?
> Bostonian Cooper, with his Hancock joined,
> Adams with Adams, one in heart and mind.
> Sprung from the soil where witches swarmed of yore,
> They come well skilled in necromantic lore;
> Intent on mischief, busily they toil,
> The magic caldron to prepare and boil;
> Arrayed in sable vests, and caps of fur,
> With wands of ebony the mess they stir;
> See! the smoke rises from the cursed drench,
> And poisons all the air with horrid stench.
>
> "Celestial muse, I fear 't will make thee hot
> To count the vile ingredients of the pot:
> Dire incantations, words of death, they mix
> With noxious plants, and water from the Styx;
> Treason's rank flowers, Ambition's swelling fruits,
> Hypocrisy in seeds, and Fraud in roots,
> Bundles of Lies fresh gathered in their prime,

And stalks of Calumny grown stale with time ;
Handfuls of Zeal's intoxicating leaves,
Riot in bunches, Cruelty in sheaves,
Slices of Cunning cut exceeding thin,
Kernels of Malice, rotten cores of Sin,
Branches of Persecution, boughs of Thrall,
And sprigs of Superstition, dipt in gall,
Opium to lull or madden all the throng,
And assafœtida profusely strong,
Milk from Tisiphone's infernal breast,
Herbs of all venom, drugs of every pest,
With min'rals from the centre brought by Gnomes,—
All seethe together till the furnace foams.

"Was this the potion, this the draught designed
To cheat the crowd, and fascinate mankind ?
O void of reason they, who thus were caught ;
O lost to virtue, who so cheap were bought ;
O folly, which all folly sure transcends,
Such bungling sorc'rers to account as friends.

"Yet though the frantic populace applaud,
'T is Satire's part to stigmatize the fraud.
Exult, ye jugglers, in your lucky tricks,
Yet on your fame the lasting brand we 'll fix.
Cheat male and female, poison age and youth,
Still we 'll pursue you with the goad of truth.
Whilst in mid-heaven shines forth the golden flame,
Hancock and Adams shall be words of shame ;
Whilst silver beams the face of night adorn,
Cooper of Boston shall be held in scorn." [1]

V.

The great American rebellion, then, is the result of a sort of insane phrensy produced by the wicked few in administering to their victims this potion of political necromancy—this hideous hell-broth made up of lies, sophistries,

[1] "The Loyalist Poetry," etc., 7–9.

ambitions, hatreds, hallucinations. Moreover, that the general madness has already made such frightful headway and havoc among the American people, has been due not to any lack of honest attempts on the part of honest men to stop it; for,

> "When civil madness first from man to man
> In these devoted climes like wildfire ran,
> There were who gave the moderating hint,
> In conversation some, and some in print;
> Wisely they spake—and what was their reward?—
> The tar, the rail, the prison, and the cord!
> Ev'n now there are, who bright in Reason's dress
> Watch the polluted Continental press;
> Confront the lies that Congress sends abroad,
> Expose the sophistry, detect the fraud." [1]

Changing, then, the image, it may be said that in this hand-to-hand battle with Error, the champions of Truth have been somewhat in the position of those brave knights of old who wandered through the world in order to fight and slay giants, enchanters, and fiery dragons,—yet with this difference, that when they had once slain the monster, slain he was, and that was the end of him:

> "But Error may not with such ease be quelled—
> She rallies fresh her force, though oft repelled;
> Cut, hacked, and mangled, she denies to yield,
> And straight returns with vigor to the field.
> Champions of Truth, our efforts are in vain;
> Fast as we slay, the foe revives again.
> Vainly the enchanted castle we surprise,
> New monsters hiss, and new enchantments rise." [2]

Moreover, the peculiar allies and agents of Error—the plotters and perpetrators of this stupendous rebellion—seem to

---

[1] "The Loyalist Poetry," etc., 26–27. [2] Ibid. 27–28.

be a race of men whose talent for mischief is inexhaustible, and who are able to provide a substitute and successor for any chieftain, however gifted, however unscrupulous, who may chance to fall:

> "Was Samuel Adams to become a ghost,
> Another Adams would assume his post;
> Was bustling Hancock numbered with the dead,
> Another full as wise might raise his head.
> What if the sands of Laurens now were run,
> How should we miss him—has he not a son?
> Or what if Washington should close his scene,
> Could none succeed him?—Is there not a Greene?
> Knave after knave as easy we could join,
> As new emissions of the paper coin.
> When it became the high United States
> To send their envoys to Versailles' proud gates,
> Were not three ministers produced at once?—
> Delicious group, fanatic, deist, dunce!
> And what if Lee, and what if Silas fell,
> Or what if Franklin should go down to hell,
> Why should we grieve?—the land, 't is understood,
> Can furnish hundreds equally as good." [1]

Then, again, so soon as American society had thrown off its ancient and rightful allegiance, it began to suffer the most horrid form of misgovernment—the rule of the worst:

> "From the back woods half savages came down,
> And awkward troops paraded every town.
> Committees and conventions met by scores;
> Justice was banished, Law turned out of doors;
> Disorder seemed to overset the land;
> They who appeared to rule, the tumult fanned;
> But Cunning stood behind with sure control,
> And in one centre caused to meet the whole." [2]

---

[1] "The Loyalist Poetry," etc., 28.

[2] Ibid. 53.

Of course, by that "one centre" where Cunning stood behind the scene, and gave direction and method to the universal madness, the poet means the Continental Congress. Congress it is which, in the name of liberty, has brought in this many-headed tyranny—the instant product of which is a vast social jumble of ignorance, violence, folly, and wretchedness:

> "Here Anarchy before the gaping crowd
> Proclaims the people's majesty aloud;
> There Folly runs with eagerness about,
> And prompts the cheated populace to shout;
> Here paper-dollars meagre Famine holds,
> There votes of Congress Tyranny unfolds;
> With doctrines strange in matter and in dress,
> Here sounds the pulpit, and there groans the press;
> Confusion blows her trump—and far and wide
> The noise is heard—the plough is laid aside;
> The awl, the needle, and the shuttle drops;
> Tools change to swords, and camps succeed to shops;
> The doctor's glister-pipe, the lawyer's quill,
> Transformed to guns, retain their power to kill;
> From garrets, cellars, rushing through the street,
> The new-born statesmen in committees meet;
> Legions of senators infest the land,
> And mushroom generals thick as mushrooms stand." [1]

So often as the satirist looks abroad over the land, searching to find out who, beyond all question, are responsible for these appalling miseries, he comes back again and again and fastens his gaze upon Congress. That body it is which, in his opinion, is the one effective organ and operator of all this public profligacy and ruin. Therefore, with eyes flashing anger, with step and gesture expressive of uttermost contempt and loathing for these men who, in the name of patriotism and freedom, have committed treason, have organized despotism, have slain the happiness of the people,

[1] "The Loyalist Poetry," etc., 2.

he demands whether it is not at last quite time to tear the masks from their faces and to expose them for the robbers and the tyrants that they are:

> "We will, we must—though mighty Laurens frown,
> Or Hancock with his rabble hunt us down;
> Champions of virtue, we 'll alike disdain
> The guards of Washington, the lies of Paine,
> And greatly bear, without one anxious throb,
> The wrath of Congress, or its lords the mob." [1]

VI.

Upon Congress, accordingly, he wreaks his satiric vengeance, unwinding over its devoted head the voluminous folds of his own copious and fructifying vocabulary of curses. In his opinion, nothing can be plainer than that the history of the Continental Congress is but a history of political duplicity and deceit; and for all its brilliant versatility in deception, that renowned body deserves to be named the very Proteus of modern politics:

> "Oh! 't is a word of power, of prime account:
> I 've seen it like the daring Osprey mount;
> I 've seen it like a dirty reptile creep,
> Rush into flame, or plunge into the deep;
> I 've heard it like a hungry lion roar,
> Who tears the prey, and bathes himself in gore;
> I 've seen it softer than the vernal rain,
> Mildly descending on the grassy plain;
> I 've heard it pious, as a saint in prayer—
> I 've heard it like an angry trooper swear;
> I 've known it suit itself to every plan—
> I 've known it lie to God, and lie to man.
>
> . . . .
>
> Whoe'er the word of Congress shall peruse,
> In every piece will see it change its views;

[1] "The Loyalist Poetry," etc., 1–2.

Now swell with duty to the king elate,
Now melt with kindness to the parent state,
Then back to treason suddenly revolve,
And join in Suffolk's infamous resolve.
Trace it through all the windings of the press,
Vote or appeal, petition or address,
Trace it in every act, in every speech,
Too sure you 'll find duplicity in each.
Mark now its soothing, now its threat'ning strain;
Mark its hypocrisy, deceit, chicane;
From the soft breathings of the new-formed board,
To that fell hour when Independence roared,
Forced, you 'll acknowledge, since creation's dawn
Earth never yet produced so vile a spawn."[1]

But the satirist is by no means satisfied when he has poured his execration upon Congress as a collective body of criminals: he needs to single out by name, and to blast individually, the men who compose it, and the men, also, who outside its walls are its conspicuous servants,—

"The blust'rer, the poltroon, the vile, the weak,
Who fight for Congress, or in Congress speak."[2]

One of those clearly entitled to this distinction at Odell's hands is Thomas Paine, whose service of Congress as a writer was most memorable:

"Swarms of deceivers, practised in the trade,
Were sent abroad to gull, cajole, persuade;

. . . .

Others apart in some obscure recess,
The studied lie for publication dress:
Prepare the vague report, fallacious tale,
Invent fresh calumnies, revive the stale,
Pervert all records sacred and profane,—

---

[1] "The Loyalist Poetry," etc., 39; 49–50.

[2] Ibid. 44.

And chief among them stands the villain Paine.
This scribbling imp, 't is said, from London came,
That seat of glory intermixed with shame.

. . . .

Our hireling author having changed his soil,
True son of Grub Street, here renewed his toil.
What cannot ceaseless impudence produce?
Old Franklin [1] knows its value, and its use:
He caught at Paine, relieved his wretched plight,
And gave him notes, and set him down to write.
Fire from the Doctor's hints the miscreant took,
Discarded truth, and soon produced a book,—
A pamphlet which, without the least pretence
To reason, bore the name of 'Common Sense.'

. . . .

The work, like wildfire, through the country ran,
And Folly bowed the knee to Franklin's plan.
Sense, reason, judgment were abashed and fled,
And Congress reigned triumphant in their stead." [2]

Another personage upon whom this stern limner bestows his skill, is General John Sullivan, first a member of Congress, and afterward its military servant,—his most noted exploit being as leader of the famous expedition into the Indian country beyond the Susquehanna:

"Amidst ten thousand eminently base,
Thou, Sullivan, assume the highest place!
Sailor, and farmer, barrister of vogue,
Each state was thine, and thou in each a rogue.
Ambition came, and swallowed in a trice,
Like Aaron's rod, the reptile fry of vice.
One giant passion then his soul possessed,
And dreams of lawless sway disturbed his rest.
He gave each wild imagination scope,

---

[1] In the text, this name is not given.

[2] "The Loyalist Poetry," etc., 51–52.

And flew to Congress on the wings of hope.
Behold him there, but still behold him curst—
He sate in Congress, but he sate not first.
What could the fever of his mind compose?
Make him a general: general straight he grows.
Head of a shirtless, shoeless gang he strides—
While Wisdom stares and Folly shakes her sides.

"And must I sing the wonders of his might?
What are they? Rout, captivity, and flight!
Rhode Island saw him to her forts advance,
Assisted by the ships of faithless France:
Rhode Island saw him shamefully retreat,
In imitation of the Gallic fleet.
His banners last on Susquehanna waved,
Where, lucky to excess, his scalp he saved."[1]

Thus, the portraits of distinguished writers and generals are dashed off by Odell in bold, ferocious, and sometimes witty caricature, and are hung up by him against the panels of his rogues' gallery. Besides, not even the pettiness, not even the obscurity, of any miscreant can protect him from the attentions of this artist:

"Not always generals offer to our aim,—
By turns we must advert t' inferior game.
Yet hard to rescue from oblivion's grasp
The worthless beetle and the noxious asp;
And full as hard to save from after-times
The names of men known only for their crimes.
Left to themselves they soon would be forgot;
But yet 't is right that rogues should hang and rot."[2]

While, however, there is such catholicity in the range of his hatred, and a mob of minor malefactors do receive the painful honor of his notice, it is upon the supreme political criminals—the splendid and now immortal chiefs of the

---

[1] "The Loyalist Poetry," etc., 46–47.

[2] Ibid. 13.

Revolution—that he bestows his most studied skill in execration. In "The American Times," the most polished and the most powerful of his satires, he contrives to bring these great criminals before him by means of a poetic device for which he is evidently indebted to the idea of Milton, namely, that the fallen angels, using their temporary privilege of absence from Pandemonium, are accustomed to take human forms and to enact renowned and malefic careers on the field of human history. In the development of this conception, Odell enacts a tremendous scene. Amid all this babel of clattering impudence in America,—standing indignant but unappalled in the very heart of this tumult wherein a mob of political jugglers are plotting crime and sorrow for their victims,—he summons into his presence from Pandemonium those mighty demons who, masquerading in this part of the earth under the shapes and names of mortal men, have really wrought here the chief infamy and wretchedness of the American rebellion:

> "O! for some magic voice, some powerful spell,
> To call the Furies from profoundest hell!
> Arise, ye Fiends, from dark Cocytus's brink;
> Soot all my paper, sulphurize my ink;
> So with my theme the colors shall agree,
> Brimstone and black—the livery of Lee."[1]

Instantly, in response to his potent call, they rise and swarm around him, a flock of malignant monsters from the nethermost pit, and receive from him their sentence: first, William Livingston of New Jersey, against whom Odell had very special grounds for abhorrence; then the serene and wise John Jay; then Samuel Chase, the robust lawyer and statesman of Maryland; then Robert Morris, the financier; then his coadjutor in finance, the brilliant and exuberant Gouverneur Morris:

---

[1] "The Loyalist Poetry," etc., 3. Of course, the "Lee" here named is General Charles Lee, who, as is now known, was a greater scoundrel than even Odell thought him.

"Whence and what art thou, execrable form,
Rough as a bear, and roaring as a storm?
Ay, now I know thee—Livingston art thou—
Gall in thy heart, and malice on thy brow;
Coward, yet cruel—zealous, yet profane;
Havoc, and spoil, and ruin are thy gain.
Go, glut like Death thy vast unhide-bound maw;
Remorseless swallow liberty and law;
At one enormous stroke a nation slay—
But thou thyself shall perish with thy prey.

"What Fiend is this, of countenance acute,
More of the knave who seems, and less of brute;
Whose words are cutting like a shower of hail,
And blasting as the mildew in the vale?
'T is Jay—to him these characters belong:
Sure sense of right, with fixed pursuit of wrong;
An outside keen, where malice makes abode;
Voice of a lark, and venom of a toad;
Semblance of worth, not substance, he puts on,
And Satan owns him for his darling son.

"Flit not around me thus, pernicious elf,
Whose love of country terminates in self;
Back to the gloomy shades, detested sprite,
Mangler of rhetoric, enemy of right:
Cursed of thy father, sum of all that 's base,
Thy sight is odious and thy name is Chase.

"What spectre 's that, with eyes on earth intent,
Whose god is gold, whose glory cent. per cent.;
Whose soul, devoted to the love of gain,
Revolts from feelings noble or humane?
Let friends, let family, let country groan,
Despairing widows shriek, and orphans moan;
Turned to the centre where his riches grow,
His eye regards not spectacles of woe.
Morris, look up—for so thy name we spell—
On earth, Bob Morris, Mammon 't is in hell.

Wretch, who hast meanly sold thy native land,
Tremble, thou wretch, for vengeance is at hand;
Soon shall thy treasures fly on eagle's wings,
And conscience goad thee with her thousand stings.

"Of head erect, and self-sufficient mien,
Another Morris presses to be seen.
Demons of vanity, you know him sure;
This is your pupil, this is Gouverneur.
Some little knowledge, and some little sense,
More affectation far, and more pretense;
Such is the man—his tongue he never balks,
On all things talkable he boldly talks;
A specious orator, of law he prates;
A pompous nothing, mingles in debates;
Consummate impudence, sheer brass of soul,
Crowns every sentence, and completes the whole;
In other times, unnoticed he might drop—
Confusion makes a statesman of a fop."[1]

VII.

With characters so powerful or so interesting as these, the poet is not always occupied,—as when he condescends to bestow four lines of contempt on that blundering and bibulous American officer, the titular Lord Stirling:

"What matters what of Stirling may become?
The quintessence of whiskey, soul of rum;
Fractious at nine, quite gay at twelve o'clock;
From thence till bed-time stupid as a block."[2]

For a fresh assortment of villains to choose from, the satirist has but to repeat his invocation, and up come another gang of them, among whom happens to be conspicuous the Polish revolutionist and outlaw, Pulaski, who was accused of plan-

---

[1] "The Loyalist Poetry," etc., 4–6.
[2] "The Loyalist Poetry," etc., 14.

ning the abduction of his king, and who was actually killed on an American battle-field a few months after that very fate was predicted for him in these lines:

> "Turn out, black monsters—let us take our choice!
> What devilish figure 's this, with devilish voice?
> Oh! 't is Pulaski—'t is a foreign chief;
> On him we 'll comment—be our comment brief.
> What are his merits, judges may dispute;
> We 'll solve the doubt, and praise him—for a brute.
> 'No quarter' is his motto—sweet and short:
> Good Britons, give him a severe retort.
> As yet he 'scapes the shot deserved so well—
> His nobler horse in Carolina fell;
> He fears not, in the field where heroes bleed,
> He starts at nothing—but a generous deed.
> Escaped from Poland, where his murd'rous knife,
> 'T is said, was raised against his sovereign's life,
> Perhaps he scoffs, with fashionable mirth,
> The notion of a God who rules the earth.
> Fool! not to see that something more than lot
> Conducts the traitor to this destined spot,—
> Rank with congenial crimes that call for blood,
> Where justice soon must pour the purple flood,
> A parricide, with parricides to die,
> And vindicate the Power that reigns on high." [1]

With even a keener zest for bestowing deserved punishment, the poet also recognizes among the rabble of fiends that he has called up from the pit, one whose earth-name is Witherspoon:

> "Known in the pulpit by seditious toils,
> Grown into consequence by civil broils,
> Three times he tried, and miserably failed,
> To overset the laws—the fourth prevailed.
> Whether as tool he acted, or as guide,
> Is yet a doubt—his conscience must decide.

[1] "The Loyalist Poetry," etc., 14–15.

Meanwhile unhappy Jersey mourns her thrall,
Ordained by vilest of the vile to fall;
To fall by Witherspoon!—O name, the curse
Of sound religion, and disgrace of verse.
Member of Congress, we must hail him next:
'Come out of Babylon,' was now his text.
Fierce as the fiercest, foremost of the first,
He 'd rail at kings, with venom well-nigh burst.
Not uniformly grand—for some bye-end,
To dirtiest acts of treason he 'd descend:
I 've known him seek the dungeon dark as night,
Imprisoned Tories to convert, or fright;
Whilst to myself I 've hummed, in dismal tune,
I 'd rather be a dog than Witherspoon.
Be patient, reader—for the issue trust;
His day will come—remember, Heaven is just!"[1]

Thus, one by one, these monsters of political crime, as they flutter about the poet, are described and damned,—members of Congress, generals of the army, governors of States, subordinate officers of government, and even its hired scribblers:

"Wretches, whose acts the very French abhor;
Commissioners of loans, and boards of war,
Marine committees, commissaries, scribes,
Assemblies, councils, senatorial tribes.

. . . .

Ask you the names of these egregious wights?
I could as soon recount Glendower's sprites.
Thick as mosquitoes, venomously keen,
Thicker than locusts, spoilers of the green;
Swarming like maggots who the carcass scour
Of some poor ox, and as they crawl, devour,—
They 'd mock the labors of a hundred pens—
'Back, owly-headed monsters, to your dens.'"[2]

---

[1] "The Loyalist Poetry," etc., 17–18. [2] Ibid. 20.

Scarcely any man of prominence in the Revolutionary cause has the felicity to be overlooked by this terrible judge; and no one, once looked upon by him, escapes without a sentence which seems to make soul and body writhe in torment. To one character only—and he a civilian, even a member of Congress, even the president of Congress—is the satirist willing to concede one solitary trait of goodness. That character is Henry Laurens, the noble South Carolinian. Having ordered back to the pit from which they came, all these clamorous monsters, the poet turns with a sort of sad respect to Laurens:

"At length, they 're silenced! Laurens, thou draw near;
What I shall utter, thou attentive hear!
I loathe all conference with thy boisterous clan,
But now with thee I 'll argue as a man.

"What could incite thee, Laurens, to rebel?—
Thy soul thou wouldst not for a trifle sell.
'T was not of power the wild, insatiate lust;
Mistaken as thou art, I deem thee just.
Saw'st thou thy king tyrannically rule?
Thou could'st not think it—thou art not a fool.
Thou wast no bankrupt, no enthusiast thou;
The clearness of thy fame e'en foes allow.
For months I watched thee with a jealous eye,
Yet could no turpitude of mind espy.
In private life I hold thee far from base—
Thy public conduct wears another face.
In thee a stern republican I view;
This of thy actions is the only clew.
Admit thy principles—could these demand,
Could these give right, to desolate a land?
Could it be right, with arbitrary will,
To fine, imprison, plunder, torture, kill?
Impose new oaths, make stubborn conscience yield,
And force out thousands to the bloody field?
Could it be right to do these monstrous things—
Because thy nature was averse to kings?

Well, but a stern republican thou art;
Heaven send thee soon to meet with thy desert!
Thee, Laurens, foe to monarchy we call,
And thou, or legal government, must fall.
Who wept for Cato, was not Cato's friend;
Who pitied Brutus, Brutus would offend.
So, Laurens, to conclude my grave harangue,
I would not pity, though I saw thee hang." [1]

But in all this bustling throng of political criminals upon whom the poet has bestowed his imprecation, right hearty and blistering, where is Washington? And did the American Loyalists of 1779—did even Jonathan Odell, the most implacable of them all—dare to assault him, to dispute his integrity, to deny to him that purity of character, those stately virtues, for which he is now canonized by the human race? Let us for a moment hearken!

"Strike up, hell's music! roar, infernal drums!
Discharge the cannon! Lo, the warrior comes!
He comes, not tame as on Ohio's banks
But rampant at the head of ragged ranks.
Hunger and itch are with him—Gates and Wayne!
And all the lice of Egypt in his train.
Sure these are Falstaff's soldiers, poor and bare,
Or else the rotten reg'ments of Rag-Fair.

. . . .

Wilt thou, great chief of Freedom's lawless sons,
Great captain of the western Goths and Huns,
Wilt thou for once permit a private man
To parley with thee, and thy conduct scan?
At Reason's bar has Catiline been heard:
At Reason's bar e'en Cromwell has appeared.

. . . .

"Hear thy indictment, Washington, at large;
Attend and listen to the solemn charge:

[1] "The Loyalist Poetry," etc., 21–22.

Thou hast supported an atrocious cause
Against thy king, thy country, and the laws;
Committed perjury, encouraged lies,
Forced conscience, broken the most sacred ties;
Myriads of wives and fathers at thy hand
Their slaughtered husbands, slaughtered sons, demand;
That pastures hear no more the lowing kine,
That towns are desolate, all—all is thine;
The frequent sacrilege that pained my sight,
The blasphemies my pen abhors to write,
Innumerable crimes on thee must fall—
For thou maintainest, thou defendest all.

. . . .

What could, when half-way up the hill to fame,
Induce thee to go back, and link with shame?
Was it ambition, vanity, or spite
That prompted thee with Congress to unite;
Or did all three within thy bosom roll,
'Thou heart of hero with a traitor's soul'?
Go, wretched author of thy country's grief,
Patron of villainy, of villains chief;
Seek with thy cursed crew the central gloom,
Ere Truth's avenging sword begin thy doom;
Or sudden vengeance of celestial dart
Precipitate thee with augmented smart."[1]

VIII.

Through all the songs and satires of Jonathan Odell there runs one thread of passionate sentiment which has to be recognized as something profoundly characteristic of him and of the great Loyalist party of which he was a leader, namely, an absolute, a cloudless, confidence in the ultimate and perfect triumph of their party through the ultimate and perfect triumph of the British arms in America. How could it be otherwise? Who that had mastered the first four rules of arithmetic, could doubt that Great Britain

[1] "The Loyalist Poetry," etc., 9–12.

would put down and stamp out this American rebellion? Accordingly, from that June afternoon in 1776, when the captive British officers, on an island in the Delaware, sang the rousing ode in which Odell had put into lyric form his assurance of the speedy discomfiture of the rebels, down to the year 1783, when the impossible came to pass, in the acknowledgment by England of the complete success of the American rebellion, it is apparent that Jonathan Odell held firmly to his faith that the arms of England must, as a matter of course, shatter and annihilate all organized opposition in the colonies.

> "Though faction by falsehood awhile may prevail,
> And Loyalty suffers, a captive in jail,
> Britain is roused, rebellion is falling:
> God save the king!
> The captive shall soon be released from his chain,
> And conquest restore us to Britain again,
> Ever to join in chanting merrily
> Glory and joy crown the king!"[1]

Such was a part of Odell's song for the king's birthday in the year 1777. Nevertheless, that year and the year following passed away, and the power of armed rebellion in America did not pass away. In spite of this strange delay, Odell doubted not that the rebellion was doomed, and that its doom was very near. Nay, in the autumn of 1778, after the grotesque failure of the French squadron in their first campaign of alliance with the Americans, Odell flung into a tumult of jeering verse his exultation over the proofs then so plentiful, that the rebel cause had not another leg to stand on:

> "The farce of empire will be finished soon,
> And each mock monarch dwindle to a loon;
> Mock-money and mock-States shall melt away,
> And the mock-troops disband for want of pay.
> . . . .

[1] "The Loyal Verses," etc., 12.

Now War, suspended by the scorching heat,
Springs from his tent, and shines in arms complete;
Now Sickness, that of late made heroes pale,
Flies from the keenness of the northern gale;
Firmness and Enterprise, united, wait
The last command to strike the stroke of Fate;
Now Boston trembles, Philadelphia quakes,
And Carolina to the centre shakes!

. . . .

What now is left of Continental brags?—
Taxes unpaid, though payable in rags.
What now remains of Continental force?—
Battalions mould'ring, waste without resource.
What rests there yet of Continental sway?—
A ruined people—ripe to disobey.
Hate now of men, and soon to be the jest!
Such is your fate, ye Monsters of the West!"[1]

Indeed, so plain was it to Odell that the last flicker of light was now to be seen in the dying embers of the rebellion, that he was able, near the close of the year 1778, to fix the exact date for its final extinction, namely, the year 1779. Therefore, for a company of Loyalists who, with convivial rites, were watching the old year out and the new year in, he conveyed this prediction in the form of a capital song, entitled "The Old Year and the New: a Prophecy":

"What though last year be past and gone,
Why should we grieve or mourn about it?
As good a year is now begun,
And better, too,—let no one doubt it.
'T is New Year's morn; why should we part?
Why not enjoy what heaven has sent us?
Let wine expand the social heart,
Let friends, and mirth, and wine content us.

"War's rude alarms disturbed last year;
Our country bled and wept around us;

[1] "The Loyal Verses," etc., 48–50.

But this each honest heart shall cheer,
And peace and plenty shall surround us.

"Last year 'King Congo,' through the land,
Displayed his thirteen stripes to fright us;
But George's power, in Clinton's hand,
In this New Year shall surely right us.

"Last year saw many honest men
Torn from each dear and sweet connection;
But this shall see them home again,
And happy in their king's protection.

"Last year vain Frenchmen braved our coasts,
And baffled Howe, and 'scaped from Byron;
But this shall bring their vanquished hosts
To crouch beneath the British lion.

"Last year rebellion proudly stood,
Elate, in her meridian glory;
But this shall quench her pride in blood,—
George will avenge each martyred Tory.

"Then bring us wine, full bumpers bring:
Hail this New Year in joyful chorus;
God bless great George our gracious king,
And crush rebellion down before us.
'T is New Year's morn; why should we part?
Why not enjoy what heaven has sent us?
Let wine expand the social heart,
Let friends, and mirth, and wine content us." [1]

---

[1] "The Loyalist Poetry," etc., 99–101. Though I have nowhere seen this song mentioned as Odell's, I do not hesitate to ascribe it to him. It is exactly in his best manner. Moreover, from a contemporary reference, we know that the song was written by a clergyman; and it is impossible to name any other Loyalist clergyman then in the country, who is known to have produced verse of the quality of this. I am confident, also, that a considerable part of Odell's work as a song-writer and satirist during the Revolution has thus far escaped recognition as his.

As one comes to the end of the American Revolution—an end that brought with it to the American Loyalists a shock of sickening disappointment and of irreparable disaster—we find them presently breaking up into two sections: first, those who after a time relented, sought reconciliation with the victors, or were glad, at any rate, to come back and dwell in peace in the young republic whose existence had been won in spite of them; and, secondly, those who never relented, who never sought reconciliation, and who, in England, in Nova Scotia, in Upper Canada, or in some other portion of the British empire, found a shelter and finally a grave for a political hostility which no lapse of time could quench or even soften. To the first section, Joseph Stansbury belonged: to the second, belonged Jonathan Odell. His principle as an American Loyalist had in it an invincible tenacity, a deathless love, a deathless hate. Even after the surrender of Cornwallis in 1781, and so long as England kept a solitary soldier in America, Odell continued to talk of aggression—of renewing the struggle,—of getting vengeance and victory even yet. When, finally, the contemptuous wrath of England gave way, and she forced her reluctant king to make terms with the late American rebels, Odell would not make terms with them; he still denounced and defied them; and with other inappeasable opponents of American Independence, he abandoned the land of his birth and of his ancestry, and settled himself in Nova Scotia, where he sustained a distinguished civil career, and where at last, in extreme old age, he died, without ever taking back a word, or uttering an apology, or flinching from an opinion,—a proud, gritty member of a political party that had been defeated, but never conquered or convinced.

CHAPTER XXX.

FRANCIS HOPKINSON AS HUMOROUS CHAMPION OF AMERICAN INDEPENDENCE: 1776–1781.

I.—Hopkinson chosen to represent New Jersey in Congress, then discussing the resolution for Independence—His serious work in legislation, in executive business—Becomes Judge of the Court of Admiralty in Pennsylvania—Finds relief from official labors in his sprightly contributions to Revolutionary literature.

II.—Obstacles to American Independence presented by certain mental and sentimental habits of the Americans—The survival among them of the colonial attitude toward the mother country—For political free-mindedness, a critical disposition is needed—To this Hopkinson contributes in December, 1776, by his "Letter Written by a Foreigner on the Character of the English Nation"—Facetious description of the typical Englishman—Playful account of the origin of the English quarrel with America—The intellectual capacity of the British voters who sustain the ministry in their war against America.

III.—General account of Hopkinson's contributions to Revolutionary literature—His revision of them in his "Miscellaneous Essays and Occasional Writings"—After July 4, 1776, the chief objects of attack for a Whig satirist are the military invaders of the country, and their American allies—Hopkinson's tone toward both these enemies of Independence.

IV.—Hopkinson's "Letter to Lord Howe," December, 1776—His "Political Catechism," and his "Camp Ballad," early in 1777—His ridicule of the two great British invasions of 1777—The terror inspired by that under General Burgoyne—Hopkinson's burlesque of Burgoyne's grandiloquent proclamation—Britannia's humiliation through Burgoyne's failure, set forth in the ballad, "Date Obolum Belisario."

V.—Hopkinson's ridicule of Howe's invasion of Pennsylvania—Circumstances which suggested "The Battle of the Kegs"—The effectiveness of that ballad—Its inferior literary quality.

VI.—Hopkinson's ridicule of the Loyalists—Their social prepossessions—Their alleged snobbishness—His "Two Letters" as by Loyalists avowing their most offensive opinions and purposes—His last work as a Revolutionary humorist, an "Advertisement," November, 1781, in ridicule of the Tory printer and bookseller, James Rivington.

I.

THE prominent part taken by Francis Hopkinson, in April, 1776, in the literary debate over the question of Independence,[1] made it natural that the political party in New Jersey which favored that measure should a few weeks afterward choose him as their representative in Congress, then engaged, as it was, in the final consideration of the same tremendous topic.

Upon taking his seat there, he was at once made a member of the committee for framing the articles of confederation.[2] In the following September, he was designated by the governor of New Jersey as one of the justices of the superior court of that State—a position which he seems to have declined.[3] In November of the same year, his associates in Congress laid upon him the sole responsibility of executing "the business of the navy," under the direction of the marine committee.[4] At a later period, he served Congress as treasurer of the continental loan office.[5] Finally, in July, 1779, he received from the president of Pennyslvania the high place of judge of the court of admiralty in that State,[6]—a position which he filled for the subsequent ten years.

It does not appear that the assumption by Hopkinson of these high and grave tasks had any effect in diminishing his facility or sprightliness as a humorous political writer. On the contrary, he seems to have found relief from the fatigue and the solemn stiffness of public business, in such escapades of fancy and mirth—always made, of course, under an incognito. At any rate, the most frolicsome of his writings were precisely those which were thrown off, as mere sports of the mind, in the midst of the gravity and high dignity of his labors as a legislator and a judge. He was a

---

[1] This subject is dealt with in chapter xxii. of the present work.

[2] "Journals of Congress," i. 390–391.

[3] Hildeburn, in "Pa. Mag. of Hist. and Biog.," ii. 321–322.

[4] "Journals of Congress," i. 551.

[5] Hildeburn, in "Pa. Mag. of Hist. and Biog.," ii. 323.

[6] Ibid. 322.

devotee to the law, who never took farewell of the muses. And thus it came about that, from the autumn of 1774 on until the very close of the long struggle, the cause of the Revolution, at nearly every stage and emergency of it, was rescued from depression, was quickened, was cheered forward, was given strength, by the vivacity of this delightful writer.

II.

Even after Congress had pronounced the terrific word Independence,—thus rending and trampling under foot the most solemn protestations made by the American people during the preceding ten years,—there still remained in their imaginations and in their hearts a prodigious obstacle to the full adoption and support of that audacious political heresy. There, to begin with, was the ancient and most passionate love of the American colonists for England itself, —for England, the cradle of their race, the one spot in all the world which, during nearly two hundred years of absence from it, they had continued to speak of as Home. There, also, was their deep, even if very provincial, regard for everything English, in opinion, in costume, in manner, in speech, in precedent. There, likewise, was American reverence for the king—a reverence perhaps always increasing in the ratio of distance from him; reverence for the king, and his chief ministers, his parliament, his generals, his troops. There, too, was American unconsciousness of their own real power in resistance and in attack—of their latent resources in civil and military organization and self-control. There, again, was the social prestige of the royal cause in America. There were the chances for promotion in rank and in office, by remaining on the king's side,—all the lures of hope, ambition, ease, wealth, respectability, held out by that side. And besides all these, there was the appeal to fear,—an appeal never very far from any man in those days,—the vision presented to the eye with awful distinctness as a thing not at all unlikely to become real some day,—the vision of a long cloudy vista, stretching far down across red battle-fields, and over mangled corpses piled up in heaps, and finally, at the further end of it, a row of scaffolds, and on each scaffold a vanquished rebel pendent. In very truth, all these were considerations which, even with honest and high-spirited people, sadly weighed, in those days, against the resolution to go over to this plucky but sudden and dubious project for Independence. Who could grapple with all these intimidating forces? Certainly, no one did so more effectually than the men who wielded the printing-press,—particularly the wits and satirists and pamphleteers on the venturesome side!

The doctrine of Independence, then, was a proposition quickly to alienate a whole people from an object which for ages had seemed to them to be very great and venerable, toward which they were still drawn by a something that throbbed in every drop of their blood,—by the instincts of race, by ancient traditions, by hereditary habits, by sentiments of ineffable depth and tenderness, by a set of spiritual forces among the strongest that can kindle and sway the human heart. Furthermore, any attempt to disturb and to reverse these deep-seated tendencies on the part of a whole people, had to encounter at the beginning, a serious difficulty springing from the very nature of the colonial mind—the undeveloped state of its critical faculty as regards the personal traits, the provoking limitations, the less pleasing idiosyncracies, of the mother race from which the colonists have themselves sprung, and with which until then they had always been eager and proud to be identified. For, always, the colonial mind in its normal condition does not judge keenly, much less does it ridicule, the faults and foibles of the parent nation. The colony that has begun to ridicule its national parent is not far from Independence. Accordingly, for the development among the Americans in 1776 of the robust political courage invoked by their new doctrine of national separation, it was necessary that this amiable note of provincialism—this filial obtuseness of the colonial mind

—should be broken up, and that the Englishmen who lived in America should begin to find food for mirth and even for derision in the peculiarities of the Englishmen who lived in England.

Toward this important political result, Hopkinson made some contribution in his so-called "Letter written by a Foreigner on the Character of the English Nation."[1] Under an old device for securing disinterested judgments on national peculiarities, Hopkinson here represents a cultivated foreigner as spending some time in England in the latter part of 1776, and as giving to a friend in his own country a cool but very satirical analysis of the alleged vices, foibles, and absurdities of the English people, and of the weak and wrong things in their treatment of their late colonists in America. "The general character of the English," says this philosophical observer, "is certainly the most fantastic and absurd that ever fell to the lot of any known nation. As they are made up of contradictions, it would be unjust to give them any uniform designation. There is scarce a virtue that adorns the mind, or a vice that disgraces human nature, but may be ascribed to them as part of their national character. But the former are often rendered ineffectual by misapplication, and the latter qualified by a levity of manners, which shews them not to be constitutionally prevalent. An Englishman will treat his enemy with great generosity, and his friend with ingratitude and inhumanity. He will be lavish of his wealth when he has but little of it, and become a miserly wretch when fortune pours her favors into his purse. He will brave the utmost hardships, and encounter the severest trials with heroic fortitude; and will drown or hang himself because the wind is in the east. He will lend large sums to a stranger on the slightest security, and refuse his nearest relation the means of subsistence. To-day his heart expands

[1] This is the title given in the Contents to vol. i. of "The Miscellaneous Essays." Over the text of the letter itself is this title: "Translation of a Letter Written by a Foreigner on his Travels," i. 98.

with social benevolence; to-morrow he is cold, sullen, and morose. To-day he possesses the wealth of a nabob; to-morrow he refuses a sixpence to a beggar, lest he should himself be reduced to the want of that sixpence. In a word, contradiction and absurdity make an Englishman." [1]

In the course of this supposed letter from London, the disinterested foreign gentleman who is represented as writing it, very naturally refers to the quarrel then going on between the king and his American subjects; and he is thus led to give to his correspondent an explanation—a very luminous and amusing explanation it is—of the origin of the quarrel, only substituting for the constitutional formula, "No taxation without representation," the arithmetical formula, "Two and two make four,"—the one formula being, according to the satirist, quite as obvious as the other. "This best of all kings," he writes, "has now turned his attention to America. There he had three millions of subjects, who loved, honored, and obeyed him. He governed them by officers of his own appointment; he had the whole regulation of their commerce; and the overflowings of their wealth were conducted, by easy channels, into his coffers, and into the purses of the merchants and manufacturers of his kingdom. But he has quarreled with these loyal and beneficial subjects, because they are so obstinate that they will not acknowledge that two and two make five. Whole volumes have been written on this subject, and all the force of reason and eloquence exerted to convince this wise king that he is in an error. The Americans have most emphatically beseeched him to accept of the undissembled loyalty of their hearts; declaring that they are

[1] "The Miscellaneous Essays," etc., i. 98–99. If we would now do justice to the skill and the success with which England, by the deft hands of her king and parliament, then conducted that fine motherly process of race-weaning which history embodies under the name of the American Revolution, we should here note that the genial American writer who, in 1776, thus defined an Englishman as a person made up of "contradiction and absurdity," was the same one who, just ten years before, had been anxious to have it understood that "we of America are in all respects Englishmen."

satisfied that the fruits of their industry should center with him and his people as heretofore, to enrich and aggrandize them; but humbly pray that they may not be compelled to acknowledge that two and two make five, which would be to them a most dangerous and distressing violation of truth. But this wise and humane monarch is far from being disposed to give up the point. He has rejected their petitions with scorn, and spurned at their offers of affection and fidelity; and declares, that he will even risk the crown of his ancestors, but he will make the obstinate Americans subscribe to his new dogma.

"To this end he hath sent over not only his own fleets and armies, but has hired a banditti of foreign mercenaries from a petty prince who supports the splendor of his court by selling the blood of his subjects; and he has also employed negroes and wild Indians to persecute the poor Americans without mercy, until they shall acknowledge that two and two make five.

"America is at this time a scene of desolation and distress—a theatre whereon is acted a real tragedy, exhibiting every species of cruelty and injustice. The royal army of this most enlightened of all nations are ravishing the women, murdering the men, and laying waste that fertile and beautiful country, under the conduct of Lord and General Howe; who are executing their bloody mandate, with all the composure in the world. His most gracious majesty receives, from time to time, such accounts of their proceedings as they please to give him, and is as happy as such a monarch can be.

"Who would have thought that the peaceful plains of America would be desolated because the inhabitants will not believe that two and two make five, when their good king and his wise parliament require them to do so?

"On the contrary, the Americans, highly resenting this treatment, have declared that they will no longer be pensioners of the smiles of such a king, or submit to a government in which they have no share, and over which they have no control, and which is, therefore, with respect to them, a government of mere will and pleasure. They have determined to be henceforth a free people; and have publicly avowed that they will enjoy the inestimable privileges of believing, and saying, that two and two make only four, according to the common sense of mankind." [1]

Such, according to this philosophic observer, late in the year 1776, is the origin of the American war. And how must such a war terminate? Is not the king's claim too preposterous to be long supported, even by his own subjects in England? At a distance, one might think so. "But the truth is that the king, by means of his ministers, hath gained such an ascendancy over the parliament, which is the constitutional voice of the people, that he can obtain their sanction for any project in which their rights are not openly and directly attacked. As to the people at large, they do not trouble themselves about the right or wrong of the matter in contest. America is a great way off, and they have no feelings for what is passing there. They grumble, indeed, about the diminution of their trade, in consequence of this war, but leave the discussion of national politics to their parliament." [2]

To make quite clear to his correspondent just how all this could be, the imaginary letter-writer then goes on to sketch with a free hand the limited lives and the petty mental range of the common people of England, their patriotic incredulity as to the existence of anything great or good outside of their little island, and especially the very limited knowledge and the quite unlimited self-conceit and stupidity of the ordinary English shopkeeper and mechanic: "The extreme ignorance of the common people of this civilized country can scarce be credited. In general, they know nothing beyond the particular branch of business which their parents or the parish happened to choose for them. This, indeed, they practise with unremitting diligence; but never think of extending their knowledge farther.

[1] "The Miscellaneous Essays," etc., i. 101–104. [2] Ibid. 104.

"A manufacturer[1] has been brought up a maker of pin-heads. He has been at this business forty years, and of course makes pin-heads with great dexterity; but he cannot make a whole pin for his life. He thinks it is the perfection of human nature to make pin-heads. He leaves other matters to inferior abilities. It is enough for him, that he believes in the Athanasian creed, reverences the splendor of the court, and makes pin-heads. This he conceives to be the sum-total of religion, politics, and trade. He is sure that London is the finest city in the world; Blackfriars bridge, the most superb of all possible bridges; and the river Thames, the largest river in the[2] universe. It is in vain to tell him that there are many rivers in America, in comparison of which the Thames is but a ditch; that there are single provinces there larger than all England; and that the colonies, formerly belonging to Great Britain, now Independent States, are vastly more extensive than England, Wales, Scotland, and Ireland, taken all together. He cannot conceive this. He goes into his best parlor, and looks on a map of England, four feet square; on the other side of the room, he sees a map of North and South America, not more than two feet square; and exclaims—'How can these things be!—it is altogether impossible!' He has read the Arabian Nights' Entertainments, and he hears this wonderful account of America; he believes the one as much as the other. That a giant should rise out of the sea, or that the Delaware should be larger than the Thames, are equally incredible to him. Talk to him of the British constitution, he will tell you—'it is a glorious constitution.' Ask him what it is, and he is ignorant of its first principles; but he is sure that he can make and sell pin-heads under it. Mention the freedom of elections, and he will tell you that 'he does not meddle in these matters; that he lives in a borough; and that it is impossible but that Squire Goose-Cap must represent that borough in parliament—because Squire

[1] Grandiose for artisan or mechanic.

[2] The text omits the definite article.

Goose-Cap is acquainted with the prime minister, and his lady comes every Sunday to the parish church in a brocaded gown; and sits in a pew lined with green cloth. How, then, can it be otherwise, but these are things in which he is not concerned?' He believes in the Athanasian creed, honours the king, and makes pin-heads—and what more can be expected of man.''[1]

From these character-sketches by the supposed foreigner in London in the year 1776—themselves by no means despicable for neat workmanship and for humorous power—it is not difficult to make out just how Hopkinson's playful writings were adapted to the achievement of serious political results, as ridding colonial-minded Americans of the intellectual restraint imposed almost unconsciously by their old provincial awe of England, and helping them to subject the metropolitan race to caustic and even contemptuous handling, as a necessary condition of national free-mindedness and of bold dissent on questions of political authority and control.

III.

It was in this spirit and with such skill, that Francis Hopkinson, legislator and judge, wrought and fought for his country, year by year, in his special capacity as man of letters and particularly as satirist. There can be no doubt that very many of his writings, having been dashed off upon occasion and printed without his name, still remain unrecognized in the newspapers to which he originally sent them; for it is chiefly to his own act, in selecting those writings which make up the three volumes of his "Miscellaneous Essays and Occasional Writings," that we are indebted for our knowledge of his authorship of the larger portion of the productions which now go under his name. Moreover, in his later years and especially after the outbreak of the French Revolution, he became more than willing to forget the asperities of the old controversy with England—then

[1] "The Miscellaneous Essays," etc., i. 106–108.

taking her undaunted stand as champion of the social order of the world. When, therefore, in this mood, he came to cull out and to revise such of his humorous and satirical writings produced during the American Revolution as he then chose to avow, it was but natural that he should be inclined to tone down their partisan vivacity, and to blunt somewhat the edge of their sarcasms.[1]

We need to have constantly in mind the great sequences of thought and of passion which made up the long word-battle of the American Revolution; and we should note, in general, that after the colossal debate which began in 1764 had reached, just twelve years afterward, its tragic culmination, and an apparent majority of the American people had passed the crisis of final decision, and had solemnly cast in their lot to live or die in the effort to gain their Independence,—from that time onward to the very end, a Whig satirist, like Hopkinson, would be likely to conclude that it was his business, with that fine-edged weapon which it was given him to wield, to fight just two sorts of enemies, first, the British generals and their troops—the armed invaders and desolators of his country, and, secondly, his own hostile fellow-countrymen, the American Loyalists.

The first class of enemies, it is now obvious, were hated by the champions of the Revolution far less vehemently than the second class. Of course, the former—the armed invaders and desolators of America—were hated vigorously enough; but, in reality, human language was altogether too feeble to give utterance to the loathing, the scorn, the bottomless and boundless detestation with which the American Whigs regarded the men of their own households and neighborhoods who did not join them in their great agony

[1] Noble as was this mood in its origin and purpose, its result could not fail to be a hindrance to the historic method in dealing with any portion of any literature. No modern student of the Revolutionary writings of Hopkinson can be sure that he is handling the original document, or that he is getting the full impression which it was written to produce, if he reads any production of Hopkinson only in the form in which Hopkinson himself finally left it in his collected works.

of patriotic effort, but who, as they believed, were secretly plotting against them, were giving help and comfort to the invaders, were working, often by tortuous ways and along secret and underground passages, to compass the defeat of this reluctant but most necessary and most perilous movement for national deliverance. In this feeling toward both classes of enemies, Francis Hopkinson, no doubt, had his full share; and yet it was in accordance with his intellectual quality, to express it less grimly than did his two chief associates in political satire. As their treatment of the enemy constantly tended toward sheer invective, so his as constantly inclined toward a use of ridicule which, while it was keen and tingling, and at times even tormenting, generally had a facetious note, almost never an angry one.

IV.

Before the close of the year 1776,—the fatal year in which those Americans who stood for their rights were persuaded to cast behind them in great sorrow the last hope of reconciliation with England,—Hopkinson began that long series of his writings which deal, either seriously or humorously, with the persons and the issues of a controversy that had finally taken to itself every dark hue of fierceness and desperation. One of the first efforts of his pen under these altered conditions, was peculiarly characteristic of him, and of his ability to be severe without being either violent or uncivil: it was "A Letter to Lord Howe"[1]—a letter at once eloquent, grave, pathetic, and stinging—written in December, 1776, in the midst of the havoc and horror occasioned by Sir William Howe's advance across New Jersey in pursuit of the flying troops of Washington.

The year 1777, which was to contain such appalling events as the invasion of New York by General Burgoyne, and the invasion of Pennsylvania by Sir William Howe, was ushered in with a solitary gleam of light cast upon the desperate

[1] "The Miscellaneous Essays," etc., i. 121–126.

situation in consequence of Washington's brilliant strokes against the enemy at Trenton and at Princeton. Very shortly after these exploits, and while the royal army was still "lying in Brunswick mortified and crestfallen,"[1] Hopkinson sent out to his fellow-countrymen "A Political Catechism,"[2] in which the questions and answers, being framed after the familiar model of a religious catechism, and in language level to the minds of the unlearned and even of children, give a most lucid, terse, and pungent presentation of the history of the war down to that moment, of its two great antithetic personages, George the Third and George Washington, and finally of the rightfulness of the cause on behalf of which the manliest of Americans, as Hopkinson believed, were then putting their lives at stake.

It was, also, early in this year 1777,—a year for whose vast menace to the American cause the most heroic preparation would be needed,—that Hopkinson stirred and lifted the hearts of his fellow-countrymen by his "Camp Ballad":

"Make room, oh! ye kingdoms in hist'ry renowned,—
Whose arms have in battle with glory been crowned,—
Make room for America,—another great nation
Arising[3] to claim in your council a station.

. . . .

"With glory immortal she here sits enthroned,
Nor fears the vain vengeance of Britain disowned;
Whilst Washington guards her, with heroes surrounded,
Her foes shall with shameful defeat be confounded.

"To arms, then, to arms!—'t is fair freedom invites us;
The trumpet, shrill sounding, to battle excites us;
The banners of virtue unfurled shall wave o'er us,
Our heroes lead on, and the foe fly before us.

---

[1] "The Miscellaneous Essays," etc., i. 118. [2] Ibid. 111–120.
[3] The text reads, Arises.

"On Heaven and Washington placing reliance,
We 'll meet the bold Briton, and bid him defiance;
Our cause we 'll support, for 't is just and 't is glorious—
When men fight for freedom, they must be victorious."[1]

As, however, this year 1777 wore on from spring into summer, and while it remained still doubtful just where Sir William Howe, from his headquarters in the city of New York, intended to deliver the great blow which was expected of him, the eyes of men were turned with unspeakable anxiety toward the further north—toward Lake George—whence General Burgoyne, with a most formidable army, was about to advance upon the lower Hudson, with the purpose of cutting in two, by that single stroke, the insurrectionary colonies, and then of suppressing all further resistance in each of the two territorial sections thus disabled from helping each other.

If we would in any just measure appreciate the quality and the effectiveness of the bit of work wrought by the humor of Hopkinson in this dire emergency, we must realize the exact situation of affairs, particularly the awful gravity of the danger, in that early summer of 1777, when Burgoyne and his army hung like some frightful storm-cloud along the northern sky. Indeed, our own memories of Burgoyne are apt to concentrate themselves upon the fact that he was defeated and captured, with all his mighty host: perhaps we have never sufficiently considered how very near he came to defeating us, and how fatal to the cause of American Independence his victory over us might have been. It was not, however, until October, 1777, that Burgoyne was defeated and made prisoner. It is natural for us to think of him simply in the light of that final event—an event which extinguished him forever as a serious incident in American affairs; but during all of the summer and early autumn preceding that event, those of our ancestors who were to meet him and to fight him and who were by no

[1] "Poems on Several Subjects," 174–175.

means confident of the result of their expected interview with him, could think of Burgoyne and his army only as a dreadful menace, only as a very actual and a very terrific danger. All this needs to be taken into the account by us, when we turn to some record of the official documents of that time, and read for ourselves the gusty and pot-valiant proclamation [1] which Burgoyne issued from his camp at Ticonderoga, on the second of July, 1777,—breathing out threatenings and slaughter, nay, "devastation, famine, and every concomitant horror" against "the hardened enemies of Britain and America." [2] Undoubtedly, Burgoyne's proclamation, which opened with a magnificent list of his own titles, offices, and honors, and which was apparently composed throughout on the theory that the wretched Americans were somehow to be overwhelmed and brought to their senses by the mere reverberation of his huge-sounding threats, remains for all time a masterpiece of military gasconading and of thunder-dealing rhetoric. As such its absurdity is obvious enough to us who are aware of the ridiculous anti-climax to which it was destined on the field of Stillwater, some three months after it was published; but to those Americans who first read it, while it was a grandiloquent threat indeed, it was also a grandiloquent threat with a great army behind it. It was, therefore, even from a military point of view, no slight service that Hopkinson rendered to the cause of the Revolution, when he sent out broadcast over the land a counter-proclamation, addressed, according to the noble style assumed by the great general himself, to "John Burgoyne, Esquire, Lieutenant-General of his Majesty's Armies in America, Colonel of the Queen's Regiment of Light Dragoons, Governor of Fort William in North Britain, one of the

---

[1] It may be found in Niles, "Principles and Acts of the Rev.," 262–264, where it is followed by Hopkinson's burlesque, which Niles has printed without Hopkinson's name. It is also given by W. L. Stone, in "Ballads and Poems relating to the Burgoyne Campaign," Appendix III.

[2] These words are part of the proclamation. Niles, "Prin. and Acts," 263.

Representatives of the Commons of Great Britain, and commanding an Army and Fleet employed on an Expedition from Canada, etc., etc., etc.''[1] This counter-proclamation, which was from first to last a most delicious burlesque on Burgoyne's manifesto, fitted exactly the mood and the need of the moment: it was everywhere read amid roars of laughter over a situation in which, truly, there was much to give alarm, but with respect to which mere laughter was an antidote to a popular panic. So long as men can be made to laugh, sonorously and convulsively, over the ridiculous aspects of a dangerous situation, they are not likely to be stampeded by it in a paroxysm of fright. Precisely this contribution toward the defeat and capture of Burgoyne was rendered, in the summer of 1777, by the humor of Francis Hopkinson.[2]

In the midst of the humiliation which, both in America and in Europe, Burgoyne's surrender brought upon the British cause, Hopkinson produced a ballad bearing the suggestive title, " Date Obolum Belisario.'' In this ballad, Britannia is depicted as a wretched woman—

> "All seated on the ground,
> With oaken staff and hat of straw,
> And tatters hanging round."

As the poet approaches her, she asks an alms:

> " A wretch forlorn, kind sir, you see,
> That begs from door to door ;
> Oh ! stop and give for charity,
> A penny to the poor ! "

With the usual promtitude of beggars in autobiographic recitals, she then proceeds to lavish upon him her story,

[1] " The Miscellaneous Essays," etc., i. 146–150.

[2] Burgoyne's Proclamation was travestied in verse by Governor William Livingston. This is given by W. L. Stone, in " Burgoyne Ballads," 7–15.

telling him of the better days she had seen, of her former wealth and power and splendor, of her children and her friends, and especially of the way in which she had been brought to poverty and misery through the misconduct of her youngest son, whose name, she intimates, was George; nor does she forget, in conclusion, the little matter appertaining to the much-desired obolus:

> "A magic wand I once possessed,
> A cap aloft it bore;
> Of all my treasures this the best,
> And none I valued more.
>
> . . . . . .
>
> "A shield and lance once graced these hands,
> Perhaps you 've heard my fame;
> For I was known in distant lands—
> Britannia is my name.
>
> "Britannia now in rags you see—
> I beg from door to door;
> Oh! give, kind sir, for charity,
> A penny to the poor." [1]

V.

Such was the relation of Francis Hopkinson as a humorist to the first of the great British expeditions of the year 1777—that of Burgoyne. The second expedition, under the command of Sir William Howe, resulted in considerable temporary disaster to the American cause, namely, the defeat of Washington both at Brandywine and at Germantown, and the British occupation of Philadelphia. Never-

[1] "Poems on Several Subjects," 164–168.

theless, it was this very expedition, so full of prosperity for the British, which in its sequel gave to Hopkinson the occasion for his most successful stroke as a humorous writer. It is well known that Sir William Howe, having in his rather tardy campaign for that year gained, almost in spite of himself, a brief succession of victories over the American rebels, then forbore to take advantage of people thus fallen, through his agency, into depressed circumstances; and, finding Philadelphia an extremely agreeable place of repose for a warrior who had already had enough of war for that particular season, he concluded to settle himself down in that gracious city, there to await with his officers and men the arrival of the next summer's campaign. Thenceforward, during all the autumn and the winter and the spring, he refrained as much as possible from aggressive military enterprises, which, besides being likely to prove disagreeable to the Americans, would have brought, of course, some inconvenience upon himself. This mighty general had, indeed, a truly martial fondness for the smiles of pretty women, for balls and routs, for dinners, theatricals, heavy gaming, and heavy drinking; and he chose to dedicate those flying hours which were given to him in Philadelphia, to that mode of existence which the moralists have been wont to describe as riotous living.

With a military sybarite like this in Philadelphia, the surrounding inhabitants, who had at first regarded him and his army with no little terror, soon came to regard both with some derision, and to conceive the idea of practising upon both certain experiments which had in them an element of covert mirthfulness as it were. One of these semi-jocose experiments seems to have been prepared near the little village where Hopkinson lived,—the village of Bordentown on the Delaware, a few miles above Philadelphia[1]; and it was by a

[1] It is by no means certain that Bordentown was the place where the machines were prepared; but it is certain that they were the invention of David Bushnell of Connecticut, much devoted to improvements in submarine warfare. In this undertaking he was accompanied by a person who knew the Delaware

very imaginative and a very rollicking expansion of the actual facts of this small affair, that Hopkinson was enabled to compose his celebrated ballad, "The Battle of the Kegs."[1]

The actual facts of the case are as follows, according to Hopkinson's own later testimony in prose: "Certain machines, in the form of kegs, charged with gunpowder, were sent down the river to annoy the British shipping at Philadelphia. The danger of these machines being discovered, the British manned the wharfs and shipping, and discharged their small arms and cannons at everything they saw floating in the river during the ebb tide."[2]

Certainly, in the hands of a poet with uncommon facility at humorous invention, here was ample material for a comic ballad; and Hopkinson failed not to make proper use of his opportunity. In the first place, he contrived with no little art to prepare the public for his ballad, by publishing in "The New Jersey Gazette"[3] an amusing prose description of the alleged panic into which the mysterious kegs had thrown the British sailors and soldiers in Philadelphia, and of their excited and most redoubtable onslaught, with fire and sword and battle cry, upon these same kegs, which, as some of the brave Britons declared, "were filled with armed rebels, who were to issue forth in the dead of night, as the Grecians did of old from their wooden horse at the siege of

---

River, but in the darkness mistook the situation and occasioned the error of placing the kegs too far from the British shipping. Bushnell's own account of the affair is in "Transactions of the American Philosophical Society," iv. 312.

[1] "Poems on Several Subjects," 169–173.

[2] Ibid. 173 n.

[3] For January 21, 1778. Though no one else, so far as I am aware, has called attention to it, I do not hesitate, both from internal and from collateral evidence, to speak of this prose narrative of the "Battle of the Kegs" as one of Hopkinson's many unacknowledged writings. A reprint of it may be seen in Frank Moore, "Diary of the American Revolution," ii. 5–6; and it is from this that I here quote. On the other hand, "The Pennsylvania Ledger," for February 11, 1778, takes the trouble to deny that anybody was frightened by the mysterious kegs, declaring that they were merely fired at, in passing, from some of the transport vessels in the river. "Mag. Am. Hist.," viii. 296.

Troy, and take the city by surprise,—asserting that they had seen the points of their bayonets through the bung-holes of the kegs." This prose story, printed as the sober testimony of an eye-witness in Philadelphia, and recounting in seeming sincerity one of the most ludicrous battles ever fought since wars began, put the people everywhere, as it was intended to do, into a frame of mind appreciative of the same story when laid before them, as it was soon afterward, in the form of a jocose street-ballad. It is mere matter of history to add, that this jingling little story of "The Battle of the Kegs"—mere doggerel though it is—flew from colony to colony, in those grim early months of the year 1778, like some merry messenger of gay tidings; and that, in many a camp, and along a thousand highroads, and by ten thousand patriot firesides, it gave the weary and anxious people the luxury of genuine and hearty laughter in very scorn of the enemy. To the cause of the Revolution, it was perhaps worth as much, just then, by way of emotional tonic and of military inspiration, as the winning of a considerable battle would have been.

From a literary point of view, "The Battle of the Kegs" is very far from being the best of Hopkinson's writings. Nevertheless, for its matter and its manner and for the adaptation of both to the immediate enjoyment of the multitude of readers, it became in his own day the best known of all its author's productions, even as, since then, it is the only one that has retained any general remembrance in our literature.

VI.

Passing, now, from the writings of Hopkinson against the armed invaders of his country, it is time for us to glance rapidly at his principal writings against that party of his fellow-countrymen who were in sympathy with those invaders. We may note, at the outset, the quiet ridicule with which he deals with the Tories on the side of their social prepossessions. From the beginning to the end of the war, a prodigious obstacle to the Revolutionary cause was the social prestige, the purple dignity, the aristocratic flavor of the Tory side of the question; and Hopkinson, having the shrewdness to see that a portion of American Toryism had its origin in mere snobbish sentiment, spoke of having known a lady "who did not possess one political principle, nor had any precise idea of the real cause of the contest between Great Britain and America, and yet was a professed and confirmed Tory, merely from the fascination of sounds. 'The imperial crown,' 'the royal robes,' 'the high court of parliament,' 'the lord chancellor of England,' and so on, were words of irresistible influence; whilst 'Captain A. the tailor,' 'Colonel B. the tavern-keeper,' and even 'General Washington the farmer,' only created contempt. But I am persuaded, if some Indian chief, with a long Cherokee or Mohawk name, had commanded our armies, she would have thought much more respectably of the American cause." [1]

A more pungent specimen of his satire is "The Birds, the Beasts, and the Bat," [2] a fable in Hudibrastic verse, intended to portray the political trimmer of the Revolution, —the American who was a Whig or a Tory, from day to day, according to the state of the military weather,—that is, the creature who like the bat, was part bird and part beast; but who was always ready to proclaim himself as all bird when the birds were in luck, and as all beast when the beasts seemed likely to win.

A strong piece of work, and in a vein altogether different —that of invective—was his "Letter to Joseph Galloway, Esquire," [3] published in 1778, and accusing that preëminent Loyalist of treachery to his country and to his friends, and

---

[1] "The Miscellaneous Essays," etc., ii. 55–56. The passage above quoted appears to have been written after the war, but it is available as an illustration of his method of dealing with the Tories even during the war.

[2] "Poems on Several Subjects," 177–180.

[3] "The Miscellaneous Essays," etc., i. 127–131.

of nearly every crime by which unscrupulous ambition may seek to climb the steps of power.

At some time during the year 1776, Hopkinson touched very skilfully the nerve of American enmity toward the Loyalists, by publishing "Two Letters," written apparently by a member of that detested party, and avowing with boastful and exasperating frankness those servile political sentiments and those unscrupulous practices which were then attributed to them by their American opponents. Here, without any disguise, is the master-principle of their party:—"Mr. Printer, I am a Tory, the son of a Tory, born and bred in the pure principles of unconditional submission, and a true friend to the Hanoverian family, right or wrong and at all events. . . . But the infatuated people of this most vile portion of this most vile planet have been moved by the instigation of the devil to oppose the earnest desire of George the Third—God bless his majesty!—to govern them in all cases whatsoever, according to his good will and pleasure. For my own part, I truly abominate and abhor their rebellious obstinacy. His majesty hath been pleased, in his great goodness, and to my unspeakable satisfaction, to send over his fleets and armies to conquer and subdue this horrible country. Now, it is the indispensable duty of all those who would be called the friends of arbitrary government and of the said George the Third, to render all the assistance in their power to the fleets and armies, and to the worthy lords and generals whom this worthy and benign monarch hath commissioned to direct and manage them."[1]

Among the many methods devised by the loyal inhabitants of America for aiding their king in his noble undertaking, one is the formation of a club of Tories, the members of which are parcelled off into committees for promoting in their several ways the success of the king's troops,—such as "the committee of wiles and stratagems," "the committee of extortion," "the committee of depreciation," "the

[1] "The Miscellaneous Essays," etc., i. 132–133.

committee of false reports," and "the committee of lies." Probably none of these committees are more active or more important than the last two. The duty of "the committee of false reports" is "to circulate misrepresentations of facts respecting the armies, and things of a public nature, on the large scale,"[1] so as "to alarm and terrify timid Whigs, and distract the minds of the people."[2] The duty of the committee of lies, however, is somewhat different: it is to "frame temporary lies" for the use of the city of Philadelphia, "particularly respecting the deliberations and intentions of Congress. These lies must be fresh, and fresh every day, and always supported by a strong assertion that the information came from some leaky member of Congress, generally without mentioning the name of any individual member; yet, in cases of urgency, the real name of some leading character may be adduced, when the lie may have had its operation before it can be contradicted."[3]

Of course, in this world, all good men have their calumniators. The Tories are no exception to this rule. "Some narrow-minded people say, that we are doing all we can to ruin our country, and entail a miserable slavery on our unborn posterity. We believe we are doing the best we can for ourselves—and, pray, what has posterity done for us, that we should run the risk of confiscation and a halter for them? . . . . 'T is true, if the British generals should succeed in their enterprise, we may see our neighbors and friends imprisoned by hundreds, and hanged by dozens, their estates confiscated, and their children turned out to beggary and want; but, then, we shall ourselves escape, and enjoy in safety our lives and estates—and, perhaps, be even promoted for our present services to places of honor and emolument."[4]

No vein of satire against the enemy, and particularly against the Tories, was more expertly worked by Hopkinson than the one exhibited in these "Two Letters,"

---

[1] "The Miscellaneous Essays," etc., i. 139.
[2] Ibid. 138.
[3] Ibid. 139–140.
[4] Ibid. 141.

namely, the systematic use of lies as a weapon of war. In "A Letter to the Editor of the New Jersey Gazette," in January, 1778, he called attention once more to the immense importance attached by the enemy to this powerful weapon, declaring that "as soon as the Howes got to New York, they appointed their Liar General, who played off innumerable lies from the batteries of Rivington and Gaine"[1]; and that the same thing was done by them immediately after they had taken possession of Philadelphia.[2] Here, then, was a method of warfare not to be neglected by the people against whom it has thus far been so vigorously employed. Of course, "nothing would be more vain than to attempt to counteract these productions of the British Lying Offices in New York and Philadelphia, with serious answers of truth and reason. Like must be opposed to like. And, therefore, I hope that Congress will no longer delay to establish Lying Offices on our side of the question, with handsome salaries annexed, and would especially recommend this my project to their serious consideration. Let there be an advertisement forthwith published by authority, to the following effect: 'Wanted, for the continental service, a person well qualified for the office of Liar General to the United States. Also, three assistants, or petit-liars, in said office. Those who are willing and able to serve their country in this department, are requested to send in their names to . . . on or before the first day of March next. As it is supposed there may be a number of persons well versed in this art amongst the Tories, free pardon and good encouragement will be given to such as will exert their lying faculties in favor of their country. N. B. Specimens of ability will be required of candidates.'"[3]

Perhaps nothing that Hopkinson wrote during the Revolution can give one a truer impression of the sprightliness and the delicacy of his humor, than the jeu d'esprit which he published shortly after the surrender of Cornwallis, and

[1] "The Miscellaneous Essays," etc., i. 143–144.

[2] Ibid. 144.

[3] Ibid. 145.

with which he may be said to have closed his work as a Revolutionary satirist. This is a mock advertisement, bearing the name of James Rivington and dated at New York, November 1, 1781, wherein Hopkinson contrives, not only to exhibit with great drollery the state of mind into which poor Rivington is supposed to have been thrown by the appalling news from Yorktown, but likewise to scatter the shafts of ridicule along the entire line of the royal and ministerial project for subjugating America. Rivington's printing-office and book-shop in New York had been regarded during the whole war as the very citadel and pest-house of American Toryism; while his newspaper, "The Royal Gazette," had always been "exceedingly virulent, abusive, and illiberal" against the Americans, their Congress, their army, their officers, and their measures. "Every paper abounded" according to the Whig view of things, "with the grossest falsities, misrepresentations, and insults."[1] If there was in America any Loyalist who must realize that the downfall of the British cause meant the necessity of his own speedy exit from the scene, it was James Rivington. Accordingly, he is here represented as publishing in his newspaper an "Advertisement," over his own name, announcing that as "the late surrender of Lord Cornwallis and his army, together with a variety of other circumstances," had "rendered it convenient for the subscriber to remove to Europe," he requests the favor of an immediate settlement of all his accounts in America, and likewise offers for sale at public auction at an early day, the whole of "his remaining stock in trade," consisting of "books," "plays," "maps and prints," "philosophical apparatus," and "patent medicines." Then follows a partial catalogue:

"BOOKS.

"The History of the American War; or, the Glorious Exploits of the British Generals, Gage, Howe, Burgoyne, Cornwallis, and Clinton.

---

[1] "The Miscellaneous Essays," etc., i. 159.

The Royal Pocket Companion: Being a New System of Policy, founded on Rules deduced from the Nature of Man, and proved by Experience, whereby a Prince may in a short time render himself the Abhorrence of his Subjects, and the Contempt of all good and wise Men.

Select Fables of Æsop, with suitable Morals and Applications. Amongst which are,—'The Dog and his Shadow,' 'The Man and His Goose which laid a Golden Egg,' etc., etc.

A New System of Cruelty: Containing a Variety of modern Improvements in that Art. Embellished with an elegant Frontispiece, representing an inside View of a Prison Ship.

The Right of Great Britain to the Dominion of the Sea—a Poetical Fiction.

The State of Great Britain in October, 1760, and October, 1781, compared and contrasted.

A Geographical, Historical, and Political History of the Rights and Possessions of the Crown of Great Britain in North America. This valuable Work did consist of thirteen volumes in Folio, but is now abridged by a Royal Author to a single Pocket Duodecimo, for the greater Convenience of Himself, his Successors, and Subjects.

. . . .

Tears of Repentance: or, the Present State of the Loyal Refugees in New York, and elsewhere.

The Political Liar: a Weekly Paper, published by the Subscriber, bound in Volumes.

. . . .

"MAPS AND PRINTS.

"An Elegant Map of the British Empire in North America, upon a very small Scale.

An Accurate Chart of the Coast of North America, from New Hampshire to Florida; with the Soundings of all the principal Inlets, Bays, Harbors, and Rivers. This

Work was undertaken and completed by his Majesty's special command, and at a national expense of many millions of Guineas, thousands of Men, and hundreds of Merchantmen and Royal Ships of War.

A Survey of Lord Cornwallis's Route through the Southern Colonies, beginning at Charleston in South Carolina, and terminating at York, in Virginia. As the preceding Chart gives an accurate description of the Sea Coast, so it was intended to form a correct Map of the interior Parts of this Country; but the rude Inhabitants grew jealous of the Operation, and actually opposed his Lordship's Progress.

The Battle of Saratoga, and the Surrender at York: Two elegant Prints, cut in Copper, and dedicated to the King.

. . . .

"PHILOSOPHICAL APPARATUS.

"A curious new-invented Magic Lanthorn: very useful for those who are at the head of affairs. This machine was constructed by an able artist, under Lord North's immediate direction, for the amusement of the good people of England. The spectators are gratified with an illuminated view of the fictitious objects presented, but kept totally in the dark with respect to the real objects around them.

. . . .

Microscopes, for magnifying small objects, furnished with a select set ready fitted for use. Amongst these are a variety of real and supposed successes of the British Generals in America.

A Complete Electrical Apparatus, with improvements, for the use of the King and his Ministers. The machine should be exercised with great caution; otherwise, as experience hath shown, the operator may unexpectedly receive the shock he intends to give.

Pocket Glasses for Short-sighted Politicians.

"PATENT MEDICINES.

"Aurum Potabile. This preparation was formerly supposed to be a never-failing specific, but has been found not so well adapted to the American climate, having been frequently tried here without effect. But its reputation is again rising, as it has lately been administered with success to General Arnold.

Vivifying Balsam: excellent for weak nerves, palpitations of the heart, over-bashfulness, and diffidence. In great demand for the officers of the army.

Sp. Men. Or, the genuine Spirit of Lying. Extracted by distillation from many hundreds of 'The Royal Gazette of New York.' . . .

Cordial Drops for Low Spirits: prepared for the special use of the Honorable the Board of Loyal Refugees at New York.

Anodyne Elixir, for quieting fears and apprehensions. Very necessary for Tories in all parts of America.

With a great variety of other articles too tedious to enumerate.

N. B. To every purchaser to the value of five Pounds, will be delivered gratis, one quire of counterfeit Continental Currency. Also, two quires of Proclamations offering Pardon to Rebels."[1]

---

[1] "The Miscellaneous Essays," etc., i. 159–169.

CHAPTER XXXI.

SATIRES, SONGS, AND BALLADS FOR AMERICAN INDEPENDENCE.

I.—Revolutionist satire in its minor and incidental forms—The partisan's intolerance of moderation and neutrality—Epigram on the Middlesex resolutions—The change in American feeling toward George the Third, from reverence to execration—The King as an object of satire—Lines on his inverted portrait—The cynical tone in American verse in the months preceding the capture of Burgoyne—The "Prophecy" written on an egg-shell—"Another Prophecy," by the "Genius of America"—Epigrams on Burgoyne—Satires on the traitor Arnold.

II.—Charles Henry Wharton, and his satire on English political corruption, in "A Poetical Epistle to George Washington," 1779—The poet's ideal of an American commonwealth.

III.—Francis Lieber's estimate of the Anglican race as writers of national songs—Grouping of the political and military songs of the American Revolution.

IV.—Some of the song-writers of the Revolution,—Prime, McClurg, Howell, Oliver Arnold, Humphreys, Barlow, Dwight—The latter's "Columbia," 1777.

V.—Nathaniel Niles, and "The American Hero, a Sapphic Ode," 1775.

VI.—The nobler mood of the American mind in 1776—Its faith and fortitude as expressed in "The American Patriot's Prayer."

VII.—"The American Soldier's Hymn."

VIII.—Characteristics of the ballads of the Revolution—"Liberty's Call," 1775—"A Song for the Red-Coats," and "The Fate of John Burgoyne," 1777—"Brave Paulding and the Spy," 1780—"Battle of King's Mountain," 1781—"The Wyoming Massacre" and "Bold Hawthorne."

IX.—Captain Nathan Hale, the American Spy—Compared with André—His arrest within the British lines—His hard fate—The ballad of "Hale in the Bush."

I.

ELSEWHERE in this book, it has been shewn that at a certain stage of the Revolutionary controversy, satire became, on both sides, a principal weapon in the literary warfare then waged, and that in the use of that weapon each side was able to point to at least two or three expert and powerful masters. So far as the spirit of the great quarrel is thus preserved in satirical writings, it is to be traced, in its strongest and most authentic form, in the work of Stansbury and Odell, on the one hand, and of Hopkinson, Trumbull, and Freneau on the other.

Nevertheless, while these writers are the chief exponents of the satiric mood throughout the later period of the dispute, that mood found abundant expression, likewise, in a multitude of forms less elaborate and less masterful indeed, and yet not lacking in sprightliness and point, and not unworthy of a passing glance as examples of one very characteristic method of literary expression in a time of fiery and implacable controversy. The newspapers of the Revolutionary period are strown with such productions,—satirical poems, long and short, of nearly all degrees of merit and demerit, some of them gross and obscene, some of them simply clownish and stupid, some absolutely brutal in their partisan ferocity, some really clever—terse, polished, and edged with wit. As students of the intellectual and emotional development of the Revolution, we may not altogether disregard even these casual, unowned, and flitting tokens of a sincere literary partisanship.

Of course, to men who are themselves imbued with the Revolutionary passion, no attitude in others is apt to seem quite so intolerable as that of neutrality or even of moderation in partisanship. Our Revolution abounds with examples of this statement. Thus, in 1774, to take but a single example, an assemblage of Loyalists in Middlesex county, Virginia, passed a series of resolutions deprecating all violent measures in opposition to the government,—an incident which was made the text for an epigram, all the more cutting as being written by a woman:

> " To manhood he makes vain pretense,
> Who wants both manly force and sense :
>
> . . . .

From such a creature, Heaven defend her!
Each lady cries—'No neuter gender!'
But, when a number of such creatures,
With woman's hearts and manly features,
Their country's generous schemes perplex,
I own—I hate this Middle-sex!"[1]

The hatred for Tories and for Toryism, thus avowed in 1774, never failed or faltered in quantity or force till long after the Revolution ended, if indeed it can be said to have failed or faltered even yet. And in the fullness of Revolutionary wrath, there came a time when, to the majority of Americans, the greatest and hatefulest Tory of all, on either side of the Atlantic, was King George himself. During all the bitterness of the first decade of the struggle, the theory had been carefully cherished among us that, not upon the good king, but upon his wicked advisers, upon his false and blood-thirsty agents, was to be laid the blame for all the tyranny that had come or was coming,—a pleasant fiction which was diligently preserved and promulgated even in the manifestoes of the American Congress, and until near the close of the year 1775. So immense was the arc of emotion through which the people passed, that, after the adoption of the purpose of Independence, and as if moved by a spontaneous impulse, they everywhere tore down from their houses all emblems and memorials of the king; they changed the names of streets and public places which had commemorated their love and reverence for him and for his family; and even the halfpence which bore the image and superscription of George the Third, were either refused when offered as money or were degraded into farthings. Of all this tremendous revulsion of feeling toward the king, a very touching example was seen in many private houses, where his portrait, once held in so much honor, was left hanging in its place, but with its face turned to the wall. In one mansion, however, a

[1] F. Moore, "Songs and Ballads," 68 n.

more dramatic denunciation of the king was resorted to: the portrait of his majesty, having been lifted from the nail on which it had hung, was simply placed upon the floor and there left leaning against the wall—but with the head downward, while some lines were written beneath it, as if to deepen, if possible, this spectacular testimony of American hatred and contempt:

"Behold the man, who had it in his power
To make a kingdom tremble and adore.
Intoxicate with folly, see his head
Placed where the meanest of his subjects tread.
Like Lucifer, the giddy tyrant fell:
He lifts his heel to Heaven, but points his head to Hell."[1]

So, as the drama of the Revolution moved on from Scene to Scene, from Act to Act, there appeared to be standing by a sort of chorus of patriotic poetasters, who, with jest and scoff and invective, flung out in blunt or biting verse their free comments on such of the actors as they disapproved of, and upon such of the things done or attempted as went counter to their wishes,—first of all, Toryism, in all its shapes and manners, in all its champions and confederates; next, the principalities and powers in Great Britain which were resolved upon our subjugation; and, finally, all the civilized or savage tools of ministerial policy, and all their projects, blunders, successes, and failures, to the last action and passion of the conflict.

The spring and summer of the year 1777 seem to stand out in our annals as a season of extraordinary dread and gloom on the part of the friends of the Revolution. In some of the writings of that time is to be heard a note of almost cynical bitterness, as in these lines added to one version of a patriotic song then given to the public:

"The times, it seems, are altered quite;
The scales are cracked, the sword is broke,

[1] "Works of John Adams," ii. 434.

Right is now wrong, and wrong is right,
And justice is a standing joke." [1]

Notwithstanding the glimmer of good cheer brought in by the two little dashes of success during the previous winter, at Trenton and Princeton, the general effect of the heavy defeats suffered by our arms within the latter half of 1776, was still weighing upon the popular imagination; nor was this burden in any way lightened by the fact that two powerful armies, one under Howe, one under Burgoyne, were apparently getting ready to sever all connection between the three great groups of States then in rebellion, after which it might seem an easy thing to conquer and crush each of these groups in its turn. In spite of Howe's lack of enterprise in the campaign of 1776, and of his obvious failure to push his advantages, his reputation among us was still a most formidable fact. Under the uncertainty as to what he might do that summer with the force at his command, his name was still a name to conjure with. It is an odd token of the various methods and weapons for public influence then resorted to on both sides, that the solemn announcement was made of the discovery of an egg which had been laid by an inspired hen in the ancient town of Plymouth, and which bore upon its shell, in legible characters, "A Prophecy," in these dreadful words: "Oh, oh, America! Howe shall be thy conqueror." Of course, so appalling a prediction was not likely to be suffered to travel about the country without being met by some counter-prediction, which, accordingly, was very soon supplied by the "Genius of America" in "Another Prophecy," of which these are the closing lines:—

"When eggs can speak what fools indite,
And hens can talk, as well as write;
When crocodiles shed honest tears,
And truth with hypocrites appears;

[1] This stanza was added to a song on "The Times," beginning, "My Muse, now thy aid and assistance we claim." F. Moore, "Ballad History," 200–201.

When every man becomes a knave,
And feels the spirit of the slave ;
And when veracity again
Shall in a Tory's bosom reign ;
When vice is virtue, darkness light,
And freemen are afraid to fight ;
When they forget to play the men,
And with the spirit of a hen
Desert the just and sacred cause,
And opening Heaven smiles applause
On such a bloody, barbarous foe,—
Then I 'll be conquered by a Howe ! "[1]

As to Burgoyne, it is easy for us now, as it was for Thackeray some forty years ago, to imagine that grandiose hero " tripping off from St. James's Street to conquer the Americans, and slinking back into the club somewhat crestfallen after his beating."[2] We cannot wonder that the derisive comments of our American chorus upon the unparalleled fiasco which closed his word-thunderous career among us, were not at all tempered by delicacy or by self-restraint. To recall only two of these choric gibes will doubtless be quite enough :

(a)

" Burgoyne, alas, unknowing future fates,
Could force his way through woods, but not through Gates."[3]

(b)

" In seventeen hundred-and-seventy-seven,
General Burgoyne set out for Heaven ;

---

[1] Given in full in F. Moore, "Songs and Ballads," etc., 160–162.

[2] " The Four Georges," 69.

[3] This epigram, said to have been written by David Edwards, was published in the newspapers shortly after Burgoyne's surrender. Some account of Edwards is given by W. L. Stone, in his " Burgoyne Ballads," 66–68 n. The authorship of this epigram has also been claimed for a Westminister School-boy, who is said to have composed it in Latin on the subject of " Saratoga "—that word having been given out for the day's exercise in Latin verse. Stone thinks this claim to be " without foundation."

[4] " Burgoyne Ballads," 66. This epigram is said to have been kept in

But, as the Yankees would rebel,
He missed his route, and went—to Hell."

The discovery of the treason of Benedict Arnold, in 1780, stirred the abhorrence of the American people more deeply, perhaps, than did any other event of the war. Of course, this emotion expressed itself in an infinite variety of forms; but of those merely in the form of verse sarcastic, a fair example is afforded by certain lines "To the Traitor Arnold," published in "The Pennsylvania Packet" for October 24, 1780:[1]

"Arnold! thy name, as heretofore,
Shall now be Benedict no more;
Since, instigated by the devil,
Thy ways are turned from good to evil.
'T is fit we brand thee with a name
To suit thy infamy and shame;
And since of treason thou 'rt convicted,
Thy name should now be Maledict-ed.
. . . . . .
And odious for the blackest crimes,
Arnold shall stink to latest times."

In the same number of the paper which contained the lines just given, appeared this epigram on the visible result of the bargain between Arnold and Sir Henry Clinton:

"'T was Arnold's post Sir Harry sought,
Arnold ne'er entered in his thought.
How ends the bargain? Let us see,—
The fort is safe as safe can be:

memory in Vermont for many years after the Revolution. It is one result, perhaps, of the theological training of the period, that the wits and satirists on both sides of the controversy were so facile in despatching their antagonists to Hell,—a penal institution of easy access to all, and therefore singularly useful to a heated debater who otherwise might have been at a loss to know just how to make final disposition of the party of the other part.

[1] A copy of this paper is in the library of the Pennsylvania Historical Society.

His favorite perforce must die ;
His view 's laid bare to every eye ;
His money 's gone—and lo ! he gains
One scoundrel more for all his pains.
André was generous, true, and brave,
And in his room he buys a knave.
'T is sure ordained that Arnold cheats
All those, of course, with whom he treats.
Now let the devil suspect a bite—
Or Arnold cheats him of his right."

Henceforth, the name of Arnold was seldom mentioned by any Revolutionist writer without its being coupled with that of Satan, between whom and the traitor the intercourse was assumed to be both familiar and without intermission. Thus, the " New Jersey Gazette," for November 1, 1780, was enabled to report this quite affectionate conversation as having then recently taken place between the two distinguished personages:

" Quoth Satan to Arnold ; ' My worthy good fellow,
I love you much better that ever I did ;
You live like a prince, with Hal [1] may get mellow,—
But mind that you both do just what I bid.'

" Quoth Arnold to Satan : ' My friend, do not doubt me !
I will strictly adhere to all your great views ;
To you I 'm devoted, with all things about me—
You 'll permit me, I hope, to die in my shoes.' " [2]

II.

From these trifles in political satire, it is pleasant to turn to a deliberate and a noble poem of the year 1779, which, while breathing high eulogy of the Revolutionist cause

[1] Sir Henry Clinton. [2] F. Moore, " Diary of the Am. Rev.," ii. 333.

and especially of its Chief, is also a stern satire upon the political blindness and corruption of the English court and parliament—a condition of things out of which, according to this poet, it was possible for so foolish and fatal a project to be born, as that of exterminating the germs of a manly political life in America.

At the time of the outbreak of the war, there was living in England, as chaplain to the Roman Catholics in the city of Worcester, an American priest, Charles Henry Wharton, —a man of singular strength and purity of character, and of quite extraordinary mental gifts,—who, notwithstanding his long absence from his native land, had never been able to lay aside his love for her, or his concern that she should be able, when her great trouble came, to beat back, with victory and honor, the blows of her enemies. He was of an old Roman Catholic family in Maryland, long settled at Notley Hall, where he was born in 1748. When but twelve years of age, he had been sent abroad to the Jesuit College at St. Omers. Not many years afterward, on the expulsion of the Jesuits from France, he had been removed with his college to Bruges, where he completed his undergraduate studies, rising to eminence both as a classicist and as a mathematician. Having afterward studied at the Jesuit College at Liège, and having there received priest's orders, he was in 1773 admitted into its faculty as professor of mathematics. This position he seems not to have retained very long,—leaving it, apparently, in order to serve in spiritual offices a congregation of his own faith in England.

Living thus in an English community, in the midst of the wrath and clangor attendant on the war then in progress against his own kinsmen and countrymen in America, he could only watch afar off the bitter unfolding of events, himself quite powerless to shape or steer them by any physical intervention of his own. Through all the bewilderments of the scene, his eye seems to have fixed itself in admiration and trust upon the person of Washington. Accordingly, in 1778,—the very year in which an American cabal had been in progress for Washington's overthrow,—this sturdy priest gave utterance to the thought that was within him touching the whole situation, in "A Poetical Epistle to George Washington, Esquire, Commander-in-Chief of the Armies of the United States of America," published first in America, and subsequently in England,—in the latter case, after receiving the friendly revision of Sir William Jones.[1] It may help us to realize to how great an extent English society always refused its sanction to the king's war against their American brethren, to note that this poem was published in London, in 1780, under the express sanction of the Duchess of Devonshire,[2] and that fifteen thousand copies of it were sold there in about three weeks at two shillings and sixpence each—the money being intended for the relief of the American prisoners of war.[3]

The full note of confidence in Washington which breathes through these verses, is nowhere weakened by any gush of panegyric. The poem is at once a manly tribute to the character and ability of the American leader, a satire on the corruption and folly of the ministerial party in England, and a magnanimous lesson in civic virtue addressed to the poet's own fellow-countrymen in their great movement toward nationality. Of course, having the conventionalized diction of eighteenth-century satire, it comes to us in a metrical garb which now suggests unreality—humdrum thought and manufactured emotion. Nevertheless, there is in this poem a genuineness that is not to be smoth-

---

[1] Wharton's "Remains," i. Appendix xxiv. [2] Ibid.

[3] This fact is mentioned in the Providence edition of the poem. The editor of Wharton's "Remains" states that the poem was first printed by Bradford in Philadelphia, in 1778. I have been unable to find any trace of such publication. I have, however, met with three early copies of the poem, as follows:—(1) a London edition bearing the date of 1780, and professing to be a reprint of an American edition published at Annapolis in 1779; (2) an edition published in Philadelphia in 1781, and professing to be a reprint of a London edition; (3) an edition published in Providence in 1781, and professing to be a reprint of a London edition. The poem was certainly in manuscript in the year 1778; but I am inclined to think that Annapolis and the year 1779 are the true place and time of its original publication.

ered even by such an envelopment—the sincerity and robustness of a clear, fearless and forthright thinker. The poem, which begins in the usual fashion of satire,—gibing at follies and wrongs that surround the poet and provoke his anger,—quickly leads on to a sudden turn in the thought, involving a bit of restrained but very impressive homage to the noble person to whom it is directed:

> "While many a servile Muse her succor lends
> To flatter tyrants, or a tyrant's friends;
> While thousands, slaughtered at Ambition's shrine,
> Are made a plea to court the tuneful Nine;
> Whilst Whitehead[1] lifts his hero to the skies,
> Foretells his conquests twice a year—and lies,
> Damns half-starved rebels to eternal shame,
> Or paints them trembling at Britannia's name;
> Permit an humble bard, great Chief, to raise
> One truth-erected trophy to thy praise.
> No abject flattery shall these numbers seek,
> To raise a blush on Virtue's modest cheek;
> Rehearse no merit, no illustrious deed,
> But foes must own—and Washington may read."[2]

After portraying the political corruption then prevalent in England, and the folly of the ministry in too long disregarding the claims of the American colonists, he prays that his own country may be saved from a leadership so blind, arrogant, and ruinous as that from which England was then suffering; and he ends with a noble sketch of what he would have America become,—a sketch which it might still profit us to be somewhat better acquainted with:

> "Great without pomp, without ambition brave,
> Proud not to conquer fellow-men, but save;
> Friend to the wretched, foe to none but those
> Who plan their greatness on their brethren's woes;

[1] Poet laureate from 1757 to 1785.

[2] "A Poetical Epistle," etc., 8.

Awed by no titles, faithless to no trust,
Free without faction, obstinately just;
Too rough for flattery, dreading e'en as death
The baneful influence of Corruption's breath;
Warmed by Religion's sacred genuine ray
That points to future bliss the unerring way;
Spurning as Hell grim Superstition's laws—
Too long a tyrant in the noblest cause;
The world's great mart, yet not by gold defiled;
To mercy prone, in justice ever mild—
Save to the man who saps great Freedom's roots;
And never cursed with Mansfields, Norths, and Butes!
Such be my country!—what her sons should be,
O, may they learn, great Washington, from thee!"[1]

III.

"It is very odd," says Francis Lieber, "that the Anglican race hardly ever produces songs with life and soul, when the life of the nation throbs high. We produced no Revolutionary song worth talking of."[2] To the general purpose of this statement one may safely assent, but with the added remark that several of the Revolutionary songs that have been the most talked of, have been perhaps among the least worthy of it,—that is, not only are they lacking in "life and soul," but they belong to the pompous, rhetorical and truly ligneous variety of the article in question. Such, for example, is John Dickinson's much belauded "Liberty Song,"[3] produced in 1768; such, also, is "The American Hearts of Oak,"[4] by the Virginian, Hewlings, produced in 1775; and such is Jonathan Mitchell Sewall's song "On Independence,"[5] produced in 1776. On the other hand,

---

[1] "An Epistle," etc., 14–15. In 1881 was published in Boston an edition of this poem "From the Original MS. belonging to David Pulsifer, A.M."

[2] Perry, "Life and Letters of Francis Lieber," 277.

[3] F. Moore, "Songs and Ballads," etc., 36–39.

[4] Ibid. 103–105. [5] Ibid. 144–146.

while these songs have had among us, for a hundred years and more, a sort of conventionalized and dutiful celebrity, it would not be difficult to shew that we inherit from the Revolution several others which since then have scarcely been talked of at all, but which certainly have something of the sparkle and dash of true popular lyrics, born too of a time when the life of the nation throbbed high. Such a song, for example, is one produced in 1775, to the Scottish tune—"I winna marry ony lad but Sandy o'er the lea," and entitled "The Pennsylvania Song," of which the first stanza runs as follows:

"We are the troop that ne'er will stoop
To wretched slavery,
Nor shall our seed by our base deed
Despisèd vassals be!
Freedom we will bequeathe to them,
Or we will bravely die;
Our greatest foe ere long shall know
How much did Sandwich lie,
And all the world shall know,
Americans are free;
Nor slaves nor cowards we will prove—
Great Britain soon shall see."[1]

Such a song, also, is one entitled "Independence," produced in the spring of 1776, and beginning thus:

"Freemen! if you pant for glory,
If you sigh to live in story,
If you burn with patriot zeal,
Seize this bright auspicious hour;
Chase those venal tools of power,
Who subvert the public weal."[2]

Such a song is one produced in 1778, in praise of the courage and devotion of the patriotic women of the Revolution,

[1] The entire song is in F. Moore, "Songs and Ballads," etc., 90–91.
[2] Ibid. 139–140.

and entitled "The Old Man's Song," of which these stanzas are a part:

"Boy, fill me a bumper! as long as I live,
The patriot fair for my toast must I give:
Here's a health to the sex of every degree—
Where sweetness and beauty with firmness agree.

"No more will I babble of times that are past,
My wish is, the present forever may last;
Already I see sulky George in despair—
Should he vanquish the men—to vanquish the fair!

"Of Greeks and of Romans enough has been said,
To Codrus and Brutus full tribute been paid:
O'er musty old heroes no longer I'll dream—
Living beauty and virtue enliven my theme.

"Fill a bumper again, boy, and let it go round,
For the waters of youth in claret are found;
The younkers shall know, I've the courage to dare
Drink as deep as the best to the patriot fair." [1]

Such a song, finally, is one produced in 1780, and entitled "The Volunteer Boys," of which the first two stanzas and the last are as follows:—

"Hence with the lover who sighs o'er his wine,
  Cloes and Phillises toasting,
Hence with the slave who will whimper and whine,
  Of ardor and constancy boasting.
    Hence with love's joys,
    Follies and noise,—
The toast that I give is the Volunteer Boys.

"Nobles and beauties and such common toasts,
  Those who admire may drink, sir;
Fill up the glass to the Volunteer Hosts,
  Who never from danger will shrink, sir.

[1] F. Moore, "Songs and Ballads," etc., 206–207.

Let mirth appear,
Every heart cheer,
The toast that I give is—the Brave Volunteer.

"Thus, the bold bands for old Jersey's defence,
The Muse hath with rapture reviewed, sir;
With our Volunteer Boys, as our verses commence,
With our Volunteer Boys they conclude, sir.
Discord or noise,
Ne'er damp our joys,
But health and success to the Volunteer Boys."[1]

IV.

Respecting this large group of compositions—the political and military songs of the Revolution—the writers of the most of them still enjoy the blessing of being unknown,—a blessing in which they are not to be disturbed by any efforts of ours. Benjamin Young Prime, a physician who had some proclivity to verse-writing, and who in 1764 wrote "The Patriot Muse,"[2] is said to have produced in the course of the Revolution several political songs which enjoyed a sort of vogue in their day. Of James McClurg, also a physician, a classmate and friend of Jefferson's, there is a tradition which certifies to his skill in the writing of neat and tripping society-verses, and of clever songs for the Revolutionary cause.[3] Rednap Howell, who was a school-master in North Carolina, and who, in 1771, published a series of caustic articles upon the political controversies then raging within

[1] The whole song is in F. Moore, "Songs and Ballads," etc., 285–288.

[2] I have not met with this poem.

[3] Some impression of him, perhaps, may be formed, from a sprightly little poem called "The Belles of Williamsburg," which is said to have been the joint work of McClurg and of St. George Tucker in the year 1777, and which, by a pardonable anachronism, John Esten Cooke has contrived to weave into his chapter on "Governor Fauquier's Ball," in "The Virginia Comedians," ii. 266–269.

that colony,[1] is to be mentioned also as a writer of patriotic songs. In Connecticut, likewise, was a coterie of poets, Oliver Arnold,[2] David Humphreys, Joel Barlow,[3] and Timothy Dwight,[4] who are said to have shewn their sympathy for the Revolution by the production of many war-songs—all of which, apparently, their country has quite willingly permitted to die. Only one of these war-songs, that of "Columbia," written by Dwight while acting as chaplain to the American army in the campaign against Burgoyne, seems to have lived beyond the occasion from which it sprang; and very likely, to those who now read Dwight's "Columbia" as a detached text, and who do not re-create for themselves the very scene, the atmosphere, the needs, the moods, from the midst of which this song came into life, it will be but ponderous and humdrum verse. Of course, wingëd words these are not, and were not; and yet so true was this song to the very heart of its time, that, high above the hail and smoke and curses of the battle-field, it really lifted the hearts of men who were just then overburdened by a dreadful task, who were bewildered in the dust and cries of the fighting, and begrimed with its soilure and blood; and it actually gave to them, for some great moments, a clear vision of the triumphant issue of all this havoc and horror,—home, country, a new fatherland in the world, which should erect its power and renown, not on the antique vulgarities of slaughter and conquest, but on the happiness of men,—on liberty, justice, opportunity, science, beauty, genius:

> "A world is thy realm; for a world be thy laws,
> Enlarged as thy empire, and just as thy cause."

Therefore, with this splendid vision before him, the singer, wandering alone from his camp into a forest of cedars and

[1] "A Fan for Fanning and a Touchstone to Tryon. By Regulus." Reprinted in the "North Carolina Magazine," for Feb. and March, 1859.

[2] F. Moore, "Songs and Ballads," 82; 379. [3] C. B. Todd, "Life of Barlow," 29–30 n. [4] "Memoir," in Dwight's "Theology," i. 13.

there trying to find some lofty cheer for others, finds it also for himself:

> "Thus, as down a lone valley, with cedars o'erspread,
> From war's dread confusion I pensively strayed—
> The gloom from the face of fair heaven retired,
> The winds ceased to murmur, the thunders expired;
> Perfumes as of Eden, flowed sweetly along,
> And a voice, as of angels, enchantingly sung,—
> 'Columbia, Columbia, to glory arise,
> The queen of the world, and the child of the skies.'"[1]

V.

When the news of Bunker Hill fight, speeding southward, reached the town of Norwich, in Connecticut, it found there in Nathaniel Niles a soul prepared to receive it and whatsoever it forboded, with the fearlessness which comes of faith in things not to be won or lost in such warfare. This man, who was born in Rhode Island in 1741, who was graduated at Princeton in 1766, and who died in Vermont in 1828, was an instance of that versatility which seems to be the fatal privilege, as it is the badge, of civilization in its pioneer stages. Of towering intellect and commanding moral force, he laid his hand, during his long life, on nearly all of the great occupations which draw to themselves the service of educated men,—pedagogy, philosophy, medicine, law, divinity, mechanical invention, agriculture, politics, legislation, magistracy. Though without ordination as a minister in the religious body to which he belonged, he preached not infrequently in its pulpits; and on several occasions he published religious discourses which made their impression upon the public. All his life, too, his mind was busy with the current affairs of this world, partic-

---

[1] The whole song is in "American Poems," 62–64. These sentences concerning Dwight's "Columbia," are transferred with some alterations from a little book of mine entitled, "Three Men of Letters," 82–84.

ularly those of his own country,—on which he wrote and spoke as became a philosopher and a patriot.

This man it was who, being at his home in Norwich as the heart-shaking tidings from Bunker Hill rolled that way, and being prompted thereby to commune with those high thoughts which have in all times ministered strength and serenity in the midst of turmoil and pain, poured out his soul in a poem of sedate and touching melody,—"The American Hero,—A Sapphic Ode,"—which was straightway set to music and was sung everywhere in the churches, and proved itself to be a true lyric of fortitude and peace through all those troubled years:

"Why should vain mortals tremble at the sight of
Death and destruction in the field of battle,
Where blood and carnage clothe the field in crimson,
Sounding with death-groans?

"Death will invade us by the means appointed;
And we must all bow to the king of terrors;
Nor am I anxious, if I am preparëd,
What shape he comes in.

"Infinite wisdom teacheth us submission;
Bids us be quiet under all His dealings;
Never repining, but forever praising
God our Creator.

"Well may we praise Him: all His ways are perfect,
Though a resplendence infinitely glowing
Much hides the glory from the sight of mortals,
Struck blind by lustre.

"Good is Jehovah in bestowing sunshine;
Nor less his goodness in the storm and thunder:
Mercies and judgments both proceed from kindness—
Infinite kindness!

"Oh then exult that God forever reigneth!
Clouds that around Him hinder our perception,
Bind us the stronger to exalt His name and
Shout louder praises!

"Then to the goodness of my Lord and Master,
I will commit all that I have or wish for:
Sweetly as babes sleep, will I give my life up
When called to yield it.

"Now, War, I dare thee, clad in smoky pillars,
Bursting from bombshells, roaring from the cannon,
Rattling in grapeshot, like a storm of hailstones,
Torturing ether!

"To the bleak heavens let the spreading flame rise,
Bursting like Etna through the smoky columns,
Lowering like Egypt o'er the burning city—
Wantonly ruined.

"While all their hearts quick palpitate for havoc,
Let slip your bloodhounds, named the British lions,
Dauntless as death-stares, nimble as the whirlwind,
Dreadful as demons!

"Let ocean waft on all your floating castles,
Fraught with combustion horrible to nature;
Then, with your sails filled by a storm of vengeance,
Bear down to battle.

"From the dire caverns made by ghostly miners,
Let the explosion, dreadful as volcanoes,
Heave the broad town, with all its wealth and people,
Quick to destruction.

"Still shall the banner of the King of Heaven
Never advance where I'm afraid to follow:
While that precedes me, with an open bosom,
Mars, I defy thee!

"Fame and dear Freedom lure me on to battle ;
While a fell despot, grimmer than a death's head,
Stings me with serpents fiercer than Medusa's,
To the encounter.

"Life for my country and the cause of freedom,
Is but a cheap price for a worm to part with :
And if preservëd in so great a conflict contest,
Life is redoubled."[1]

VI.

The year 1776 opened with most solemn portents for Americans, for Englishmen, for mankind. The word Independence, held back so long, so long repudiated as a word hateful and calamitous, had been flung at last into the controversy, and was thenceforward to be spoken by many lips white with dread or tremulous with desire. No man could foresee what was coming upon the earth: all men could foresee that something was coming which the earth itself had not seen before. Thus, while in those early months of 1776, the people of this land were doubting or affirming, were cursing, weeping, fighting, or fleeing from the fight, one man, whose name we know not, set down upon paper, and sent forth in print, a few lines of verse which, perhaps, would long ago have become celebrated in literature had they been uttered anywhere else than among ourselves, and which, at any rate, may convince us that in the midst of all that hurly-burly were men and women who knew how, alway, through all confusions, right guidance lies in the path of high principle and especially of trust in the Unseen Leader. These lines, thus written and printed, frame themselves into a prayer, laconic, austere, devout; they are a stately and sweet poem, fit to be placed by the side of

[1] This poem, as commonly published, has been altered in many particulars from the original, and in most cases for the worse. My copy is taken with exactness from the original manuscript, which was courteously sent to me by Nathaniel Niles, of New York, a grandson of the writer, whose name he bears.

any other of its kind that can be met with anywhere in the many-mansioned treasure-house of our English speech:

"The American Patriot's Prayer."

"Parent of all, omnipotent
In heaven, and earth below,
Through all creation's bounds unspent,
Whose streams of goodness flow,

"Teach me to know from whence I rose,
And unto what designed;
No private aims let me propose,
Since link'd with human kind.

"But chief to hear my country's voice,
May all my thoughts incline;
'T is reason's law, 't is virtue's choice,
'T is nature's call and Thine.

"Me from fair Freedom's sacred cause
Let nothing e'er divide;
Grandeur, nor gold, nor vain applause,
Nor friendship false, misguide.

"Let me not faction's partial hate
Pursue to this land's woe;
Nor grasp the thunder of the state
To wound a private foe.

"If, for the right to wish the wrong
My country shall combine,
Single to serve th' erroneous throng,
Spite of themselves, be mine."[1]

---

[1] This remarkable poem first appeared, so far as I am able to discover, in the "Large Additions to Common Sense," appended to the third edition of that pamphlet as published by Robert Bell, in Philadelphia, February, 1776. Thomas Paine's latest and best biographer (M. D. Conway, i. 116) seems to have been led by this fact to ascribe the poem to his hero. In that opinion I

VII.

A noble specimen of the religious songs that were actually sung by the armies of the Revolution, remains to us in "The American Soldier's Hymn," a composition not unworthy to be placed by the side of Luther's "Ein feste Burg ist unser Gott," a composition in the manner of the great hymn-writers of the sixteenth and seventeenth centuries,—simple, earnest, reverent, stately, with the deep note of heroic trust in the help of the Eternal Helper:

"'T is God that girds our armor on,
And all our just designs fulfills;
Through Him our feet can swiftly run,
And nimbly climb the steepest hills.

"Lessons of war from Him we take,
And manly weapons learn to wield;
Strong bows of steel with ease we break,
Forced by our stronger arms to yield.

"'T is God that still supports our right,
His just revenge our foes pursues;
'T is He that with resistless might,
Fierce nations to His power subdues.

"Our universal safeguard He!
From Whom our lasting honors flow;
He made us great, and set us free
From our remorseless bloody foe.

---

am unable to concur. Of course, the first appearance of the poem in the addenda to "Common Sense" does not at all prove that it was written by the author of that pamphlet; since Paine wrote but few, if any, of that miscellaneous collection of pieces. When one turns to the test of internal evidence, it seems to me difficult to conclude that this poem bears the characteristic marks of Paine's work. I do not recall anything, known to have been written by him, which, whatever its merit, is not somewhere marred by at least a touch of disproportion, of excess, of pungency verging towards truculence, and of a willingness to surrender his uncommon gift of expression to mere smartness of phrase; whereas this poem is characterized throughout by spiritual ripeness, by self-restraint, and by an entire freedom from any trace either of rancor or of rhetorical glitter.

"Therefore to celebrate His fame,
Our grateful voice to Heaven we 'll raise;
And nations, strangers to His name,
Shall thus be taught to sing His praise."[1]

VIII.

Crossing the somewhat indistinct line between the song and the ballad, we find that there were produced during the Revolution a great number of those blunt and artless compositions, intended either to be sung or to be recited, wherein the more picturesque and stirring incidents of the war are told with the undisguised emotion, and in the homely diction and loose measure made dear to so many generations of our race in the old ballads of England and Scotland. It is doubtful if the American ballads which sprang into life on either side of our Revolutionary controversy, will be found to differ materially, either in quality or in form, from such products of popular feeling as have been thrown forth, in similar times of commotion, upon the highways and byways of the mother country. At any rate, among the most characteristic of these American ballads, on the Revolutionist side of the controversy, should be mentioned one of considerable sprightliness and imaginative vigor, entitled "Liberty's Call," said to have been written in 1775, and beginning with these lines:

"High on the banks of Delaware,
Fair Liberty she stood,
And waving with her lovely hand,
Cried, 'Still, thou roaring flood!'"[2]

---

[1] I use the copy given by F. Moore in his "Ballad History of the American Revolution," 221–222, and taken by him from a manuscript found among the papers of General George Clinton.

[2] First printed in "The Pennsylvania Packet" in 1775, it enjoyed great popularity during the Revolution; was attributed to several different writers, notably to Francis Hopkinson; but was probably the work of John Mason, an eccentric tradesman of Philadelphia. F. Moore, "Songs and Ballads," 83–87.

Nor should we forget " A Song for the Red Coats," which tells, with the true ballad-ring, the never-to-be-exhausted story of the successful campaign against Burgoyne in the summer and autumn of 1777:

> " Come unto me, ye heroes,
> Whose hearts are true and bold,
> Who value more your honor,
> Than others do their gold!
> Give ear unto my story,
> And I the truth will tell,
> Concerning many a soldier
> Who for his country fell."[1]

Upon the same prolific theme is the ballad of " The Fate of John Burgoyne," written likewise in 1777, and in its opening lines depicting the merry scene of this hero's departure from London for the conquest of America:

> " When Jack, the king's commander,
> Was going to his duty,
> Through all the crowd he smiled and bowed—
> To every blooming beauty ;
> The city rung with feats he 'd done
> In Portugal and Flanders,
> And all the town thought he 'd be crowned
> The first of Alexanders."[2]

For the thrilling story of the capture and fate of Major John André, a very genuine thing, self-styled a "ditty," is " Brave Paulding and the Spy," wherein the shrewdness and incorruptible integrity of Paulding are celebrated with a fervor which yet admits of downright admiration and sympathy for the unfortunate young officer whom Paulding

---

[1] F. Moore, "Songs and Ballads," 176–184.

[2] Ibid., 185. Much of the contemporary verse evoked by our victory over Burgoyne is doleful rubbish, such as a " Short Review of Burgoyne's Expedition," by Robert Dinsmore, the " rustic bard," and all the metrical stuff written by the Reverend Wheeler Case.

had to bring to his death. Thus, in singing of André upon the gallows—an enemy and a spy—this homely ballad has a robust compassion and an unshrinking honesty of praise to be expected only in an utterance so fearless as a genuine street-song:

> "When he was executed,
> He looked both meek and mild;
> He looked upon the people,
> And pleasantly he smiled.
> It moved each eye with pity,
> Caused every heart to bleed;
> And every one wished him released—
> And Arnold in his stead.
> He was a man of honor,
> In Britain he was born;
> To die upon the gallows
> Most highly he did scorn."[1]

The almost matchless victory of the rebels, achieved in 1780 on a rugged height near the northern border of South Carolina, has claimed popular commemoration ever since in a hundred forms,—in none of them more genuine than in a ballad published in 1781 and called "Battle of King's Mountain,"—a ballad which begins with this bit of charmingly outspoken vituperation:

> "'T was on a pleasant mountain
> The Tory heathens lay,—
> With a doughty major at their head,
> One Ferguson they say.
> Cornwallis had detached him,
> A thieving for to go,
> And catch the Carolina men,
> Or bring the rebels low."[2]

It may be worth while for us also to take note of two other fighting ballads, one with the flavor of the land and

[1] F. Moore, "Songs and Ballads," etc., 320–321. [2] Ibid. 335.

one with the flavor of the sea, namely, "The Wyoming Massacre," written by Uriah Terry,[1] and "Bold Hawthorne, or, The Cruise of the 'Fair American'"[2]: both of them crude enough in form, but both breathing the very breath of the life of those strong and passionate days.

IX.

Four years before the tragical adventure of André had drawn toward him the tenderness of millions of hearts on both sides of the Atlantic, a fate not unlike his, though without its immediate compensations in sympathy and glory, had befallen Nathan Hale, a most gallant and accomplished young American, of a character stronger and more original, probably, than André's, and certainly not less noble. A graduate of Yale College in 1773, a school-teacher at New London, and a candidate for the ministry, the tidings from Lexington and Concord had turned him into a soldier; and by the early autumn of 1776, he had risen to be captain of a company in the "Connecticut Rangers," forming a part of the army under the immediate command of Washington in the neighborhood of New York. In response to an earnest appeal from Washington, he consented to go in disguise within the enemy's lines for the purpose of procuring information greatly needed by the commander-in-chief: in short, he took upon himself, in the name of duty to his country, the ignominy and the peril of becoming a spy. In that service he was caught, was carried before General Howe, was hurriedly tried and condemned, and was hurriedly executed,—having been refused by the provost-marshal the attendance of a chaplain or the use of a Bible, and having suffered the added cruelty of seeing his letters of farewell to his sisters and to his betrothed torn in pieces before his face. The story of this young fellow's fearless devotion and death, has not

[1] Charles Miner, "History of Wyoming," Appendix.

[2] McCarty's "National Songs," ii. 250.

been suffered to die or to grow dim among us. Poems have been written about him.[1] Statues have been reared to him. Anniversaries have been kept in his honor. Moreover, in the very year of his self-immolation, his fate was sung in a ballad which for poetic quality—for weird pathos, for a strange sweet melody—probably deserves to be placed at the head of this entire class of writings as produced during the period of the Revolution.

Landing from his little boat upon a lonely spot within the enemy's lines, Hale had openly gone about in the disguise of a Loyalist school-master; he had visited the various British camps on Long Island and in New York; but having, according to one account, been recognized by an unrelenting kinsman who was a real Loyalist, he was tracked and captured just as he was in the act of making his escape by the way he had come. It is at this stage of the story that the ballad begins:

"The breezes went steadily through the tall pines,
A saying 'oh! hu-ush!' a saying 'oh! hu-ush!'
As stilly stole by a bold legion of horse,
For Hale in the bush, for Hale in the bush.

"'Keep still!' said the thrush as she nestled her young,
In a nest by the road, in a nest by the road;
'For the tyrants are near, and with them appear
What bodes us no good, what bodes us no good.'

"The brave captain heard it, and thought of his home
In a cot by the brook, in a cot by the brook,
With mother and sister and memories dear
He so gaily forsook, he so gaily forsook.

"Cooling shades of the night were coming apace,
The tattoo had beat, the tattoo had beat;

---

[1] No other verse inspired by the story of Nathan Hale is, in my opinion, equal to a lyric by Francis Miles Finch, beginning,—

"To drum-beat, and heart-beat,
A soldier marches by."

The noble one sprang from his dark lurking place,
To make his retreat, to make his retreat.

" He warily trod on the dry rustling leaves,
As he passed through the wood, as he passed through the wood;
And silently gained his rude launch on the shore,
As she played with the flood, as she played with the flood.

" The guards of the camp on that dark dreary night,
Had a murderous will, had a murderous will;
They took him and bore him afar from the shore,
To a hut on the hill, to a hut on the hill.

" No mother was there, nor a friend who could cheer,
In that little stone cell, in that little stone cell;
But he trusted in love from his Father above—
In his heart all was well, in his heart all was well.

" An ominous owl with his solemn bass voice,
Sat moaning hard by, sat moaning hard by:—
'The tyrant's proud minions most gladly rejoice,
For he must soon die, for he must soon die.'

. . . .

" They took him and bound him and bore him away,
Down the hill's grassy side, down the hill's grassy side:
'T was there the base hirelings, in royal array,
His cause did deride, his cause did deride.

" Five minutes were given, short moments, no more,
For him to repent, for him to repent;
He prayed for his mother—he asked not another—
To Heaven he went, to Heaven he went.

" The faith of a martyr the tragedy shewed,
As he trod the last stage, as he trod the last stage;
And Britons will shudder at gallant Hale's blood,
As his words do presage, as his words do presage:—

"'Thou pale king of terrors, thou life's gloomy foe,
Go frighten the slave, go frighten the slave;
Tell tyrants, to you their allegiance they owe—
No fears for the brave, no fears for the brave!'"[1]

[1] F. Moore, "Songs and Ballads," 130–133.

CHAPTER XXXII.

THE DRAMATIC LITERATURE OF THE REVOLUTION.

I.—The beginnings of our dramatic literature—These writings exceed all others in the frankness and realism with which they exhibit the ideas and passions of the period.

II.—The tragedy of "Ponteach, or the Savages of America," by Major Robert Rogers, 1766—The author's acquaintance with the American Indians and their wrongs—Method of this tragedy—Outline of its plot—Estimate of the work—Fails in the presentation of real savages.

III.—"Disenchantment, or, The Force of Credulity," a comic opera, by Andrew Barton, 1767.

IV.—A Loyalist colloquy, "The Americans Roused, in a Cure for the Spleen," by Jonathan Sewall, 1774.

V.—Two political satires in dramatic form by Mercy Otis Warren—"The Adulateur, a Tragedy, as it is now Acted in Upper Servia," 1773—Exhibits historical situations in New England from 1770 to 1773—Also, the prevailing fear and hatred of Governor Hutchinson—"The Group," a metrical play in two Acts, 1775—Satirizes the British and Loyalist leaders in Boston just prior to the military stage of the conflict—Her two elaborate tragedies in blank verse, "The Sack of Rome," and "The Ladies of Castile."

VI.—An American Chronicle Play, early in 1776, on "The Fall of British Tyranny, or, American Liberty Triumphant. The First Campaign. A Tragi-Comedy of Five Acts, as lately planned at the Royal Theatrum Pandemonium at St. James"—A jocular and rough Whig satire—Its chief personages—Represents the British attack on American rights as originating in the ambition of Lord Bute—Various scenes in the play—Satire on Lord Dunmore, and the British generals in America—The Epilogue alludes to "Common Sense," and avows its doctrine.

VII.—The evacuation of Boston by the British in March, 1776, celebrated in the American army by a farce entitled "The Blockheads," in reply to Burgoyne's recent farce entitled "The Blockade."

VIII.—"The Battle of Brooklyn," a Loyalist farce just after the American defeat on Long Island, August, 1776—Satirizes the American leaders as vulgar adventurers, and reflects some of the coarse personal scandals of the time.

IX.—The high literary merit of two dramatic poems by Hugh Henry Brackenridge, both dealing with military events in the first year of the war—"The

I.

TENTATIVE and crude as are nearly all of the writings in dramatic form, which were produced among us during the period of the Revolution, they are not unworthy of some slight attention, in the first place, as giving the genesis of a department of American literature now become considerable; but, chiefly, as reproducing the ideas, the passions, the motives, and the moods of that stormful time in our history, with a frankness, a liveliness, and an unshrinking realism not approached by any other species of Revolutionary literature.

II.

A very early and also a very notable example of dramatic writing in our literature, is "Ponteach, or, The Savages of America: a Tragedy," published in London in 1766, and believed to have been the work of Major Robert Rogers, an American officer in the service of England during her last great war with the French and Indians in America.[1] Written, therefore, by a man who knew the Indians in some other manner than by hearsay or through a haze of idealizing sentiment—whose acquaintance with them, in fact, was of that intimate and authentic kind which is to be had by

[1] Robert Rogers is also dealt with in Chapter vii. of the present work.

living among them and fighting with them and of course occasionally killing them—this drama nevertheless exhibits the red men of the American forests as, upon the whole, more courteous and more generous, as honester, as nobler, than the white men who, in the capacity of traders, hunters, or warriors, had invaded those forests in order to transact business with them. According to Major Rogers,—veteran bush-whacker, forest-ranger, and skull-cracker to his majesty among the American Indians,—it was they who, in all communications with the white men were usually lied to and insulted, in all bargains usually cheated, in the beginning of all quarrels usually the party suffering injury.

The tragedy of "Ponteach" is built out into Five Acts, after the conventional pattern for structures of this kind; it is, also, in blank verse, with occasional accesses of rhyme. Its tragic culmination springs from two sets of enormities—on the one hand, those of the English against the Indians, on the other, those of the Indians against one another; and it is reached along two lines of retributive fulfillment, often entangled together, yet always easily discriminated.

The First Act brings forward the first set of crimes—those of rapacity, treachery, and cruelty practised upon Indians by white men. Thus, in the opening Scene, two traders commune together over their plans for sundry large and profitable frauds upon their unsophisticated customers—exulting in all this as one might exult in something altogether laudable. In the Second Scene, a hunter named Honeyman, proposes to another hunter, named Osbourn, the jolly plan of enriching themselves without much trouble, by shooting down such straggling Indians as they might chance to fall in with—especially if found to be carrying furs to market. Honeyman's proposal leads to the following colloquy:

" *Osbourn.* Trust me for that—I 'll join with all my heart;
Nor with a nicer aim or steadier hand
Would shoot a tiger than I would an Indian.

There is a couple !—stalking now this way,
With lusty packs ! Heaven favor our design !

Honeyman. Silence ! conceal yourself, and mind your eye !

Osbourn. Are you well charged ?

Honeyman. I am. Take you the nearest,
And mind to fire exactly when I do.

Osbourn. A charming chance !

Honeyman. Hush ! let them still come nearer."

As soon as these Indians, unconscious of danger, have come somewhat nearer, the hunters shoot; then Honeyman cries out—

" They 're down, old boy, a brace of noble bucks ! "—

whereupon these two Christian gentlemen rush forward and strip their pagan victims of the rich load of furs they had with them.[1]

In the Third Scene, two officers of the English army wantonly insult the great Ottawa chieftain, Ponteach; and to his face they tell him of their expectation soon to have the pleasure of slaughtering his people, and of laying the fire-brand to their wigwams and their corn-fields.

In the Fourth Scene, we are permitted to witness a conference between three provincial governors, who arrive at the friendly agreement to rob the Indians of the money and other gifts which the king had sent out for them, and at the same time, in order to shew their impartiality, to rob the king, also, of the presents which Ponteach had entrusted to these noble governors for his royal brother in England.

This closes the First Act. In the Second Act, the Indian portion of the plot has its beginning,—in the perception by the Indians that they must have war with the English; in the plans of Ponteach for conducting such war; in the fatal rivalry, both in love and in ambition, between his two sons, Chekitan and Philip.

---

[1] "Ponteach, or The Savages of America," 9–10.

From these several causes, then, issue the events which follow in the tragedy, wherein we have an abundance of intrigue, violence, hate, love, lust, superstition, oratory, ceremony, state-craft, torture, assassination, suicide. At last, when so many of those whom he loved or cared for are weltering in their blood, and disasters overwhelm him on every hand, the hero of the tragedy stands out alone in all the grandeur of a great soul unconquered by misfortune, determined still to show to the gods an unbending purpose and a courage worthy even of themselves.

While the details of this plot are almost entirely without historical basis, the piece as a whole has a certain authenticity in its presentation of the genius and the daring of its celebrated hero, as well as of the wrongs inflicted on him and his people by the superior race then incontinently helping itself to their country. "The style of the drama is," in the opinion of Francis Parkman, "superior to the plot; and the writer displays at times no small insight into the workings of human nature."[1] On the other hand, it is hard to understand how a composition in which a man like Major Robert Rogers had a considerable share, could have escaped so perfectly as this drama has done, almost every note of the true Indian manner in thought or expression. In fact, nearly all the Indians to be met with in this play are rather cultivated persons. Even the filth and the profanity, which Parkman[2] complains of as being rather too pervasive of the talk of the white men whom we have here to listen to, are probably much truer to the life of which this drama professes to be a representation, than are those refinements of sentiment, those elaborations of conventional phrase, which the play puts into the mouths of such young savages as Chekitan, Torax, and Monelia. Indeed, of all the American Indians thus set upon the stage for us to look at and listen to, it must be said that if they are savages —as the title of this drama declares them to be—they are extremely artificial savages. As a professed delineation of

[1] "The Conspiracy of Pontiac," ii., 321. [2] Ibid. 332.

the life and thought and speech of Ottawas and Mohawks, the tragedy of "Ponteach" may be original—it can hardly claim to be aboriginal.[1]

III.

Sometime in the year 1767,—during that lull in political excitement which intervened between the repeal of the Stamp Act and the subsequent return of parliament to its policy of colonial taxation,—there was published in New York a play which is at least notable for its exemption from all the perplexities incident to affairs of state, being simply a frolicsome satire on a certain phase of character then too prominent in this part of the world, to wit, the greed and the credulity which bewitched so many men, and tempted them to spend life and fortune and hope itself in digging for treasures supposed to have been hidden in the earth by valiant pirates and other thrifty accumulators in a former time. This play bears the title of "Disenchantment; or, The Force of Credulity. A New American Comic Opera, of Three Acts. By Andrew Barton, Esquire";[2] and while the text is not at all brilliant, the drollery of some of the situations must have given to it no little effectiveness.[3]

---

[1] In "The Conspiracy of Pontiac," i., 164 note, Parkman says of this tragedy of "Ponteach": "It is very rare; and besides the copy in my possession, I know of but one other, which may be found in the library of the British Museum." As some indication of the bibliographical treasures now accumulated in the public and private libraries of Providence, Rhode Island, and of the generous courtesy with which those treasures are made available to students, I may state that the only two copies of "Ponteach" which, after considerable enquiry, I have ever been able to see, are both in that city; one of them belonging to Mr. John Nicholas Brown, the other to the library of Brown University.

[2] Perhaps an assumed name for Col. Thomas Forrest of Germantown. Manuscript note on title-page of the old copy in Library Company of Philadelphia.

[3] Indeed, its personal allusions were so effective that "Douglas's Company," playing in Philadelphia in April, 1767, withdrew it after having put it in rehearsal. P. L. Ford, "Beginnings of Am. Dram. Lit.," 13–14.

IV.

One of the earliest and certainly one of the crudest experiments in the direction of dramatic writing, during this period, is a colloquy, published probably in the autumn of 1774, and entitled " The Americans Roused, in a Cure for the Spleen. Or, Amusement for a Winter's Evening: Being the Substance of a Conversation on the Times, over a Friendly Tankard and Pipe." This production, which was probably written by Jonathan Sewall of Massachusetts, won for itself considerable notoriety, not indeed for its wit or its literary charm, but for the unshrinking candor with which, under the shield of a dramatic irresponsibility, its author denounced the work of the first Continental Congress, and the entire movement in opposition to the British ministry.

V.

Two notable efforts at political satire in dramatic form were made in the years just preceding the outbreak of military violence, by " Madam Mercy Warren, the historical, philosophical, poetical, and satirical consort of . . . General James Warren of Plymouth."[1] Of these once celebrated performances, the first is " The Adulateur: a Tragedy, as it is now Acted in Upper Servia," wherein the streets, buildings and people of that far-off country do duty for the streets, buildings, and people of Boston; wherein Brutus, Cassius, Marcus, Portius and other patriotic and grandiloquent conspirators stand for James Otis, John Adams, Samuel Adams, Hancock, Warren and the rest; wherein Bagshot, as Aga of the Janizaries, enacts the bloodthirsty part then popularly attributed to Captain Preston of His Majesty's Twenty-Ninth Regiment of Infantry; wherein Rapatio, as Governor of Upper Servia, embodies the boundless and unscrupulous ambition, the

---

[1] John Adams, " Works," x. 99.

treachery, the ingenuity, the lust for blood, then supposed to characterize Thomas Hutchinson, His Majesty's Governor of Massachusetts Bay. The play is duly elaborated into Five Acts, chiefly in unrhymed pentameter verse. It exhibits a series of historical situations in New England, ranging from some imaginary moment prior to the Boston massacre in 1770, down to some time in 1773, when the very air is hot with conspiracy, revolution, and readiness for deeds of violence, and when the habit of the Revolutionary chiefs seems to have been to talk of American liberty in the grandiose fashion of Greek and Roman patriots. Another most veracious note of this play, is the profound suspicion of Governor Thomas Hutchinson which it everywhere intimates—the fear of him, the hate of him—as the colossal marplot and head-devil of British tyranny in America. For example, one of Hutchinson's creatures, named Gripeall, boasts to the governor how he means so to use his official authority over the Upper Servians as to

> . . . "cramp their trade till pale-eyed Poverty
> Haunts all their streets and frowns destruction on,
> While many a poor man, leaning on his staff,
> Beholds a numerous famished offspring round him,
> Who weep for bread. Gods, how his bosom heaves!
> Ghastly he rolls an aching eye upon them,
> Then blasts my name, and with a groan expires."

In response to this jubilant portrayal of public misery to be wrought by his own servant upon people whose only crime is insubmission to his despotism, the governor exclaims—

> "What throbs of joy! Nero, I tower above thee!"[1]

Mercy Warren's second and more effective experiment in political satire is her metrical play, called "The Group," published early in the year 1775, apparently before the day of Lexington and Concord. By that time, Hutchinson,

---

[1] "The Adulateur," 25.

the most dreaded of the Tory leaders, was in England, whither he had been summoned to make personal report to the king; but the malign character ascribed to him by his enemies is here well sustained by his brother, Foster Hutchinson, who appears in "The Group" under the name of Judge Meagre; and along with him are a dozen or more of the New England chiefs of the Loyalist party,—Peter Oliver as Lord Chief Justice Hazlerod, Timothy Ruggles as Brigadier Hateall, the foppish Daniel Leonard as Beau Trumps, Harrison Gray as Scriblerius Fribble, Sir William Pepperell as Sir Sparrow Spendall, Nathaniel Ray Thomas as Simple Sapling, Secretary Thomas Flucker as Dupe,[1] and so on. Moreover, these Tory chiefs, thus forming the "dramatis personæ" of the play, are "attended by a swarm of court sycophants, hungry harpies, and unprincipled danglers collected from the neighboring villages, hovering over the stage in the shape of locusts, led by Massachusettensis in the form of a basilisk; the rear brought up by Proteus, bearing a torch in one hand and a powder flask in the other; the whole supported by a mighty army and navy from Blunderland, for the laudable purpose of enslaving its best friends."[2]

The play has but two Acts. The scene of the first is laid in "a little back parlor," with "guards standing at the door"[3]; while in the second Act "the scene changes to a large dining room. The table furnished with bowls, bottles, glasses, and cards. The group appear sitting round in a restless attitude. In one corner of the room is discovered a small cabinet of books for the use of the studious and contemplative, containing Hobbes's Leviathan, Sipthrop's Sermons,[4] Hutchinson's History, Fable of the Bees, Phila-

[1] I here follow the identification of characters as given by Norton Quincy. J. Adams, "Works," x. 99 note. This assignment seems to have been satisfactory to Jared Sparks, who inserted it in his own copy of "The Group," now in the library of Cornell University. In one of the copies of the play belonging to the Boston Athenæum, I observed an assignment of characters somewhat different from the above. [2] "The Group," 2.

[3] Ibid. 3. [4] A gibe at the Reverend East Apthorp.

lethes on Philanthrop with an Appendix by Massachusettensis, Hoyle on Whist, Lives of the Stuarts, Statutes of Henry the Eighth and William the Conqueror, Wedderburn's Speeches, and Acts of Parliament for 1774." [1]

Within those two rooms, accordingly, the members of this Tory club have ample opportunity to exhibit, either for the derision or for the horror of their Whig fellow-countrymen, their half-hearted ambitions, their qualms of conscience, their guilty surmises of failure, their plots, disagreements, jealousies, fears, hopes, hatreds, and their sullen contempt for the rights and the sufferings of their fellow-countrymen. In the course of the play, there enter the Tory members of the colonial council who, "with trembling servile gestures," present to Sylla—that is, to General Gage—several petitions from their "Under-Tools in the distant counties, begging each a guard of myrmidons to protect them from the armed multitudes . . . approaching to take speedy vengeance" upon them; whereat Sylla, walking up and down the room "in great perplexity," discusses the whole miserable business with Hateall, Dupe, Meagre, Simple Sapling and others, confessing frankly his own sense of the nobility and strength of the cause against which he is ordered to make war, and his own deep reluctance to do anything to precipitate the bloody conflict which seems so near:

> "shall I rashly draw my guilty sword,
> And dip its hungry hilt in the rich blood
> Of the best subjects that a Brunswick boasts,
> And for no cause, but that they nobly scorn
> To wear the fetters of his venal slaves!" [2]

As Sylla then goes from the stage with such words of misgiving upon his lips, Hazlerod exclaims "in great agitation,"—

> "This balancing of passions ne'er will do,
> And by the scale which virtue holds to reason,

---

[1] "The Group," 7. [2] Ibid. 13–17.

Weighing the business ere he executes,—
Doubting, deliberating, half resolved
To be the savior of a virtuous state,—
Instead of guarding refugees and knaves,
The buzzing reptiles that crawl about his court,
And lick his hand for some delicious crumb.

. . . .

I'll hasten after, and stir up his soul
To dire revenge and bloody resolutions,
Or the whole fabric falls on which we hang,
And down the pit of infamy we plunge,
Without the spoils we long have hoped to reap." [1]

Accordingly, as Hazlerod "crosses the stage hastily and goes after Sylla," Dupe and Meagre are left standing "at the further part of the stage"; and in the conversation which then takes place between them and which ends the play, Meagre proves by his honest avowal of the very highest sort of Toryism how worthy he is, at least according to the conception of the satirist, to be the brother of the greatest of Tories, Governor Hutchinson:

"Let not thy soft timidity of heart
Urge thee to terms, till the last stake is thrown.
'T is not my temper ever to forgive—
When once resentment 's kindled in my breast.
I hated Brutus [2] for his noble stand
Against the oppressors of his injured country.
I hate the leaders of these restless factions
For all their generous efforts to be free.
I curse the senate which defeats our bribes.

. . . .

I hate the people who, no longer gulled,
See through the schemes of our aspiring clan.

[1] "The Group," 17–18.

[2] The reference is probably to James Otis, brother of the satirist, then disqualified for further service on account of the brutal beating, and especially the sword-cut upon the head, which he received in 1769 from sundry revenue officers and others in a tavern.

> And from the rancor of my venomed mind,
> I look askance on all the human race ;
> And if they 're not to be appalled by fear,
> I wish the earth might drink that vital stream
> That warms the heart and feeds the manly glow—
> The love inherent, planted in the breast,
> To equal liberty conferred on man
> By Him who formed the peasant and the King.
> Could we erase these notions from their minds,
>
> . . . .
>
> We 'd smoothly glide on midst a race of slaves,[1]
> Nor heave one sigh—though all the human race
> Were plunged in darkness, slavery, and vice."

Besides these two dramatic poems having direct relation to the controversies of the Revolution,[2] Mercy Warren wrote, "as the amusement of solitude, at a period when every active member of society was engaged, either in the field or the cabinet, to resist the strong hand of foreign domination,"[3] two carefully wrought historical plays, "The Sack of Rome," and "The Ladies of Castile," which, however, were not published till the year 1790.

VI.

Early in the year 1776—probably in the month of March[4] —there was published in Philadelphia a drama bearing this rather emotional title,—"The Fall of British Tyranny; or, American Liberty Triumphant. The First Campaign. A Tragi-Comedy of Five Acts, as lately planned at the Royal Theatrum Pandemonium at St. James'." This production may be roughly described as an American Chronicle

[1] "The Group," 20–21.

[2] The authorship of a farce called "The Blockheads," mentioned later in this chapter, is attributed to her.

[3] Warren, "Poems, Dramatic and Miscellaneous," Dedication, p. iii.

[4] From internal evidence, it must be inferred that the writing of the play was finished after the publication of "Common Sense" in January, 1776, and before

Play. Being in no respect embarrassed by attention to the dramatic unities, it shifts the scene with a truly sovereign facility from one side of the Atlantic to the other,—from England to Massachusetts, from Massachusetts to Virginia, from Virginia to Massachusetts, from Massachusetts to Canada, and from Canada back again to Massachusetts. As to the period of the action, it may be said to begin at that moment—quite impossible to ascertain—when in the ambitious and plotting soul of Lord Bute, was born, as is here assumed, the purpose to create a disastrous American crisis in order to precipitate a still more disastrous English crisis, amid the commotions of which George the Third should be driven to an abdication of the throne,—whereupon Bute's own kinsmen, the Stuarts, should come back and enjoy their own again. From that indefinable point of beginning, the action sweeps on and on, year after year, until it culminates in the first campaign of actual war in America, including the incidents at Lexington and Concord, the battle of Bunker Hill, Lord Dunmore's negro-stealing and house-burning raids along the Virginia coast, the American invasion of Canada, and especially the spectacle,—astonishing to gods and men—of a rabble of half-armed peasants shutting up the invincible army of Britain within the city of Boston, where they are saved from starvation only by great displays of valor on their part in the stealing of chickens, sheep, and pigs from the islands and shores of the harbor. The action comes to an end just before the British evacuation of Boston,—which occurred on the 17th of March, 1776.

Of course, for this huge and very Gothic drama, no claim of artistic merit need be supposed. Nevertheless, as a presentation of the spirit and method of Revolutionary thought when first confronted with the question of Independence,

---

the news had reached Philadelphia of the evacuation of Boston, March 17, 1776. Sabin confidently attributes this play to John Leacock. ("Dictionary," etc., sub nom.) Hildeburn is more cautious, being content to remark that it is "said to have been written by Mr. Laycock of Philadelphia." ("Issues of the Press," etc., ii. 249.)

"The Fall of British Tyranny" is of the highest interest and value. It is simply a tremendous Whig satire, in dramatic form, first, on the one deep, treasonable motive attributed to the Tory conspirators who, in England and America, had forced the two countries into so monstrous a conflict; and, secondly, on the imbecility, the cowardice, and the grotesque failure thus far displayed by the military agents of these Tory conspirators in the execution of their horrid plot.

Even in the long list of the "dramatis personæ" of the play, one may catch something of its rough humor, and especially of its jocular indifference to the majesty of all great names in England below that of the king,—the latter being here spared contumelious mention except as a victim of the political profligacy of his own chief servants:

Lord Paramount, Mr. Bute.
Lord Mocklaw, Mr. Mansfield.
Lord Hypocrite, Mr. Dartmouth.
Lord Poltroon, Mr. Sandwich.
Lord Catspaw, Mr. North.
Lord Wisdom, Mr. Chatham.
Lord Religion, Bishop of St. Asaph.
Lord Justice, Mr. Camden.
Lord Patriot, Mr. Wilkes.
Bold Irishman, Mr. Burke.
Judas, Mr. Hutchinson.
Charlie, Mr. Jenkinson.
Brazen, Mr. Wedderburn.
Colonel, Mr. Barré.
Lord Boston, Mr. Gage.
Admiral Tombstone, Mr. Graves.
Elbow Room, Mr. Howe.
Mr. Caper, Mr. Burgoyne.
Lord Kidnapper, Mr. Dunmore.

Besides the foregoing persons, are Washington, Charles Lee, Putnam, Earl Percy, and several other characters, who appear in the play under their own names.

In developing the vast series of actions participated in by this army of dramatic personages, the play opens with a scene intended to fasten the attention powerfully upon the alleged origin of the American Revolution, namely, in the Jacobite designs, in the perfidy and subtlety, of Lord Bute. It is a room in the palace of St. James, where he—Lord Paramount, solus—is strutting about in an ecstacy of self-admiration, discoursing betimes upon his own greatness:—"Many long years have rolled delightfully on, whilst I have been basking in the sunshine of grandeur and power,—whilst I have imperceptibly, though not unsuspected, guided the chariot of state, and greased with the nation's gold the imperial wheels. 'T is I that move the mighty engine of royalty; and with the tincture of my somniferous opiate, or, in the language of a courtier, by the virtue of my secret influence, I have lulled the axletree to sleep, and brought on a pleasing insensibility. Let their champion, Lord Wisdom, groan; he is now become feeble and impotent—a mere cripple in politics. Their Lord Patriot's squint has lost its basilisk effect. And the Bold Irishman may bellow the Keenew till he is hoarse,—he 's no more, when compared to me, than an Irish salmon to a Scotch herring. I care not a bawbee for them all. I 'll reign in Britain—I 'll be king of their councils, and chief among the princes. Oh Ambition! thou darling of my soul, stop not till I rise superior to all superlative,—till I mount triumphantly the pinnacle of glory,—or at least open the way for one of my own family and name to enter without opposition." [1]

This soliloquy is broken by the entrance of the astute and unscrupulous Lord Mocklaw, whom Paramount had summoned as his confidential adviser, and to whom he now discloses the outline of his scheme. At the first glance, Mocklaw sees great difficulties in the way:—"You have need, my lord, of all your wisdom, fortitude and power, when you consider with whom you have to contend. Let

[1] "The Fall," etc., 1–2.

me see! Lord Wisdom, Lord Religion, Lord Justice, Lord Patriot, the Bold Irishman, and so forth, and so forth, and so forth, and the wisdom of the United Colonies of America in Congress to cope with. As individuals, they are trifling; but in league combined, may become potent enemies." To this Paramount replies: "Granted, but are you so little of a lawyer as not to know the virtue of a certain specific I 'm possessed of, that will accomplish anything, even to performing miracles? Don't you know, there 's such sweet music in the shaking of the Treasury keys, that they will instantly lock the most babbling patriot's tongue, transform a Tory into a Whig, and a Whig into a Tory, make a superannuated old miser dance, and an old cynic philosopher smile? How many thousand times has your tongue danced at Westminster Hall to the sound of such music?"

Thus the interview continues, until Lord Paramount brings it to a close by whispering to his confidant the leading details of his plan:—"Now, then, for a line of politics. I propose to begin, first, by taxing America as a blind. That will create an eternal animosity between us, and by sending over continually ships and troops, this will of course produce a civil war, weaken Britain by leaving her coasts defenceless, and impoverish America,—so that we need not fear anything from that quarter. Then, the united fleets of France and Spain, with troops, to appear in the channel and make a descent, while my kinsman, with thirty thousand men, lands in Scotland, marches to London, and joins the others. What, then, can prevent the scheme from having the wished-for effect? This is the main point,—which keep to yourself."[1]

In the subsequent Scenes of the First Act, we are permitted to watch the several moves of the game which Bute has undertaken to play, and which reaches an important stage in the closing Scene. Here we are witnesses of a meeting of the privy council, at which Judas of Massachusetts is present by special invitation. With much apparent

[1] "The Fall," etc., 4–5.

indignation, Lord Paramount lays before the Council the series of seditious acts perpetrated by the Americans in opposition to royal authority, and demands that vigorous measures be taken to put down such insolent proceedings,—a proposition which is loudly echoed, as a matter of course, by his creatures—Mocklaw, Brazen, and Poltroon. "My advice," says the latter, "is that Lord Boston and Admiral Tombstone be immediately sent to Boston, with two or three regiments,—though one would be more than sufficient,—and a few ships to shut up their ports. Disannul their charters, stop their trade; and the pusilanimous beggars,—those rascals, whose predominant passion is fear,—would immediately give up, on the first landing of the regulars, and fly before 'em like a hare before the hounds. That this would be the case, I pawn my honor to your Lordships; nay, I 'll sacrifice my life."[1] This proposition is adopted. The troops and the warships are ordered off to America; and with this ample and admirable preparation of national disaster, the First Act ends.

The Second Act presents, in one Scene, a vigorous debate in the house of lords on the American question, with speeches by Lord Wisdom, Lord Religion, and Lord Justice—all strongly against the harsh and harmful measures of the ministry; and, in another Scene, a lively conversation on the same subject between Lord Patriot, the Bold Irishman, and the Colonel. The Third Act carries the action across the Atlantic, where the logical results of Lord Bute's policy begin to shew themselves. Here we have, in one Scene, the city of Boston just after the application to it of the port bill in 1774, and the call of the first Continental Congress; in another, a preacher making announcement that their charter had been taken away, themselves proclaimed rebels, and their property doomed to confiscation; in another, the excitement and confusion in the streets of Boston on the arrival of Lord Boston with his troops and

[1] "The Fall," etc., 12.

ships; in another, Lord Boston himself, on the 19th of April, 1775, surrounded by his guards, and awaiting in great complacency the victorious return of the expedition sent out by him toward Lexington and Concord under Colonel Smith the night before. "If Colonel Smith succeeds in his embassy," says Lord Boston, musingly, "and I think there 's no doubt of it, I shall have the pleasure this evening, I expect, of having my friends Hancock and Adams's good company. I 'll make each of them a present of a pair of handsome iron ruffles, and Major Provost shall provide a suitable entertainment for them in his apartment." "Sure," says an officer in reply, "they 'll not be so unpolite as to refuse your excellency's kind invitation." Lord Boston rejoins in his bland and merry way,—"Should they, Colonel Smith and Major Pitcairn have my orders to make use of all their rhetoric, and the persuasive eloquence of British thunder."[1] And while the smiles which applaud this witticism are still playing over the faces of the guards, in rushes a messenger in hot haste with news that the troops are in full retreat before the rebels. A touch of comedy is given by the Scene in which two shepherds near Lexington, Dick and Roger, talk over in bucolic language the rout and flight of the regulars; while the pathos of all this ghastly business transacted for the political accommodation of Lord Bute, comes out in the last Scene, wherein an American matron grieves over the loss of her husband, son and brother, all slain in Bunker Hill fight, which is then graphically described by a neighbor who witnessed it.

The earlier portion of the Fourth Act is laid in Virginia, and exhibits in realistic fashion the ravages of Lord Dunmore along that coast,—his alleged rapacity, cruelty, and shameless lust. After six Scenes devoted to Dunmore, the action returns to Boston, immediately after the battle of Bunker Hill. Then follows one of the most effective passages of the play—a council of war at which the chief offi-

---

[1] "The Fall," etc., 27–28.

cers of the army, Lord Boston, Elbow Room, Caper, Percy, and Clinton, appear to be grotesquely terrified and even paralyzed by the unexpected military capacity of the rebels, while Admiral Tombstone, bursting with a truly marine contempt for his military associates, these cowardly and baffled lubbers of the land, utters his opinion of them in frequent jets of extremely nautical phraseology. "I fully expected," maunders Lord Boston, "with the help of the last re-enforcement you brought me over, and the advice and assistance of three accomplished and experienced generals, I should have been able to have subdued the rebels, and gained immortal laurels to myself,—to have returned to Old England like a Roman consul, with a score or two of the rebel generals, colonels, and majors to have graced my triumph." Upon this slur, the conversation is taken up by Elbow Room, Percy, Clinton, and Caper, and soon becomes a bedlam of angry recrimination between them,—whereupon the bluff Admiral breaks in:—"Damn it, don't let us kick up a dust among ourselves, to be laughed at fore and aft. This is a hell of a council of war,—though I believe it will turn out one before we 've done."

Clinton: Pray, gentlemen, drop this discourse. Consider, the honor of England is at stake, and our safety depends upon this day's consultation. . . .

Lord Boston: Well, gentlemen, what are we met here for?

Admiral Tombstone: Who the devil should know, if you don't? Damn it, did n't you send for us?

Lord Boston: Our late great loss of men has tore up the foundation of our plan, and rendered all further attempts impracticable. 'T will be a long time ere we can expect any more re-enforcements; and if they should arrive, I 'm doubtful of their success.

Clinton: The provincials are vastly strong, and seem no novices in the art of war. 'T is true, we gained the hill at last, but of what advantage is it to us? None. The loss of fourteen hundred as brave men as Britain can boast of, is a melancholy consideration, and must make our most sanguinary friends in England abate of their vigor.

Elbow Room: I never saw or read of any battle equal to it. Never was more martial courage displayed; and the provincials—to do the dogs justice—fought like heroes; fought, indeed, more like devils than men. Such carnage and destruction not exceeded by Blenheim, Minden, Fontenoy, Ramilies, Dettingen, the Battle of the Boyne; and the late affair of the Spaniards and Algerines a mere cock fight to it! No laurels there!

Mr. Caper: No, nor triumphs neither. I regret in particular the number of brave officers that fell that day, many of whom were of the first families in England.

Admiral Tombstone: Aye, a damned affair, indeed! Many powdered beaux—petit maitres—fops—fribbles—skip jackets—macaronies—jack puddings—noblemen's bastards and whores' sons fell that day; and my poor marines stood no more chance with 'em than a cat in hell without claws.

Lord Boston: It can't be helped, Admiral. What is to be done next?

Admiral Tombstone: Done?—why, what the devil have you done? Nothing yet, but eat Paramount's beef, and steal a few Yankee sheep; and that, it seems, is now become a damned lousy beggarly trade, too; for you have n't left yourselves a mouthful to eat.

(Aside.) 'Bold at the council board
But cautious in the field, he shunned the sword.'

Lord Boston: But what can we do, Admiral?

Admiral Tombstone: Do? Why, suck your paws;—that 's all you 're like to get."[1]

For the last Act, one Scene presents to us the American forces at the capture of Montreal; another, Ethan Allen groping about in a British dungeon, and stormily execrating his keepers, who have entered to lay him in irons; another,

[1] "The Fall," etc. 51–54.

the American army at Cambridge; and still another, Washington's grief over the news of the death of General Montgomery, and the solemn act wherein he and his generals renew their vows of devotion to the American cause, even unto death. Finally, the real purpose of the play is brought out in a pithy epilogue, with its telling allusion to a political pamphlet, the title of which was just then resounding through the land:

> "Are we not men? Pray, who made men, but God?
> Yet men made kings—to tremble at their nod!
> What nonsense this! let 's wrong with right oppose,
> Since naught will do but sound, impartial blows.
> Let 's act in earnest, not with vain pretense;
> Adopt the language of sound COMMON SENSE,
> And with one voice proclaim—INDEPENDENCE!"[1]

VII.

During the winter of 1775 and 1776, while the British army lay shut up in the town of Boston, their officers made efforts to drive dull care away, in part, by giving theatrical performances in Faneuil Hall; and for such an entertainment, General Burgoyne, already well-known as a dramatic writer, supplied a farce ironically called "The Blockade," and intended to make light of the valor of the rebel soldiers, and of the gravity of their own situation. Shortly after their departure from the town, in March, 1776, was published there a retort in the form of a farce in three Acts, with a title that is itself a slant upon that of the play of which it is itself a mirthful reverberation. It is called "The Blockheads, or, The Affrighted Officers,"[2] and is a bit of rough fun-making which must have been greatly relished at the time, when played, as it probably was, by some of the vic-

[1] "The Fall," etc. 66.

[2] This farce is attributed to Mercy Warren, by P. L. Ford. "Beginnings of American Dramatic Literature," 16–19.

torious American soldiers for the diversion of their own comrades. The time of the play is that memorable morning on which Washington was discovered with his extemporized intrenchments on Dorchester Heights, and ready to sweep with his guns the town and the shipping. Doubtless, for many a day after the presentation of this piece, the quarters occupied by the American troops in Boston and the neighborhood rang with their shouts of merriment over the numerous and by no means delicate hits herein given at the political and military aspects of the situation,—more especially at the alleged cowardice, stupidity, and profligacy of the British soldiers, at their ridiculous sufferings from hunger during the long siege, and, finally, at the disgust and dismay of the Amercan Loyalists in Boston upon learning that their invincible protectors were about to flee for their lives.

VIII.

One proof of the effectiveness of Whig satire on the Loyalists, as contained in "The Fall of British Tyranny," is to be met with in a Loyalist retort in kind, which appears to have been written just after the American defeat on Long Island, the 27th of August, 1776, and is entitled "The Battle of Brooklyn, a Farce." The intention of this performance is to retaliate upon the rebel cause, by holding up to derision the contemptible character of its chief leaders—they being, in most cases, bar-tenders, horse-jockeys, blacklegs, ploughmen, and cobblers, transformed into colonels and generals; actuated by groveling motives; wielding their military authority in the spirit of pick-pockets and common swindlers; of low, obscene, and profligate lives. The satirical method of the play is fairly revealed in its "dramatis personæ," these being divided into two groups, contemptuously designated as "Men" and as "Women." The former are headed by four "Rebel Chiefs"—Washington, Putnam, Sullivan, and Stirling.. These are followed by three "Colonels," to wit, "Lasher, a shoemaker of New York; Clark, a retailer of rum in Connecticut; Remsen, a farmer of Newtown, Long Island." These several dignitaries are ministered to in various capacities by "Ebenezer Snuffle, a New England parson, Chaplain to General Putnam; Joe King, servant to Sterling; Noah, servant to Sullivan; Skinner, a thief employed by Putnam."

The list of "Women" includes but two names,—"Lady Gates" and "Betty, her servant"; and the interchanges of confidence as here reported between these two women are extremely candid examples of retail traffic in the grosser scandals of the period as affecting Washington and other American leaders both military and civil. In the development of this farce, Lord Sterling is set before us as a mere pretender whose natural stupidity is quite needlessly enhanced by perpetual drunkenness. General Putnam, on the other hand, appears as a patriotic and clever scoundrel who has taken up arms for his country mainly on account of the facilities he thereby gets for petty plundering, and who is here represented as calling to sharp account one of his officers, Lieutenant Skinner, because the latter had failed to share with his chief the watches, rings and other valuables filched from the houses to which Putnam had sent him for the purpose. The military incompetence of the rebel officers and the almost universal cowardice of their men are exhibited in the immense object-lesson furnished by their defeat on Long Island and their hurried flight across the North River. In all this lavish distribution of infamy, it is perhaps possible to detect some slight forbearance toward Washington, to whom is attributed a certain superiority to the men whom he leads—a superiority, however, not extending to such particulars as low lust and political hypocrisy. The whole production is unutterably coarse—mere provender for bovine and porcine appetites—a triumphant exhibition of vigor in the flinging back of filth at the enemy—in these respects, therefore, an authentic memorial of the very spirit and procedure of the time.

IX.

The dramatic writings thus far noticed, must continue to have an interest for us, not only as illustrating the beginnings of this species of literature in America, but likewise as embodying in authentic form the thoughts and passions which warred fiercely in the minds of the American people during their Revolutionary conflict. The literary defects of these writings need not be dwelt upon, —they are obvious. It is in spite of their literary defects, —their crudity, dullness, coarseness, provincialism,—that they are worth the moment's glance which we here give to them; for they are vestiges of one entire stage of our literary development as a people, and are frank witnesses to the throes of mental and moral anguish through which we had to pass in order to become a nation. But we now approach two examples of dramatic writing having a literary merit so positive and so remarkable as to justify our study of them even on that account alone.

Hugh Henry Brackenridge demands and deserves our notice on account of two dramatic poems produced by him soon after the opening of the physical conflict of the Revolution, and having in themselves a striking distinctness of method and of purpose. Like every other writer of this period, he seems to have been deeply stirred by the significance of the military events of the first year of that conflict—the year 1775—their pathos, their tragic horror, and their prodigious messages both of warning and of good-cheer. From all these events he selects two, each as the subject of a serious dramatic poem,—the one being the first real clash between American and Briton as displayed on the seventeenth of June, upon a height in full view from Boston; the other being the death of the high-minded American leader, General Montgomery, in his baffled attempt at the capture of Quebec. Both of these dramas are wrought out with strict attention to the classic unities of time, place, and action; and both are intended merely as dramatic poems to be read, not at all as plays to be acted.

The chief purpose of the earlier poem—" The Battle of Bunker's Hill"—published in 1776, was one exactly fitted to the need of the hour in which it sprang into life: it was to inspire Americans with military confidence by setting forth, in opposition to the old taunts of cowardice and incapacity, the remarkable fighting qualities—the almost unrivaled military effectiveness—exhibited by their brethren in that battle. This is the controlling idea of the poem; and while it is indicated from the very beginning of the action, the full development of it is delayed till near the end, when it is accomplished with striking effect in the form of spontaneous admissions from the lips of the victorious British officers then commenting on the battle they had just won at so great a cost. Finally, the lesson of military confidence which the poem is meant to teach, has an added impressiveness from the fact that the poet, while recognizing the physical conditions on which military success depends, gives great prominence, also, to the moral conditions of such success. Thus, the object for which a man fights, is sure to tell on his success in fighting. Certainly, the justice or the injustice of one's cause must count for something. There is a power in the world which makes for the victory of righteousness—even upon a battle-field. And it is to this higher sphere of prediction, even with reference to the ultimate result of the physical struggle in which they were then engaged, that the poet seeks to raise his fellow-countrymen, as he develops in this drama the immense moral contrast between the objects of the two opposing armies,—the implication being that the moral superiority of the American cause must be taken into the account as some offset to its inferiority in physical force.

On the evening of a certain day in June, 1775, two military councils are held: the one in Cambridge, by three high officers of the American army—Putnam, Warren, and Gardiner; the other only a few miles away, in Boston, by the

British commander, Gage, and his two generals, Howe and Burgoyne. The result of the former council is a forward movement of a portion of the American army, that very night, to the heights of Bunker Hill, in the hope of drawing out the enemy from their shelter within the city. The result of the latter council is an order reluctantly given by Gage at the demand of his two generals, for an advance of a portion of the British army the very next morning against the rebel force supposed to be still lying inactive in Cambridge. Of course, by the dawn of day, the British discover that the rebels have already come more than half way to meet them,—a fact which is thus hurriedly announced by Burgoyne to the commanding General:

"The rebel foe, grown yet more insolent
By that small loss or rout at Lexington,
Prevent our purpose; and the night by-past
Have pushed intrenchments and some flimsy works,
With rude achievement, on the rocky brow
Of that tall hill. A ship-boy, with the day,
From the tall mast-head of the admiral,
Descried their aim, and gave the swift alarm.
Our glasses mark but one small regiment there;
Yet every hour we languish in delay
Inspires fresh hope, and fills their pigmy souls
With thoughts of holding it. You hear the sound
Of spades and pick-axes upon the hill,
Incessant, pounding like old Vulcan's forge
Urged by the Cyclops." [1]

These words of Burgoyne are scarcely spoken, when General Howe rushes upon the scene, exclaiming:

"To your alarm posts, officers! Come, gallant souls,
Let 's out, and drive them from that eminence
On which the foe doth earth himself.
I relish not such haughty neighborhood.
Give orders swiftly to the admiral,

---

[1] "The Battle," etc. 18–19.

That some stout ship heave up the narrow bay,
And pour indignant from the full-tide wave
Fierce cannonade, across the isthmus point,
That no assistance may be brought to them.
If but seven hundred, we can treat with them—
Yes, strew the hill with death and carcasses,
And offer up this band a hecatomb
To Britain's glory, and the cause of kings."[1]

As they hasten from the place, poor Gage, who is the one ludicrous character in the poem, being portrayed as an indolent and cowardly voluptuary, is left alone, maundering to himself of his guilt and fear:

"May Heaven protect us from their rage, I say.
When but a boy, I dreamed of Death in bed;
And ever since that time, I hated things
Which put him, like a pair of spectacles,
Before my eyes. The thought lies deep in fate,
Nor can a mortal see the bottom of it.
'T is here—'t is there—I could philosophize—
Eternity, is like a winding sheet—
The seven Commandments like—I think there 's seven.
. . . .
Oh Bute and Dartmouth, knew ye what I feel,
You sure would pity an old drinking-man
That has more heart-ache than philosophy!"[2]

By this time, General Howe has conducted a division of the army across the bay which separates them from that steep hill on which the enemy have taken position; and pausing at the shore, he prepares their minds for a task that is likely to prove a costly one:

"Behold yon hill, where fell Rebellion rears
Her snake-streamed ensign, and would seem to brave,
With scarce seven hundred, this sea-bounded camp,

[1] "The Battle," etc. 19.
[2] Ibid. 20.

Where may be counted full ten thousand men
That in the war with France so late acquired
Loud fame, and shook the other continent.
Come on, brave soldiers, seize your gleaming arms,
And let this day in after times be held
As Minden famous, and each hostile field
Where British valor shone victorious.
The time moves slow which enviously detains
Our just resentment from these traitors' heads.
Their richest farms and cultured settlements,
By winding river or extensive bay,
Shall be your just reward. Our noble king,
As things confiscate, holds their property,
And in rich measure will bestow on you
Who face the frowns and labor of this day.
He that outlives this battle, shall ascend
In titled honor to the height of state;
Dukedoms and baronies, midst these our foes
In tributary vassalage kept down,
Shall be your fair inheritance. Come on,
Beat up the heroic sound of war! The word
Is—'George our sovereign, and Britannia's arms.'"[1]

Meanwhile, from behind their intrenchments on the hill-top, the Americans can see the British upon the opposite shore, mustering for the attack. Warren first addresses the little band, trying to lift them by his words to the height of any sacrifice, and saying, as he closes,

"The word is 'Liberty'—
And Heaven smile on us in so just a cause!"[2]

Thereupon, Colonel Gardiner, as he leads his men to the engagement, says to them:

"Fear not, brave soldiers, though their infantry,
In deep array, so far out-number us.
The justness of our cause will brace each arm,

---

[1] "The Battle," etc. 21–22. [2] Ibid. 24.

And steel the soul with fortitude; while they,
Whose guilt hangs trembling on their consciences,
Must fail in battle, and receive that death
Which, in high vengeance, we prepare for them.
Let, then, each spirit, to the height wound up,
Shew noble vigor and full force this day.
For, on the merit of our swords is placed
The virgin honor and true character
Of this whole continent ; and one short hour
May give complexion to the whole event,
Fixing the judgment whether as base slaves
We serve these masters, or more nobly live—
Free as the breeze that on the hill-top plays,
With these sweet fields and tenements our own.
Oh fellow soldiers, let this battle speak
Dire disappointment to the insulting foe,
Who claim our fair possessions, and set down
These cultured farms and bowery hills and plains
As the rich prize of certain victory.
Shall we, the sons of Massachusetts-Bay,
New Hampshire and Connecticut, shall we
Fall back, dishonored, from our native plains,
Mix with the savages, and roam for food
On western mountains, or the desert shores
Of Canada's cold lakes ? or, state more vile,
Sit down in humble vassalage, content
To till the ground for these proud conquerors ?" [1]

Thus, to the end of the poem, the scene shifts in quick succession from one side of the fight to the other; and at every stage of its progress comes out in deeper colors the contrast in moral significance between the objects of the two armies. This effect reaches its culmination in a noble scene wherein the very defeat of the Americans is consecrated by the blood of their chieftain, Warren. This leader—a hero of the antique mold, one of Plutarch's men—having received his death wound, falls upon his right knee, and " covering his

[1] "The Battle," etc. 25–26.

breast with his right hand, and supporting himself with his firelock in his left,'' spends his fast-ebbing strength in this appeal to his comrades:

> "By the last parting breath
> And blood of this your fellow soldier slain,
> Be now adjured never to yield the right,—
> The grand deposit of all-giving Heaven
> To man's free nature,—that he rules himself!
> With these rude Britons wage life-scorning war,
> Till they admit it, and like hell fall off,
> With ebbing billows, from this troubled coast,
> Where, but for them, firm concord and true love
> Should individual hold their court and reign.
> The infernal enginery of state resist
> To death, that unborn times may be secure;
> And while men flourish in the peace you win,
> Write each fair name with worthies of the earth.
> . . . .
> Weep not for him who first espoused the cause,
> And risking life, hath met the enemy
> In fatal opposition—but rejoice!
> For now I go to mingle with the dead,—
> Great Brutus, Hampden, Sidney, and the rest,
> Of old or modern memory, who lived
> A mound to tyrants, and strong hedge to kings,
> Bounding the inundation of their rage
> Against the happiness and peace of man."

Then, as the film thickens over his eyes, more distinct becomes the vision of that overarching sphere to which he sees himself beckoned by hands that cannot receive the indignity of death:

> "I see these heroes where they walk serene,
> By crystal currents, on the vale of Heaven,
> High in full converse of immortal acts
> Achieved for truth and innocence on earth.
> Meantime the harmony and thrilling sound

Of mellow lutes, sweet viols, and guitars
Dwell on the soul, and ravish every nerve.
Anon the murmur of the tight-braced drum,
With finely varied fifes to martial airs,
Winds up the spirit to the mighty proof
Of siege and battle, and attempt in arms.
Illustrious group! They beckon me along,
To ray my visage with immortal light,
And bind the amaranth around my brow.
I come, I come, ye first-born of true fame
Fight on, my countrymen, be free, be free!" [1]

At last, therefore, having thrice repulsed the enemy, driving them thrice with almost unexampled slaughter down the hill, the little army of the rebels "overpowered by numbers are obliged to retreat;" whereupon, amid the huzzas of victory, the British leaders concede and emphasize the military significance of these displays of prowess and of soldierlike efficiency on the part of men till that day set down for cowards. Thus, Richardson, a young British officer, on the parapet, exclaims,

"The day is ours, huzza, the day is ours;
This last attack has forced them to retreat.

CLINTON.

'T is true, full victory declares for us,
But we have dearly, dearly purchased it.
Full fifteen hundred of our men lie dead,
Who, with their officers, do swell the list
Of this day's carnage. On the well-fought hill,
Whole ranks cut down lie struggling with their wounds,
Or close their bright eyes in the shades of night.
No wonder! such incessant musketry
And fire of cannon, from the hill-top poured,
Seemed not the agency of mortal men,
But heaven itself with snares and vengeance armed

[1] "The Battle," etc. 28–29.

T' oppose our gaining it. E'en when was spent
Their ammunition, and fierce Warren slain,
Huge stones were hurlëd from the rocky brow,
And war renewed by these inveterate,
Till Gard'ner wounded, the left wing gave way,
And with their shattered infantry, the whole,
Drawn off by Putnam, to the causeway fled;
When from the ships and batt'ries on the wave
They met deep loss, and strewed the narrow bridge
With lifeless carcasses. . . .

LORD PIGOT.

The day is ours, but with heart-piercing loss
Of soldiers slain and gallant officers.

. . . .

Should every hill, by the rebellious foe
So well defended, cost thus dear to us,
Not the united forces of the world
Could master them, and the proud rage subdue
Of these AMERICANS.

HOWE.

E'en in an enemy I honor worth
And valor eminent. The vanquished foe
In feats of prowess shew their ancestry,
And speak their birth legitimate,—
The sons of Britons, with the genuine flame
Of British heat and valor in their veins." [1]

X.

The second of the two dramatic poems of Brackenridge, "The Death of General Montgomery, at the Siege of Quebec," was published in 1777. Its chief purpose was to stimulate American military ardor by stimulating American hatred of the enemy; and this it sought to accomplish through a presentation of their detestable character, espe-

[1] "The Battle," etc. 33-35.

cially their sordidness, perfidy, and cruelty. Thus, in the two poems, the argument is made complete: first, that we have the ability to fight the British; and, secondly, that we have every possible motive for fighting them—since they are monsters of greed, treachery, and inhumanity.

The entire action of this tragedy takes place in the hours between midnight and dawn of the last day of the year 1775,—the time which was actually fixed by General Montgomery for his attempt to capture by escalade that stout city which he had tried in vain, during the previous four weeks, to capture by siege. In the first Scene, is given a view of the American camp before Quebec, in the deep silence of a long December night, with Montgomery and Benedict Arnold holding conference together,—a conference of which the first words that reach us are these, as spoken by Montgomery:

"The third hour turning from the midnight watch,
By no ray visited of moon or star,
Marks to our enterprise its proper date.
Now from above, on every hill and copse,
The airy element descends in snow,
And with the dark winds from the howling North,
Commixed and driven on the bounded sight,
Gives tumult privacy, and shrouds the march;
So that our troops, in reg'ment or brigade,
May undistinguished to the very walls
Move up secure, and scale the battlements,—
May force the barred gates of this lofty town,
On all sides bound with artificial rock,
Of cloud-capped eminence impregnable—
Impregnable so long, and fully proof
To all our battery and sharp cannonade;
But yet, assailed with vigor and full force,
This morn, I trust, we enter it in storm,
And from its bosom long defiled, pluck
This scorpion progeny, this mixëd brood
Of wild-wood savages and Englishmen
Who 'gainst their brethren, in unrighteous cause,

With cruel perfidy have wagëd war.
Against their brethren, did I say? O God!
Are we the offspring of that cruel foe
Who late at Montreal, with symbol dire,
Did call the savages to taste of blood,
Life-warm and streaming from the bullock slain,
And with fell language—told it was the blood
Of a Bostonian—made the sacrament?
At this the hell-hounds, with infernal gust,
To the snuffed wind held up their blood-stained mouths,
And filled with howlings the adjacent hills." [1]

With such vigor, with such unhesitant tones of abhorrence, does the poet give us the key-note of this drama. Presently, Montgomery communicates to Arnold the details of his plan for the assault upon the city, which was to be made simultaneously at three different points; whereupon Arnold takes his exit in order to prepare for the part assigned to him. Then follow two or three Scenes of great tenderness and nobility, in which the poet contrives to exhibit, in sharp opposition to the execrable and loathsome qualities attributed to the enemy, the fine and high traits of the American leaders in this daring enterprise,—their superiority to sordid motives, their pure love of country and of fame, their kinship with the great military heroes of England's past, and above all their sensibility in that particular spot to all that is lofty, radiant, and inspiring in the memory of Wolfe. Two of Montgomery's staff are Macpherson and Chessman—young fellows noted in their day for great personal attractiveness, and especially for chivalry of character. Of Macpherson the General is particularly fond; and it is to him, in that deep stillness before the crash and agony of battle, that the elder man now reveals his own prescience of the near fate which then awaited them both, as well as the ideals of glory in pursuit of which they could meet that fate with serenity:

---

[1] "The Death," etc. 9–10.

" It seems to me, Macpherson, that we tread
The ground of some romantic fairy land,
Where knights in armor, and high combatants
Have met in war. This is the plain where Wolfe,
Victorious Wolfe, fought with the brave Montcalm;
And even yet, the dreary snow-clad tomb
Of many a hero, slaughtered on that day,
Recalls the memory of the bloody strife.
I believe not superstition, or the dreams
Of high-wrought fantasy that fill the brain,
But yet methinks, Macpherson, that I feel
Within this hour some knowledge of my end,—
Some sure presentiment that you and I,
This day, shall be with them, shall leave
Our breathless bodies on this mortal soil.
But this allotment, should it be our case,
Fear not, young soldier, for our cause is just ;
And all those failings we are conscious of,
Shall in the bosom of our God repose,
Who looks with mercy on the sons of men,
And hides their imperfections with his love.
Say not, young soldier, that thy life was short—
In the first bloom of manhood swift cut off.
All things are mortal—but the warrior's fame ;
This lives eternal in the mouths of men.

MACPHERSON.

The light is sweet, and death is terrible ;
But when I left my father and my friends,
I thought of this, and counted it but gain,
If fighting bravely in my country's cause,
I tasted death, and met an equal fame
With those at Lexington, and Bunker's Hill.

MONTGOMERY.

Sweet fame, young hero, shall attend thy years ;
And linked in friendship, as we are linked in death,
Our souls shall mount, and visit those fair hills

Where never-dying bards and heroes stray.
There Wolfe shall hail us, and the great Montcalm
Shall bind the amaranth around our brows;
For mighty warriors, though opposëd here,
There live serene, in heavenly amity,
And walk and taste of conference sublime.
Go, then, young soldier, and these orders bear
To Colonel Campbell, and to Livingston.
The disposition for the attack is here.
Bid them be ready, when the morning breaks,
To try this city by an escalade." [1]

In the progress of the drama, the chief incidents of the attack on Quebec are indicated; Montgomery, Chessman, and Macpherson are slain; heroic valor in the fight is shown by Arnold, Burr, Oswald, Morgan, Lamb, and the rest of the American warriors; the ghost of General Montgomery appears upon the field of his glorious death, pronouncing woe upon the king and parliament, and predicting final victory for the Americans and the birth of a great, free empire in the new world; and at last, Carleton, the British general, comes upon the "wall of the Upper Town, exposing the body of Montgomery," and calling upon the Americans to surrender under promise of honorable and generous treatment. Upon these terms, they lay down their arms; whereupon Carleton, violating his promise, turns upon them with these fiendish words:

"Now, in my power, disarmëd and reduced,
I will give scope, and scorn you with my tongue.
You vile rebellious progeny of wrath,
Fierce and malignant in Don Quixotism
Of moon-mad liberty! You bedlam-brood,
You viper-lipped and serpent-hearted race,
Bred on the poison of foul fraud and hate,
Scum and offscouring of humanity,
Whom laws of government to the sure cord

---

[1] "The Death," etc. 14–16.

Have ever destinëd ! And were it not
That the black vengeance of your countrymen
Might dare retaliate, and gibbet up
Some British prisoner, each soul should hang,
And die this day, in execrable form,
The death of traitors. Yet, whatever shape
Of suffering horrible can be devised,
In dreary dungeon, and in obscure jail,
Cold, dark, and comfortless, and lacking bread,
Shall be your lot, snake-venomed parricides.
And first, three victims from your shattered band
Must to the savages be given up,—
Some three Bostonians sacrificed and slain,
To glut the appetites of Indian chiefs
Who at our cantico at Montreal,
Drank of the ox-blood, roasting his large limbs,
Symbolical of rebels burnt with fire.
Take these three men, ye Indian warriors,
And use them wantonly, with every pain
Which flame's fierce element can exercise ;
And with the sound of each loud instrument,
The drum, the horn, in wildest symphony
With your own howlings, shall the scene be graced,
Save that in terror oftentimes awhile
The noise shall cease, and their own cries be heard." [1]

---

[1] In the original publication of this tragedy, there is a footnote by the author referring to these and other words attributed to General Carleton : " Want of candor is very blameable, even in the account given of an enemy. For this reason I have been sometimes uneasy lest these words put into the mouth of General Carleton, should seem to give a coloring to his character beyond the real complexion of his Excellency's conduct. But I find my conscience pretty much at ease in this matter, when I give my memory time to recollect the inhumanity of the officers and soldiers under his command to our prisoners, from the moment our affairs began to be on the decline in Canada. . . . I have conversed with those who saws the scalps warm from the heads of our countrymen. I have had the relation from their mouths who beheld the fires lighted up, and heard, with a soul-paining sympathy, the horrid shrieks and gloomy howlings of the savage tribes in the execution of the poor captives who, according to the threat of Carleton, were burned on an island in the river St. Lawrence after our unfortunate surrender at the Cedars." P. 51.

Of course, the captives remind Carleton of his promise, and appeal to him to be just to them, even if not merciful; but he hardens his heart against them, reiterates his orders, and increases his threats of further vengeance. In view of all this, the gallant Virginian officer, Morgan, speaks these words, which form a fitting close to the poem:

> "Sad thought of cruelty and outrage dire!
> Not to be paralleled 'mongst human kind,
> Save in the tales of flesh-devouring men,
> The one-eyed Cyclops, and fierce Cannibal.
> For what we hear of Saracen or Turk,
> Mogul, or Tartar of Siberia,
> Is far behind the deed of infamy
> And horror mixed, which Britons meditate.
> Nature herself, degenerate from the fall,
> In the cursed earth can scarcely furnish out
> So much black poison from the beasts and herbs,
> As swells the dark hearts of these Royalists.
> The toad's foul mouth, the snake's envenomed bite,
> Black spider, asp, or froth of rabid dog
> Is not so deadly as these murderers.
> When men far off, in civilizëd states,
> Shall know the perfidy and breach of faith,
> The thought remorseless and dire act of these,
> In every language they shall execrate
> The earth-disgracing name of Englishmen;
> And at the Last Day, when the Pit receives
> Her gloomy brood, and seen among the rest
> Some spirit distinguishëd by ampler swell
> Of malice, envy, and soul-griping hate,
> Pointing to him, the foul and ugly ghosts
> Of hell shall say—'That was an Englishman.'" [1]

---

[1] "The Death," etc. 48–53.

XI.

In 1778 Addison's "Tragedy of Cato" was played at the Bow Street Theatre, Portsmouth, New Hampshire. An epilogue for the play was written by Jonathan Mitchell Sewall, which shews how even quite disinterested theatrical representations then responded to the military themes that were then universal. This epilogue is a parallel between Rome in the time of Cato, and America in the time of its Revolutionary struggle; and its concluding lines have never yet been forgotten among us:

> "Rise, then, my countrymen! for fight prepare,
> Gird on your swords, and fearless rush to war!
> For your grieved country nobly dare to die,
> And empty all your veins for liberty.
> No pent-up Utica contracts your powers,
> But the whole boundless continent is yours!" [1]

XII.

"The Motley Assembly: a Farce, published for the Entertainment of the Curious," in Boston, in 1779, is but a slight affair in itself, but of no little significance to us now as an American satire upon certain Americans in high life whose patriotism had then grown cool under the shade of misfortune to the American cause. It is particularly aimed at the upper circles of society in Boston, where it seems then to have become fashionable to sneer at the Revolutionary cause, to speak patronizingly of Washington, to denounce the French allies as both inefficient and perfidious, and to indulge in pensive regrets for the good old days of the British occupation, when Boston society was made gorgeous by the presence of innumerable British officers. Into such a company of high-bred Bostonians, where

[1] "Occasional Addresses." Edited by Laurence Hutton and William Carey. New York, 1890.

"Whigs and Tories, joined by wayward chance,
Should hand in hand lead on the sprightly dance,"[1]

comes one day "Captain Aid," a gallant young officer of the Revolutionary army. He accepts a glass of wine; and having drunk to the health of the ladies, and of "Mr. Runt," the only person of his own sex whom he finds there, he very properly proposes the health of "his most Christian Majesty, and godlike, glorious Washington." To this toast, Mrs. Flourish, the hostess, responds with an almost inaudible assent; whereupon the excellent little "Mr. Runt" speaks up:

"With all my heart, Captain. I really take that Washington to be a very clever fellow.

Aid: Let us be silent on that subject, Mr. Runt—we have neither time nor talents to do it justice.

Mrs. Flourish: Why, he is no more than man, Captain Aid.

Aid: Then all mankind beside are less, madam.

Mrs. Flourish: You have not seen all mankind, sir. I believe Mr. Washington, or General Washington, if you please, is a very honest, good kind of a man, and has taken infinite pains to keep your army together, and I wish he may find his account in it. But doubtless there are his equals—so say no more.

Aid: If you meant that as a compliment, madam, it is really so cold a one, that it has made me shiver. I will, therefore, with your leave, drop the subject, and take another glass of wine.

Runt: Ay, ay, that 's right, Captain—I think there are more fit subjects for a young gentleman's contemplation in this room.

Aid: Still gallant, Mr. Runt. But the ladies must pardon me if I cannot readily assent to the justice of your rebuke, when I assure them that such charms as theirs would justify my inattention to any other subject but what concerns my general or my country.

---

[1] "The Motley Assembly," 15. These lines are a part of the epilogue.

Miss Taxall: I believe we are all very ready to pardon your inattention to us at all times.

Aid: Curse your impudence. [Aside.] Knowing my inclination and particular attention to please and oblige the ladies, you say what you please without the hazard of offending. And—as you seem disposed at this time to be merry at my expense—I am extremely sorry to deprive you of the opportunity by being obliged to leave you. [Exit Aid.]" [1]

XIII.

Our record of the dramatic writings produced here during the Revolutionary time, comes to a rather inglorious end in a piece of crudity which, for its title, repeats one already made use of: "The Blockheads, or, Fortunate Contractor. An Opera, in Two Acts, as it was performed at New York. The music entirely new, composed by several of the most eminent masters in Europe." Printed in London in 1782,[2] it professes to be a reprint of an edition already issued in New York. It embodies in light, colloquial form, and with some amusing parts in dialect—as between a Frenchman and a Dutchman—those satirical views of the French alliance which were then sincerely cherished by the Loyalists in New York and elsewhere.

[1] "The Motley Assembly," 9–10. That this play was by Mercy Warren, is the not improbable suggestion of P. L. Ford. "Beginnings of American Dramatic Literature," 24.

[2] A copy of this rare tract is in the Lenox Library. I do not know that any one has yet come across a copy of the earlier New York edition, which, after all, may have been a myth.

CHAPTER XXXIII.

PRISON LITERATURE.

I.—Special interest attaching to narratives of American prisoners of war in the hands of the British—Ethan Allen—His complex character, and his achievements with sword and tongue—A prisoner of war from 1775 to 1778—"A Narrative of Colonel Ethan Allen's Captivity"—Its quality as a book—Reasons for the severities bestowed upon him—His experience with General Prescott in Canada—His voyage to England—His treatment there—The astonishment excited by him among the natives of that isle—His compulsory voyages on various British vessels—At Cape Fear, Halifax, New York—On parole in New York—His sight of the sufferings of American prisoners there.

II.—"A Narrative of the Capitivity and Treatment of John Dodge by the English at Detroit," 1779.

III.—The bad preëminence of the British prison-ships in New York harbor—"The Old Jersey Captive, or, a Narrative of the Captivity of Thomas Andros on board the Old Jersey Prison-Ship," 1781—The career of Andros from the outbreak of hostilities till 1781—His capture—His descriptions of the "Old Jersey," and of the ways of life and death thereon.

IV.—"A Narrative of the Capture of Henry Laurens, and of His Confinement in the Tower of London"—The high character of Laurens—His career as merchant and statesman—President of Congress—Sails as American commissioner to Holland in 1780—His capture at sea—His imprisonment in the Tower from 1780 to 1782—The charm of his story of this experience.

I.

PERHAPS no aspect of the Revolutionary war has touched more powerfully the imagination and sympathy of the American people, than that relating to the sufferings borne by their own sailors and soldiers who chanced to fall as prisoners into the hands of the enemy; and for many years after the war, the bitterness which it brought into the hearts of men, was kept alive and was hardened into a perdurable race-tradition through the tales which were told by the survivors of the British prison-pens and especially of the British prison-ships.

The most celebrated of all these narratives of military captivity was that produced in 1779 by Ethan Allen, a blustering frontier hero of not unchallenged political integrity[1]; described by a fellow-patriot in the first year of the war as "a high-flying genius," who "pursues every scheme on its first impression, without consideration, and [with] much less judgment"[2]; an able-minded ignoramus, of rough and ready humor, of boundless self-confidence, and of a shrewdness in thought and action equal to almost any emergency; a warrior who, "when barred up in gold lace . . . felt himself as grand as the Great Mogul,"[3] and who, having fighting abilities of the dramatic and oratorical kind, was not incapable, upon occasion, of playing the part of military wind-bag and braggart conqueror.

Having won great notoriety by his exploit in the capture of Ticonderoga in May, 1775, he was, in the following autumn, invited to accompany the little army under General Montgomery upon its march into Canada. Before very long, while in command of a small party of troops not far from Montreal, he was put to flight, overtaken, and forced to surrender; he then remained as a prisoner in the hands of the enemy for nearly three years,—gaining his liberty, upon exchange, in May, 1778. Before the end of March, 1779, he had written out his story of this long and bitter experience, which he published under the title of "A Narrative of Colonel Ethan Allen's Captivity."[4]

---

[1] The question of Ethan Allen's alleged treason to the American cause is briefly stated in "The Magazine of Am. Hist.," viii., 221–222; and on pages 438–439 of the same volume is an article by H. E. Hayden, discrediting the charge.

[2] "The New England Chronicle," for 2 Nov., 1775.

[3] So described in 1781 by an eye-witness of his splendor, Ann Eliza Bleecker, in her "Works," 153.

[4] First published in Philadelphia in 1779, and repeatedly there and elsewhere during the Revolution; since then at Philadelphia in 1799, at Walpole in 1807, at Albany in 1814, at Burlington in 1838 and 1846, in Boston in 1845 and 1849,

Of this little book, it may fairly be said, that it is a mirror not only of its author's character, but of that of many of his compatriots—especially along the rougher edge of our American society. As a literary crudity, we may easily deride it, and fling it aside as beneath our notice; but it instructs us, it amuses us, it does not bore us; and with all its grotesque faults, it is an authentic American product of the period. We cannot wonder at its popularity: it is a series of staunch, blunt, boastful, blundering, fearless words from out of the heart of a typical American man, and it easily finds it way again to the hearts of all such. Indeed, there is in Ethan Allen's "Narrative" so much of the best and of the worst qualities of his Revolutionary fellow-countrymen—so much talent, energy, ingenuity, audacity, such composure in the presence of danger and pain, such rampant scorn of authority or discipline, such humor and good humor, such invincible hope, such impatience, such irascibility, such colossal egotism, that we can hardly go wrong in accepting it as a thing having the very age and body of the time—his form and pressure.

As Ethan Allen was captured nearly a year before the Declaration of Independence, and while as yet the colonial uprising was under the first opprobrium attaching to a flagrant case of rebellion, it was inevitable that he, as a most conspicuous and a most dangerous rebel, should have had to

---

at Dayton in 1849, and probably at other times and places beyond present record. I have looked into many of these editions, but for the present purpose have used the Burlington edition of 1846—absurdly calling itself the "fourth edition." Ethan Allen was fond of nearly all sorts of big things, especially of big book-titles, of which his own title to this book is a model: "A Narrative of Colonel Ethan Allen's Captivity, from the Time of his being taken by the British, near Montreal, on the 25th Day of September, 1775, to the Time of his Exchange, on the 6th Day of May, 1778: Containing his Voyages and Travels, with the most remarkable Occurrences respecting himself and many other Continental Prisoners of different Ranks and Characters, which fell under his Observation, in the course of the same; particularly, the Destruction of the Prisoners at New York, by General Sir William Howe, in the Years 1776 and 1777. Interspersed with some political Observations. Written by Himself and now published for the Information of the Curious in all Nations."

bear the very brunt of all the contempt and wrath—of all that craving for instant and savage vengeance upon him—which his captors would so naturally feel. It is probable that in all the Thirteen Colonies was then to be found no other man better fitted by boldness, adroitness, toughness, pride, fortitude, cheerfulness, and by terrific volubility in invective, to be a pioneer prisoner in the hands of the British, and to educate them, as it were, in the graces and virtues of a proper conduct towards us, by giving every Briton to his face scorn for scorn, a pride like his own or like Lucifer's, a fearlessness that could defy the Tower or Tyburn or Tophet, a tenacity of will that was able to wear out any tormentor; finally, an amplitude and an appalling humor in profane swearing well calculated to disconcert and abash the very men who called themselves his masters. From the beginning he seems to have fixed upon the line of conduct which he should hold towards them: no meekness, no deference, no apology, no acknowledgment of wrong or of inferiority, no submission to insult or abuse, no solicitation of kindness as a mere favor, above all, no whining, and an imperturbable demand for his rights as a patriot, a prisoner of war, and a gentleman. "No abuse was offered me," says he, in giving an account of his capture, "till I came to the barrack yard at Montreal, where I met General Prescott, who asked me my name—which I told him. He then asked me whether I was that Colonel Allen who took Ticonderoga. I told him I was the very same man. Then he shook his cane over my head, calling many hard names—among which he frequently used the word 'rebel'—and put himself in a great rage. I told him he would do well not to cane me—for I was not accustomed to it—and shook my fist at him, telling him that was the beetle of mortality for him if he offered to strike; upon which Captain M'Cloud, of the British, pulled him by the skirt and whispered to him, as he afterwards told me, to this import—that it was inconsistent with his honor to strike a prisoner."[1] After some delay

[1] "Narrative," etc. 29.

and various exciting incidents, General Prescott "made me the following reply: 'I will not execute you now, but you shall grace a halter at Tyburn, God damn you.' I remember I disdained his mentioning such a place. I was, notwithstanding, a little pleased with the expression, as it significantly conveyed to me the idea of postponing the present appearance of death. Besides, his sentence was by no means final as to 'gracing a halter,'—although I had some anxiety about it after I landed in England, as the reader will find in the course of this history. General Prescott then ordered one of his officers to take me on board the 'Gaspee' schooner of war, and confine me, hands and feet, in irons,—which was done the same afternoon I was taken."[1] "The handcuff was of the common size and form; but my leg-irons, I should imagine, would weigh thirty pounds. The bar was eight feet long, and very substantial; the shackles, which encompassed my ankles, were very tight. I was told by the officer who put them on, that it was the king's plate; and I heard other of their officers say, that it would weigh forty-weight. The irons were so close upon my ankles that I could not lay down in any other manner than on my back. I was put into the lowest and most wretched part of the vessel, where I got the favor of a chest to sit on. The same answered for my bed at night; . . . . I was confined in the manner I have related, on board the 'Gaspee' schooner, about six weeks; during which time I was obliged to throw out plenty of extravagant language, which answered certain purposes at that time, better than to grace a history. To give an instance: upon being insulted, in a fit of anger I twisted off a nail with my teeth —which I took to be a ten-penny nail; it went through the mortise of the bar of my handcuff. And at the same time, I swaggered over those who abused me; particularly a Doctor Dace, who told me that I was outlawed by New York, and deserved death for several years past, was at last fully ripened for the halter, and in a fair way to obtain it.

[2] "Narrative," etc. 30–31.

When I challenged him, he excused himself in consequence, as he said, of my being a criminal; but I flung such a flood of language at him that it shocked him and the spectators —for my anger was very great. I heard one say—' Damn him, can he eat iron ?' "[1]

Frequently in the course of his story—as in the foregoing passages—the hero refers with no little satisfaction to his own extraordinary gift for the use of strong language—those explosive and sulphurous vocables with which, in cases of conflict with his fellow-men, he seems to have flooded the entire neighborhood, and to have imparted to his antagonists a horror-stricken desire for some form of rapid retreating motion. After a voyage of about forty days, during which he received the most brutal treatment, the vessel came within sight of the English coast; " soon after which," says he, " the prisoners were taken from their gloomy abode, being permitted to see the light of the sun, and breathe fresh air, which to us was very refreshing. The day following, we landed at Falmouth. . . . When the prisoners were landed, multitudes of the citizens of Falmouth, excited by curiosity, crowded to see us, which was equally gratifying to us. I saw numbers on the tops of houses; and the rising adjacent grounds were covered with them. The throng was so great, that the king's officers were obliged to draw their swords and force a passage to Pendennis Castle, which was near a mile from the town, where we were closely confined, in consequence of orders from General Carleton, who then commanded in Canada. . . . The reader will readily conceive I was anxious about my preservation, knowing that I was in the power of a haughty and cruel nation. . . . Those that daily came in great numbers out of curiosity to see me, both gentle and simple, united in this—that I would be hanged. A gentleman from America, by the name of Temple, and who was friendly to me, just whispered me in the ear, and told me that bets were laid in London that I would be exe-

[1] " Narrative," etc. 30–34.

cuted; he likewise privately gave me a guinea, but durst say but little to me."[1] "I could not but feel inwardly extremely anxious for my fate. This I, however, concealed from the prisoners, as well as from the enemy who were perpetually shaking the halter at me. I nevertheless treated them with scorn and contempt. . . . I now clearly recollect that my mind was so resolved, that I would not have trembled or shewn the least fear, as I was sensible it could not alter my fate, nor do more than reproach my memory, make my last act despicable to my enemies, and eclipse the other actions of my life. For I reasoned thus: that nothing was more common than for men to die with their friends around them, weeping and lamenting over them, but not able to help them, which was in reality not different in the consequence of it from such a death as I was apprehensive of; and as death was the natural consequence of animal life, to which the laws of nature subject mankind, to be timorous and uneasy as to the event and manner of it, was inconsistent with the character of a philosopher and soldier. The cause I was engaged in, I ever viewed worthy hazarding my life for; nor was I, in the most critical moments of trouble, sorry that I engaged in it; and as to the world of spirits, though I knew nothing of the mode or manner of it, I expected nevertheless, when I should arrive at such a world, that I should be as well treated as other gentlemen of my merit."[2]

It fell in with his sense of the comic element so plentifully mixed with all this tragedy, that the ingenuous natives of the English isle were apparently impressed with a notion that he was some uncouth monster of the American forests, gifted with powers extraordinary, possibly supernatural, very likely dangerous; and it gave him amusement to minister to this impression, while never failing to demand for himself the treatment due to his character as an American patriot and hero. "I am apprehensive," he says, "my Canadian dress contributed not a little to the surprise

[1] "Narrative," etc. 40–42. [2] Ibid. 44–46.

and excitement of curiosity. To see a gentleman in England regularly dressed and well behaved, would be no sight at all; but such a rebel as they were pleased to call me, it is probable, was never before seen in England."[1] "Among the great numbers of people who came to the castle to see the prisoners, some gentlemen told me that they had come fifty miles on purpose to see me, and desired to ask me a number of questions. . . . Then one of them asked me, what my occupation in life had been. I answered him, that in my younger days I had studied divinity, but was a conjurer by profession. He replied, that I conjured wrong at the time I was taken; and I was obliged to own that I mistook a figure at that time, but that I had conjured them out of Ticonderoga. This was a place of great notoriety in England, so that the joke seemed to go in my favor.

"It was a common thing for me to be taken out of close confinement into a spacious green in the castle, or rather parade, where numbers of gentlemen and ladies were ready to see and hear me. I often entertained such audiences with harangues on the impracticability of Great Britain's conquering the then colonies of America. At one of these times I asked a gentleman for a bowl of punch, and he ordered his servant to bring it,—which he did, and offered it to me; but I refused to take it from the hand of his servant. He then gave it to me with his own hand,—refusing to drink with me in consequence of my being a state-criminal. However, I took the punch, and drank it all down at one draught, and handed the gentleman the bowl. This made the spectators, as well as myself, merry."[2]

As it turned out, the Londoners who had staked their money on the faith that he would be hanged, lost it; for, in January, 1776, instead of gracing a halter at Tyburn, he was, with other prisoners, put on board an English frigate, and was thus started again upon his long and painful wanderings over land and sea, being now in the harbor of Cape Fear, and now in New York, now in Halifax, and now

---

[1] "Narrative," etc. 48. [2] Ibid. 46–47.

again in New York. There, at last, in October, 1776, he was permitted to go out upon parole, within the limits of the city: "I soon projected means to live in some measure agreeably to my rank, though I was destitute of cash. My constitution was almost worn out by such a long and barbarous captivity. The enemy gave out that I was crazy and wholly unmanned; but my vitals held sound, nor was I delirious any more than I had been from my youth up; but my extreme circumstances, at certain times, rendered it politic to act in some measure the mad man."[1]

Coming thus to the headquarters of the enemy in the midst of their great successes upon Long Island, in New York City, and elsewhere in that neighborhood, he was able to speak as an eye-witness of the sufferings of the American prisoners there, and to bear some testimony well fitted to kindle the sympathy and the undying wrath of his fellow-countrymen: "I next invite the reader to a retrospective sight and consideration of the doleful scene of inhumanity exercised by General Sir William Howe, and the army under his command, towards the prisoners taken on Long Island on the 27th day of August, 1776; sundry of whom were in an inhuman and barbarous manner murdered after they had surrendered their arms:—particularly a General Odel, or Woodhull, of the militia, who was hacked to pieces with cutlasses, when alive, by the light horsemen; and a Captain Fellows, of the continental army, who was thrust through with a bayonet, of which wound he died instantly. Sundry others were hanged up by the neck till they were dead,—five on the limb of a white-oak tree, and without any reason assigned, except that they were fighting for the only blessing worth preserving. And, indeed, those who had the misfortune to fall into their hands at Fort Washington, in the month of November following, met with but little better usage, except that they were reserved from immediate death, to famish and die with hunger. In fine, the word 'rebel,' applied to any vanquished persons, without regard

[1] "Narrative," etc. 77.

to rank, who were in the continental service on the 27th of August aforesaid, was thought by the enemy sufficient to sanctify whatever cruelties they were pleased to inflict, death itself not excepted."[1] "The private soldiers who were brought to New York, were crowded into churches, and environed with slavish Hessian guards, a people of a strange language, who were sent to America for no other design but cruelty and desolation; and, at others, by merciless Britons, whose mode of communicating ideas being intelligible in this country, served only to tantalize and insult the helpless and perishing; but above all, the hellish delight and triumph of the Tories over them, as they were dying by hundreds. This was too much for me to bear as a spectator; for I saw the Tories exulting over the dead bodies of their murdered countrymen. I have gone into the churches and seen sundry of the prisoners in the agonies of death, in consequence of very hunger, and others speechless, and very near death, biting pieces of chips; others pleading, for God's sake, for something to eat, and at the same time shivering with cold. Hollow groans saluted my ears, and despair seemed to be imprinted on every of their countenances. The filth in these churches . . . was almost beyond description. . . . I have seen in one of these churches seven dead at the same time, lying among the excrements of their bodies. . . . The provision dealt out to the prisoners was by no means sufficient for the support of life. . . . I saw some of them sucking bones after they were speechless; others, who could yet speak and had the use of their reason, urged me in the strongest and most pathetic manner, to use my interest in their behalf."[2]

---

[1] "Narrative," etc. 78–79.

[2] Ibid. 79–81. A good example of Ethan Allen's power in robust controversy may be seen in a little book of his published in 1779,—"A Vindication of the Opposition of Vermont to the Government of New York." As a controversial writer whose rage in assertion was unchastened either by adequate knowledge, or by any suspicion of his lack of it, his reputation, doubtless, rests on a work published in 1784, under this entirely characteristic title:—"Reason the Only Oracle of Man; or, A Compenduous System of Natural Religion.

II.

Another authentic and very stirring specimen of this sort of prison-literature, is " A Narrative of the Capture and Treatment of John Dodge, by the English at Detroit," written by Dodge himself and published at Philadelphia in 1779. The author, a native of Connecticut, had settled as an Indian trader at Sandusky in 1770; had acquired much facility in the Indian dialects thereabout, and much influence over the Indians themselves; and having, on account of his stanch and too competent Americanism, become an object of suspicion to the English officers in that region, had been pounced upon by them and thrown for safe-keeping into their prison-den at Detroit, where the most barbarous treatment awaited him, and where he was in constant peril of murder. Of all these ugly doings and sufferings, this little book tells the story, and it does so with graphic simplicity and after the manner of a man who is speaking the truth.

III.

Perhaps all American prisoners at Montreal, or Dartmoor, at Halifax, or Detroit, had some right to deem themselves the very children of good luck, by comparison with any of their countrymen in captivity who chanced to form an acquaintance with the inside of the British prison-ships in the harbor of New York. Of these prison-ships was born a very considerable literature,—a literature in itself most pathetic and implacable,—the literature of a realm shut away apparently from the pity of God or man and given over to be the very dwelling-place of rage and brutality, of filth, foul air, hunger, thirst, pestilence, blasphemy, madness.

No better example of such naïve chronicles can be chosen, than " The Old Jersey Captive, or, a Narrative of the Cap-

---

Alternately adorned with Confutations of a Variety of Doctrines incompatible with it; Deduced from the most exalted Ideas which we are able to form of the Divine and Human Characters, and from the Universe in General."

tivity of Thomas Andros, . . . on Board the Old Jersey Prison-Ship at New York, 1781." At the breaking out of hostilities in 1775, Thomas Andros was but a lad of sixteen, laboring on a farm near Plainfield in Connecticut, his mother being then a widow and in much poverty. As the news from Lexington and Concord passed that way, this boy enlisted as a soldier, and thereafter served in several campaigns. In 1781, having taken employment on board an American privateer, and being one of a crew put in charge of a prize-vessel which they were to carry into port, he and all his mates were captured by the enemy on the 27th of August, 1781, were taken to New York, and were there cast into that floating prison, the ship "Old Jersey," around which are gathered so many baleful memories of the Revolution. "This was," writes Andros, "an old sixty-four gun ship, which through age had become unfit for further actual service. She was stripped of every spar and all her rigging, . . . and nothing remained but an old, unsightly, rotten hulk. Her dark and filthy external appearance perfectly corresponded with the death and despair that reigned within. . . . She was moored about three quarters of a mile to the eastward of Brooklyn ferry near a tide-mill on the Long Island shore. The nearest distance to land was about twenty rods. And doubtless no other ship in the British navy ever proved the means of the destruction of so many human beings. It is computed that not less than eleven thousand American seamen perished in her. But after it was known that it was next to certain death to confine a prisoner here the inhumanity and wickedness of doing it was about the same as if he had been taken into the city and deliberately shot on some public square. But as if mercy had fled from the earth, here we were doomed to dwell. And never while I was on board, did any Howard or angel of pity appear to inquire into or alleviate our woes. Once or twice, by the order of a stranger on the quarter deck, a bag of apples were hurled promiscuously into the midst of hundreds of prisoners crowded together as thick as they could stand, and life and limbs were endangered by the scramble. This, instead of compassion, was a cruel sport. When I saw it about to commence, I fled to the most distant part of the ship.

"On the commencement of the first evening, we were driven down to darkness between decks, secured by iron gratings and an armed soldiery. And now a scene of horror which baffles all description presented itself. On every side wretched, desponding shapes of men could be seen. Around the well room an armed guard were forcing up the prisoners to the winches, to clear the ship of water and prevent her sinking, and little else could be heard but a roar of mutual execrations, reproaches, and insults. During this operation, there was a small dim light admitted below, but it served to make darkness more visible, and horror more terrific. In my reflections I said this must be a complete image and anticipation of hell. Milton's description of the dark world rushed upon my mind—

> 'Sights of woe, regions of sorrow, doleful
> Shades where peace and rest can never dwell.'

". . . . When I first became an inmate of this abode of suffering, despair, and death, there were about four hundred prisoners on board, but in a short time they amounted to twelve hundred. And in proportion to our numbers, the mortality increased. All the most deadly diseases were pressed into the service of the king of terrors, but his prime ministers were dysentery, small pox, and yellow fever. . . . The diseased and the healthy were mingled together in the main ship. In a short time, we had two hundred or more, sick and dying, lodged in the fore part of the lower gun-deck, where all the prisoners were confined at night. Utter derangement was a common symptom of yellow fever; and to increase the horror of the darkness that shrouded us (for we were allowed no light betwixt decks) the voice of warning would be heard—' Take heed to yourselves,—there is a mad man stalking through the ship with a knife in his hand.' . . . While so many were sick with raging fever, there was a loud cry for water, but none could be had except on the upper deck, and but one allowed to ascend at a time. The suffering then from the rage of thirst during the night was very great. Nor was it at all times safe to attempt to go up. Provoked by the continual cry for leave to ascend, when there was already one on deck, the sentry would push them back with his bayonet. . . . In the morning the hatchways were thrown open and we were allowed to ascend all at once, and remain on the upper deck during the day. But the first object that met our view in the morning, was a most appalling spectacle,—a boat loaded with dead bodies, conveying them to the Long Island shore, where they were very slightly covered with sand. . . . Let our disease be what it would, we were abandoned to our fate. . . . No English physician, or any one from the city, ever, to my knowledge, came near us. . . . The prisoners were furnished with buckets and brushes to cleanse the ship, and with vinegar to sprinkle her inside. But their indolence and despair were such that they would not use them, or but rarely. And, indeed, at this time the encouragement to do it was small. For the whole ship, from keel to the taffarel, was equally affected, and contained pestilence sufficient to desolate a world : disease and death were wrought into her very timbers. At the time I left, it is to be presumed a more filthy, contagious, and deadly abode for human beings, never existed among a Christianized people. It fell but little short of the Black Hole at Calcutta. . . . The lower hold and the orlop deck were such a terror, that no man would venture down into them. Humanity would have dictated a more merciful treatment to a band of pirates. . . . But in the view of the English, we were rebels and traitors: we had risen against the mother country in an unjust and wanton civil war. On this ground, they considered us as not entitled to that humanity which might be expected by prisoners taken in a war with a foreign nation. . . . As to religion, I do not remember of beholding any trace of it in the ship. I saw no Bible—heard no prayer, no religious conversation; no clergyman visited us, though no set of afflicted and dying men more needed the light and consolations of religion. . . . I know not that God's name was ever mentioned, unless it was in profaneness and blasphemy. . . . I wish it to be understood that what I have said of this horrid prison, relates almost exclusively to the time I was on board. Of what took place before or afterward, I say little. . . . Nor would I heap the cruel horrors of this prison-ship as a reproach upon the whole nation without exception. It is indeed a blot which a thousand ages cannot eradicate from the name of Britain; but no doubt, when the pious and humane among them came to know what had been done, they utterly reprobated such cruelty." [1]

IV.

A piece of writing having such worth and charm as to entitle it to far greater fame than it has yet had, is "A Narrative of the Capture of Henry Laurens, of His Confinement in the Tower of London, and So Forth, 1780, 1781, 1782," [2]—this being the story of a very considerable international incident as told by the principal actor and sufferer

[1] "The Old Jersey Captive," 8–20. The most thrilling part of this strong narrative is that which tells the story of its writer's escape. After marvels of suffering and adventure, the poor fellow at last got home to his mother near Plainfield, where he lay dangerously ill a long time; and then, as an offering of conscience and gratitude, he devoted himself to the sacred ministry—a service for which he fitted himself under great disadvantages, and in which he achieved a long and beneficent career, dying at the age of eighty-six in the town of Berkeley where he had lived as minister for seven-and-fifty years. Interesting accounts of this extraordinary person are to be seen in Enoch Sanford's "History of the Town of Berkeley," 9–27; and in S. H. Emery's "Ministry of Taunton," ii. 254–277. In a note to page 262 of the latter work is a good, though not complete, list of Andros's many published sermons and other writings.

[2] "Collections of the South Carolina Historical Society," i. 18–68.

in it, and told with simplicity, sprightliness, and grace, also with a sureness of intellectual movement born of the splendid sincerity, virility, wholesomeness, and competence of this man—himself the noblest Roman of them all—the unsurpassed embodiment of the proudest, finest, wittiest, most efficient, and most chivalrous Americanism of his time.

Henry Laurens was of Huguenot ancestry, and was born in Charleston, South Carolina, in 1723. Early in life he was placed in a counting-house in his native town; afterward he was transferred to a similar position in London, where he remained several years. Returning to Charleston, he engaged in business on his own account and met with extraordinary success; he became one of the merchant-princes of his country, the possessor, also, of large wealth in lands and in slaves.[1] Prior to the final asperities of the Revolution, he had begun to take a high-spirited part in the affairs of his own colony,—even serving in a campaign against the Cherokees. In 1771, he retired from business, and went abroad for travel and for the education of his children. In 1774, being in London, he was one of the thirty-eight Americans who there signed a petition intended, if possible, to dissuade parliament from entering upon the harsh colonial policy embodied in the Boston port bill. With the final failure of that honest American effort to save the mother country from a fatal misjudgment of her American children, Henry Laurens came back to his own land to take his full share in whatsoever fate might be in

---

[1] Yet he had an abhorrence of slave-holding; and one of the noblest passages in early anti-slavery literature is that portion of a letter which was written by him at Charleston, August 14, 1776, informing his eldest son, the gallant John Laurens, of his purpose, at whatever cost, to emancipate his slaves. "Correspondence of Henry Laurens," 19–21. This is the first volume of "Materials for History Printed from Original Manuscripts," and edited by Frank Moore, for the Zenger Club. No subsequent volume was ever issued. In 1861—at a time when the anti-slavery testimony of this illustrious South Carolinian had a singular pertinence—his letter of August, 1776, was separately reprinted, under the title of "A Protest against Slavery."

store for it. Being elected to the first provincial congress of South Carolina in 1775, he drew up the form of association to be signed by all citizens of that colony who were resolute in their opposition to ministerial encroachments. Of the council of safety—a revolutionary body of almost unlimited power—he became president. In 1776, he was made vice-president of the new State of South Carolina. In 1777, he was made a member of the Continental Congress.[1] Coming at last upon the arena of national politics, he was soon recognized for what he was—a trusty, sagacious, lofty, imperturbable character—a man whom Washington could love and lean upon; of whom even the bitterest of the Loyalists had to speak with admiration and forbearance. Soon after the retirement of John Hancock from the presidency of Congress, Henry Laurens was made president in his place, and served as such from the first of November, 1777, until the ninth of December, 1778. In the latter part of the year 1779, he was chosen by Congress as its commissioner to negotiate a treaty of amity and commerce with Holland, and to procure a loan in that country.[2] For the performance of this high duty, he set sail from Philadelphia, August 13, 1780, in the brigantine, "Mercury"—a packet belonging to Congress; and on the third of September, the "Mercury" with all on board was captured by Captain Keppel of the British frigate, "Vestal." Near the end of that month, Laurens arrived in England as a prisoner of state and was sent to the Tower. There he remained "closely confined and inhumanly treated"[3] for about fifteen months, being finally let out on bail, and subsequently set free in exchange for Lord Cornwallis. In the latter part of his incarceration, a British surgeon remarked to the prisoner as he lay ill in bed, that "it was very difficult to put a man to death in

---

[1] Elected 10 Jan., 1777. He took his seat 22 July. "Journals of the American Congress," ii. 44, 202.

[2] "Secret Journals of Congress," ii. 282–318; especially for Oct. 21, 26, 30; Nov. 1, 5, 8, 1779; and for June 20, 1780.

[3] "A Narrative," etc. 57.

this country." "There is, however, in this country," said Laurens in reply, "a facility in murdering a man by inches: I have experienced it in a degree not to be paralleled in modern British history."[1]

All this hard experience of his as a prisoner of state in the hands of the British, was borne by him not only with fortitude, but with gayety, and with a quick discomfiture of all devices for his intimidation or corruption. Such experience, also, furnished the subject and the materials for his "Narrative,"[2]—a modest and fascinating story of an heroic episode in the history of the Revolution, a fragment of autobiography fit to become a classic in the literature of a people ready to pay homage to whatever is magnanimous, exquisite, and indomitable in the manly character.

---

[1] "A Narrative," etc. 56.

[2] In "Collections of the South Carolina Historical Society," i. 69–83, at the end of the "Narrative," is given an "Appendix, containing Documents, Letters, etc., relating to Mr. Laurens's Imprisonment in the Tower." In "The Magazine of American History" for December, 1884, may be seen a rebus letter written by Laurens to Lord George Gordon, whom he knew as a fellow-prisoner in the Tower.

CHAPTER XXXIV.

PHILIP FRENEAU AS POET AND SATIRIST IN THE WAR FOR INDEPENDENCE: 1778–1783.

I.—Two periods of Freneau's activity in immediate contact with the Revolution—The first period embraces the latter half of the year 1775—The second period extends from 1778 to 1783—Freneau's abandonment of the country in 1776 and his stay in the West Indies till 1778—His poetic work there—Denounces slavery.

II.—His return to his country, and to literary activity in its service, in 1778—His confidence in the success of the Revolution—"Stanzas on the New American Frigate 'Alliance'"—"America Independent"—Fierce onslaughts upon King George the Third—His invectives against Burgoyne and the American Loyalists.

III.—His poem "To the Dog Sancho."

IV.—His contributions to "The United States Magazine" in 1779—Two more attacks on the King.

V.—His capture and imprisonment by the British—He is stimulated thereby to new and fiercer satires against the enemy—"The British Prison Ship."

VI.—His principal poems for the years 1781, 1782, and 1783.

VII.—"The Political Balance; or, The Fates of Britain and America Compared."

VIII.—"The Prophecy."

IX.—His final word to the British King.

X.—Freneau's proper rank as a poet—A pioneer in the reform of eighteenth-century English verse—The first American poet of Democracy, and his fidelity to that character.

I.

THE work of Philip Freneau as poet and satirist in direct contact with the American Revolution, was broken into two periods,—these periods being separated from each other by an interval of about two years. The first period, which has been dealt with in a former part of this work,[1] embraces those months of the year 1775 wherein his own fierce pas-

[1] See chapter ix.

sions, like the passions of his countrymen, were set aflame by the outbreak of hostilities. Thereafter occurred a mysterious lapse in his activity as a writer on themes connected with the great struggle, to which he had professed his undying devotion;—he was absent from the country until some time in the year 1778. With the middle of the year 1778 began the second period of his work as Revolutionary poet and satirist, and it did not come to an end, except with the end of the Revolution itself. If we are right in assigning to the later months of the year 1775 Freneau's "MacSwiggen, a Satire," we shall find in that poem some clew to the mood of literary disgust and discouragement which seems then to have seized him, impelling him for a time to leave his native land:

> "Long have I sat on this disastrous shore,
> And, sighing, sought to gain a passage o'er
> To Europe's towns, where, as our travellers say,
> Poets may flourish—or perhaps they may." [1]

Not to Europe, however, did the down-hearted political prophet make his escape,—the Tarshish to which he fled was in the West Indies:

> "Sick of all feuds, to Reason I appeal
> From wars of paper, and from wars of steel;
> Let others here their hopes and wishes end,
> I to the sea with weary steps descend;
> . . . .
> In distant isles some happier scene I 'll choose,
> And court in softer shades the unwilling Muse." [2]

This resolution, which seems weak-spirited enough and wholly unworthy of him, Freneau carried out, sailing away to the tropics some time in the year 1776, and remaining there, probably, during the remainder of that year, and the

[1] "The Poems of Philip Freneau," 83. [2] Ibid. 87–88.

year 1777, and even a part of the year 1778. Then it was that he wrote some of his longest and most powerful non-political poems,—"The House of Night,"[1] "The Beauties of Santa Cruz,"[2] and "The Jamaica Funeral,"[3]—the latter notable for one passage of scorching satire on the frivolity and sensuality then so often to be met with in the clergy of the colonial Church. Even in his remoteness from the scene of his country's danger and anguish, he could not forget either that anguish or that danger; and his fine little poem "On the Death of Captain Nicholas Biddle, Commander of the 'Randolph' Frigate," is some token of Freneau's continued remembrance of the cause of his countrymen—whom, however, he seemed to have abandoned. There is one stanza of this poem over which the reader will be tempted to linger as having a weird beauty, a sort of spectral suggestiveness, quite characteristic of Freneau in his nobler work. Referring to the American ship, which had been blown up and sunk in the very moment of its victory over the British cruiser, he says:

> "The 'Randolph' soon on Stygian streams
> Shall coast along the land of dreams,
>   The islands of the dead!
> But fate, that parts them on the deep,
> Shall save the Briton, still to weep
>   His ancient honors fled."[4]

Even his long poem, "The Beauties of Santa Cruz," wherein he tries to give himself up to the delights of tropical nature, is not without some touch revealing his sorrowful consciousness of the disasters which, in the summer and autumn of that year, 1776, were overwhelming his native land:

> "Far o'er the waste of yonder surgy field
> My native climes in fancied prospect lie,

[1] "Poems of Philip Freneau," 88–108.
[2] Ibid. 117–133.
[3] Ibid. 109–117.
[4] Ibid. 147.

> Now hid in shades, and now by clouds concealed,
> And now by tempests ravished from my eye.
>
> "There, triumphs to enjoy, are Britain, thine,
> There thy proud navy awes the pillaged shore;
> Nor sees the day when nations shall combine
> That pride to humble, and our rights restore." [1]

Perhaps it was in mere disgust, perhaps it was in anger and despair, that the poet had been able to persuade himself to leave behind him what he calls the "bloody plains" and the "iron glooms" of his country, and, as he says,

> "Quit the cold northern star, and here enjoy
> Beneath the smiling skies, this land of love"; [2]

yet even in that "land of love" his heart was soon embittered by sights and sounds of hate,—sights and sounds which seemed to transform that paradise into a pandemonium:

> "If there exists a hell—the case is clear—
> Sir Toby's slaves enjoy that portion here.
>
> . . . .
>
> Here whips on whips excite a thousand fears,
> And mingled howlings vibrate on my ears:
> Here nature's plagues abound, of all degrees,
> Snakes, scorpions, despots, lizards, centipees." [3]

Chiefly, the ineffable horrors of slavery in the West Indies gave to this poet of liberty such sorrow as made it impossible for him there to enter without reserve into the mere enjoyment of nature. In a bit of noble prose with which, three years afterward, he prefaced his poem on "The Beauties of Santa Cruz," he said: "The only disagreeable circumstance attending this island, which it has in common

---

[1] "The Poems of Philip Freneau," 131. [2] Ibid.

[3] "Poems on Several Occasions," 391.

with the rest, is the cruel and detestable slavery of the negroes. . . . No class of mankind in the known world undergo so complete a servitude as the common negroes in the West Indies. It casts a shade over the native charms of the country; it blots out the beauties of the eternal spring which Providence has there ordained to reign; and amidst all the profusion of bounties which nature has scattered,—the brightness of the heaven, the mildness of the air, and the luxuriancy of the vegetable kingdom,—it leaves me melancholy and disconsolate, convinced that there is no pleasure in this world without its share of pain. And thus the earth, which, were it not for the lust of pride and dominion, might be an earthly paradise, is, by the ambition and overbearing nature of mankind, rendered an eternal scene of desolation, woe, and horror: the weak goes to the wall, while the strong prevails; and after our ambitious frenzy has turned the world upside down, we are contented with a narrow spot, and leave our follies and cruelties to be acted over again by every succeeding generation."[1]

II.

Even though lacking other biographical data, we can find in Freneau's verse sufficient evidence that he was at home again by the middle of the year 1778,—his return to his native land having been signalized by his return to the most vigorous literary activity in its service:

> "Returned a prisoner to my native shore,
> How changed I find those scenes that pleased before!
> How changed those groves where fancy loved to stray,
> When spring's young blossoms bloomed along the way.
> From every eye distils the frequent tear,
> From every mouth the doleful tale I hear!
> Some mourn a father, brother, husband, friend;
> Some mourn, imprisoned in their native land,

[1] First printed in "The United States Magazine," 1779. These sentences are given in "Poems relating to the American Revolution by Philip Freneau, with an Introductory Memoir by Evert A. Duyckinck," xiii–xiv.

In sickly ships what numerous hosts confined—
At once their lives and liberties resigned!"[1]

Notwithstanding this tone of sadness over the havoc wrought by the war, there rings through the three or four poems which he wrote during the latter half of the year 1778, a note of absolute confidence—of exultant and even of jeering confidence—in the success of the American cause, all to be accomplished through American capacity and valor backed by the aid of France. It is to the one great event of this year, the French alliance—to the king and the people of France, our old foes, our new friends—that he now pays many a jubilant and grateful tribute. Perhaps no finer expression of this new note of exultation is to be met with, than in his "Stanzas on the new American Frigate 'Alliance,'" wherein he represents Neptune as looking abroad over his watery dominions toward the west, and with such surprise as a god may be capable of, seeing there a mighty war-ship that was altogether new to him:

"As nearer still the monarch drew,—
Her starry flag displayed to view,—
He asked a Triton of his train,
'What flag was this that rode the main?—

"'A ship of such a gallant mien
This many a day I have not seen;
To no mean power can she belong,
So swift, so warlike, stout, and strong!'"[2]

In reply to this enquiry of the sea-god, the Triton proceeds to give Neptune some valuable information about the latest phases of mundane politics,—explaining, especially, that this ship belongs to a new nation which had just been formed in the far West, and which, in resentment for wrongs inflicted by Britain, is now victoriously confronting that arrogant power even on the sea—on the sea where

[1] "The Poems of Philip Freneau," 141. [2] Ibid. 144.

Britain has been accustomed to think of itself as without a rival. In the last stanza, this admirable Triton manages to compress the neatest possible compliment to the spirit of the people who have sent forth this fine ship. Apostrophizing the most famous vessel of antiquity, he exclaims:

> "Not, Argo, in thy womb was found
> Such hearts of brass as here abound:
> They for their golden fleece did fly—
> These sail to vanquish tyranny."[1]

The poet's assurance of the success of the American cause breathes a sort of ferocious exultation through the longest and strongest of the poems produced by him in 1778,—"America Independent, and Her Everlasting Deliverance from British Tyranny and Oppression:"

> "'T is done! and Britain for her madness sighs!
> Take warning tyrants, and henceforth be wise:
> If o'er mankind man gives you legal sway,
> Take not the rights of human kind away.
> When God from chaos gave this world to be,
> Man then he formed, and formed him to be free;
> In his own image stampt the favorite race—
> How dar'st thou, tyrant, the fair stamp deface?"[2]

Thus assuming that the contest was then entirely over and the British already expelled from the land, he proceeds to doom them at once to infamy and to insignificance among the peoples of the earth:

> "This be their doom, in vengeance for the slain,
> To pass their days in poverty and pain;
> . . . .
> And to their insect isle henceforth confined,
> No longer lord it o'er the human kind."[3]

---

[1] "The Poems of Philip Freneau," 146. [2] Ibid. 134–135.
[3] Ibid. 135.

According to this poet, nothing good can be said for kings in general, even in spite of the fact that both Solomon and David belonged to that order of men; for,

> "Though one was wise, and one Goliath slew,
> Kings are the choicest curse that man e'er knew."[1]

But for George the Third of Britain it was left to exhibit to the world to what extremes of hypocrisy, tyranny, and stupidity even a king might attain:

> "In him we see the depths of baseness joined—
> Whate'er disgraced the dregs of human kind;
> Cain, Nimrod, Nero—fiends in human guise—
> Herod, Domitian—these in judgment rise;
> And, envious of his deeds, I hear them say,
> None but a George could be more vile than they.
> . . . .
> Yet he to arms, and war, and blood, inclined,
> A fair-day warrior with a feeble mind,
> Fearless, while others meet the shock of fate,
> And dare that death which clips his thread too late,—
> He to the fane—O hypocrite!—would go
> While not an angel there but was his foe;
> There did he kneel, and sigh, and sob, and pray—
> Yet not to lave his thousand sins away.
> Far other motives swayed his spotted soul;
> 'T was not for those the secret sorrow stole
> Down his pale cheek—'t was vengeance and despair
> Dissolved his eye, and planted sorrow there!
> How could he hope to bribe the impartial sky
> By his base prayers, and mean hypocrisy?
> . . . .
> What were his prayers?—his prayers could be no more
> Than a thief's wishes to recruit his store!"[2]

Possibly, however, the bitterest invective contained in this most bitter poem, is in the passages which are devoted

[1] "The Poems of Philip Freneau," 136. [2] Ibid. 136–137.

to Burgoyne, and especially, as in the following lines, to the poet's own countrymen, the Tories:

> "So vile a crew the world ne'er saw before,
> And, grant, ye pitying heavens, it may no more!
> If ghosts from hell infest our poisoned air,
> Those ghosts have entered these base bodies here.
> Murder and blood is still their dear delight—
> Scream round their roofs, ye ravens of the night!
> Whene'er they wed, may demons and despair
> And grief and woe and blackest night be there;
> Fiends leagued from hell the nuptial lamp display,
> Swift to perdition light them on their way,
> Round the wide world their devilish squadrons chase—
> To find no realm that grants one resting place." [1]

But though these people, driven out from America, are to find in all the world no real resting-place, there is, the poet tells us, at least one spot of earth sufficiently hideous and desolate to be their proper place of abode. Perhaps the very climax of Freneau's power, both in description and in execration, is reached in the passage wherein he assigns to Burgoyne and to the American Tories their future earthly home:

> "Far to the north, on Scotland's utmost end,
> An isle there lies, the haunt of every fiend;
> There screeching owls and screaming vultures rest,
> And not a tree adorns its barren breast.
> No sheperds there attend their bleating flocks,
> But withered witches rove among the rocks;
> Shrouded in ice, the blasted mountains show
> Their cloven heads, to fright the seas below;
> The lamp of heaven in his diurnal race
> Here scarcely deigns to unveil his radiant face,
> Or if one day he circling treads the sky,
> He views this island with an angry eye;

[1] "The Poems of Philip Freneau," 139.

Or ambient fogs their broad moist wings expand,
Damp his bright ray, and cloud the infernal land ;
The blackening wind, incessant storms prolong,
Dull as their night, and dreary as my song.
When stormy winds with rain refuse to blow,
Then from the dark sky drives the unpitying snow ;
When drifting snows from iron clouds forbear,
Then down the hailstones rattle through the air ;
No peace, no rest, the elements bestow,
But seas forever rage, and storms forever blow.

" Here, miscreants, here with Loyal hearts retire,
Here pitch your tents, and kindle here your fire ;
Here desert nature will her stings display,
And fiercest hunger on your vitals prey ;
And with yourselves let John Burgoyne retire
To reign the monarch whom your hearts admire ! "[1]

III.

From these savageries of satire, it is a relief to turn for a moment to a playful and gracious little poem—also a product of the year 1778—a poem in which Freneau, while still not forgetful of the vices which make so many human beings detestable to him, shews both admiration and tenderness for the virtues which adorn the dog—that humble and faithful friend of man. In the circumstances that gave occasion for his poem " To the Dog Sancho," one gets some glimpse of the lawlessness and violence which the barbarities of war had by that time made rampant among us, especially on the outer edges of our civilization. Sometime in that year, 1778, a lonely cabin occupied by Freneau, near the Neversink Hills in New Jersey, was attacked at midnight by robbers, who came armed with a musket and a cutlass, which they used with almost fatal effect on poor Sancho, he having courageously challenged their right to be there. The easy and playful movement of this poem well suits its humanity

[1] " The Poems of Philip Freneau," 139-140.

of tone,—the affability, in fact, of the poet's ways toward a companion so truly loved and respected by him:

> "The world, my dear Sancho, is full of distress,
> And you have your share, I allow and confess;
> For twice with a musket, and now a cutteau—
> You had nearly gone off to dog-heaven below.
>
> "Was this your reward, to be slashed, to be cut,
> For defending at midnight the door of a hut?
> You had little to fight for, had little to win,
> Yet you boldly held out, till the robbers broke in.
>
> "The blade which was meant the bold robber to face,
> To guard a fair lady, or serve in the chase,
> Was drenched in the blood of an innocent cur,
> Who said in dog language, 'What want you, good Sir?'
>
> "Poor fellow, I pity your pitiful case!
> In fact they have ruined the round of your face;
> And die when you will, be it early or late,
> You will go to your grave with a scar on your pate.
>
> "If ever a dog be permitted to pass
> Where folks I could mention, have fixed on a place,
> (But which, I suspect, they will hardly attain
> While rights of pre-emption in Satan remain.)
>
> "Good Sancho had merit to put in his plea,
> And claim with the claimants a portion in fee,
> On the ground, that in life he was one of the few
> Who, in watching and barking, were trusty and true.
>
> "To warn us of danger, he ventured his beef,
> And, in his own lingo, cried—'Robber and Thief!'
> So now, in return for the good he has done,
> For the vigils he kept, and the battles he won,

"I 'll give him a verse with the great of the age,
And if he quite dies, he must die in my page;
And long may he live in despite of the mob,
And the fools who his master, a poet, would rob!

"Wherever I take up my evening retreat,
Dear Sancho, I 'll have you to lie at my feet;
And whether at home or in regions remote,
For a bed, I 'll allot you the skirt of a coat.

"With my dog at my feet, and my gun at my head,
I am equally safe in a fort or a shed;
From a snap of his teeth and the shot of a gun,
Thrice happy the thief that is able to run!"[1]

IV.

For the year 1779, Freneau's most characteristic work found expression in the pages of "The United States Magazine," of which his classmate, Brackenridge, was the editor, and to which he contributed much both in prose and verse, particularly two of the long poems written by him during his recent abode in the West Indies.[2] There, also, appeared his two satires on the ever-enticing topic of King George the Third: "A Dialogue between his Britannic Majesty and Mr. Fox, supposed to have passed about the time of the approach of the combined fleets of France and Spain to the British coasts, August, 1779";[3] and "George the Third His Soliloquy for 1779."[4] In both of these satires, the king is made to bewail with grotesque frankness the desperate plight into which he has fallen through his zeal to suppress the spirit of liberty in America:

---

[1] Freneau, "Poems Written and Published during the Revolutionary War," i., 260–261.

[2] Paul Leicester Ford, "Check-List of American Magazines printed in the Eighteenth Century," 7; Albert H. Smyth, "The Philadelphia Magazines and their Contributors 1741–1850," 60–61; Evert A. Duyckinck, in "Introductory Memoir" to Freneau's "Poems relating to the American Revolution," xii.–xv.

[3] "The Poems of Philip Freneau," 156–164.

[4] Ibid. 151–153.

"France aids them now, a desperate game I play,
And hostile Spain will do the same, they say.
My armies vanquished and my heroes fled,
My people murmuring, and my commerce dead,
My shattered navy pelted, bruised, and clubbed,
By Dutchmen bullied and by Frenchmen drubbed,
My name abhorred, my nation in disgrace,
How should I act in such a mournful case!
My hopes and joys are vanished with my coin,
My ruined army, and my lost Burgoyne!"[1]

V.

It is possible that the discontinuance of "The United States Magazine," which occurred with the close of the year 1779, may have left Freneau without definite literary employment; and for this reason or some other he resolved to leave the country once more, setting sail early in 1780 upon a voyage from Philadelphia to St. Eustacia. The voyage was both a brief and a disastrous one. While just off the Capes of the Delaware, the ship was captured by a British cruiser and was carried to New York. Then it was that the poet entered upon the most tragic and the most deplorable experience of his life—an experience of personal indignity and suffering as a prisoner in the hands of the enemy—an experience which had the natural effect of stimulating to almost inconceivable proportions his hatred of them, and thus of qualifying him to write the most energetic and the most envenomed of all his satires. Though but a passenger on the captured vessel, he was thrown into one of those celebrated prison-ships which then lay in New York harbor,—a loathsome hulk called the "Scorpion," where, by reason of the combined horrors of foul air, foul food, foul water, and foul treatment, he soon fell violently ill of a fever,—in consequence of which he was transferred to a so-called hospital ship, the "Hunter." This change of place proved to be but a change of miseries—not an amelioration

[1] "The Poems of Philip Freneau," 152.

of them. After a time, he succeeded in making his escape from these floating hells ; and then, without waiting to regain his bodily strength, but using the strength of his great wrath, he addressed himself to the work of vengeance by writing, before the close of the year 1780, his most savage satire, " The British Prison-Ship,"—a satire actually writhing and scorching with a hatred which no one will be likely to consider as either artificial or feigned:

> " The various horrors of these hulks to tell,—
> These Prison Ships where pain and horror dwell,
> Where Death in tenfold vengeance holds his reign,
> And injured ghosts, yet unavenged, complain,—
> This be my task ! Ungenerous Britons, you
> Conspire to murder those you can't subdue !
>
> " Weak as I am, I 'll try my strength to-day,
> And my best arrows at these hell-hounds play ;
> To future years one scene of death prolong,
> And hang them up to infamy, in song ! "[1]

As originally published, in 1781, the poem was in four cantos, afterward recast into three. Of these, the least effective is the first, which tells the story of his capture. It is in the second and third cantos, wherein he describes the horrors of the prison-ship and of the hospital, that he finds his supreme opportunity for satire and invective:

> " Remembrance shudders at this scene of fears :
> Still in my view some English brute appears—
> Some base-born Hessian slave walks threat'ning by—
> Some servile Scot, with murder in his eye,
> Still haunts my sight, as vainly they bemoan
> Rebellions managed so unlike their own !
>
> " Oh may I never feel the poignant pain,
> To live subjected to such fiends again,—
> Stewards and mates that hostile Britain bore,

---

[1] " The Poems of Philip Freneau," 170–171.

Cut from the gallows on their native shore;
Their ghastly looks and vengeance-beaming eyes
Still to my view in dismal colors rise.
Oh may I ne'er review these dire abodes,
These piles for slaughter, floating on the floods!
And you that o'er the troubled ocean go,
Strike not your standards to this miscreant foe.
Better the greedy wave should swallow all,
Better to meet the death-conducted ball,
Better to sleep on ocean's deepest bed,
At once destroyed and numbered with the dead,
Than thus to perish in the face of day—
Where twice ten-thousand deaths one death repay.

. . . .

Hunger and thirst to work our woe combine,
And mouldy bread, and flesh of rotten swine,
The mangled carcase, and the battered brain,
The doctor's poison, and the captain's cane,
The soldier's musket, and the steward's debt,
The evening shackle, and the noon-day threat!"[1]

One of the most harrowing passages of the poem is that in which he tells how, at the close of every day, they were driven from the hot and crowded decks down into the hold—still hotter and still more crowded:

"Swift from the guarded decks we rushed along,
And vainly sought repose—so vast our throng.
Three hundred wretches here, denied all light,
In crowded mansions pass the infernal night;
Some for a bed their tattered vestments join,
And some on chests, and some on floors recline.
Shut from the blessings of the evening air,
Pensive we lay with mangled corpses there;
Meagre and wan, and scorched with heat, below,
We loomed like ghosts, ere death had made us so!"[2]

It is, however, in individual portraiture—it is in the tributes of choice and vitriolic execration which he pays to three or

[1] "The Poems of Philip Freneau," 172–173, 175. [2] Ibid. 173.

four of the officers whom he had the unhappiness to encounter on board these horrid ships—that the power of this artist is best shewn. One of these detested men was the mate of the "Hunter,"—

> "That wretch who, banished from the navy crew,
> Grown old in blood, did here his trade renew.
> His serpent's tongue, when on his charge let loose,
> Uttered reproaches, scandal, and abuse,
> Gave all to hell who dared his king disown,
> And swore mankind were made for George alone.
> Ten thousand times, to irritate our woe,
> He wished us foundered in the gulph below;
> Ten-thousand times he brandished high his stick,
> And swore, as often, that we were not sick—
> And yet so pale! that we were thought by some
> A freight of ghosts from Death's dominion come."[1]

Another creature on whom the poet here bestows his attentions is a Hessian doctor, the assistant-surgeon of the hospital ship:

> "Fair Science never called the wretch her son,
> And Art disdained the stupid man to own;
>
> . . . .
>
> Yet still he doomed his genius to the rack,
> And, as you may suppose, was owned a quack!
> He on his charge the healing work begun
> With antimonial mixtures— by the tun;
> Ten minutes was the time he deigned to stay,—
> The time of grace allotted once a day,—
> He drenched us well with bitter draughts, 't is true,
> Nostrums from Hell, and cortex from Peru;
> Some with his pills he sent to Pluto's reign,
> And some he blistered with his flies of Spain;
> His Cream of Tartar walked its deadly round,
> Till the lean patient at the potion frowned,
> And swore that hemlock, death, or what you will,
> Were nonsense to the drugs that stuffed his bill.

[1] "The Poems of Philip Freneau," 176.

On those refusing, he bestowed a kick,
Or menaced vengeance with his walking-stick ;
Here, uncontrolled, he exercised his trade,
And grew experienced by the deaths he made ;
By frequent blows we from his cane endured,
He killed at least as many as he cured,
On our lost comrades built his future fame,
And scattered fate where'er his footsteps came.
Some did not seem obedient to his will,
And swore he mingled poison with his pill ;
But I acquit him by a fair confession—
He was no Englishman—he was a Hessian !
Although a dunce, he had some sense of sin,
Or else—the Lord knows where we now had been,—
Perhaps in that far country sent to range
Where never prisoner meets with an exchange !"[1]

But "this dog of Hesse," as the poet calls him, is but a subordinate officer of the medical staff, and has for his one redeeming quality that he is not an Englishman. Not even so much as that can be said on behalf of the man who stood above him, as surgeon-in-chief :

"One master o'er the murdering tribe was placed,—
By him the rest were honored or disgraced.
Once, and but once, by some strange fortune led,
He came to see the dying and the dead ;
He came—but anger so deformed his eye,
And such a faulchion glittered on his thigh,
And such a gloom his visage darkened o'er,
And two such pistols in his hand he bore,
That, by the gods !—with such a load of steel
He came, we thought, to murder, not to heal !
Hell in his heart, and mischief in his head,
He gloomed destruction, and had smote us dead,
Had he so dared—but fate withheld his hand :
He came—blasphemed—and turned again to land !"[2]

---

[1] "The Poems of Philip Freneau," 178–179. [2] Ibid. 179.

VI.

From the time of Freneau's deliverance from imprisonment until the ratification of the treaty of peace, there seems to have been for him no interval of inactivity in his work as a satirist; and one now finds the years 1781, 1782, and 1783 thickly strown with his keen and poisoned verses. Indeed, a running commentary on the writings of this poet during the last three or four years of the Revolution, would be a running commentary on the most important aspects of our history during those years. Even the titles of his chief poems for that time have a value, as helping us to form some rude notion of the variety and range of the subjects with which he then dealt: "On the Memorable Victory obtained by the Gallant Captain Paul Jones, of the 'Good Man Richard,' over the 'Seraphis,' etc. under the command of Captain Pearson";[1] "To the Memory of the Brave Americans, under General Greene, who fell in the Action of September 8, 1781";[2] "To his Excellency General Washington";[3] "Dialogue between the Lords Dunmore and Mansfield";[4] "To Lord Cornwallis, at York, Virginia, October 8, 1781";[5] "An Epistle from Lord Cornwallis to Sir Henry Clinton";[6] "On the Fall of General Earl Cornwallis";[7] "Copy of an Intercepted Letter from a New York Tory to his Friend in Philadelphia";[8] "The Tenth Ode of Horace's Book of Epodes Imitated," for the departure of Benedict Arnold from New York, in December, 1781;[9] "A Speech that should have been spoken by the King of the Island of Britain to his Parliament," at the close of the campaign of 1781;[10] "Sir Harry's Call";[11] "Lord Dunmore's Petition to the Legislature of Virginia";[12] "Epigram occasioned by the Title of Rivington's Royal Gazette being Scarcely Legible";[13] "Song on

---

[1] "The Poems of Philip Freneau," 183–187.
[2] Ibid. 203–204.
[3] Ibid. 187–189.
[4] Ibid. 192–193.
[5] Ibid. 191–192.
[6] Ibid. 194–195.
[7] Ibid. 197–203.
[8] Ibid. 190–191.
[9] Ibid. 257–258.
[10] Ibid. 217–219.
[11] Ibid. 232–233.
[12] Ibid. 213–214.
[13] Ibid. 215.

Captain Barney's Victory over the Ship 'General Monk'";[1] "On Sir Henry Clinton's Recall";[2] "Sir Guy Carleton's Address to the Americans";[3] "Lines Occasioned by General Robertson's Proclamation";[4] "Satan's Remonstrance Occasioned by Mr. Rivington's Late Apology for Lying";[5] "Rivington's Reflections, December, 1782";[6] "Stanzas Occasioned by the Departure of the British from Charleston";[7] "Hugh Gaine's Account of His Life";[8] "The New York Refugees' Petition to Sir Guy Carleton";[9] "A New York Tory's Epistle to One of his Friends in Pennsylvania, written previous to his Departure for Nova Scotia";[10] and "Rivington's Confessions, Addressed to the Whigs of New York," [11] December 31, 1783.

VII.

In addition to the poems thus named as Freneau's chief productions for the last few years of the Revolution, are three others belonging to the same period, but so remarkable for their satiric quality, so rich in their interpretations of the later moods of the Revolutionist party, as to claim in this place our more particular consideration. The first, which probably was written in the year 1780, or in the first half of the year 1781, is entitled "The Political Balance, or, the Fates of Britain and America Compared," [12] and, for imaginative force and delicacy, for humor, for pungent wit, for spontaneity and liveliness of action, and for its easy mastery of the technique of comic verse, may be accounted as the most brilliant of all this author's writings.

At the outset, the reader gets from the couplet which forms its motto, a fair hint of the purpose and method of this sprightly composition:

---

[1] "The Poems of Philip Freneau," 241–244. [2] Ibid. 244–247.
[3] Ibid. 247–249. [4] Ibid. 255–256. [5] Ibid. 264–265.
[6] Ibid. 275–280. [7] Ibid. 291–293. [8] Ibid. 281–291.
[9] Ibid. 269–270. [10] Ibid. 295–298. [11] Ibid. 299–302; 305–309.
[12] Ibid. 224–232.

" Deciding fates, in Homer's style, I shew,
And bring contending gods once more to view."

It is, indeed, what its author calls it, " A Tale,"—a merry mock-classic tale in verse, wherein the principal gods of Olympus make a sudden and unexpected irruption into the sphere of modern and western life, and, looking down with sovereign derision upon its strutting and vulgar pretensions to greatness, proclaim judgments which, for the insurgent Americans of that time, must have had the effect of the most delicious paradox—upsetting all those tests and standards of personal or national value then imposed upon the world—particularly upon the American world—by the immense predominance of Great Britain:

" As Jove, the Olympian, (who both I and you know,
Was brother to Neptune, and husband to Juno)
Was lately reviewing his papers of state,
He happened to light on the records of Fate.

" In alphabet order this volume was written,
So he opened at B., for the article 'Britain.'
'She struggles so well,' said the god, 'I will see
What the sisters in Pluto's dominions decree!'

" And first on the top of a column he read—
'Of a king with a mighty soft place in his head,
Who should join in his temper the ass and the mule,
The Third of his name, and by far the worst fool:

" 'His reign shall be famous for multiplication,
The sire and the king of a whelp generation;
But such is the will and the purpose of Fate,
For each child he begets he shall forfeit a state.

" 'In the course of events, he shall find to his cost
That he cannot regain what he foolishly lost;
Of the nations around he shall be the derision,
And know by experience the rule of division.'

"So Jupiter read—a god of first rank—
And still had read on, but he came to a blank;
For the Fates had neglected the rest to reveal—
They either forgot it, or chose to conceal."[1]

Naturally annoyed at this neglect or refusal of the Fates to provide him with further information about the future of Great Britain, especially in its contention with America, Jupiter determines to obtain the information for himself, by just weighing the two contending parties in a huge pair of "Scales" which he knows of as existing somewhere in his sky. Accordingly, summoning Vulcan, he orders him at once to make a globe, with the several portions of the earth so adjusted to it that he could take them out one by one, and put them into the balance:

"How else should I know what the portions will weigh,
Or which of the combatants carry the day?"

With Jove's command, the ingenious blacksmith at once proceeded to comply:

"Made centre and circles as round as a pancake,
And here the Pacific, and there the Atlantic.

"An axis he hammered, whose ends were the Poles,
(On which the whole body perpetually rolls)
A brazen meridian he added to these,
On which were engraven twice ninety degrees.

"I am sure you had laughed to have seen his droll attitude,
When he bent round the surface the circles of latitude,
The zones, and the tropics, meridians, equator,
And other fine things that are drawn on salt water.

"Away to the southward—instructed by Pallas—
He placed in the ocean the Terra Australis,
New Holland, New Guinea and so of the rest—
America lay by herself in the west.

. . . .

---

[1] "The Poems of Philip Freneau," 224–225.

"Adjacent to Europe he struck up an island,
One part of it low, but the other was high land,
With many a comical creature upon it,
And one wore a hat, and another a bonnet.

"Like emmets or ants in a fine summer's day,
They ever were marching in battle array,
Or skipping about on the face of the brine
Like witches in egg-shells,—their ships of the line.

"These poor little creatures were all in a flame,
To the lands of America urging their claim,
Still biting, or stinging, or spreading their sails,—
For Vulcan had formed them with stings in their tails.

"So poor and so lean, you might count all their ribs,[1]
Yet were so enraptured with crackers and squibs,
That Vulcan with laughter almost split asunder—
'Because they imagined their crackers were thunder.'

"Due westward from these, with a channel between,
A servant to slaves, Hibernia was seen,
Once crowded with monarchs, and high in renown,—
But all she retained was the Harp and the Crown!

"Her genius, a female, reclined in the shade,
And, merely for music, so mournfully played,
That Jove was uneasy to hear her complain,
And ordered his blacksmith to loosen her chain.

. . . .

"At length, to discourage all stupid pretensions,
Jove looked at the globe, and approved its dimensions,
And cried in a transport—'Why! what have we here?
Friend Vulcan, it is a most beautiful sphere!

"'Now, while I am busy in taking apart
This globe that is formed with such exquisite art,
Go, Hermes, to Libra—you 're one of her gallants—
And ask, in my name, for the loan of her Balance.'

---

[1] "Their national debt being above £200,000,000 sterling." Freneau.

"Away posted Hermes as swift as the gales,
And as swiftly returned with the ponderous Scales,
And hung them aloft to a beam in the air,
So equally poised they had turned with a hair."[1]

Thus, having all things in readiness, Jove undertakes alone to lift "Columbia" into its scale, but to his amazement he finds that even his Olympian strength is unequal to the task. Accordingly, "turning about to their godships," he bids them all to join forces with him, and together to try to hoist the mighty mass:

"So to it they went, with handspikes and levers,
And upward she sprung, with her mountains and rivers,
Rocks, cities, and islands, deep waters and shallows,
Ships, armies, and forests, high heads and fine fellows!

"'Stick to it,' cries Jove, 'now heave one and all!
At least we are lifting one eighth of the Ball!
If backward she tumbles, then trouble begins,
And then have a care, my dear boys, of your shins!'

"When gods are determined, what project can fail?
So they gave a fresh shove, and she mounted the scale;
Suspended aloft, Jove viewed her with awe—
And the gods for their pay, had a hearty huzza!"[2]

At the mere appearance of an intention on Jove's part to do so preposterous a thing as to put Britain into the scale opposite that which held the enormous mass of Columbia, Neptune, who seems to have been standing by, perhaps without lending a hand, rudely bawls out—saluting his august brother as "a noddy!" Whereupon,

"'Away to your waters, you blustering bully,'
Said Jove, 'or I'll make you repent of your folly!
Is Jupiter, sir, to be tutored by you?—
Get out of my sight, for I know what I do!'

---

[1] "The Poems of Philip Freneau," 225–228. [2] Ibid. 228–229.

"Then searching about with his fingers for Britain,
Thought he, 'This same island I cannot well hit on;
The devil take him who first called her the Great!
If she was—she is vastly diminished of late.'

"Like a man that is searching his thigh for a flea,
He peeped, and he fumbled, but nothing could see;
At last he exclaimed—'I 'm surely upon it—
I think I have hold of a highlander's bonnet.'

"But finding his error he said with a sigh,
'This bonnet is only the island of Skie!'
So away to his namesake, the planet, he goes,
And borrowed two moons to hang on his nose:

"Through these, as through glasses, he saw her quite clear,
And in raptures cried out—'I have found her—she 's here!
If this be not Britain, then call me an ass—
She looks like a gem in an ocean of glass;

"But, faith, she 's so small I must mind how I shake her—
In a box I 'll inclose her, for fear I should break her:
Though a god, I might suffer for being aggressor,
Since scorpions, and vipers, and hornets possess her.

"'The white cliffs of Albion are full in my view—
And the hills of Plinlimmon I think I could shew;
But, Vulcan, inform me what creatures are these,
That smell so of onions and garlick and cheese?'

"Old Vulcan replied—'Odds splutter a nails!
Why these are the Welsh, and the country is Wales!
When Taffy is vexed, no devil is ruder—
Take care how you handle the offspring of Tudor!

"'On the crags of the mountains hur living hur seeks,
Hur country is planted with garlic and leeks;
So great is hur choler, beware how you tease hur,
For these are the Britons—unconquered—by Cæsar!'

"Jove peeped through his moons, and examined their features,
And said, 'By my troth, they are wonderful creatures!—
The beards are so long they encircle their throats,
That—unless they are Welshmen—I swear they are goats.

"'But now, my dear Juno, pray give me my mittens—
The insects I am going to handle are Britons—
I 'll draw up their isle with a finger and thumb,
As the doctor extracts an old tooth from your gum.'

"Then he raised her aloft—but to shorten our tale—
She looked like a clod in the opposite scale,
Britannia so small, and Columbia so large—
A ship of first rate, and a ferryman's barge!"

Of course, the result of this grotesque experiment was only too obvious; and as he put back into their proper places the two contending sections of his globe,

"said Jove with a smile,
'Columbia shall never be ruled by an isle;
But vapors and darkness around her shall rise,
And tempests conceal her awhile from our eyes.

. . . . . .

"'Then cease your endeavors, ye vermin of Britain'—
And here in derision their island he spit on—
''T is madness to seek what you never can find,
Or think of uniting what nature disjoined;

"'But still you may flutter awhile with your wings,
And spit out your venom, and brandish your stings;
Your hearts are as black and as bitter as gall—
A curse to yourselves, and a blot on the Ball!'"[1]

VIII.

Some months after the American victory at Yorktown had made it plain to all the world that the war, even though it should be still further prolonged, was certainly to end at

[1] "The Poems of Philip Freneau," 229–332.

last in American Independence, Freneau sent forth the second of the three poems to which special attention has here been called,—a capital jeu d'esprit, called "The Prophecy," —a prophecy which, in mock imitation of an ancient oracle, is expressed in mystic terms, initials, and other transparent disguises,—a prophecy, also, which is written in that safest of all prophetic ways, namely, after the occurrence of the chief events which it assumes to foretell. Within the twenty-three lines of this delightful trifle, as in a poetic microcosm, one finds the whole American Revolution, in its great successive stages, humorously summed up and concluded, from the Whig point of view:

"When a certain great king, whose initial is G,
Shall force stamps upon paper, and folks to drink tea;
When these folks burn his tea and stampt paper, like stubble,
You may guess that this king is then coming to trouble.
But when a petition he treads under his feet,
And sends over the ocean an army and fleet;
When that army, half-starved, and frantic with rage,
Shall be cooped up with a leader whose name rhymes to cage;
When that leader goes home dejected and sad,
You may then be assured the king's prospects are bad.
But when B and C with their armies are taken,
This king will do well if he saves his own bacon.
In the year seventeen hundred and eighty and two,[1]
A stroke he shall get that will make him look blue;
In the years eighty-three, eighty-four, eighty-five,
You hardly shall know that the king is alive;
In the year eighty-six the affair will be over,
And he shall eat turnips that grow in Hanover.
The face of the Lion shall then become pale,
He shall yield fifteen teeth, and be sheared of his tail.
O king, my dear king, you shall be very sore;
The Stars and the Lily shall run you on shore,
And your Lion shall growl—but never bite more!"[2]

[1] Perhaps alludes to the provisional articles for a treaty of peace, recognizing American Independence.

[2] "The Poems of Philip Freneau," 223.

IX.

Not, however, in jest or playfulness, but in uttermost sincerity of scorn, in the ruthlessness of unforgiving hate, was this poet of alienated America to say his last word to the unfortunate monarch whose blundering conscientiousness in king-craft, whose well-intentioned and prayerful obstinacy in baleful leadership, had at last brought to England the loss of her most valuable dependency, and to the English-speaking race a disruption that should bear for unborn millions on both sides of the Atlantic a legacy, perhaps an endless legacy, of mutual ill-will. Freneau's last word to King George of England—a poet's ban and malediction upon him and his people—was spoken in March, 1783, on the news of "the King's Speech, recommending Peace with the American States":

> "Grown sick of war, and war's alarms,
> Good George has changed his note at last—
> Conquest and Death have lost their charms;
> He and his nation stand aghast
> To see what horrid lengths they 've gone,
> And what a brink they stand upon.
>
> . . . .
>
> "Let jarring powers make war or peace,
> Monster!—no peace shall greet thy breast:
> Our murdered friends shall never cease
> To hover round and break thy rest!
> The Furies shall thy bosom tear,
> Remorse, Distraction, and Despair,
> And Hell with all its fiends, be there!
>
> "Curs'd be the ship that e'er set sail
> Hence, freighted for thy odious shore;
> May tempests o'er her strength prevail,
> Destruction round her roar!
> May Nature all her aids deny,

The sun refuse his light,
The needle from its object fly,
No star appear by night,
Till the base pilot, conscious of his crime,
Directs the prow to some more grateful clime.

"Genius! that first our race designed,
To other kings impart
The finer feelings of the mind,
The virtues of the heart!
When'er the honors of a throne
Fall to the bloody and the base,
Like Britain's monster, pull them down!—
Like his, be their disgrace!

"Hibernia, seize each native right!
Neptune, exclude him from the main;
Like her that sunk with all her freight,
The 'Royal George,' take all his fleet,
And never let them rise again;
Confine him to his gloomy isle,
Let Scotland rule her half;
Spare him to curse his fate awhile,
And Whitehead—thou to write his epitaph!"[1]

X.

After a considerate inspection of the writers and the writings of our Revolutionary era, it is likely that most readers will be inclined to name Philip Freneau as the one American poet of all that time who, though fallen on evil days and driven from his true course somewhat by stormy weather, yet had a high and questionless vocation for poetry. Of his own claim to recognition he was proudly conscious, as sometimes appeared when, in blunt and facetious fashion, he was retorting upon some of his literary brethren who both robbed and calumniated him:

---

[1] "The Poems of Philip Freneau," 293–295.

"The sun 's in the west,
And I am opprest
With fellows attempting to blacken my muse,
Who hardly have genius to blacken my shoes."[1]

Nor was he unconscious of all that was malign to his poetic destiny, both in the time and in the place on which his lot was cast:

"What doom the Fates intend, is hard to say,—
Whether to live to some far-distant day,
Or, sickening in your prime,
In this bard-baiting clime,
Take pet, make wings, say prayers, and flit away."[2]

Even in the larger relations which an American poet in the eighteenth century might hold to the development of English poetry everywhere, Freneau did some work, both early and late, so fresh, so original, so unhackneyed, so defiant of the traditions that then hampered and deadened English verse, so delightful in its fearless appropriation of common things for the divine service of poetry, as to entitle him to be called a pioneer of the new poetic age that was then breaking upon the world, and therefore to be classed with Cowper, Burns, Wordsworth, and their mighty comrades,—those poetic iconoclasts who, entering the temple of eighteenth-century English verse, broke up its wooden idols, rejected its conventionalized diction, and silenced forever its pompous, monotonous, and insincere tune.

Finally, of Freneau, it remains to be said that, in a certain eminent sense, he was the first American poet of Democracy; and that from the beginning to the end of his career, and in spite of every form of temptation, he remained true—fiercely, savagely true—to the conviction, that his part and lot in the world was to be a protagonist on behalf of mere human nature, as against all its assailants

---

[1] "The Poems of Philip Freneau," 155.
[2] "Poems on Several Occasions," 394.

whether in church or state. In the year 1795—during Washington's second term in the presidency—this combat-loving poet sent forth a second and an enlarged edition of his poems, which had been first issued seven years before; and in some verses which he therein inserted, entitled "To My Book," one may still hear the proud voice with which he claimed for himself that, whether in other ways successful or not, he was at least a poet militant—ever doing battle on the people's side:

> "Seven years are now elapsed, dear rambling volume,[1]
> Since, to all knavish wights a foe,
> I sent you forth to vex and gall 'em,
> Or drive them to the shades below,—

---

[1] "Poems on Several Occasions," 394–395. It does not come within the scope of this book to deal with the literary work of Freneau after 1783; but as some of his publications after that date included work done by him during the Revolution, it may be proper to mention that in 1788, at Philadelphia, was published "Miscellaneous Works of Mr. Philip Freneau, Containing his Essays and Additional Poems." The only copy of this book which I have ever met with, formerly belonged to George Ticknor, and by his gift is now the property of the Massachusetts Historical Society. It has prose and verse intermingled,—some of it, doubtless, produced during the Revolution. Freneau was the master of a delightful prose style, easy, sinewy, touched with delicate humor, crisp, and keen-edged. As good examples of his work, I noted in this volume "Advice to Authors, by the late Robert Slender," 42–48; "Robert Slender's Idea of the Human Soul," 87–91; "The Market Man," 93–94; "The Debtor," 96–97; "Rules and Directions How to Avoid Creditors, Sheriffs, Constables, etc." 97–106; "The City Poet," 111–119; "Directions for Courtship," 133–140. In 1809, at Philadelphia, was published in two volumes, the third edition of his collected poems, entitled "Poems Written and Published During the American Revolutionary War, and now Republished from the Original Manuscripts, interspersed with Translations from the Ancients, and other Pieces not heretofore in Print." There is need of a thorough life of Freneau, based upon letters of his and other materials never yet used. We ought, also, to have a carefully edited collection of his writings in prose and verse. At present, we have only sketches of him,—as by John W. Francis, in Duyckinck's "Cyclopædia of American Literature," i. 332–333; in the "Introduction" to the London reprint of his "Poems," A.D. 1861; in Evert A. Duyckinck's "Introductory Memoir" to Freneau's "Poems Relating to the American Revolution"; and by Edward F. DeLancey, in "Philip Freneau the Huguenot Patriot-Poet of the Revolution and his Poetry."

With spirit still of Democratic proof,
And still despising Shylock's cankered hoof.

. . . .

For seven years past, a host of busy foes
Have buzzed about your nose,
White, black, and grey, by night and day,
Garbling, lying, singing, sighing.
These eastern gales a cloud of insects bring
That, fluttering, snivelling, whimpering, on the wing,
And wafted still as Discord's demon guides,
Flock round the flame that yet shall singe their hides.

"Well!—let the Fates decree whate'er they please:
Whether you 're doomed to drink Oblivion's cup,
Or Praise-God-Barebones eats you up,
This I can say, you 've spread your wings afar,
Hostile to garter, ribbon, crown, and star,—
Still on the People's, still on Freedom's side,
With full determined aim, to baffle every claim
Of well-born wights that aim to mount and ride."

CHAPTER XXXV.

PULPIT-CHAMPIONS OF THE AMERICAN REVOLUTION.

I.—The tradition of leadership inherited by the pulpit of the Revolution—The political power of the preachers as recognized by Otis and others—Public occasions for political discourse from the pulpit.

II.—Charles Chauncy's services to the Revolution as preacher, author, and political monitor—His special enjoyment of theological controversy.

III.—Sermon before the Revolutionary assembly of Massachusetts, May 31, 1775, by Samuel Langdon, president of Harvard College.

IV.—Our first national Fast Day, July 20, 1775, as the occasion for sermons in all the colonies on the political and military crisis—At the camp in Roxbury, by Ezra Sampson—At Philadelphia, by Thomas Coombe, assistant rector of Christ Church and St. Peter's.

V.—The first national Fast Day as observed by Congress at Philadelphia—The sermon by Jacob Duché—His history and character—His brilliant oratory—"The first prayer in Congress"—The eclat of his various services for the Revolutionary cause—Under the military reverses of the summer of 1776, he loses heart, and advises Washington to stop the war—Duché's retreat to England, and popularity there—His "Discourses on Various Subjects," 1777—His once famous "Caspipina's Letters."

VI.—Jacob Green, a preacher of Revolutionary politics, in New Jersey.

VII.—Pulpit warnings against the moral and spiritual dangers of the times—Oliver Hart, of Charleston, South Carolina, preaches against the sin of dancing—Israel Evans preaches to the troops in Pennsylvania against the religious apathy and immorality then prevalent.

VIII.—Hugh Henry Brackenridge as chaplain in Washington's army in 1777—His previous career as student, teacher, and poet—His "Six Political Discourses Founded on Scripture"—His chant of patriotic hatred and vengeance—His prophetic woes on the enemies of American peace and freedom.

IX.—Samuel Cooper of Boston—His unusual influence in letters, society, and affairs—His political essays—His published discourses.

X.—Sermon by Nathan Fiske of Brookfield, on the capture of Lord Cornwallis.

XI.—Zabdiel Adams's election sermon in Massachusetts, 1782.

XII.—Nathaniel Whitaker of Salem—His sermons in imprecation of the Tories.

XIII.—Sermons on the day of national Thanksgiving for Independence and Peace, December 11, 1783—By Eliphalet Porter, at Roxbury—By David Osgood at Medbury—By John Rodgers in New York,

XIV.—George Duffield of Philadelphia—His career—His prominence as a political preacher—Extolled by John Adams, in 1775 and 1776—His services as army chaplain—As a mark for Odell's satire—His sermon on the advent of Peace.

I.

"In America, as in the Grand Rebellion in England," said a Loyalist writer of our Revolutionary time, "much execution was done by sermons." [1] Had it been otherwise, there would now be cause for wonder. Indeed, the preachers were then in full possession of that immense leadership, intellectual and moral, which had belonged to their order, in America ever since its settlement, in England ever since the middle of the sixteenth century; and though this tradition of leadership was beginning to suffer under the rivalry of the printing-press and under the ever-thickening blows of rationalism, yet, when aroused and concentrated upon any object, they still wielded an enormous influence over the opinions and actions of men,—even as to the business of this world. Without the aid "of the black regiment," as James Otis facetiously called them, he declared his inability to carry his points.[2] Late in the year 1774 the Loyalist, Daniel Leonard, in an essay accounting for the swift and alarming growth of the spirit of resistance and even of revolution in America, gave a prominent place to the part then played in the agitation by "our dissenting ministers." "What effect must it have had upon the audience," said he, "to hear the same sentiments and principles, which they had before read in a newspaper, delivered on Sundays from the sacred desk, with a religious awe, and the most solemn appeals to heaven, from lips which they had been taught from their cradles, to believe could utter nothing but eternal truths!" [3]

The literary history of the pulpit of the American Revolution is virtually a history of the pulpit-champions of that movement; since those preachers who were not its champions could seldom find a printer bold enough to put their sermons to press, or even an opportunity to speak them

[1] J. Boucher, "Autobiography" in "Notes and Queries," 5th Series, vi. 142.

[2] Tudor, "Life of Otis," 492 n.

[3] "Nov. and Massachusettensis," 151.

from the pulpit.[1] Nor was it necessary that ministers should seem to go out of their way in order to discourse upon those bitter secular themes: indeed, they would have been forced to go out of their way in order to avoid doing so. Fast days, thanksgiving days, election days, the anniversaries of battles and of important acts of Congress and of other momentous events in the progress of the struggle, brought such topics to the very doors of their studies, and even laid them upon the open Bibles in their pulpits. Moreover, if any clergyman held back from political preaching, he was not likely to escape some reminder, more or less gentle, as to what was expected of him in such a time of awful stress and peril. "Does Mr. Wibird preach against oppression and the other cardinal vices of the time?" wrote John Adams to his wife, from Philadelphia, shortly after the battle of Bunker Hill. "Tell him, the clergy here of every denomination, not excepting the Episcopalian, thunder and lighten every Sabbath. They pray for Boston and the Massachusetts. They thank God most explicitly and fervently for our remarkable successes. They pray for the American army."[2]

II.

One of the purest and most undaunted public characters to confront us on the threshold of this period, is Charles Chauncy,[3] pastor of the First Church in Boston, who as preacher, author, and political monitor brought to the service of the Revolution a keen and a ripe intellect, unbounded courage, and the prestige of long and manifold

[1] In Chapter xiv. of the present work, Jonathan Boucher is taken as the representative of the Loyalist preachers of the Revolution; even as Jonathan Mayhew is dealt with in Chapter vi. as the representative of the preachers who, in the first years of the Revolution, educated public opinion for its bold doctrines and duties.

[2] "Letters of John Adams, Addressed to His Wife," i. 50.

[3] His character, and his career as a writer prior to the American Revolution, are dealt with by me in "A History of American Literature during the Colonial Time," ii. 199–203.

literary industry. He brought to the service of the Revolution, also, an invincible confidence in its final triumph. "Our cause is so just," said he again and again, "that if human efforts should fail, a host of angels would be sent to support it."[1]

With the Revolutionary movement, in every stage and phase of it, particularly as interpreted by the radical politicians of New England, he was in perfect sympathy. Perhaps his most characteristic contribution to its development was made through the part he took in that violent controversy which raged during the earliest years of the Revolution, over the projected introduction of Anglican bishops into America,[2]—a controversy which had no little effect in creating and inflaming American suspicion as to the dangerous and, in fact, damnable designs of the British government for a universal suppression of human rights in America. From year to year, however, during this whole period, there was scarcely an aspect of the moving scene, upon which this apostle of civic righteousness and fortitude did not utter some notable comment, giving to his imperiled countrymen the most ample help in the form of counsel, warning, and reproof. Thus, in 1766, he published "A Discourse on 'the Good News from a Far Country,'" delivered on the day of public thanksgiving for the repeal of the Stamp Act, and discussing the whole problem of Anglo-American relations, with the tone of a man of affairs as well as of a cloistered thinker and a divine.[3] In 1770, he sounded his

[1] Tudor, "The Life of James Otis," 148.

[2] The titles of his publications touching the Episcopal controversy, which are too numerous for mention in the text, may be easily found by those who have the curiosity therefor, in any one of the several extant lists of his published writings for his entire career, as follows:

(1) John Clarke, "A Discourse . . . at the Interment of the Rev. Charles Chauncy," etc., Boston: 1787.

(2) Sprague, "Annals," etc., viii. 10–11.

(3) William Chauncey Fowler, "Memorials of the Chaunceys," 51–54.

(4) Sabin, "A Dictionary of Books relating to America," iii. 546–553.

(5) Paul Leicester Ford, "Bibliotheca Chaunciana." The last is by far the most complete and the most accurate.

[3] A reprint of this sermon may be seen in John Wingate Thornton, "The Pulpit of the American Revolution," 105–146.

usual high note of political courage, in a sermon entitled "Trust in God the Duty of a People in a Day of Trouble." In 1774, he published "A Letter to a Friend," giving an account "of the hardships and sufferings the town of Boston . . . must undergo in consequence of the late act of the British parliament." In 1778, he published a sermon against "sordid avarice" as "the accursed Thing" which "must be taken away from among a people, if they would reasonably hope to stand before their enemies."

When, at last, the triumph of the Revolution loomed in clear vision just before him, this master and lover of debate was quite free to give himself up to the bliss of a new theological controversy—more lively, if possible, than the political and military one then drawing to its end—a controversy over the doctrine of future punishment. Upon this question Chauncy, who took the less glowing but more genial side, published, in 1782, a little book entitled, "Salvation of All Men, Illustrated and Vindicated as a Scripture Doctrine"; in 1783, a little book entitled, "Divine Glory brought to View, in the Final Salvation of All Men"; in 1784, a large book entitled, "The Mystery hid from Ages and Generations, made manifest by the Gospel-Revelation; or, the Salvation of All Men the Grand Thing aimed at in the Scheme of God." In setting forth his own optimistic faith as to the divine management of the universe, he had sometimes a sparkling and a grimly playful zest, as when, for example, he opposed his own view to that of an antagonist who had laid down the doctrine, that the everlasting misery of a portion of the human race "was consistent with the justice of God, and essential to His glory." "I have such a veneration for my Creator," says Chauncy, "as to suppose He needs no foil to set off His perfections; such an opinion of the Saints, as to imagine they could relish their felicity, without being spectators of the misery of the damned. I place such a value upon the merits and death of my Redeemer, as to conclude all will be happy for whom He suffered on the Cross. And I pay such a regard to the positive declarations of Scripture, as to anticipate the restitution of all things, when the ruins of the Fall shall be more than repaired, and the creature which now groans shall groan no more." He is but too glad, also, to admit that the God whom he serves, is "very unlike" the God of his antagonist: "The God to whom you pay your religious homage, needs the introduction of sin and misery, in order to illustrate His own character, and display His divine perfections. I bow my knee to a Power intrinsically excellent, who can shine without contrast, whose glory is essential, whose happiness is immutable, and who would be the admiration of His creatures, even were guilt and suffering banished the universe. You expect to look down from Heaven upon numbers of wretched objects, confined in the Pit of Hell, and blaspheming their Creator forever. I hope to see the prison-doors opened, and to hear those tongues which are now profaning the name of God, chaunting His praise. In one word, you imagine the Divine Glory will be advanced by immortalizing sin and misery: I, by exterminating both natural and moral evil, and introducing universal happiness. Which of our systems is best supported, let reason and Scripture determine." [1]

III.

On the thirty-first of May, 1775,—in the grim interval between Concord and Bunker Hill,—there was convened at the village of Watertown, a few miles west of Cambridge, an assemblage of delegates from the several towns of Massachusetts, to act as a provisional government for the colony in place of their General Court which, under the circumstances, could not be held. It was the anniversary of the day fixed by royal charter for the election, by the lower house, of the members of the colonial council: a day on which, for nearly a century and a half, it had been customary for the members of the legislature to go in a body to the

[1] "Divine Glory brought to View," etc., 3-4.

house of worship and listen to a sermon from some eminent preacher expressly chosen for the purpose. The stately and venerable associations of the day were not forgotten by those sturdy representatives at Watertown; and though a rude intermission had then befallen their regular government, they determined to keep alive as many as possible of its ancient forms. Accordingly on this day, having proceeded to the old village meeting-house, they were addressed by Samuel Langdon, president of Harvard College, who, in the very first sentences of his discourse, gave voice to the stern grief, the indignation, the undaunted purpose that were in all their hearts. "On this day," said he, "the people have from year to year assembled from all our towns, in a vast congregation, with gladness and festivity, with every ensign of joy displayed in our metropolis, which now, alas, is made a garrison of mercenary troops, the stronghold of despotism! But how shall I now address you from this desk, remote from the capital, and remind you of the important business which distinguished this day in our calendar, without spreading a gloom over this assemblage by exhibiting the melancholy change made in the face of our public affairs? We have lived to see the time when British liberty is just ready to expire; when that constitution of government which has so long been the glory and strength of the English nation, is deeply undermined and ready to tumble into ruins; when America is threatened with cruel oppression, and the arm of power is stretched out against New England, and especially against this colony, to compel us to submit to the arbitrary acts of legislators who are not our representatives, and who will not themselves bear the least part of the burdens which without mercy they are laying upon us. The most formal and solemn grants of kings to our ancestors are deemed by our oppressors as of little value; and they have mutilated the charter of this colony in the most essential parts, upon false representations and new-invented maxims of policy, without the least regard to any legal process. We are no longer permitted to fix our eyes on the faithful of the land, and trust in the wisdom of their counsels and the equity of their judgment; but men in whom we can have no confidence—whose principles are subversive of our liberties . . . men who are ready to serve any master and execute the most unrighteous decrees, for high wages—whose faces we never saw before, and whose interests and connections may be far divided from us by the wide Atlantic—are to be set over us as councilors and judges, at the pleasure of those who have the riches and power of the nation in their hands, and whose noblest plan is to subjugate the colonies first, and then the whole nation, to their will." [1]

IV.

In view of the "critical, alarming, and calamitous state" of America, after the battles of Lexington and Concord, the 20th of July, 1775, had been appointed by the Continental Congress "for all the English colonies on this continent as a day of public humiliation, fasting, and prayer"; [2] and in at least thirteen of those colonies the day was observed accordingly,—being, indeed, "the first general fast ever kept on one day since the settlement" of the country; [3] and being, likewise, a notable proof that these same American colonies had finally passed from the stage of local separatism into the stage of incipient national unity. On that day, therefore, from New Hampshire to Georgia, the pulpit became the organ of this new national consciousness—of this universal alarm and pain and hate and aspiration; it then spoke out in every tone natural to Englishmen, to freemen, and to Christians.

On that day, at the camp at Roxbury, Massachusetts, a most stirring sermon [4] was preached to the officers and men of Colonel Cotton's regiment by the youthful pastor of the Congregational Church at Plympton, Ezra Sampson, a graduate of Yale, a man of abilities so remarkable that he

---

[1] "A Sermon," etc., 5–7.

[2] "Journals of the Am. Cong.," i. 81–82.

[3] A. Holmes, "Annals," etc., ii. 215.

[4] Published at Watertown: 1775.

was described by one of his classmates "as being both Sampson by name and Sampson by nature."[1] "It is recorded of a Turkish general," exclaimed the preacher, "that being called to engage a Christian army which had broken through the most solemn ties, he stood up at the head of his troops, and then taking out the treaty that they had violated and holding it up to view, thus addressed the Throne of Heaven: 'O Almighty Being, if thou art, as they say thou art, these Christians' God, thou lovest what is right and hatest perfidy. Look down, therefore, and behold this treaty which they have broken; and as thou canst not favor what is wrong, render their arms successless, and make mine victorious.' He ended. Immediately the sword was drawn; the two parties vigorously engaged, and the perfidious Christians were beaten off the field. And may not we also hold up a broken charter, the cruel port bill, and the most impious and infamous Quebec bill, adding to these the inhuman, unequaled treachery exercised toward the distressed inhabitants of Boston, as witnesses of the perfidy of our enemies and what their designs upon us are?"[2]

On that day, Thomas Coombe, assistant minister of Christ Church and St. Peter's in Philadelphia, an orator trained to a most flowing and impressive pulpit-style, preached a sermon[3] suitable to the time; for though afterward he

---

[1] Letter of Edward Robinson, in Sprague, "Annals," ii. 124.

[2] "A Sermon," etc., 19–20. This preacher lived to the year 1823, and became well known, not only for his published sermons but for his numerous articles in "The Balance" and in the "Connecticut Courant," and for several books, namely, "The Beauties of the Bible," "The Historical Dictionary," and "The Brief Remarker." His is another example of the strong impulse given to literary activity at Yale College during the decade immediately preceding the Declaration of Independence.

[3] Published in Philadelphia in 1775. In the year previous, he had also published the substance of two sermons on "The Harmony between the Old and New Testament respecting the Messiah." He was also a writer of verse. Thus he published in Philadelphia in 1775, "Edwin or the Emigrant, an Eclogue," wherein Edwin sings of "Auburn's vale," of his own deceased wife Emma, and of other poetic subjects—all in strains melodiously mixed of Goldsmith and

shrank back from the proposition for Independence, he fully justified the course of the colonists thus far in their opposition to ministerial encroachments. Moreover, in this sermon preached upon an occasion of state, he did not fail to point out the frequent and fatal connection between public calamity and private misdoing. In the very year in which the physical conflict of the Revolution began, in the very city in which that conflict was officially directed on behalf of the Revolutionists, this preacher saw reason to lament over the frivolity, the self-indulgence, the gross and sordid vices of the people: "What a rage for pleasure, what extravagance in dress and dissipation, what an unworthy pride of going beyond each other in splendor of appearance. . . . O Philadelphia, dear native city! . . . thy inhabitants, like those of ancient Babylon, dwell carelessly in their habitations; . . . thy young men have far exceeded the bounds of decent or honorable amusement, and scarce any are to be found of either sex stemming the general corruption." [1]

V.

On the morning of the day thus set apart for a solemn consideration by the American people of their sins, dangers, duties, the members of Congress took the trouble to conform to their own recommendation by assembling at half-past nine o'clock, at their usual place of meeting, and going thence in a body "to attend divine service at Mr. Duché's church," [2] where, as was expected, the sermon was preached

water. I have seen a copy of this poem published likewise in Philadelphia, but without date and under a title somewhat altered, namely "The Peasant of Auburn, or the Emigrant. A Poem." This alteration has led to the mistake that these two titles stand for two different poems. For example, "Appletons' Cyclopædia of Am. Biog.," sub. nom.

[1] "A Sermon," etc., 13.

[2] These words, as if from some official minutes which he does not designate, are cited by E. D. Neill, in "The Pa. Mag. of Hist. and Biog.," ii. 66. In my copy of the "Journals of the Am. Cong.," i. 120, the entry of their agreement "to attend divine service" does not mention the church to which they are to go.

by Mr. Duché himself. Representing America as a vine still united to the parent-stalk of Britain, the preacher gave them a vivid and impassioned discourse, wherein, doubtless, every radical Revolutionary politician in Congress had the gratification of hearing his own opinions proclaimed, with melodious fervor, by the most eloquent and fashionable Anglican clergyman in the land. The orator spoke of himself and his countrymen as "injured and oppressed," and as "unmeriting the harsh and rigorous treatment" they were receiving from the mother country; and he thrilled his hearers with fresh indignation and horror at the unnaturalness of this severity: "'T is not now," he exclaimed, "a foreign enemy, or the savages of our own wilderness, that have made the cruel and unrighteous assault; but it is even thou, Britain, that with merciless and unhallowed hands wouldst cut down and destroy this branch of thine own vine."[1]

The preacher who spoke these flaming words, was the Reverend Jacob Duché, rector of the united parishes of Christ Church and St. Peter's, himself at that time thirty-eight years of age, of an old and influential family in Pennsylvania, a member of the first class graduated from the College of Philadelphia, a man noted for his affectionate and generous nature, and for his high cultivation,—his many brilliant and captivating gifts being made still more captivating by the extraordinary sweetness of his voice and his own rather wonderful mastery of it.[2] Alas, as the event proved, it was the misfortune of this pleasant gentleman, that, living in times which called for virile and stern qualities—sound sense, toughness, tenacity, the power to resist flattery and to take blows—he lacked all these, and yet pos-

[1] "The American Vine," 20–21. A Sermon preached before Congress, 20 July, 1775. Philadelphia: 1775.

[2] The first Bishop of Pennsylvania considered Whitefield as the best reader of the Prayer Book he had ever heard, and next to Whitefield, Jacob Duché. He also attributed much of Duché's popularity as a preacher to his "remarkably fine voice and graceful action." Bird Wilson, "Mem. of Bishop White," 28; and Sprague, "Annals," etc., v. 185.

sessed exactly the sort of talent to render his lack of them conspicuous and lamentable.

Nearly a year before the time of Duché's fast-day sermon, he had come into great prominence before the country by an act of devout patriotism which, indeed, at once endeared him to all friends of the Revolution, and which made him the central figure in a noble and pathetic scene still celebrated in our history: he it was who uttered "the first prayer in Congress."

That illustrious body had met for the first time in its existence on Monday, the fifth of September, 1774. On the day following, Cushing of Massachusetts had moved that their daily sessions should be opened with prayer. To this proposal an objection was made by Jay of New York and by Rutledge of South Carolina, on the ground that, proper as the act would be, it was rendered impracticable by their diversity in religious sentiments and usages—some of the members being Congregationalists, some Presbyterians, some Anabaptists, some Episcopalians, some Quakers. Whereupon the sturdy Puritan, Samuel Adams, stood up in his place and said, that while he was a Congregationalist, "he was no bigot, and could hear a prayer from a gentleman of piety and virtue, who was at the same time a friend to his country. He was a stranger in Philadelphia, but had heard that Mr. Duché deserved that character; and therefore he moved that Mr. Duché, an Episcopal clergyman, might be desired to read prayers to the Congress to-morrow morning."[1] Under this gust of magnanimous feeling, the motion prevailed;[2] and, accordingly, the clergyman thus mentioned, having been waited on in person by Peyton Randolph, the President of Congress, graciously consented to their wishes. It happened, likewise, almost at the very moment when Randolph was laying before Duché the invitation of Congress, that the whole town was thrown into consternation by the news which, happily, turned out

[1] "Letters of John Adams," etc., i. 23.

[2] "Journals of the Am. Congress," i. 8.

to be false—that the British forces in the neighborhood of Boston had opened fire upon that beleagured and distressed city. Under such circumstances it was, that on the following morning, Wednesday, the seventh of September, the rector of Christ Church and St. Peter's arrived at the door of Carpenter's Hall. "He appeared with his clerk and in his pontificals," as John Adams wrote in a letter a few days afterward, "and read several prayers in the established form, and then read the collect[1] for the seventh day of September, which was the thirty-fifth Psalm. You must remember, this was the next morning after we heard the horrible rumor of the cannonade of Boston. I never saw a greater effect upon an audience. It seemed as if Heaven had ordained that Psalm to be read on that morning. After this, Mr. Duché, unexpectedly to everybody, struck out into an extemporary prayer, which filled the bosom of every man present. I must confess, I never heard a better prayer, or one so well pronounced. . . . Dr. Cooper himself never prayed with such fervor, such ardor, such earnestness and pathos, and in language so elegant and sublime, for America, for the Congress, for the province of Massachusetts Bay, and especially the town of Boston. It has had an excellent effect upon everybody here. . . . Mr. Duché is one of the most ingenious men, and best characters, and greatest orators, in the Episcopal order upon this continent—yet a zealous friend of liberty and his country."[2]

Outside of Congress, also, the eclat of this performance was very great; and thenceforward throughout the remainder of that year, and throughout the years 1775 and 1776, Duché was a burning and a shining light among American

---

[1] As John Adams's devotions had not been of a kind to make him familiar with the Prayer Book, he may be easily pardoned for calling the Psalter for the day, its "collect." He mentions the thirty-fifth Psalm only; but the Psalter for the seventh day of the month includes the thirty-sixth Psalm also, which was undoubtedly read by Duché, and which must have increased the impression of the astonishing applicability of the portion of ancient Scriptures ages before set apart for that particular day.

[2] "Letters of John Adams," etc., i. 23–24.

civilians and soldiers then engaged in making resistance to the colonial policy of England, and finally in throwing off her authority altogether. Thus, in a fiery sermon preached by him within the walls of Christ Church, about a fortnight after the battle of Bunker Hill, he exhorts the first battalion of Philadelphia troops there present, to remember the duty of standing fast in their spiritual and temporal liberties—of standing fast even in that terrific conflict which England, in her jealousy, as he says, of the rising greatness of America, was then forcing upon her American children. "Stand fast," cried out this surpliced Captain Bobadil to a throng of men then banded and weaponed for an enterprise that was likely to prove a very serious one to them, "stand fast by a steady constancy and perseverance. Difficulties unlooked for may yet arise, and trials present themselves sufficient to shake the utmost firmness of human fortitude. Be prepared, therefore, for the worst. Suffer not your spirits to evaporate by too violent an ebullition now. Be not too eager to bring matters to an extremity, lest you should be wearied out by a continued exertion, and your constancy should fail you at the most important crisis. Coolly and deliberately wait for those events which are in the hands of Providence; and depend upon Him alone for strength and expedients suited to your necessities. In a word, my brethren, though the worst should come, though we should be deprived of all the conveniences and elegancies of life, though we should be cut off from all our usual sources of commerce, and constrained, as many of our brethren have already been, to abandon our present comfortable habitations, let us, nevertheless, stand fast as the guardians of liberty."[1] Brave advice was this, and bravely spoken; and probably no man needed it more, or violated it sooner, than the man himself from whose quivering lips it fell upon that rapt congregation.

A few days after the Declaration of Independence, Duché

[1] This sermon, dedicated to Washington, was published in 1775 both in Philadelphia and in London. The words quoted are on pages 23–24.

was officially notified that, in consideration of his "piety" as well as of his "uniform and zealous attachment to the rights of America," the Congress of the United States had appointed him their chaplain, and would be pleased to have him attend on them every morning at nine o'clock.[1] Attend on them, accordingly, he did, every morning for the next three months, and prayed most fervently for the Divine blessing upon their acts in rejection of the authority of the king and in resistance of his power: "Look down in mercy, we beseech Thee, on these our American States, who have fled to Thee from the rod of the oppressor, and thrown themselves on Thy gracious protection, desiring to be henceforth dependent only on Thee. To Thee have they appealed for the righteousness of their cause; to Thee do they now look up for that countenance and support which Thou alone canst give. Take them, therefore, Heavenly Father, under Thy nurturing care. Give them wisdom in council, and valor in the field; defeat the malicious designs of our cruel adversaries; convince them of the unrighteousness of their cause; and if they still persist in their sanguinary purposes, oh! let the voice of Thine own unerring justice, sounding in their hearts, constrain them to drop the weapons of war from their unnerved hands in the day of battle."[2] Not long, however, after this prayer had been first uttered, the cause on behalf of which it was made began to suffer that series of military reverses which brought on the times that tried men's souls—times in which the soul of poor Duché was tried, and found wanting. For when, at last, these reverses to the American cause culminated in the possession of Philadelphia by the British, Duché promptly turned the political coat which he wore under his surplice; and opening his church for the use

---

[1] John Hancock's letter notifying Duché of the appointment is given by Neill, in "Pennsylvania Mag.," etc., ii. 67. The appointment was made 9 July, 1776. "Jour. Am. Cong.," i. 402. An error seems to have crept into the date of Hancock's letter, in Neill's copy.

[2] The whole prayer is given in Sabine, "Loyalists of the Am. Rev.," i. 389.

of those "cruel adversaries" against whom he had prayed with so much energy, he at once restored to the service such portions of the Prayer Book as he had latterly omitted,[1] and especially gave to the prayers for the king and the royal family the benefit of his most sympathetic and thrilling vocal expression. Soon after that feat of moral versatility, Duché did almost the only logical thing that was left for him to do—he addressed a letter to his friend, the commander-in-chief of the American army, exhorting him by all that was sacred and prudent, "to represent to Congress the indispensable necessity of rescinding the hasty and ill-advised Declaration of Independency." "Your interposition and advice, I am confident, would meet with a favorable reception from the authority under which you act; if it should not, you have an infallible recourse still left—negotiate for your country at the head of your army."[2]

Certainly, as soon as these facts got abroad, this country could hardly be expected to afford a comfortable habitation for the Reverend Jacob Duché. Indeed, a few weeks after his letter to Washington, the newspapers appropriately announced his departure for England, in the distinguished company of Lord Cornwallis, General Cliveland, and Sir George Osborne. Moreover, the country which, in its dire distress, Duché thus abandoned, he never saw again—he was never permitted to see again—until, in 1792, being then old, paralytic, and harmless, he appeared once more in the

[1] "Pennsylvania Mag.," etc., ii. 69.

[2] "The Duché Letter to General Washington," n. p.; n. d., 6–7. This reprint seems to have been made from a copy found among the Duché MSS. offered for sale in Philadelphia in 1893. The very letter which was sent to Washington by Duché is now in the Department of State, and an exact reprint of it has been issued by Worthington Chauncey Ford, in his collection of eight letters from and to Washington and relating to Duché's political attitude during the Revolution; "The Washington-Duché Letters." Between Ford's version and the one given in Sparks, "Corr. of the Am. Rev.," i. 448–458, are many variations. The Philadelphia copy, from which I have quoted above, is almost identical with the text of Sparks's version. Neither, therefore, is quite so valid as Ford's version, which I had not at hand at the time of making my citations.

city of his birth, where it was given him to witness the stately beginnings of the national life of the young Republic under the presidency of that very General whom, in its dark days, he had exhorted to betray both himself and it to the enemy. Six years afterward, his body was laid by the side of his wife's in the churchyard of St. Peter's.

As to Duché's part in the literature of the Revolution, it may be mentioned, that besides the occasional sermons which he sent to the press before he took leave of his country, he published in London, in 1779, two beautiful volumes entitled "Discourses on Various Subjects,"—these discourses being products of his long career in Philadelphia, each volume, also, being adorned with a frontispiece from a painting by the former Philadelphian, Benjamin West. In 1790, this work had passed to its third edition.

By far the most notable contribution made by him to our literature, was a little book commonly known as "Caspipina's Letters," first published in Philadelphia, 1774; republished in Bath, 1777, in London, 1791, and in Dublin, 1792. It was also translated into German and published at Leipsic in 1778.[1] Its exact title is "Observations on a Variety of Subjects, Literary, Moral, and Religious, in a Series of original Letters written by a Gentleman of Foreign Extraction, who resided some Time in Philadelphia." The hypothetical writer of these letters is a young Englishman, bearing the astounding name of Tamoc Caspipina,[2] a student of Magdalen College, Oxford, who, having been sent to America for a couple of years, helps himself to kill the time by giving an account of the country and its people, in letters to such very desirable corre-

[1] For these dates, excepting for the first one, I depend on Sabin. To the first English reprint, was added a life of William Penn; and it was from this reprint that the German translation was made: "Briefe, welche Beobachtungen über verschiedene Gegenstande der Literatur, Religion, und Moral enthalten, nebst dem Leben des Herren Penn. Aus dem Englischen. Leipzig: 1778."

[2] An acrostic upon the full title of the office which Duché then held: "The Assistant Minister of Christ Church and St. Peter's in Philadelphia in North America."

spondents as "The Right Honorable Lord Viscount P.," "Lady Caroline S.," and "The Lord Bishop of B——l." The prevailing tone of the letters is one of refinement, gentility, devoutness; of unswerving deference to the English Church and the English aristocracy; with a genial forbearance towards almost everything in America—except Methodism. This precious and mealy-mouthed Caspipina seems to be a well-developed prig; his observations are wholly without keenness, depth, or force; and though treating of personal and social topics in a new country, it seems never to occur to him that the grandiose solemnity of his platitudes might sometimes be qualified by a stroke of satire, or a ripple of mirth.

VI.

Jacob Green, a graduate of Harvard College in 1744, was molded for the Christian ministry under the influence of Whitefield and Gilbert Tennent, and for the last forty-five years of his life was pastor of the Presbyterian Church in Hanover, New Jersey. An early and a fearless champion of the doctrine of American Independence, he not only preached it from his pulpit, but published a pamphlet[1] in support of it—at a time, too, when any general approval of the doctrine was doubtful. His parish held an exposed

[1] I state this on the testimony of his son, Ashbel Green, in Sprague, "Annals," etc., iii. 138, where he does not mention the title of the pamphlet. Elsewhere, however, he attempts to give the title from memory, but without being confident of his own accuracy, as "Observations on the Present Controversy between Great Britain and Her American Colonies." Quoted in Hildeburn, "Issues of the Pennsylvania Press," ii. 91, as from "Life of Ashbel Green," 46. Hildeburn suggests that the pamphlet referred to, may have been the one published at Philadelphia, in 1769, entitled, "The Controversy between Great Britain and her Colonies Reviewed," etc. On the other hand, Mr. Franklin Burdge has suggested that Green's pamphlet may be the one published in Philadelphia, in 1776, entitled "Observations on the Reconciliation of Great Britain and the Colonies." From internal evidence, as I think, neither of these pamphlets could have been by Jacob Green; neither takes the side of the controversy which his son declares that he took.

situation; yet through the entire period of the war, and amid many perils and hardships, he remained undauntedly at his post; and in all that time of anguish, even as before and afterward, he wrought strongly, according to the light that was in him, on behalf of every interest of man. His most notable publication was "A Vision of Hell: and a Discovery of Some of the Consultations and Devices there, in the Year 1767."[1] In spite of what might be inferred from its title, this little book has no immediate reference to earthly politics, being, in fact, a very animated report of a conference, apparently overheard by the writer, between Satan and the other big devils, touching the outlook for their business in this world, especial emphasis being laid by them on the impediments just then presented to their favorite work of catching souls.

VII.

To some of the patriotic preachers it seemed a shocking impiety that people in so hard a stress of toil and danger as were the Americans, should have any disposition to indulge in the frivolous and baleful device of dancing. For example, Oliver Hart, for thirty years pastor of the Baptist Church in Charleston, South Carolina, was stirred to indignation and grief that in his own city, enveloped as it then was by storm-clouds of calamity, this saltatory abomination was not only "revived," but was "attended to in a frantic manner, at a time when everything in Providence is calling us to different exercises. The judgments of God are now opened over the land, and the inhabitants ought to learn righteousness. The alarm of war, the clangor of arms, the garments rolled in blood, the sufferings of our brethren in the Northern States and of others in a state of captivity, together with the late dreadful conflagration in this town,

[1] The true authorship of this brochure is disguised under the pseudonym of Theodorus Van Shermain. I found a copy of it in the Congregational Library, Boston.

are so many loud calls to repentance, reformation of life, and prayer that the wrath of God may be turned away from us. Instead of which, we are smothered up in pleasure and dissipation. It will hardly be credited that the fire was scarcely extinguished in Charleston, before we had balls, assemblies, and dances in every quarter, and even in some of those houses which miraculously escaped the flames. . . . Is it thus we requite the Lord for our deliverance? The monumental ruins of the town will rise up in judgment against the inhabitants, and condemn them for such impieties. . . . I am no prophet, nor the son of a prophet, and yet will venture to predict that other and perhaps greater judgments will yet light upon us unless we repent."[1] Accordingly, on the 22d of March, 1778, he preached a sermon, blazing with the pure old Puritan fire, entitled "Dancing Exploded: a Sermon shewing the Unlawfulness, Sinfulness, and Bad Consequences of Balls, Assemblies, and Dances in General."

In October, 1779, the eloquent army chaplain, Israel Evans, preaching at Easton, Pennsylvania, to a great throng of soldiers just back from a campaign against the Six Nations, spoke out, like an old Hebrew prophet, against the apathy and immorality then so prevalent among his own countrymen, and their appalling decline in patriotism: "Alas, the spirit of liberty is now rather struggling with the vicious manners and the selfish principles of the times, than with the tyrant of Britain. The love of wealth and the pursuit of pleasure have almost extinguished that flame of patriotism which blazed forth with such ardor at the beginning of this war. Virtue and patriotism, the guardians of liberty, are in many places and by many men made the subject of scorn and contempt, and that by those who would be esteemed wise politicians and friends to their country. . . . A republic without virtue is an absurdity

[1] Part of the Preface to his sermon, "Dancing Exploded," 1778. My quotation is made from the reprint given in "The Patriot Preachers of the American Rev.," 232–257.

in politics, and can no more stand than a building when the foundation is removed." [1]

VIII.

Upon the opening of the military campaign under Washington in the spring of 1777, there appeared among the Pennsylvania troops a young chaplain named Hugh Henry Brackenridge,[2] tall and commanding in person, with the voice, the eye, and the soul of an orator: so penetrated, likewise, by the passion of rage against the enemy and of zeal to destroy him, that his sermons—so far as now known to us—seem to have breathed almost every sort of sentiment excepting such as would remind one of the Sermon on the Mount.

The personal history of this young chaplain had already been an interesting one, and was characteristic of the fiery, aspiring, and indomitable spirit within him. Born in Scotland in 1748, he was brought to America when but five years of age. So poor were his parents that the cost of the sea-voyage had taken their last penny; and on leaving the ship the father had sold the very coat from off his back in order to buy bread and procure conveyance out into the woods of York County, Pennsylvania, beyond the Susquehanna. This little boy, Hugh, not at all lacking in the usual boy-appetite for bread, very soon gave evidence of an unusual appetite for knowledge and of a marvelous precocity and indefatigableness in acquiring it. He would sometimes trudge thirty miles to Fogg's Manor to procure a book, and on coming home would read it in the long winter evening, by the light of burning chips and splinters.

[1] "A Discourse," etc., 25–26.

[2] In his earliest acknowledged publication, and in an advertisement of his school in 1778, his middle name was given as Montgomery. Subsequently, he dropped this name, and took that of Henry. The best biographical account of him which I have met with is by his son, Henry Marie Brackenridge, originally printed in "The Southern Literary Messenger"; reprinted in the elder Brackenridge's prose satire, "Modern Chivalry," ed. 1846, Appendix.

He bargained with a neighboring clergyman for lessons in Latin and Greek, in return for personal labor. Afterward he bargained with a young man near by for lessons in mathematics, in return for his own lessons in Latin and Greek. Thus, by the time he had reached the age of fifteen years, he was ready to set up as a public teacher of those several branches of knowledge. After due examination, he was given the appointment of teacher to a free-school at Gunpowder Falls in Maryland,—a school having in it a number of young men older and bigger than himself. Of these, one very soon came to think that it would be fine to try issues with their stripling-pedagogue, and, accordingly offering him some impertinence, defied his authority. Of course, to young Brackenridge it was quite plain that that particular question of authority was the very one which needed to be settled then and there to the satisfaction of all concerned; and without waste of time or words, he seized a burning stick from the fire, and with it smote his hulk of an antagonist such a blow as felled him to the floor—thereby convincing him and the rest of the school that their new master had valid credentials to teach and to rule in that place. After a peaceful reign among them for several years, Brackenridge gathered up his small earnings, and marched away to Princeton College, where President Witherspoon had just entered upon his duties, and where the young man was enabled to arrange for a part payment of costs, by himself undertaking to teach classes in the college for two hours a day. While giving to the President some account of his own life thus far, he happened to quote the familiar words of Juvenal:

> "Haud facile emergunt, quorum virtutibus obstat
> Res angusta domi"; [1]

whereupon Witherspoon finely replied,—"There you are wrong, young man! it is only your 'res-angusta-domi'-men that do emerge."

[1] Juvenalis Saturarum Liber Primus, iii. 164–165.

Having among his classmates James Madison and Philip Freneau—with whom his friendship seems to have become a life-long influence—he took his bachelor's degree at Princeton in 1771. There, also, he remained for some time after graduation, serving as college-tutor, studying divinity, receiving likewise his license as a preacher. He then went back to Maryland and took charge of an academy on the Eastern Shore; and it was while thus engaged that, in 1776, he wrote for his pupils the tragedy of "The Battle of Bunker's Hill."[1] As public disasters thickened, and the paths of the fighting-men became more and more beset with bafflement and anguish, it was not unlike Brackenridge to turn his back upon his far-off school, and make his way to the camp—there to partake with the troops in all the allotments of fate, to the endurance of which they were to be helped by his strong and thrilling speech and his undaunted bearing.

Then it was that he composed for them the "Six Political Discourses Founded on the Scripture," which, in 1778, were given forth in print to all who cared to read them; the range and method of which may partly be guessed from their titles: "The Bloody Vestiges of Tyranny," "The Nature and Artifice of Toryism," "The Fate of Tyranny and Toryism," "The Agency of Heaven in the Cause of Liberty," "The Blasphemy of Gasconade and Self-Dependence in a Certain General," "The Great Wrath of the Tyrant and the Cause of it." These discourses do indeed announce themselves as "Founded on the Scripture." It may be so; but it is chiefly to Old Testament Scripture that the reference must be meant, and particularly to those portions of it which recite the slaughter of the Canaanites by Joshua, the pitiless deed of Jael the wife of Heber, the imprecations of the Psalmist David, the fierce valor and terribleness of the Maccabees.

---

[1] Published in 1776, and followed in 1777 by his tragedy of "The Death of General Montgomery." For an account of these tragedies, the reader is referred to Chapter xxxii. on "The Dramatic Literature of the Revolution."

Thus, the first discourse, entitled "The Bloody Vestiges of Tyranny," was written and spoken just after the rout and slaughter of our men at the battle of Brandywine, and is a weird rhythmic chant of rage and patriotic hate and vengeance. Taking for his text a part of the eleventh of Jude: "Woe unto them, for they have gone in the way of Cain," he proceeds to name one by one the several renowned successors of him who was "first in the line of murderers"[1]—Nimrod, Pharaoh, Ahab, the Alexanders, the Jenghis Khans, the Tamerlanes. These he then passes by. "I leave behind me," he adds, "all that is related of the Hun, the Vandal, or the Goth, and all the cruel, persecuting, and bloody princes and people in more modern times, when Europe floated as one sea of blood. I pass them by, and hasten on, for I have an object of greater wickedness in view,—an object of such accomplished fraud, perfidy, and murder, that every one heretofore mentioned is lost and disappears. I mean him of England—the fierce, cruel, unrelenting, and bloody king of Britain."[2] Thus, arraigning that poor, dull-witted, obstinate, conscientious and religious George the Third, as the ultimate and supreme successor of the first murderer and the first fratricide, he goes on to sketch, with tremendous power both in outline and in color, a picture of the havoc upon human nature wrought in America by this wicked king's messengers: "Let the town of Boston be witness to their cruelty,—the town of Boston, with the cries of infants, and the groans of distressed mothers. . . . Let the heights of Canada, and the environs of Quebec, call to mind, and publish, the bloody vestiges of tyranny in that unhappy country. . . . From the heights of Canada to the distant barrier of Fort Sullivan, let the intermediate States give in remembrance to remotest times, what they have suffered from the Hessian ravisher, and from the inroad of the cruel Englishman wasting their plantations. Let the Jersey State be witness to their vestiges! Let the blood of Haslet on the plain of

[1] "Six Political Discourses," 5-6.

[2] Ibid. 7.

Princeton cry aloud to God for a day of retribution. Let the fourteen wounds of Mercer with the bayonet point, on the same victorious eminence, open their dumb mouths afresh, and cry aloud for justice."[1] But the cruelties of these invaders "are now transacted on our own plains. They have landed—they have traveled through a part of the adjacent country—they have burned dwelling houses—they have destroyed provision and the means of life—they have tortured for money those whom they suspected of possessing it—they have driven the peaceful inhabitants from their places of abode—they have violated the chastity of women who fell into their hands—they are bending on and breathing slaughter to the whole state. They meditate destruction at the risk of their own lives. It is their determination to destroy or to perish. Rather than suffer us to live, they will cease to live themselves. . . . Can anything be more diabolical, . . . more in the spirit of the first-born Cain?"[2]

And this voice of the prophet, as it begins with words of imprecation denounced upon the enemies of American peace and freedom, how shall it do otherwise than end in the same manner? "Woe unto them, for they have rejected the frequency and humility of our petitions. They have rejected them with a fierce disdain. They have been deaf to all entreaty, and the softest words of soft expostulation. They have pursued, without remorse, the dire intention to destroy us. They have pursued it in a cruel manner. They have warred with a rage unknown to civilized nations. They have mangled the bodies of our heroes on the field of battle. They have defaced our colleges and schools of learning. They have burned houses of religious worship. They have stabbed and shed the blood of an unarmed and supplicating clergyman. This they have done to persons of the same language and religion with themselves. Woe unto them, for they have shed a brother's blood. They have gone in the way of Cain."[3] Moreover,

[1] "Six Political Discourses," 12. [2] Ibid. 13. [3] Ibid. 13–15.

"let us be careful to recollect and commemorate their conduct. Let every class of men join to execrate the tyrant, and the tyranny, and to rank the George of England with the Cains and the murderers of mankind. Let fathers teach their sons the degenerate nature,—and the name of Englishmen,—let mothers still with this the children on the breast, and make the name a bugbear. In thought, in word, let indignation have a place; but chiefly in our actions, let strong resentment shew itself. Let the aged father send his son to battle, with cheerfulness and resignation. Let the wife permit her husband, and perplex him not with womanish exclamation, or with tears. Let the soldier in the field—and to such I principally address myself—let the soldier in the field behave with fortitude. Let him forget the effeminacy of a tender and luxurious life. Let him summon up the blood—give indignation to the visage—and let the spirit of resentment flash from the enraged eye. Let him, in obedience to his orders, shew himself steady—in execution of them prompt—in every enterprise undaunted. Let the arm be stretched with vigor, and give full revenge its scope. Duty, honor, and the love of virtue calls to battle. A bleeding and a ravished country calls to battle. The wounded soldier and the dying hero calls to battle. The voice of the brigades so lately[1] injured by superior numbers, calls to battle. The happiness and glory of the rising generations, calls to battle. Let every man give audience to the voice. Let every man become a soldier. Let every soldier acquit himself as valiant. Let him determine victory or death. Let him be of the mind to fight from hill to hill, from vale to vale, and on every plain, until the enemy is driven back, and forced to depart,—until the tyrant shall give up his claim, and be obliged to confess that free men, that Americans, are not to be subdued."[2]

IX.

Probably no other American preacher of the Revolutionary time united in so high a degree the talents and accom-

[1] At Brandywine.

[2] "Six Political Discourses," 15–16.

plishments suited to his sacred calling, with those suited to the clever man of the world, as did Samuel Cooper, born in Boston in 1724, and from 1744 until his death in 1783, pastor of the Brattle Street Church.[1] Of a noble commanding person, with a voice of great melody and power, a manner of speech full of animation and grace, with personal ways at once courtly, genial, and captivating, he acquired almost from his youth an extraordinary hold upon the admiration and confidence of the community to which he ministered,—a community then swayed by the traditions of clerical leadership. In his day, also, he had great distinction on account of his literary gifts; and to his contemporaries, it seemed no exaggeration to say, that by his "accurate taste, the brilliancy of his imagination, and the clearness of his judgment," he had "adorned and enriched the republic of letters."[2] It comported with his character, likewise, for him to be intimate with men prominent in all the great doings of the world—in science, letters, commerce, politics, war; to have an active part in managing the affairs of his own country, both before and during the Revolution; to represent his own city, likewise, in gracious attentions to distinguished visitors; in short, to be guide, philosopher, and friend to all men, both for this world and for the next.

According to the fashion of the time among men of position and influence, he was a constant writer for the newspapers, dealing with current topics in every sphere of interest. Perhaps nothing that he did in this way is more commonly cited than an essay called "The Crisis," published in 1754, in opposition to a proposal for a colonial excise.[3] During

---

[1] The best accounts of Cooper I have met with, are by two of his contemporaries: John Clarke, in a sermon preached at his funeral, published in Boston, 1784; and John Eliot, in "A Biographical Dictionary," 129–133. Other sources of information concerning him are given in Sprague, "Annals," etc., i., 440–444, especially in note to page 440.

[2] John Clarke, "Sermon at Interment of Cooper," 16–17.

[3] After all, the most notable thing about this pamphlet of Cooper's, is that it anticipates the title made renowned by Thomas Paine twenty-two years later. Oddly enough, Cushing, in "Anonyms," attributes to Cooper the English pamphlet called "The Crisis," published in London in 1766, which, I think, was

the controversies of the Revolution, he is said to have written for the "Boston Gazette" many of the most trenchant articles that appeared in that fearless and influential journal.

His published discourses,[1] though not so numerous as those of several of his contemporaries, are sufficient to preserve for us his chief traits as a sermon-writer: affluence and grace of diction, sincerity of tone, vivacity, impressiveness, the note of social amenity and of worldly wisdom, with frequent applications of his thought to the great political and military events of the day. Of these discourses, by far the ablest is the one preached by him, in 1780, before the governor and legislature of Massachusetts, on the inauguration of the new government of that State under its first written constitution,—an occasion worthy of the speech of a political philosopher. Cooper uses it like one; and while he is not lacking in the congratulations and compliments demanded by the great fact which had brought together that assemblage, he ministers to them something always more needful than congratulations or compliments. "Nations who are jealous of their own liberties," he warns them, "often sport with those of others."[2] Exultant and proud aspirations for national greatness,—so natural among any people near the victorious close of a vast and perilous struggle such as theirs had been,—he does not discourage among his countrymen. Nay, he insists upon such aspirations; but he likewise requires of his countrymen a high conception of the nature and of the obligations of that national greatness to which he would have them aspire. "It is

never before spoken of as Cooper's; but fails to mention this American pamphlet called "The Crisis," which, I think, has always been understood to be Cooper's.

[1] I have made note of only eight discourses by Samuel Cooper, all of which I examined at the Congregational Library, Boston:—Artillery Sermon, 1751; Industry Sermon, 1753; Election Sermon, 1756; Quebec Sermon, 1759; Ordination Sermon, 1760; Sermon on Death of George II., 1761; Dudleian Lecture, 1773; Sermon at Inauguration of the new government of Massachusetts, 1780.

[2] "A Sermon," etc., 15.

laudable," he tells them, " to lay the foundations of our republics with extended views. . . . Conquest is not indeed the aim of these rising States—sound policy must ever forbid it. We have before us an object more truly great and honorable. We seem called by Heaven to make a large portion of this globe a seat of knowledge and liberty, of agriculture, commerce and arts, and, what is more important than all, of Christian piety and virtue. . . . Our mountains, our rivers and lakes, have a singular air of dignity and grandeur. May our conduct correspond to the face of our country. At present, an immense part of it lies as nature hath left it; and human labor and art have done but little, and brightened only some small specks of a continent that can afford ample means of subsistence to many, many millions of the human race. It remains with us and our posterity . . . to establish the honor and happiness of this new world, as far as it may be justly our own, and to invite the injured and oppressed, the worthy and the good, to these shores, by the most liberal governments, by wise political institutions, by cultivating the confidence and friendship of other nations, and by a sacred attention to that Gospel that breathes ' peace on earth, and good will towards men.' Thus will our country resemble the new city which St. John saw ' coming down from God out of Heaven, adorned as a bride for her husband.' Is there a benevolent spirit on earth or on high, whom such a prospect would not delight ? But what are those illustrious forms that seem to hover over us on the present great occasion, and to look down with pleasure on the memorable transactions of this day ? Are they not the founders and law-givers, the skilful pilots and brave defenders of free states, . . . who thought no toils or vigilance too great to establish and protect the rights of human nature, no riches too large to be exchanged for them, no blood too precious to be shed for their redemption ? But who are they who seem to approach nearer to us, and in whose countenances we discern a peculiar mixture of gravity and joy upon this solemnity? Are they not the venerable Fathers of the Massachusetts, who though not perfect while they dwelt in flesh, were yet greatly distinguished by an ardent piety, by all the manly virtues, and by an unquenchable love of liberty,—they who, to form a retreat for it, crossed the ocean, through innumerable difficulties, to a savage land,—they who brought with them a broad charter of liberty, over which they wept when it was wrenched from them by the hand of power, and an insidious one placed in its room? With what pleasure do they seem to behold their children, like the ancient seed of Abraham, this day restored to their original foundations of freedom,—their governor 'as at the first, and their counselors as at the beginning'? Do they not seem to call upon us to defend these foundations at every hazard, and to perpetuate their honor in the liberty and virtue of the state they planted?"[1]

X.

On the 14th of November, 1781, the people of Brookfield, Massachusetts, came together in formal assemblage to express their joy over "the capture of Lord Cornwallis and his whole army"; and, as was fitting, their own pastor, Nathan Fiske, a man of uncommon literary gifts, stood forth and spoke to them at large of the great event. "What a radiance will this struggle for liberty, which has produced such exertions of genius and prowess, throw around America! 'T is enough to make us proud of our country and to glory in the name of Americans; yea, even to make it criminal to be destitute of pride." "Happy country! the scene of such wonders, the nurse of such heroes, the defender of liberty, and the care of Jehovah. . . . Soon, we trust, will commence the era of our quiet enjoyment of those liberties which our fathers purchased with the toil of

---

[1] "A Sermon, October 25, 1780, on the Commencement of the Constitution and Inauguration of the New Government," 52–55.

their whole lives, with their treasure, with their blood. Safe from the enemy of the wilderness, safe from the griping hand of arbitrary sway, here shall be the late-founded seat of peace and freedom. Here shall arts and sciences, the companions of tranquillity, flourish. Here shall dwell uncorrupted faith, the pure worship of God in its primitive simplicity — unawed, unrestrained, uninterrupted. Here shall religion and liberty extend their benign influences to savage, enslaved, and benighted nations. How can we forbear rejoicing in such happy prospects! . . . But the blessing is too divine, the joy is too great—too sacred, to be affronted by profaneness, or polluted and debased by sensuality." [1]

---

[1] "An Oration," etc., 6–8. The chief literary activity of Nathan Fiske belongs to the years following the period here under view. He was a man of great note in his time,—strong, broad, brilliant, and loveable. Born in 1733, he became pastor in Brookfield in 1758, and so remained as long as he lived. A wide and eager reader, an impressive speaker, a writer of rare pith and skill; disliking metaphysics in the pulpit, and controversy everywhere; refined, benevolent, affable; a leader and laborer in every practical work for the good of his fellow-creatures; himself a man of joy, and frowning not at joy in others —even when expressed in certain harmless amusements previously under ban; it may be said of him that he lived in this world the life of a sane and friendly man, and died the death of one. On Sunday, November 24, 1799, he preached to his people from the text, Prov., iv., 18: "But the path of the just is as the shining light, that shineth more and more unto the perfect day." Having for forty-one years given in his own life among the same people a clear illustration of that text, he was permitted to let the record close victoriously at that point; for that same night, in his bed at home, he slept the eternal sleep. In any account of American Literature between 1783 and 1800, Nathan Fiske deserves a permanent place, especially for his many essays fashioned somewhat upon the plan of "The Spectator" and published in "The Massachusetts Spy" and in "The Massachusetts Magazine." After his death, about one hundred and fifty of these essays were culled out and republished in two volumes under the title of "The Moral Monitor." Sketches of this man, who is not unworthy of some sort of literary resurrection, may be seen in Sprague, "Annals," i., 573–574; "Monthly Anthology," i., 639–642; J. I. Foot, "Hist. Disc."; and especially in the first vol. of "The Moral Monitor." In "Appletons' Cycl. of Am. Biog.," this Nathan Fiske is made to be the father of Professor Nathan Welby Fiske of Amherst College, and the grandfather of Helen Fiske, who became Helen Hunt Jackson. Doubtless these two people were quite worthy of such an ancestor; but Nature did not happen to arrange it so.

XI.

In the Spring of the year immediately following the surrender of. Cornwallis, the election sermon in Massachusetts was preached by Zabdiel Adams, a cousin of John Adams, gifted with the energy of mind and the boldness in act and utterance characteristic of that clan. Having in view the achievements of the war, and likewise the uncertainty which then beclouded its close, he urged his fellow-countrymen to remain firm, to yield to no illusions, to think nothing gained till all was gained, to be ready for any labors or sacrifices that might still await them in their long battle for Independence. "We are now," said he, "in sight of the promised land. How humiliating it would be to have our Independence, just brought to the birth, fail for want of strength to be delivered!" "Expense is not to be regarded in a contest of such magnitude. What can possibly be a compensation for our liberties? It is better to be free among the dead, than slaves among the living. The ghosts of our friends slain in war, the spirits of our illustrious ancestors long since gone to rest, . . . a regard to children still unborn,—all call upon us to make greater exertions, and will rise up in judgment against us, if through cowardice we desert the noble cause in which for many years past we have been engaged."[1]

XII.

Nathaniel Whitaker, for many years pastor of a congregation in Salem, Massachusetts, an able and a good man, was, however, as a Revolutionary politician little less than ferocious,—for the reason that he had succeeded in sanctifying his own hatred of the American Tories by discovering a close resemblance between them and certain children of evil in the Old Testament on whom had fallen the wrath of God and the curses of the prophets. Thus, the only sermons of

[1] "Mass. Election Sermon," 57, 59.

his which attained to any note during those years, were two in exposition and championship of this gospel of implacable hate.

The first of these sermons, preached in 1777, was "An Antidote against Toryism; or, the Curse of Meroz."[1] Condensing his thought into these few fine words of savagery—"Cursed be he that holdeth back his hand from blood"—he sees in the conduct of the Tories, who refused to draw the sword in the cause of the Revolution, precisely the crime which should bring down upon their heads that appalling imprecation. Their crime, bad enough in itself, had these two aggravations: that it was a violation of the laws of nature; and that it was also a sin against posterity. When dealing with the latter aspect of it, he says: "What a scene opens to view! Behold these delightful and stately mansions for which we labored, possessed by the minions of power. See yonder spacious fields, subdued to fruitfulness by the sweat and toil of our fathers or ourselves, yielding their increase to clothe, pamper, and enrich the tyrant's favorites, who are base enough to assist him in his cursed plots to enslave us. Does this rouse your resentment? Stop a moment, and I 'll show you a spectacle more shocking than this. What meagre visages do I see in yonder field, toiling and covered with sweat to cultivate the soil? Who are those in rags, bearing burdens and drawing water for these haughty lords, and then cringing to them for a morsel of bread? They are—(O gracious God! support my spirits)—they are my sons, and my daughters, . . . loaded with irons and dragging after them, wherever they go, the heavy, galling, ignominious chains of slavery! But, may we not hope for an end of these miseries? Alas, what hope? Slavery debases the human faculties, and spreads a torpor and stupidity over the whole frame. They sink in despair under their load. They see no way, they feel no power, to recover themselves from this pit of misery, but pine away, and die in it, and leave to their children the

[1] Published, Newburyport, 1777.

same wretched inheritance. What, then, does he deserve, or, rather, what curse is too heavy for the wretch, that can tamely see our country enslaved?"[1]

Again, in May, 1783, as the peace drew near, and with it the danger of some softening of the American heart toward the Tories, this apostle of political vindictiveness once more in his pulpit sought to stir and to blow into flame the embers of the popular wrath against those unhappy people. His sermon, entitled "The Reward of Toryism,"[2] was an elaborate and a red-hot argument for the expulsion of the Tories from the country, or their exclusion from all political privileges within it. "The Tories of these States, whether still residing among us or gone over to the enemy, are guilty of the sin of Meroz." "It is the command of God that in cursing we curse them."[3]

XIII.

The eleventh of December, 1783, had been designated by Congress as a day of thanksgiving for the double blessing of Peace and Independence. Accordingly, at the Congregational Church in Roxbury, Massachusetts, the day was greeted by an assemblage of citizens over whose faces was spread "an appearance of undissembled joy." Their minister, Eliphalet Porter, then but twenty-five years of age and at the beginning of a pastorate which lasted more than fifty years, touched with a strong hand the chords of public gratitude and of jubilant national confidence. "It is no common event, no vulgar occasion," said he, "that now calls for our gratitude. Not only the common mercies of the last revolving year, but the favorable interposition of Providence on our behalf through a long and tedious conflict with a powerful enemy, the maintenance of our rights and liberties, the ultimate acknowledgement of our freedom, sovereignty, and Independence, a period to the calam-

---

[1] "An Antidote," etc., 24-25.
[2] Published, Newburyport, 1783.
[3] "The Reward," etc., 9.

ities and the distresses of war, and the return of Peace—lovely Peace—with her attendant blessings, are the events we are this day called to celebrate. These are the events for which our hearts should expand with grateful joy. These are the events for which the united thousands of America are required this day, with one heart and one voice, to ascribe blessing and praise to the God of their salvation. And these, no doubt, are events for which the more numerous hosts on high—those lovers of peace, and well-wishers to mankind—give honor and glory to Him that sitteth on the throne, and who ruleth in the kingdom of men." [1]

At the Congregational Church in Medford, Massachusetts,—a town near to the very track taken by the British soldiers on their famous night-march to Lexington in 1775,—the young pastor, David Osgood, delivered a sermon [2] remarkable for its vigor both of thought and of expression, in which he retraced year by year the course of the long war; and portrayed its results in great civic blessings achieved or made possible.

In the city of New York, where, for local reasons, exultation over the peace was uncommonly fervent, John Rodgers, pastor of the old Wall Street Presbyterian Church, discoursed to his flock on " The Divine Goodness Displayed in the American Revolution,"—holding up to his fellow-countrymen the need of authenticating their professions of national gratitude by fidelity to all national obligations: " Would you reap the fruits of your toils, your losses and your blood, it is indispensably necessary that the federal union of these States be cemented and strengthened; that the honor of the great council of the nation be supported, and its salutary measures carried into execution, with unanimity and despatch, without regard to partial views or local interests; that the credit of this new empire be established on the principles of the strictest justice; and its faith maintained sacred and inviolable, in whatever way or to

---

[1] " Sermon," 3-4.

[2] Published in Boston, 1784.

whatever description of persons it has been pledged, or may at any time be pledged." [1]

XIV.

Among the sturdiest and most vivacious of the Revolutionary preachers in the middle colonies was George Duffield, a Presbyterian pastor, born in 1732, of Anglo-Irish and Huguenot ancestry, a graduate of Princeton in 1752, one of the party of "New Lights" in his denomination.[2] For the peculiar activities and perils of his career during the Revolution, he had received admirable preparation in his early ministry along the western frontier of Pennsylvania, where the onsets of the Indians were just then so frequent as to compel all the male members of his flock to go armed, and where he himself often accompanied his parishioners upon their military raids. At one of his preaching-places, also, the meeting-house had to be surrounded by fortifications, behind which the stout-hearted pastor was accustomed to minister to his people, while their sentinels were standing upon the ramparts to give warning of the approach of the enemy.[3] Acquiring renown for zeal, eloquence, and intrepidity, he accepted, about the year 1766, the pastorate of the Third Presbyterian Church of Philadelphia,—a position which he continued to hold until his death in 1790.

His stanch opinions touching the great dispute, and the boldness with which he proclaimed them, drew to his church many of the leaders of the Revolutionary movement, who, perhaps, in their admiration for his politics, were disposed to waive any objections that they may have had to his theology; and in great crises of the struggle—in days alike of disaster and of triumph—they flocked to his

---

[1] "A Sermon," etc., as reprinted in "The Patriot Preachers of the Am. Rev.," 340.

[2] Sketch of Duffield, by his grandson, George Duffield of Detroit, in Sprague, "Annals," etc., iii., 186–192. Also, S. D. Alexander, "Princeton College," etc., 17.

[3] Sprague, "Annals," etc., iii., 187–188.

services for the good cheer and the guidance they found in his undaunted faith and in his thrilling words. Thus, on the 11th of June, 1775, in the midst of the popular emotion following the events of Lexington and Concord and preceding those of Bunker Hill, John Adams, then in attendance upon the Continental Congress at Philadelphia, wrote home to his wife some account of this notable man: "I have been this morning to hear Mr. Duffield, a preacher in this city, whose principles, prayers, and sermons more nearly resemble those of our New England clergy than any that I have heard. His discourse was a kind of exposition on the thirty-fifth chapter of Isaiah. America was the wilderness, and the solitary place, and he said it would be glad, 'rejoice and blossom as the rose.' He labored 'to strengthen the weak hands and confirm the feeble knees.' He 'said to them that were of a fearful heart, Be strong, fear not. Behold, your God will come with vengeance, even God with a recompense; he will come and save you.' . . . He applied the whole prophecy to this country, and gave us as animating an entertainment as I ever heard. He filled and swelled the bosom of every hearer."[1] About six weeks afterward, Adams wrote again of this Whig John Knox, whom he had evidently taken to his heart: "This day I have heard my parish priest, Mr. Duffield, from 2 Chronicles, xv., 1, 2. This gentleman never fails to adapt his discourse to the times. He pressed upon his audience the necessity of piety and virtue, in the present times of adversity, and held up to their view the army before Boston as an example. . . . You may well suppose that this language was exceedingly pleasing to me."[2]

On the arrival of the enemy near New York in the summer of 1776, Duffield served as chaplain in the American army gathered there to oppose them; and, on one occasion, for lack of a more convenient pulpit, he climbed into a tree, and, supporting himself upon its forks, preached to the

[1] "Familiar Letters of John Adams and His Wife," etc., 65.

[2] Ibid., 90.

men until a shot from the enemy, crashing through the branches, suggested to him and his congregation the propriety of retiring behind a neighboring hillock for the completion of their religious exercises.[1] He is said to have remained with the army during the whole of the disastrous campaign of the autumn of 1776[2]; after which, hurrying back to Philadelphia, he resumed his duties to his own congregation there. His stay with them at that time was very soon interrupted; for just before Washington's celebrated attack upon the enemy at Trenton, Duffield publicly "rebuked his people because there were so many men in the house, saying there 'would be one less to-morrow, and no lecture on Wednesday evening.'"[3]

Late in the summer of the following year, in the midst of the alarm of Congress over the impending movement of General Howe upon Philadelphia, John Adams witnessed the march of General Washington and his army through that town in the direction of the foe,—a scene which he at once described in a letter to his wife, adding these words: "After viewing this fine spectacle and firm defence, I went to Mr. Duffield's meeting to hear him pray, as he did most fervently, and I believe he was most sincerely joined by all present, for its success."[4] Upon the flight of Congress from Philadelphia to York,—a place less accessible to the enemy,—Duffield served as one of its chaplains, in which capacity he had the honor to draw upon himself the lightning of the Tory satirist, Odell, in this flash of verse:

"A saint of old, as learned monks have said,
Preached to the fish—the fish his voice obeyed.
The same good man convened the grunting herd—
Who bowed obedient to his pow'rful word.
Such energy had truth, in days of yore;
Falsehood and nonsense, in our days, have more.

---

[1] Sprague, "Annals," etc. iii., 190–191.

[2] Ibid. 191.

[3] R. Webster, "Presb. Church in America," 672.

[4] "Familiar Letters," etc. 298.

Duffield avows them to be all in all,
And mounts or quits the pulpit, at their call.
In vain 'New Light' displays her heavenly shine,
In vain attract him oracles divine:
Chaplain of Congress give him to become,
Light may be dark, and oracles be dumb.
It pleased Saint Anthony to preach to brutes—
To preach to devils best with Duffield suits." [1]

By temperament, he was an orator rather than a writer; and the verbal form of his discourses was usually the work of the instant in which they were spoken. Only one production of his seems to have found its way into print,[2]—a sermon preached in his own church on the 11th of December, 1783, the day of national thanksgiving for deliverance and peace. This discourse has all the marks of direct and vivid oral address. Its topics are the obvious ones for such an occasion; and, as might be expected, it has the usual exultant forecast of the era of imperial liberty and happiness for mankind then about to begin under the ægis of the victorious American Republic: "Here has our God erected a banner of civil and religious liberty, and prepared an asylum for the poor and oppressed from every part of the earth. Here, if wisdom guide our affairs, shall a happy equality reign; and joyous freedom bless the inhabitants wide and far, from age to age. Here, far removed from the noise and tumult of contending kingdoms and empires, far from the wars of Europe and Asia and the barbarous African coast, here shall the husbandman enjoy the fruits of his labor; the merchant trade, secure of his gain; the mechanic

---

[1] "The Loyalist Poetry," etc. 40–41.

[2] In the best existing sketch of Duffield, it is said that "he published an account of his tour with Mr. Beatty along the frontiers of Pennsylvania." Sprague, "Annals," etc. iii. 192. I have met with no such publication. There was published in London in 1768 "The Journal of a Two Months' Tour with a View of promoting Religion among the Frontier Inhabitants of Pennsylvania." This little book was by Charles Beatty, who frequently mentions Duffield as his companion and co-worker in the tour.

indulge his inventive genius; and the sons of science pursue their delightful employment, till the light of knowledge pervade yonder yet uncultivated western wilds, and form the savage inhabitants into men."[1]

[1] "A Sermon at Third Presbyterian Church," etc. 16-17. These sentences are taken from the original edition of the sermon, published in 1784. A reprint of the entire sermon may be seen in "The Patriot Preachers of the American Revolution," 344-368.

CHAPTER XXXVI.

THREE ACADEMIC PREACHERS AND PUBLICISTS.

I.—William Smith, Provost of the College of Philadelphia—His many discourses on occasions of state—"On the Duties of the Christian Soldier"—"On the Present Situation of American Affairs," June 23, 1775—His retirement at the approach of Independence—His discourses in the latter part of the Revolution—His quality as a writer.

II.—John Witherspoon, President of the College of New Jersey—His arrival in America in 1768, and prompt identification of himself with the nobler moods of American society—Outline of his previous career—Éclat attending his entrance upon his work at the college.

III.—Witherspoon's fitness for the varied services that lay before him in his new position—His eminence as a preacher—The stimulus he gave to the development of the College of New Jersey.

IV.—Witherspoon's career as political writer and practical statesman—Enters Congress in June, 1776—Reasons for his great influence in that body—His sermons on public questions—His miscellaneous political writings, grave and humorous.

V.—Witherspoon's treatment of the leading questions then in dispute—Special value of his writings on public finance—He forsees the perils that were to follow American Independence.

VI.—Ezra Stiles, President of Yale College — His ambition for universal scholarship.

VII.—Stiles's numerous unpublished writings—His few published writings—His lack of ability in sustained literary expression—His defects in literary taste.

VIII.—Estimate of Stiles's services to civilization in America—His attitude toward the chief tendencies of modern thought—His free-mindedness—His confidence in the victory of truth—His great charity—His sagacious judgments concerning secular affairs—In 1760 and 1761, he predicts the entire movement toward American union, Independence, and national development.

I.

A PREACHER of great celebrity in his day, in America as in England, was William Smith, the provost of the College of Philadelphia, who, being without parochial duties, being also eminent in many spheres of intellectual activity, was many times brought forward for semi-sacred discourses upon occasions of political and military importance. Thus, in the spring and summer of 1768, in the Great Hall of the College of Philadelphia, he preached to the Royal Regiment of Ireland a series of five discourses[1] on the duties of the Christian soldier,—it being apparently supposed that some specimens of that rare kind of man were to be met with in the aforesaid regiment. Beyond all question, his most notable performance in political pulpit oratory was made on the twenty-third of June, 1775, two days after the departure of Washington to take command of the American forces at Cambridge, when the eloquent provost preached at Christ Church, and in the presence of the members of Congress, a sermon "On the Present Situation of American Affairs."[2] This sermon, which was addressed to the Third Battalion of Philadelphia Volunteers, contained the boldest words on the questions of the day, which had then been spoken in America from an Anglican pulpit, and brought upon its author an embarrassing amount of attention, whether laudatory or damnatory, from Dr. Priestly, Dr. Price, John Wesley, from "The Monthly Review," "The London Magazine," "The London Chronicle," "The Public Advertiser," and even from Junius himself.[3] About a month afterward, on July 20, 1775, for the first public fast proclaimed by Congress, this facile orator made still another appearance, preaching at All Saints' Church a sermon[4] which had the effect of an anti-climax,—for it was altogether lacking in definite application to any living problem, and indicated on the writer's part a staggering fear of the extreme courses into which many of his political associates

[1] "The Works of William Smith," ii. 179–250.

[2] Ibid. 251-286.

[3] An extended account of the contemporary praise and abuse of this sermon may be seen in "Preface to the First Edition" with supplementary materials, in "The Works of William Smith," ii. 252–264. The sermon itself follows: 265–286.

[4] Ibid. 112–126.

were getting ready to plunge. Soon, there came stalking to the front the issue of Independence,—in the presence of which this pulpit-orator shrank back into silence.[1] Thenceforward, no political word is any more heard proceeding out of his mouth, until, at his place of retirement in Maryland, he preaches a sermon for the public fast,[2] in May, 1781, and another for the public thanksgiving,[3] in December, of the same year.

There can be no doubt that the various pulpit harangues of Provost William Smith during the Revolution had, at the instant of their utterance, a sort of life and power, derived partly from the eloquent manner of the speaker, partly from the vitality of the great topics with which he in some fashion dealt—topics which already thrilled his hearers before he began to speak about them. Lacking such collateral force, it must be confessed that these printed reports of what he said seem now to be little else than well-dressed and orderly platoons of windy words.[4]

II.

Although John Witherspoon did not come to America until the year 1768,—after he had himself passed the middle line of human life,—yet so quickly did he then enter into the spirit of American society, so perfectly did he identify himself with its nobler moods of discontent and aspiration, so powerfully did he contribute by speech and act to the right development of this new nation out of the old cluster of dispersed and dependent communities, that it would be altogether futile to attempt to frame a just account of the great intellectual movements of our Revolution without

[1] As the conceded author of the "Letters of Cato," he did indeed have something to say against Independence.

[2] "The Works of William Smith," i. 127–140.

[3] Ibid. 141–154.

[4] The notable influence of William Smith as a preacher, teacher, writer, and man of miscellaneous activity, prior to 1765, has been treated of by me in "A History of American Literature during the Colonial Time," ii. 233–234.

taking some note of the part played in it by this eloquent, wise, and efficient Scotsman—at once teacher, preacher, politician, law-maker, and philosopher, upon the whole not undeserving of the praise which has been bestowed upon him as "one of the great men of the age and of the world." [1]

Born in 1722, in the parish of Yester, fourteen miles east of Edinburgh,—a parish of which his father was minister,—he was able upon his mother's side to trace his lineage, through an unbroken line of Presbyterian ministers, back to John Knox. That such a man should ever, in any country, come to lend his support to a system of rather bold conduct respecting royal personages in general, was hardly a thing to shock or surprise any single drop of blood in his body. At the age of twenty, he was graduated from the University of Edinburgh, where he had for associates Hugh Blair, James Robertson, and John Erskine. At the age of twenty-two, he became minister of the parish of Beith in the west of Scotland. At the age of thirty-four, he became pastor of the Low Church in Paisley. At the age of forty-six, after having declined calls to Presbyterian congregations in Dundee, Dublin, and Rotterdam, he accepted an invitation to the presidency of the College of New Jersey—an invitation which he had already declined two years before. At the time of his removal to America, therefore, he had achieved distinction as a preacher and an ecclesiastical leader. Even as an author, also, he had become well known, his chief publications, at that time, being "An Essay on Justification"; "A Practical Treatise on Regeneration"; "A Serious Enquriy into the Nature and Effects of the Stage"; a prose satire, called "Ecclesiastical Characteristics"; besides several volumes of sermons, and a collection of miscellaneous writings in three volumes, entitled "Essays on Important Subjects." [2]

---

[1] Sprague, "Annals," etc. iii. 289.

[2] The most of these publications, together with his later writings, are to be found in his collected "Works," of which two editions have appeared: the one in four volumes, Philadelphia, 1800-1801; the other in nine volumes, Edinburgh, 1804-1805. The latter is the edition used by me. For biographical

His advent to the college over which he was to preside was like that of a prince coming to his throne. From the moment of his landing in Philadelphia until that of his arrival in Princeton, his movements were attended by every circumstance that could manifest affection and homage; and on the evening of the day on which he made his entry into what was thenceforward to be his home, "the college edifice was brilliantly illuminated; and not only the whole village, but the adjacent country, and even the province at large, shared in the joy of the occasion."[1] It is pleasant to know that in the six-and-twenty years of public service that then lay before him in America, the person of whom so much was expected, not only did not disappoint, but by far exceeded, the high hopes that had thus been set upon him. For once in this world, as it turned out, a man of extraordinary force, versatility, and charm had found the place exactly suited to give full swing and scope to every element of power within him.

III.

He seems to have come at the right moment, to the right spot, in the right way. Being perhaps equally apt for thought and for action, and having quite remarkable gifts as preacher, debater, conversationalist, politician, and man of affairs, happily he found himself, in the fulness of his ripened powers, in a station of great dignity and prominence, near the centre of the new national life of America, in the midst of a kindred people just rousing themselves with fierce young energy to the tasks and risks of a stupendous crisis in their history. Thenceforth, whatsoever John

---

sketches of Witherspoon, the reader is referred to these editions of his "Works"; also, to the sermon preached at his funeral by John Rodgers, with a valuable appendix by Samuel Stanhope Smith; to J. Sanderson, "The Signers of the Declaration of Independence," v. 99–186; to Sprague, "Annals," etc. iii. 288–300. The article on Witherspoon, in "Appletons' Cyclopædia of American Biography," vi. 584–585, is worth attention.

[1] Sprague, "Annals," etc. iii. 292.

Witherspoon had it in him to do, in things sacred or secular, in life academic or practical, in the pulpit, in the provincial convention, in the Continental Congress, for the shaping, in war and peace, of the thought and character and destiny of this primitive, passionate, indomitable people, he then had the opportunity to do. That opportunity, so precious and so rare in the experience of men, he did not fail to use to the utmost.

Even in the exterior personal gifts which make for influence, he was not lacking. It was said of him that, with the exception of Washington, he had more of the quality called presence than, perhaps, any other man of his time in America. He was, moreover, kindly and companionable in private intercourse, and fascinated men by talk sparkling with anecdote, epigram, and repartee.

In the due order of things, his earliest appearance before the public was in the pulpit, which, to the very end of his career, continued to be the true seat and organ of his best activity and influence. Having the gift of easily remembering whatever he wrote, and of speaking naturally what he thus remembered, he was able to give to his sermons the double attraction of premeditated and of extemporaneous speech; and both for the matter and the manner of discourse, he soon took rank here as one of the foremost preachers of his time. As a contemporary of his has testified: " President Witherspoon's popularity as a preacher was great. The knowledge that he was to conduct a public service, usually filled the largest churches in our cities and populous towns, and he never failed to command the profound attention of his audience." [1] Notwithstanding the prodigious variety of those public and private engagements which were soon laid upon him, he maintained to the very end the supremacy of his sacred calling, and never, either by dress, or speech, or conduct, permitted his career as a civilian even to seem to involve any lapse or suspension of his character as a clergyman.

---

[1] Ashbel Green, in Sprague, " Annals," etc. iii. 299.

As the call that had brought him to America was the call to preside over the College of New Jersey, its interests very properly had the first claim upon his attention; and, before he had been long in charge of them, it became evident that, through him, the college was about to enter upon a new and a larger life. He addressed himself, first of all, to that need which is the primary, classic, and perennial need of every college fit to exist at all,—the need of money; and the extraordinary success he had therein was due partly to his own extraordinary energy and tact, and partly to the sheer confidence of the public in anything for which he chose to concern himself. He also brought about an enlargement of the curriculum by the introduction of new courses, particularly in Hebrew and in French; and through his own brilliant example as a lecturer on eloquence, history, philosophy, and divinity, he encouraged methods of instruction far more manly, vital, and stimulating than those previously in voguc there. Finally, his fame as a divine, and soon, also, as a statesmen and a patriot, continually added to the reputation of the college, and attracted to it during his time some of the brightest and noblest of American youths. Perhaps John Witherspoon was the first man among us to illustrate in a high degree the possibilities for influence to be found in this very modern and peculiar function of an American college president.

IV.

Before many years, also, as the struggle with the British ministry took on more and more of its tragic aspect, Witherspoon's labors as preacher and as college officer began to be overlaid by his labors as a political writer and a statesman. It has been well said of him that "he became an American the moment he landed on our shores"[1]; and, having quickly mastered the questions in dispute, he showed from the outset a rational, temperate, but unflinching sympathy with the rising spirit of American opposition. By the spring of the

[1] Sanderson, "The Signers," etc. v. 115.

year 1776, it was no longer possible for him to hold back from more direct employment in the Revolution; and he then began his political career by taking his place as a member of the convention for framing the first constitution for New Jersey.[1] His service in that body gave a new éclat to his reputation, and great access to the public confidence in him; and, on the 21st of June, 1776, he received promotion by being transferred from the convention of New Jersey to the Continental Congress, in which body he took his seat in time to give his voice and his vote in favor of the Declaration of Independence.

Thus, at last, was John Witherspoon brought as an active force into the highest sphere of American statesmanship, and at a period of supreme opportunity in our affairs. In that sphere he remained and wrought, with but a single brief interval, until the virtual close of the Revolution. From the beginning, he took and held the foremost rank among his associates. In the mere erudition required for statesmanship, especially at such a crisis, probably few of them were so well equipped as he. This, perhaps, was to have been expected, in view of his previous personal history. They, however, who had supposed that this great academic personage—this renowned divine and philosopher—would in Congress prove himself to be a mere amateur in statesmanship, a doctrinaire and a dreamer, were permitted to enjoy a great surprise. His long training in ecclesiastical politics in Scotland had left to him few things to learn as regards the handling of secular politics in America: he was familiar with the usages of legislative bodies, he had consummate skill in debate, he knew how to influence men to think and act with himself. Throughout all those years in which there were in Congress advocates for an imbecile military policy, for financial shuffling and dishonor, even for the annihilation of all genuine national life, the wit, the wisdom, the moral force of this shrewd Scotsman were to be found on the side of wholesome measures,—an assured union of the

[1] Poore, "The Federal and State Constitutions," ii. 1310–1314.

insurgent States; more power at the centre of government; terms of enlistment long enough to make an army worth having after it had become an army; the management of the public finances on the only principles that have ever proved sound or profitable in the conduct of any business public or private.[1] Moreover, it became soon apparent that, in his view, the chief duty of a congressman was not to talk, but to work. At the sessions of Congress, no member was more constant in attendance; in committees, no one wrought harder, or had harder tasks entrusted to him.[2]

The powerful influence which, through his published writings, Witherspoon exerted upon the course of Revolutionary thought, may be traced in the very few sermons of his which touch upon the political problems of that time, in various congressional papers, and especially in the numerous essays, long or short, serious or mirthful, which he gave to the press between the years 1775 and 1783, and commonly without his name.

His most memorable sermon during this period was that preached by him at Princeton on the 17th of May, 1776, being the general fast appointed by Congress throughout the United Colonies,—an opportunity for solemn delay and for reflection before that great step should be taken which could not be taken back. Witherspoon's discourse bore an imposing title, "The Dominion of Providence over the Passions of Men,"[3] and contained a calm and very striking statement of his reasons for concurring in the American demand for the control by Americans of their own affairs. It was much read on both sides of the Atlantic; and at Glasgow it was sent forth embellished with notes of dis-

---

[1] For example, see his speeches in Congress "On the Confederation," "Works," ix. 135–141; "On a Motion for Paying the Interest of Loan-Office Certificates," ibid. 117–124; "On the Finances," ibid. 125–134; also his remarkable "Essay on Money," ibid. 9–25.

[2] A fairly good idea of the nature and value of Witherspoon's services as a member of the Congress from 1776 to 1782, may be gathered from Sanderson, "The Signers," etc. v. 116–157.

[3] "Works," v. 176–216.

sent and indignation wherein the reverend author was called a rebel and a traitor.[1] To the American edition of the sermon, Witherspoon added an "Address to the Natives of Scotland residing in America,"[2]—an effective and a much-needed treatment of that series of events, in both countries, which had resulted in so extensive an alienation of American Scotsmen from the cause of American self-government.

As a writer of political and miscellaneous essays, commonly published in the newspapers, it is probable that Witherspoon's activity was far greater than can now be ascertained; but his hand can be traced with certainty in a large group of keen and sprightly productions of that sort,—"Reflections on the Present State of Public Affairs and on the Duty and Interest of America in this Important Crisis,"[3] "Thoughts on American Liberty,"[4] "On the Controversy about Independence,"[5] "On Conducting the American Controversy,"[6] "Aristides,"[7] "On the Contest between Great Britain and America,"[8] "On the Affairs of the United States,"[9] "Observations on the Improvement of America,"[10] and a series of periodical papers called "The Druid."[11] His gift for personal and political satire is shown in "The Humble and Earnest Supplication of J. Rivington, Printer and Bookseller in New York,"[12] and in "Recantation of Benjamin Towne."[13] By far the most masterly secular writing of Witherspoon's is his "Essay on Money as a Medium of Commerce, with Remarks on the Advantages and Disadvantages of Paper admitted into General Circulation,"[14] principally made up of portions of

---

[1] Sprague, "Annals," etc. iii. 293–294.

[2] "Works," v. 217–236.

[3] Ibid. ix. 66–72.

[4] Ibid. 73–77.

[5] Ibid. 78–82.

[6] Ibid. 83–87.

[7] Ibid. 88–98.

[8] Ibid. 166–170.

[9] Ibid. 171–177.

[10] Ibid. 178, 179.

[11] Ibid. 224–291.

[12] Ibid. 180–191.

[13] Ibid. 192–198; also Albert H. Smyth, "The Philadelphia Magazines," etc. 56, 57.

[14] "Works," ix. 9–65.

speeches delivered by him in Congress, and conveying much invaluable and unfamiliar truth to the American people, then, as so often since then, mired in the bog of financial fallacies and impostures.

V.

Of all these writings of Witherspoon, dealing in grave or playful fashion with Revolutionary themes, the chief note is that of a virile mind, well-balanced, well-trained, and holding itself steadily to its own independent conclusions,—in short, of enlightened and imperturbable common-sense, speaking out in a form always temperate and lucid, often terse and epigrammatic. "There is not a single instance in history," says he, "in which civil liberty was lost, and religious liberty preserved entire. If, therefore, we yield up our temporal property, we at the same time deliver the conscience into bondage."[1] As to the ministers, parliament, and people of Great Britain, "I do not refuse submission to their unjust claims because they are corrupt or profligate, although probably many of them are so, but because they are men, and therefore liable to all the selfish bias inseparable from human nature; . . . because they are separated from us, independent of us, and have an interest in opposing us."[2] "It has been my opinion from the beginning that we did not carry our reasoning fully home when we complained of an arbitrary prince, or of the insolence, cruelty, and obstinacy of Lord North, Lord Bute, or Lord Mansfield. What we have to fear, and what we have to grapple with, is the ignorance, prejudice, partiality, and injustice of human nature."[3] "The question then is: Shall we make resistance with the greatest force,—as rebel subjects of a government which we acknowledge, or as Independent States against an usurped power which we detest and abhor?"[4] "Is there a probable prospect of recon-

---

[1] "Works," v. 203.
[2] Ibid.
[3] Ibid. ix. 80.
[4] Ibid. 92.

ciliation on constitutional principles? What are these constitutional principles? Will anybody show that Great Britain can be sufficiently sure of our dependence, and yet we sure of our liberties?"[1] "It is proper to observe that the British settlements have been improved in a proportion far beyond the settlements of other European nations. To what can this be ascribed? Not to the climate, for they are of all climates; not to the people, for they are a mixture of all nations. It must, therefore, be resolved singly into the degree of British liberty which they brought from home, and which pervaded more or less their several constitutions."[2] "Can any person of a liberal mind wish that these great and growing countries should be brought back to a state of subjection to a distant power? And can any man deny that, if they had yielded to the claims of the British parliament, they would have been no better than a parcel of tributary states, ruled by lordly tyrants, and exhausted by unfeeling pensioners, under the commission of one too distant to hear the cry of oppression, and surrounded by those who had an interest in deceiving him?"[3] "It ought, therefore, in my opinion, to meet with the cordial approbation of every impartial person, as I am confident it will of posterity, that they have united for common defense, and resolved that they will be both free and independent, because they cannot be the one without the other."[4] As to American Independence, "I mean to shew—1. That it was necessary. 2. That it will be honorable and profitable. And, 3. That in all probability it will be no injury, but a real advantage, to the island of Great Britain."[5]

Of this newly born and newly announced nation, thus starting out in life with a very serious war on its infant hands, the direst need was, not of men to do the fighting, but of money to sustain the men while they were fighting; and in the way of all this stood, not only the organic impotence of

[1] "Works," ix. 97. [2] Ibid. v. 223. [3] Ibid. 224.
[4] Ibid. 224. [5] Ibid.

the general government, but the ignorant, false, and reckless notions as to money and as to the relation of government to money, which these people had brought over with them from their colonial stage, and which, in fact, they had long been putting into practice to their own incalculable loss and shame. Under such circumstances, what greater service to the American cause could have been rendered by a man like Witherspoon, than by exposing, as he did, the financial sophistries of Revolutionary demagogues and blatherskites, and by putting into pithy, lucid, and fearless words the essential and immutable truths as to what is possible and desirable in public finance? "No paper of any kind is, properly speaking, money. It ought never to be made a legal tender. It ought not to be forced upon anybody, because it cannot be forced upon everybody."[1] "The cry of the scarcity of money is generally putting the effect for the cause. No business can be done, say some, because money is scarce. It may be said, with more truth, money is scarce because little business is done. Yet their influence, like that of many other causes and effects, is reciprocal."[2] "Too much money may be emitted upon loan; but to emit money in any other way than upon loan, is to do all evil and no good."[3] "The excessive quantity of paper emitted by the different States of America, will probably be a loss to the whole. They cannot, however, take advantage of one another in that way. That State which emits most will lose most, and vice versa."[4] "Those who refuse doubtful paper, and thereby disgrace it, or prevent its circulation, are not enemies, but friends, to their country."[5]

Happy was it for us, that this clear-headed thinker, this expert in the art of popular exposition, was in full sympathy with those deep human currents of patriotic thought and feeling which then swept towards an Independent national life in this land. Happy was it for us, also, that while he was capable beyond most men of seeing the

[1] "Works" ix. 63. [2] Ibid. [3] Ibid. 64.
[4] Ibid. [5] Ibid.

historic and cosmopolitan significance of the movement for American Independence, he had the moral greatness to risk even his own great favor with the American people, by telling them that the acquisition of Independence, was not to be the end of their troubles, but rather, in some sense, the beginning of them; since greater perils than those brought in by Red Coats and Hessians were then to meet them, in the form of shallow and anarchical politics, corruption among voters, unscrupulous partisanship, new and hitherto unimagined forms of demagogism, and the boisterous incompetence of men entrusted with power in the regulation and guidance of the state. He who declared that the American Revolution would be "an important era in the history of mankind,"[1] also said: "I am much mistaken if the time is not just at hand when there shall be greater need than ever in America for the most accurate discussion of the principles of society, the rights of nations, and the policy of states"; and that only by making a people "virtuous," can they be made "invincible."[2]

VI.

On the eighth of July, 1778, Ezra Stiles, then fifty years of age, being inducted into the presidency of Yale College, delivered an oration in Latin, "on the encyclopedia of literature,"—meaning thereby the state of human knowledge, on all subjects, up to date; and ever afterward, until very near his death, he was accustomed, in his lectures to the students, after prayers, in the chapel, to launch out from time to time into the vasty deep of the same shoreless theme. To be what he called "a universal scholar," was his ruling passion. There was nothing knowable which he did not very strenuously desire to know. "I consider myself," he wrote in a private memorandum, at the age of twenty, "as a citizen of the intellectual world, and a subject of its almighty Law-giver and Judge. By Him I am

[1] "Works," v. 222.

[2] Ibid. ix. 231.

placed upon an honorable theatre of action, to sustain, in the sight of mortal and immortal beings, that character and part which He shall assign me, in order to my being trained up for perfection and immortality ; and shall, therefore, from this time forth, devote my life to the service of God, my country, and mankind." [1] In this spirit, he threw open every window of his mind, toward every quarter of the heavens and the earth: toward the languages of men, their opinions, deeds, laws, institutions, in all ages, in all lands; especially toward the person and character of the Creator as unfolded in His visible universe—in atoms and planets, in space, in time, in force, in the developments of His Providence over all sentient creatures. Thus it was, that as his life lengthened, and as his zeal for learning strengthened, he came to have some valid claim, according to the standards of his time, to be called mathematician, astronomer, chemist, electrician, meteorologist, linguist, orientalist, antiquarian, jurist, theologian, Biblical translator and exegete.

When, accordingly, in 1771, his portrait was painted, he very naturally caused it to be "charged with emblems" descriptive of this omnivorous appetency of his mind. He himself is represented as "in a teaching attitude," with his right hand on his breast, and his left hand holding the Bible. Just behind him, on the left side, is a partial glimpse of his book-shelves, on one of which we see Eusebius, Livy, Du Halde's History of China, the Zohar, the Babylonian Talmud, Aben Ezra, Rabbi Selomo Jarchi, Rabbi Moses Ben Maimon, and Moreh Nevochim; while on another shelf are Newton's Principia, Plato, Watts, Doddridge, Cudworth's Intellectual System, besides five learned New England divines, Hooker, Chauncey, Davenport, Mather, and John Cotton. Upon his right side is a pillar, on the shaft of which is wrought a circle encompassing "a solar point, as an emblem of the Newtonian or Pythagorean system of the sun, planets, and comets." Moreover, at the top of the pillar and on the wall is "an

[1] Holmes, "Life of Stiles," 18.

emblem of the Intellectual World," containing, in a central glory, in Hebrew, the Sacred Name "surrounded with white spots in a field of azure. From each spot ascend three hair-lines, denoting the tendencies of mind to Deity, and communion with the Trinity in the divine light. These spots denote systems of worlds, and their tendencies to the eternal, central, yet omnipresent light. The motto is,—ALL HAPPY IN GOD." [1]

VII.

Now, all that Ezra Stiles did to appease this hunger of his soul in the pursuit of knowledge, and how for this he toiled from youth to age, by day and night, on Sundays and on week-days, in readings, in observations, experiments, conversations, in elaborate and most persistent letters to the learned in many distant lands,—is it not written in the chronicles of Ezra Stiles himself, to wit, in some fifty volumes or more of manuscripts, being his "Itineraries and Memoirs," his "Literary Diary," his memoranda of scientific observations and experiments, his notes for an "Ecclesiastical History of New England," his "Memoirs concerning Mr. Robert Sandeman," his letters, his sermons, his innumerable miscellaneous scraps and jottings, all still reposing under the legal custody of the president of Yale University? [2]

---

[1] Holmes, "Life of Stiles," 151–154.

[2] The Stiles Manuscripts may be described as consisting of two portions, those that are bound and those that are unbound. Of the latter, the following are the principal items: (1) Some hundreds of letters to and from Stiles. (2) About forty of his sermons. (3) Loose sheets of material not otherwise classified. Of the former and larger portion of these manuscripts, the following are the principal items: (1) "Literary Diary," from January 1, 1769, to May 6, 1795, 15 vols., quarto. (2) "Itineraries and Memoirs," from May 23, 1760, to November 8, 1794, 6 vols., quarto. (3) Memoranda mainly scientific. About 10 vols. (4) Miscellaneous memoranda. About 10 vols. (5) Material for an "Ecclesiastical History of New England," 1 vol., quarto. (6) Extracts from manuscripts, made by Stiles, 1 vol., quarto. (7) Letters to and from Stiles, 13 vols., quarto and folio. (8) "Memoirs concerning Mr. Robert Sandeman," 1 vol., quarto. (9) The Journal of Rev. John Sergeant of Stockbridge, from April 1, 1739, to March 30, 1740, 1 vol., quarto. This

As to his published writings, any possible list of them would be a very small one, consisting of two or three Latin orations;[1] of a few sermons, such as that "On the Christian Union," in 1761; that "On Saving Knowledge," in 1770; that for the funeral of Napthali Daggett, in 1780; that for "the anniversary election" in Connecticut, in 1783; that for the funeral of Chauncey Whittelsey, in 1787; that for the ordination of Henry Channing, in the same year; and besides these, of a single book only, "A History of Three of the Judges of King Charles I.," in 1794.

A notable contrast, surely, between this man's boundless and tireless intellectual preparation, and any deliberately uttered result! Indeed, he seems to have had no faculty for sustained literary expression. His delight was in the perpetual acquisition of knowledge, never in any record of it, save in his log-book of extemporized notes. On every subject, he was inclined to postpone elaborate report till the data should all be in,—which was to postpone it forever;

---

note is founded on my own memoranda made during an inspection of the Stiles Papers, and on information subsequently sent me by Professor Franklin B. Dexter, who also furnished to Henry M. Dexter the description of the Stiles Papers, given in "Congregationalism as Seen in its Literature," App. 288. I infer that many of the manuscript sermons of Stiles are still in existence. One of them, belonging to me, is "No. 454." Stiles's "Literary Diary" ought by all means to be printed without delay, for the light it throws on the intellectual and political life of the eighteenth century.

[1] Besides these, he delivered at least three Latin orations which seem not to have been printed: one in 1752, on the completion of the first half-century from the founding of Yale College; in 1753, on the death of Bishop Berkeley; and, in 1781, on the renewal of public commencements at the college, after an interruption of seven years, caused by the war. On the latter occasion, President Stiles's fondness for exercising in public his gift for languages unknown to the most of his auditors, had an extraordinary gratification: he ushered in the exercises of the morning by an oration in Hebrew, and those of the afternoon by one in Latin. He wrote and spoke Latin with great facility, and as his contemporary, Professor Meigs, thought, "with a purity and elegance that would have honored the age of Augustus." The specimens of his Latin which have come down to us, do not justify this praise: it was far from being immaculate, and one would prefer to extol it as doing honor to the age of George the Third, than to that of Augustus. With Meigs's opinion, in Holmes's "Life of Stiles," 22–23, compare that of a real Latinist, Kingsley, in his "Life of Stiles," 73.

and if, by chance, for such a report he ever made a beginning, he was apt soon to fall away from it, before the enticements of fresh opportunities for knowledge. Besides, he was deficient in the sense of form, proportion, congruity, in literary judgment, poise, and self-restraint; and with respect to his erudition, he was nearly always its victim rather than its master. Of these traits, the monumental example is his solitary book, published in old age,—a medley born of the vagrant and gossiping industry of more than thirty years,—a heterogeneous collection of facts, fictions, rumors, traditions, guesses, appertaining more or less to the three regicides, Whalley, Goffe, and Dixwell, who had found in New England kindly shelter and quiet graves: a book not without value, not without interest, not without a sort of fascination, yet admitting so many puerile incidents, and so many pottering discussions, as to have led John Adams, soon after its publication, to describe it as "a wild thing," and a sign of its author's mental decay.[1]

It may be said of Stiles, moreover, that he often wrote well, except when he tried to do so. In some moods of literary unconsciousness, his thought was clear, and his language simple, incisive, impressive; but upon any occasion of unusual importance, the balance of his discretion was liable to very serious disturbance. At such times, deeming it his duty to produce before the world his learning, he commonly appalled it by his excesses of pedantry; while some fatal supposition, on his part, that he was then expected to be eloquent, had the effect of precipitating him into rhetorical hysterics—into the very orgasm of bombast. "O Washington!" exclaimed he, in his election sermon, in 1783, delivered in the presence of the governor and general assembly of Connecticut, "O Washington! how do I love thy name! How have I often adored and blessed thy God, for creating and forming thee the great ornament of human kind! . . . The world and posterity will, with admiration, contemplate thy deliberate, cool, and stable judgment,

[1] "Correspondence of Miss Adams," vol. ii., part ii. 144–145.

thy virtues, thy valor and heroic achievements, as far surpassing those of Cyrus, whom the world loved and adored. The sound of thy fame shall go out into all the earth, and extend to distant ages. . . . Such has been thy military wisdom in the struggles of this arduous conflict, such the noble rectitude, amiableness, and mansuetude of thy character, something is there so singularly glorious and venerable thrown by Heaven about thee, that not only does thy country love thee, but our very enemies stop the madness of their fire in full volley, stop the illiberality of their slander at thy name, as if rebuked from Heaven with a—' Touch not mine Anointed, and do my Hero no harm!' Thy fame is of sweeter perfume than Arabian spices in the gardens of Persia. A Baron de Steuben shall waft its fragrance to the monarch of Prussia: a Marquis dē Lafayette shall waft it to a far greater monarch, and diffuse thy renown throughout Europe. Listening angels shall catch the odor, waft it to heaven, and perfume the universe!"[1]

VIII.

Nevertheless, the man who, in the seclusion of his study, deliberately forged this apostrophe, and then with vociferous self-satisfaction, hurled it at the heads of the unhappy governor and legislators of Connecticut, was by no means a fool; nay, but one of the wisest, acutest, and noblest men of that period, who did great things in his day for the enlightenment of men and the advancement of civilization,—for science, for the arts and industries, for literature, for education, for the reign of justice, freedom, and good-will in this world.

The real quality of his intellect we may partly gather from his life-long attitude toward that enormous movement of skepticism which swept through the entire period in which he lived. Having himself, as regards the Christian doctrine, " gone through all the conflicts that it is possible

---

[1] "The United States elevated to Glory and Honor," 42–43.

for the human mind to be perplexed with,"[1] he had achieved a clear vision of its truth, wherein, as he said, "revelation" appeared to him as proceeding "from the most perfect and consummate reason,"[2] and to invite and welcome, rather than to repel, any form of rational criticism. When, accordingly, in 1759, President Clap of Yale College declined to receive for its library a gift of books, "some of which were deistical," Ezra Stiles, then a pastor at Newport, took this ground in opposition: "Deism has gained such head, in this age of licentious liberty, that it would be in vain to try to suppress it by hiding the deistical writings: the only way is, to come forth into the open field, and dispute the matter on even footing. The evidences of revelation are, in my opinion, nearly as demonstrative as Newton's Principia, and these are the weapons to be used."[3] Having perfect faith in the victory of truth in every open and fair fight, he could not consent that the large political liberty which America was then winning for itself, should ever be lessened by any pettiness of theological restraint. It is in America, as he said, just at the close of the Revolutionary War, that "the unfettered mind can think with a noble enlargement; and with an unbounded freedom, go wherever the light of truth directs. Here will be no bloody tribunals, no cardinals inquisitors-general, to bend the human mind, forcibly to control the understanding, and put out the light of reason, the candle of the Lord, in man. . . . Religion may here receive its last, most liberal and impartial examination. . . . Here deism will have its full chance; nor need libertines more to complain of being overcome by any weapons but the gentle, the powerful, ones of argument and truth. Revelation will be found to stand the test of the ten-thousandth examination."[4]

As he thus welcomed for Christianity the fullest criticism on the part of its opponents, so he would have among

---

[1] Stiles, MS., quoted in Holmes's "Life of Stiles," 85.

[2] Stiles, letter to Wright, in Holmes's "Life of Stiles," 123.

[3] Letter to Clap, in Holmes's "Life of Stiles," 79.

[4] Election Sermon, in 1783, p. 56.

all religious sects mutual forbearance: and his charity was a mantle as wide as the brotherhood of man. "It has been a principle with me for thirty-five years past," so he wrote in 1781, "to walk and live in a decent, civil, and respectful communication with all, although in some of our sentiments in philosophy, religion, and politics, of diametrically opposite opinions. Hence, I can freely live and converse in civil friendship, with Jews, Romanists, and all the sects of Protestants, and even with Deists. I am, all along, blamed by bigots for this liberality, though, I think, none impeach me now of hypocrisy; because I most freely, fully, and plainly give my sentiments on everything in science, religion, and politics. I have my own judgment, and do not conceal it. I have no secrets. I hold it beneath the dignity of a philosopher, to suppress his sentiments upon anything. It is, indeed, unworthy of him to make up hasty opinions on every new subject which occurs. Upon these, therefore, he should discourse, in the way of search and enquiry, till he has formed his judgment: then let him express it, but without reprobating others, or treating them with acrimonious reflections, because they think differently."[1] Nobly did Channing describe Ezra Stiles as one whose "heart was of no sect," and who "desired to heal the wounds of the divided church of Christ, not by a common creed, but by the spirit of love."[2]

This same large and fearless spirit abode with him, likewise, in his judgments concerning purely secular affairs—such as forms of government, and the duties and rights of the people. He was an early specimen of the American radical. On taking his bachelor's degree, just thirty years before the Declaration of Independence, he defended this thesis: "Jus regum non est jure divino hæreditarium"[3]; and in the year which saw the close of our long struggle with the king of England, he shewed that with respect to kings

---

[1] "Literary Diary," in Holmes's "Life of Stiles," 274–275.

[2] "The Works of William Ellery Channing," iv. 340–341, where occurs an exquisite eulogy of Stiles, whom Channing personally knew.

[3] Holmes, "Life of Stiles," 14.

in general, his opinion had in the meantime suffered no conservative relapse: "It is next to an impossibility to tame a monarch, and few have ruled without ferocity."[1] It is doubtful if any statesman of that age saw earlier or more clearly than did this New England divine, the inevitable direction and the irresistible force of that prodigious undercurrent in American society which was setting toward union, Independence, and national greatness. In 1760, in a discourse occasioned by the English capture of Montreal, and their reduction of all Canada, he saw for England a gain in which was coiled up a far greater loss: "It is probable that in time there will be formed a Provincial Confederacy and a Common Council, standing on free provincial suffrage; and this may in time terminate in an imperial diet, when the imperial dominion will subsist, as it ought, in election."[2] In 1761, in a sermon on the accession of George the Third, he spoke of "the possible exigencies of New England, which may fall within the period of his majesty's reign"; adding that if the "men, who have a mighty opinion of retrenching the liberties of these colonies, or throwing a net of policy over them, . . . should gain access to his majesty's ears, mistaken representations may induce his majesty to accede to measures of unhappy consequences to the liberty of America."[3] In 1774, he wrote to the English historian, Catharine Macaulay: "There will be a Runnymede in America."[4]

---

[1] Election Sermon for 1783, p. 17.

[2] Thanksgiving Sermon, in Holmes's "Life of Stiles," 99–100.

[3] Quoted in Holmes's "Life of Stiles," 101–102.

[4] Holmes, "Life of Stiles," 180. Other instances of Stiles's political sagacity and foresight are to be met with in Holmes's book; while his unpublished "Literary Diary" abounds in them. See, also, Gordon, "History of the American Revolution," i. 115; and William E. Foster, "Stephen Hopkins," ii. foot notes on pp. 86, 87, 95, 118–119, together with a letter from Stiles in Appendix T. A good short sketch of Stiles is given by Sprague, "Annals," i. 470–479, particularly valuable for reminiscences of this Yale president by two of his pupils. A sprightly account of him, under the title of "An Old New England Divine," written by his great-granddaughter, Kate Gannett Wells, with the advantage of family papers, is in "The Atlantic Monthly," for Aug., 1884, pp. 247–257.

CHAPTER XXXVII.

TWO APOSTLES OF QUIETNESS AND GOOD WILL: JOHN WOOLMAN AND ST. JOHN CREVECŒUR.

I.—Comparison between Franklin's "Autobiography" and John Woolman's "Journal"—The spirit of Woolman's life—He is weaned from the desire for outward greatness—Begins his first journey to visit Friends.

II.—John Woolman's apostleship—The kindly burden thereof as set forth in his "Journal."

III.—John Woolman's death in 1772—His several ethical and religious essays—An unlettered writer whose purity of style is born of the purity of his heart—The love and praise of him by Charles Lamb, Channing, Crabb Robinson, and Whittier.

IV.—St. John Crevecœur's "Letters from an American Farmer" published in 1782—Their sweetness of tone and literary grace—Personal history of the author—His personal and literary traits as American farmer, philosopher, dreamer, and altruist.

V.—Crevecœur's description of the American colonies—The limited range of his topics—His definition of an American—His sympathetic studies of nature—His classic contributions to the literature of natural history.

VI.—The note of peace in Crevecœur's book—He celebrates the comfort of American rural life, its opportunity, thoughtfulness, equality, dignity, friendliness, its happy companionship with all innocent things.

VII.—The note of pain in Crevecœur's book—The inevitable barbarism of negro slavery—His pathetic picture of the caged negro—The Indian wrong and terror—This quietist appalled by the wrangles and violence of the Revolution—His idealized descriptions of American felicity both fascinated and misled many readers in Europe—His influence upon the English poets, especially the inventors of "Pantisocracy."

I.

IT is no slight distinction attaching to American literature for the period of the Revolution, that in a time so often characterized as barren of important literary achievement, were produced two of the most perfect examples of autobiography to be met with in any literature. One of these, of course, is Franklin's "Autobiography," the first, the largest, and the best part of which was written in 1771,—a work that has long since taken its place among the most celebrated and most widely read of modern books. Almost at the very time at which that fascinating story was begun, the other great example of autobiography in our Revolutionary literature was finished—"The Journal of John Woolman," a book which William Ellery Channing long afterward described as "beyond comparison the sweetest and purest autobiography in the language."[1] It is a notable fact, however, that while these two masterpieces in the same form of literature are products of the same period, they are, in respect of personal quality, very nearly antipodal to each other; for, as Franklin's account of himself delineates a career of shrewd and somewhat selfish geniality, of unperturbed carnal content, of kindly systematic and most successful worldliness, so the autobiography of Woolman sets forth a career which turns out to be one of utter unworldliness, of entire self-effacement, all in obedience to an Unseen Leadership, and in meek and most tender devotion to the happiness of others—especially slaves, poor toiling white people, and speechless creatures unable to defend themselves against the inhumanity of man.

John Woolman, who was of a spirit so unpresuming that he would have wondered and have been troubled to be told that any writing of his was ever to be dealt with as literature, was born in 1720 in Northampton, New Jersey, his father being a farmer, and of the Society of Friends. Until his twenty-first year, he lived at home with his parents, and, as he expresses it, "wrought on the plantation." Having reached his majority, he took employment in the neighboring village of Mount Holly, in a shop for general merchandise. In this occupation he passed several years; after which, as he writes, "I was thoughtful of

[1] This was said by Channing not long before his death, in a conversation with Whittier. Introd. to "The Journal of John Woolman," 2.

some other way of business; perceiving merchandize to be attended with much cumber in the way of trading in these parts. My mind, through the power of truth, was in a good degree weaned from the desire of outward greatness, and I was learning to be content with real conveniences that were not costly; so that a way of life free from much entanglements, appeared best for me, though the income might be small. . . . I saw that an humble man, with the blessing of the Lord, might live on a little; and that where the heart was set on greatness, success in business did not satisfy the craving, but that commonly, with an increase of wealth, the desire of wealth increased. There was a care on my mind so to pass my time, that nothing might hinder me from the most steady attention to the voice of the true Shepherd. My employer, though now a retailer of goods, was by trade a tailor, and kept a servant man at that business; and I began to think about learning the trade, expecting that if I should settle, I might by this trade and a little retailing of goods, get a living in a plain way without the load of great business. I mentioned it to my employer, and we soon agreed on terms; and then, when I had leisure from the affairs of merchandize, I worked with his man. I believed the hand of Providence pointed out this business for me, and was taught to be content with it, though I felt at times a disposition that would have sought for something greater. But, through the revelation of Jesus Christ, I had seen the happiness of humility, and there was an earnest desire in me to enter deep into it; and at times this desire arose to a degree of fervent supplication, wherein my soul was so environed with heavenly light and consolation, that things were made easy to me which had been otherwise. . . . I then wrought at my trade as a tailor; carefully attended meetings for worship and discipline; and found an enlargement of gospel love in my mind, and therein a concern to visit Friends in some of the back settlements of Pennsylvania and Virginia; and being thoughtful about a companion, I expressed it to my beloved friend, Isaac Andrews, who then told me that he had drawings to the same places, and also to go through Maryland, Virginia, and Carolina. . . . I opened the case in our monthly-meeting; and Friends expressing their unity therewith, we obtained certificates to travel as companions,—his from Haddonfield, and mine from Burlington." [1]

II.

The story of John Woolman, as thus far told, brings us to the point where he began to give himself almost wholly to the true work of his life—that of an apostle, with a need to go from land to land in fulfillment of his apostleship, and able, like one of the greatest of all apostles, to minister to his own necessities by the labors of a lowly trade. For, long before he set out upon these travels, even from his early childhood, he had entered, as he thought, into the possession of certain treasures of the spirit which he could not hoard up for himself alone,—which, if he could but share them with others, would make others rich and happy beyond desire or even imagination. As we study John Woolman along the pages upon which he has made record of his inmost nature, we shall be inclined to infer that the traits which made him the man he was, were these: first, a singularly vivid perception of the reality and worth of things spiritual; secondly, such a passion of desire for all that is like God, that whatsoever he met with in himself or in others which was otherwise, grieved him with an ineffable sorrow; thirdly, love, taking every form of adoration for the Highest Love, and of sympathy and effort on behalf of all God's creatures, great and small; next, humility; next, directness, simplicity, sincerity; next, refinement. Certainly, the power of this book cannot be conveyed by detached passages, and in all cases must be without effect, save upon natures that are prepared for it; yet of what has just now been said, some verification may be had in sentences

[1] "A Journal of the Life," etc., 19–21.

like these, taken here and there from it. "I was taught to read near as soon as I was capable of it; and as I went from school one seventh day, I remember, while my companions went to play by the way, I went forward out of sight, and sitting down I read the twenty-second chapter of the Revelation: 'He shewed me a pure river of water of life, clear as crystal, proceeding out of the throne of God and of the Lamb, &c.' And in reading it, my mind was drawn to seek after that pure habitation."[1] "I . . . was early convinced in my mind, that true religion consisted in an inward life, wherein the heart doth love and reverence God the Creator, and learns to exercise true justice and goodness, not only toward all men, but also toward the brute creatures; that as the mind was moved, by an inward principle, to love God as an invisible incomprehensible Being, by the same principle it was moved to love Him in all His manifestations in the visible world; that, as by His breath the flame of life was kindled in all animal sensible creatures, to say we love God as unseen, and at the same time exercise cruelty toward the least creature moving by His life, or by life derived from Him, was a contradiction in itself."[2] "I looked upon the works of God in this visible creation, and an awfulness covered me; my heart was tender and often contrite, and universal love to my fellow creatures increased in me."[3] "Some glances of real beauty may be seen in their faces, who dwell in true meekness."[4] "When I eat, drank, and lodged free-cost with people who lived in ease on the hard labor of slaves, I felt uneasy; and as my mind was inward to the Lord, I found from place to place this uneasiness return upon me at times through the whole visit."[5] "This trade of importing slaves from their native country . . . was frequently the subject of my serious thoughts. And I saw in these southern provinces so many vices and corruptions, increased by this trade and this way of life, that it appeared to me as a dark gloominess hanging over the

[1] "A Journal of the Life," etc., 2. [2] Ibid. 8–9.
[3] Ibid. 9. [4] Ibid. 9. [5] Ibid. 23.

land. And though now many willingly run into it, yet in future the consequence will be grievous to posterity: I express it as it hath appeared to me, not once nor twice, but as a matter fixed on my mind."[1] "I was then carried in spirit to the mines, where poor oppressed people were digging rich treasures for those called Christians; and heard them blaspheme the name of Christ, at which I was grieved —for His name to me was precious."[2] "About this time, a person at some distance lying sick, his brother came to me to write his will. I knew he had slaves, and asking his brother, was told he intended to leave them as slaves to his children. As writing is a profitable employ, and as offending sober people was disagreeable to my inclination, I was straitened in my mind; but as I looked to the Lord, He inclined my heart to His testimony. And I told the man, that I believed the practice of continuing slavery to this people was not right, and had a scruple in my mind against doing writings of that kind; that though many in our society kept them as slaves, still I was not easy to be concerned in it, and desired to be excused from going to write the will. I spake to him in the fear of the Lord, and he made no reply to what I said, but went away. He also had some concerns in the practice, and I thought he was displeased with me. In this case, I had a fresh confirmation, that acting contrary to present outward interest, from a motive of divine love and inward regard to truth and righteousness, and thereby incurring the resentments of people, opens the way to a treasure better than silver, and to a friendship exceeding the friendship of men."[3] "A neighbor received a bad bruise in his body, and sent for me to bleed him; which being done, he desired me to write his will. I took notes; and amongst other things, he told me to which of his children he gave his young negro. I considered the pain and distress he was in, and knew not how it would end; so I wrote his will, save only that part concerning his slave, and carrying it to his bed-side, read it to him, and then told

[1] "A Journal of the Life," etc., 24. [2] Ibid. 233. [3] Ibid. 35.

him, in a friendly way, that I could not write any instruments by which my fellow creatures were made slaves, without bringing trouble on my own mind. I let him know that I charged nothing for what I had done, and desired to be excused from doing the other part in the way he proposed. We then had a serious conference on the subject. At length, he agreeing to set her free, I finished his will."[1] "We were taught by renewed experience to labor for an inward stillness; at no time to seek for words, but live in the spirit of truth, and utter that to the people which truth opened in us."[2] "The natural man loveth eloquence, and many love to hear eloquent orations; and if there is not a careful attention to the gift, men who have once labored in the pure Gospel ministry, growing weary of suffering and ashamed of appearing weak, may kindle a fire, compass themselves about with sparks, and walk in the light—not of Christ who is under suffering, but of that fire which they, going from the gift, have kindled; and that, in hearers, which is gone from the meek suffering state into the worldly wisdom, may be warmed with this fire, and speak highly of these labors. That which is of God gathers to God, and that which is of the world, is owned by the world."[3]

III.

Thus, the autobiography of John Woolman was the gradual and secret growth of many years, beginning when he was of the age of thirty-six, and added to from time to time until, at the age of fifty-two, being in the city of York, in England, about the business of his Master, he was stricken down of the small pox, whereof he died. Besides this story of his life, he left several ethical and religious essays:—"Some Considerations on the Keeping of Negroes"[4]; "Considerations on Pure Wisdom, and Human Policy, on Labor, on Schools, and on the Right Use of the

[1] "A Journal of the Life," etc., 42–43. [2] Ibid. 30. [3] Ibid. 243–244.
[4] Part I. first printed in 1754; Part II. in 1762.

Lord's Outward Gifts"[1]; "Considerations on the True Harmony of Mankind, and How it is to be Maintained"[2]; finally, "A Word of Remembrance and Caution to the Rich,"[3]—the last being in some respects the most impressive of all his essays, with a striking applicability to problems now vexing the civilized world.

While these essays set forth, without reserve and without censoriousness, the very altruism of Jesus Christ, which, as Woolman thought, must first live in the hearts of men, both rich and poor, before the distinctions of outward condition will cease to occasion bitterness and violence upon earth, it is fitting here to add, that, like the autobiography, all these writings are, as Whittier has said, in the style "of a man unlettered, but with natural refinement and delicate sense of fitness, the purity of whose heart enters into his language."[4] "The secret of Woolman's purity of style," said Channing, "is that his eye was single, and that conscience dictated the words."[5] There is about John Woolman's writings that unconventionality of thought, that charity without pretense, that saintliness without sanctimony or sourness, that delicacy, that untaught beauty of phrase, by which we are helped to understand the ardor of Charles Lamb's love for him, as uttered in his impulsive exhortation to the readers of the Essays of Elia: "Get the writings of John Woolman by heart."[6] "A perfect gem!" wrote Henry Crabb Robinson, in 1824, of Woolman's "Journal," which Lamb had shortly before made known to him. "His is a 'schöne Seele.' An illiterate tailor, he writes in a style of the most exquisite purity and grace. His moral qualities are transferred to his writings."[7] Perhaps, after all, the

---

[1] First printed in 1768.

[2] First printed in 1770.

[3] First printed in 1793, and reprinted as a part of the Appendix to Whittier's edition of "The Journal of John Woolman."

[4] "The Journal of John Woolman," Introd., 33.

[5] Cited by Whittier, Ibid. 34.

[6] This occurs in the ninth of the Essays of Elia, entitled "A Quakers' Meeting." "The Works of Charles Lamb," iii. 84.

[7] "Diary . . . of Henry Crabb Robinson," i. 403.

aroma that lingers about Woolman's words is best described by Woolman's true spiritual successor in American literature, in the saying, that he who reads these writings becomes sensible "of a sweetness as of violets."[1]

IV.

In 1782, just as the people of England were beginning to adjust themselves to the fact that their obstreperous American children had finally come of age, and were giving rather too many proofs of their capacity to set up political housekeeping on their own account, there was published in London an American book about these same American children and their big country, but written with a sweetness of tone and, likewise, with a literary grace and a power of fascination, then quite unexpected from the western side of the Atlantic. It presented itself to the public behind this ample title-page:—"Letters from an American Farmer, describing certain provincial situations, manners, and customs, not generally known, and conveying some idea of the late and present interior circumstances of the British Colonies in North America: written for the information of a friend in England, by J. Hector St. John, a farmer in Pennsylvania."[2]

The name of the author as thus given upon his title-page, was not his name in full, but only the baptismal portion of it. By omitting from the book his surname, which was Crevecœur, he had chosen to disguise to the English public the fact—which could hardly have added to his welcome among them—that though he was an American, he was not an English American, but a French one,—having been born in Normandy, and of a noble family there, in 1731. Moreover, this is not his only device for self-concealment; for, throughout the book, he writes under the character of a simple-hearted American farmer who, born in America, and with but slight education, and with no opportunity for

[1] Whittier, Introd. to "The Journal of John Woolman," 34.

[2] The copy used by me is the edition of 1783, "Printed for Thomas Davies, in Russell Street, Covent Garden."

travel beyond the bounds of his native land, has inherited his farm from his American father, and has learned, almost within the horizon of that farm, his best lessons concerning this world and other worlds and the meaning of life everywhere.

In reality, however, while really an American farmer, Crevecœur was a man of education, of refinement, of varied experience in the world. When but a lad of sixteen, he had removed from France to England; when but twenty-three, he had emigrated to America. Here, in due time, he had taken unto himself an American farm, and an American wife, and with true French graciousness and tact had quickly assimilated the ways of life, especially of rural life, in his adopted country. It is probable that he was of the Society of Friends—which may partly account for his coming to America and especially to Pennsylvania, as well as for many peculiarities of his book,—some of its local and personal allusions, its gentle tone, its spirituality, its mysticism, its tender but firm championship of the poor Indian and the poor slave, and, above all, its prevailing reticence concerning the ferocious political and military controversies of the Revolution. At any rate, being a man of quite uncommon literary cultivation, and having the vivacity and the imaginative flexibility of his race, having also a fondness both for human fellowship and for solitude, and the power to look upon life, even in a wilderness, through the eyes of a scholar, a philosopher, and an idealist, he threw himself with full delight into the primitive free spirit of the new world,—its consciousness of ample room and of escape from tradition, its helpfulness, its frank customs, crude labors, artless pleasures,—and all these he was able, at last, to interpret to the old world in a series of idyllic descriptions which, surely, could not be fallacious or misleading—except, of course, to people who were not scholars, philosophers, and idealists, or who, at least, had not his faculty of seeing in this world those beautiful realities that are invisible always to the mere bodily sight.

V.

As an account of the American colonies, this book makes no pretension either to system or to completeness; and yet it does attain to a sort of breadth of treatment by seizing upon certain representative traits of the three great groups of colonies. For the northern group, he has five letters, devoted to Nantucket, Martha's Vineyard, and Cape Cod. For the middle group, he has two letters, evidently founded upon his own experience as the possessor of a farm in Pennsylvania, on "the edge of the great wilderness, three hundred miles from the sea": one of these letters being descriptive of "the situation, feelings, and pleasures of an American farmer," and the other of the "distresses of a frontier-man." For the southern group, he has but one letter, dealing with Charleston, South Carolina, and with the more harrowing and tragic form of the slave-labor system as prevalent in that region. The remaining letters—four in number—are taken up with a variety of topics, all having their interpretative value; such as the genius and the achievements of John Bartram the American botanist, his own observations upon natural history in America, and especially some aspects of the race-problem there, which he deals with in answer to the question—"What is an American?"

If we would come at once into contact with Crevecœur's habit and tone of thought,—a delicate and joyous perception of phenomena, and a divination of their meaning as seen by him through a haze of noble idealizing sentiment,—we can perhaps do no better than to turn to his discussion of this very question—a question still often asked and perhaps never yet fully answered. Premising that the people of the colonies "are a mixture of English, Scotch, Irish, French, Dutch, Germans, and Swedes," and that "from this promiscuous breed that race now called Americans have arisen," he repeats the enquiry—"What, then, is the American, this new man? He is neither an European, nor the descendant of an European: hence that strange mixture of blood, which you will find in no other country. I could point out to you a family, whose grandfather was an Englishman, whose wife was Dutch, whose son married a French woman, and whose present four sons have now four wives of different nations. He is an American, who, leaving behind him all his ancient prejudices and manners, receives new ones from the new mode of life he has embraced, the new government he obeys, and the new rank he holds. He becomes an American by being received in the broad lap of our great 'alma mater.' Here individuals of all nations are melted into a new race of men, whose labors and posterity will one day cause great changes in the world. Americans are the western pilgrims, who are carrying along with them that great mass of arts, sciences, vigor, and industry, which began long since in the east. They will finish the great circle. The Americans were once scattered all over Europe. Here they are incorporated into one of the finest systems of population which has ever appeared, and which will hereafter become distinct by the power of the different climates they inhabit. The American ought therefore to love this country much better than that wherein either he or his forefathers were born. Here the rewards of his industry follow, with equal steps, the progress of his labor. His labor is founded on the basis of nature—self-interest: can it want a stronger allurement? Wives and children, who before in vain demanded of him a morsel of bread, now, fat and frolicsome, gladly help their father to clear those fields whence exuberant crops are to arise, to feed and to clothe them all, without any part being claimed either by a despotic prince, a rich abbot, or a mighty lord. Here religion demands but little of him,—a small voluntary salary to the minister, and gratitude to God: can he refuse these? The American is a new man, who acts upon new principles; he must therefore entertain new ideas, and form new opinions. From involuntary idleness, servile dependence, penury, and useless labor, he has passed to toils of a very different nature, rewarded by ample subsistence.—This is an American."[1]

[1] "Letters," etc., 48; 51–53.

It is probable that not many passages in these letters were more enjoyed at the time, or are more likely to last in our literature as delightful examples of description at first hand, than those in which the author gives the results of his keen and sympathetic watchfulness of nature in the New World, —such as his account of the intrusive swallow and the submissive wren,[1] or of the bee-hunt,[2] or of the battle between the water-snake and the black-snake,[3]—all of which, indeed, are contributions to natural history as well as to literature.

VI.

There are in this book two distinct notes—one of great peace, another of great pain. The earlier and larger portion of the book gives forth this note of peace: it is a prose pastoral of life in the New World, as that life must have revealed itself to a well-appointed American farmer of poetic and optimistic temper, in the final stage of our colonial era, and just before the influx of the riot and bitterness of the great disruption.[4] What he thus writes breathes such deep tranquillity as might have its pulse in some leafy dale of Arcadia. Evidently this American farmer has found some happy valley—some peace-encircled spot—where, in modest competence, and with a " holiday-rejoicing spirit," he can plough his fields, and angle in his brooks, and take note of the splendors of sun-rise, and become acquainted with his birds and bees and squirrels and other furtive creatures—including even his own wife and children. Those political busy-bodies who, in the enjoyment of the utmost freedom, have yet thrown themselves into the anguish of imaginary slavery through their gratuitous speculations over the taxing-power of parliament, have no message for him. At

---

[1] " Letters," etc., 40–41.

[2] Ibid. 34–36.

[3] Ibid. 243–246.

[4] He himself says that several of the letters in his book were written before " the troubles that lately convulsed the American colonies " had " broke out." " Letters," etc., 7 n.

present he hears them not. He celebrates the comfort of American life—its opportunity—its thoughtfulness—its dignity—its beneficence. From his far-away plantation he stretches out his hands and shares in the "secret communion among good men throughout the world."[1] Happy with enough, he has no hatred for those who have more. "I envy no man's prosperity, and wish no other portion of happiness than that I may live to teach the same philosophy to my children."[2] He exults in the largeness, equality, facility, of life in this land: "Here we have in some measure, regained the ancient dignity of our species: our laws are simple and just; we are a race of cultivators; our cultivation is unrestrained, and therefore everything is prosperous and flourishing. For my part, I had rather admire the ample barn of one of our opulent farmers, who himself felled the first tree in his plantation, and was first founder of his settlement, than study the dimensions of the temple of Ceres. I had rather record the progressive steps of this industrious farmer, throughout all the stages of his labors and other operations, than examine how modern Italian convents can be supported without doing anything but singing and praying."[3] He is glad to think that American society "is not composed, as in Europe, of great lords who possess everything, and of a herd of people who have nothing. Here are no aristocratical families, no courts, no kings, no bishops, no ecclesiastical dominion, no invisible power giving to a few a very visible one."[4] "We are a people of cultivators, scattered over an immense territory, communicating with each other by means of good roads and navigable rivers, united by the silken bands of mild government, all respecting the laws, without dreading their power, because they are equitable."[5] He loves to think of America "as the asylum of freedom, as the cradle of future nations, and the refuge of distressed Europeans."[6] "We know, properly speaking, no strangers: this is every person's country."[7] He is fond of giving us

---

[1] "Letters," etc., Dedication. [2] Ibid. 45. [3] Ibid. 8–9.
[4] Ibid. 46. [5] Ibid, 47. [6] Ibid. Dedication. [7] Ibid. 70.

glimpses of his own serene and manly relation to life, as he sits "smoking a contemplative pipe"[1] on his piazza, or as he plows his low ground holding his "little boy on a chair which screws to the beam of the plow."[2] No struggle for existence, no carking care, keeps him from enjoying the sights and sounds of nature about him: "The pleasure I receive from the warblings of the birds in the spring is superior to my poor description, as the continual succession of their tuneful notes is for ever new to me. I generally rise from bed about that indistinct interval which, properly speaking, is neither night nor day; for this is the moment of the most universal vocal choir. Who can listen unmoved to the sweet love-tales of our robins, told from tree to tree, or to the shrill cat-birds? The sublime accents of the thrush, from on high, always retard my steps, that I may listen to the delicious music. The variegated appearances of the dew-drops, as they hang to the different objects, must present, even to a clownish imagination, the most voluptuous ideas. The astonishing art which all birds display in the construction of their nests, ill-provided as we may suppose them with proper tools, their neatness, their convenience, always make me ashamed of the slovenliness of our houses. Their love to their dame, their incessant careful attention, and the peculiar songs they address to her while she tediously incubates their eggs, remind me of my duty, could I ever forget it. Their affection to their helpless little ones is a lovely precept; and, in short, the whole economy of what we proudly call the brute creation, is admirable in every circumstance; and vain man, though adorned with the additional gift of reason, might learn from the perfection of instinct, how to regulate the follies, and how to temper the errors, which this second gift often makes him commit. This is a subject on which I have often bestowed the most serious thoughts. I have often blushed within myself, and been greatly astonished, when I have compared the unerring path they all follow,—all just, all proper, all wise, up to the nec-

[1] "Letters," etc., 40.

[2] Ibid. 26–27.

essary degree of perfection—with the coarse, the imperfect, systems of men."[1]

VII.

This note of peace holds undisturbed through the first half of the book, and more. Not until, in the latter half of it, the author comes to describe slavery in the far-south,[2] likewise the harsh relations between the colonists and the Indians,[3] finally the outbreak of the tempest of civil war, does his book give out its second note—the note of pain. His observations upon slavery are penetrating, and while never censorious, are yet pitiless in their justice and their moral purity. Moreover, the barbarism—perhaps, the necessary barbarism—of its penal methods, is set forth by him in a single picture, that of the caged negro; a picture, which has genuine literary power—quietness of stroke, absolute sureness, vividness, and pathos, and a self-enforcing logic which no dialectics can refute or escape. "I was not long since invited to dine with a planter who lived three miles from ——, . . . In order to avoid the heat of the sun, I resolved to go on foot, sheltered in a small path leading through a pleasant wood. I was leisurely travelling along, attentively examining some peculiar plants which I had collected, when all at once I felt the air strongly agitated, though the day was perfectly calm and sultry. I immediately cast my eyes toward the cleared ground, from which I was but a small distance, in order to see whether it was not occasioned by a sudden shower; when at that instant a sound, resembling a deep rough voice, uttered, as I thought, a few inarticulate monosyllables. Alarmed and surprised, I precipitately looked all around, when I perceived, at about six rods distance, something resembling a cage, suspended to the limbs of a tree, all the branches of which appeared covered with large birds of prey, fluttering about and anx-

---

[1] "Letters," etc., 38–39.

[2] See, for example, pages 219–224.

[3] As in pages 272–275.

iously endeavoring to perch on the cage. Actuated by an involuntary motion of my hands, more than by any design of my mind, I fired at them: they all flew to a short distance, with a most hideous noise, when, horrid to think and painful to repeat, I perceived a negro suspended in the cage, and left there to expire! I shudder when I recollect that the birds had already picked out his eyes; his cheek bones were bare; his arms had been attacked in several places; and his body seemed covered with a multitude of wounds. From the edges of the hollow sockets, and from the lacerations with which he was disfigured, the blood slowly dropped and tinged the ground beneath. No sooner were the birds flown, than swarms of insects covered the whole body of this unfortunate wretch, eager to feed on his mangled flesh and to drink his blood. I found myself suddenly arrested by the power of affright and terror; my nerves were convulsed; I trembled, I stood motionless, involuntarily contemplating the fate of this negro in all its dismal latitude. The living spectre, though deprived of his eyes, could still distinctly hear, and in his uncouth dialect begged me to give him some water to allay his thirst. Humanity herself would have recoiled back with horror; she would have balanced whether to lessen such reliefless distress, or mercifully with one blow to end this dreadful scene of agonizing torture. Had I had a ball in my gun, I certainly should have despatched him; but, finding myself unable to perform so kind an office, I sought, though trembling, to relieve him as well as I could. A shell ready fixed to a pole, which had been used by some negroes, presented itself to me; I filled it with water, and with trembling hands I guided it to the quivering lips of the wretched sufferer. Urged by the irresistible power of thirst, he endeavored to meet it, as he instinctively guessed its approach by the noise it made in passing through the bars of the cage. 'Tankè you, whitè man; tankè you; putè somè poison and givè me.' 'How long have you been hanging there?'—I asked him. 'Two days, and me no die; the birds, the birds, aaah me!' Oppressed with the reflections which this shocking spectacle afforded me, I mustered strength enough to walk away, and soon reached the house where I intended to dine. There I heard that the reason for this slave's being thus punished, was on account of his having killed the overseer of the plantation. They told me that the laws of self-preservation rendered such executions necessary, and supported the doctrine with the arguments generally made use of to justify the practice, with the repetition of which I will not trouble you at present." [1]

In the final chapter of the book, entitled "Distresses of a Frontier Man," the note of pain, which has begun to be heard still earlier, rises into something like a wail; for, the twofold horrors, first of impending attacks by Indians, and, secondly, of civil war between white men, have at last reached the once happy home of this bucolic philosopher and quietist. "The hour is come at last, that I must fly from my house and abandon my farm. But what course shall I steer, enclosed as I am? . . . Whichever way I look, nothing but the most frightful precipices present themselves to my view, in which hundreds of my friends and acquaintances have already perished. Of all animals that live on the surface of this planet, what is man when no longer connected with society, or when he finds himself surrounded by a convulsed and a half-dissolved one!" [2] "I am a lover of peace,—what must I do? . . . I am conscious that I was happy before this unfortunate Revolution. I feel that I am no longer so; therefore I regret the change. . . . If I attach myself to the mother-country, which is three thousand miles from me, I become what is called an enemy to my own region; if I follow the rest of my countrymen, I become opposed to our ancient masters. Both extremes appear equally dangerous to a person of so little weight and consequence as I am, whose energy and example are of no avail. As to the argument, on which the dispute is founded, I know but little about it. Much has been said and written on both sides, but who has a judgment capacious

[1] "Letters," etc., 232–235. [2] Ibid. 270–271.

and clear enough to decide? . . . Books tell me so much, that they inform me of nothing. . . . Alas, how should I unravel an argument in which reason herself has given way to brutality and bloodshed? What then must I do? I ask the wisest lawyers, the ablest casuists, the warmest patriots, for I mean honestly. Great Source of Wisdom! inspire me with light sufficient to guide my benighted steps out of this intricate maze! Shall I discard all my ancient principles, shall I renounce that name, that nation, which I held once so respectable? . . . On the other hand, shall I arm myself against that country where I first drew breath, against the play-mates of my youth, my bosom-friends, my acquaintances? . . . Must I be called a parricide, a traitor, a villain; lose the esteem of all those whom I love, to preserve my own; be shunned like a rattle-snake, or be pointed at like a bear?"[1]

By its inclusion of these sombre and agonizing aspects of life in America, the book gains, as is most obvious, both in authenticity and in literary strength. Nevertheless, with even these tremendous abatements from the general scene of human felicity presented by the New World, the reader is tempted to infer that, after all, felicity is the permanent fact there, and that suffering is but a temporary accident. It is not hard to understand why, at such a time, a book like this should soon have made its way into the languages of Europe, particularly those of France,[2] Germany,[3] and Holland;[4] nor why it should have fascinated multitudes of

[1] "Letters," etc., 276–278.

[2] "Lettres d'un cultivateur Américain, écrites à W. S. Écuyer, Depuis l'année 1770, jusqu' à 1781. Traduites de L'Anglois par . . ." Paris: 1784. This translation was made by Crevecœur himself, who had been so long unaccustomed to French that his work abounds in Anglicisms. In 1787, there appeared in Paris a greatly enlarged edition, with map, plates, etc.

[3] "Briefe eines Amerikanischen Landmanns . . . Aus dem Englischen ins Französische von . . . und jetzt aus dem Französischen übersetst und mit einigen Anmerkungen begleitet, von Johann August Ephraim Götze." Drei Bänder. Leipzig: 1788.

[4] "Brieven van eenen Amerikaenschen Landman van Carlisle in Pennsilvanien, geschteven aen eenen zijner vrienden in Engeland. Uit het Engelsch." Ley-

readers in all parts of the continent, even beguiling many of them—too many of them, perhaps—to try their fortunes in that blithe and hospitable portion of the planet where the struggle for existence seemed almost a thing unknown. In England, likewise, the book won for itself, as was natural, a wide and a gracious consideration; its praises lasted among English men of letters as long, at least, as until the time of Hazlitt and Charles Lamb; while its idealized treatment of rural life in America wrought quite traceable effects upon the imaginations of Campbell, Byron, Southey, Coleridge, and furnished not a few materials for such captivating and airy schemes of literary colonization in America as that of "Pantisocracy."[1]

---

den: 1784. Several titles in French, German, and Dutch are given by Sabin, "Dictionary," etc., v. 76–77.

[1] In 1801 was published in Paris, in three volumes, a copious work entitled "Voyage Dans La Haute Pensylvanie et Dans l'État de New York, par un Membre adoptif de la Nation Onéida. Traduit et publié par l'auteur des Lettres de 'un Cultivateur Americain." This assumed relation to the book was probably only a characteristic literary device of Crevecœur's for veiling his actual authorship of it.

CHAPTER XXXVIII.

FRANKLIN IN THE LITERATURE OF THE REVOLUTION.

I.—Franklin's absence from America during the larger part of the Revolution—His vast influence on both sides of the Atlantic—Political uses of his fame as an electrician.

II.—His renown prior to 1764—What he had then done as a wiiter—Development of his literary powers down to old age—Quality of his humor.

III.—Classification of his writings during the period of the Revolution—Account of those apart from that controversy—His proposal to Madame Helvetius.

IV.—His urbane and humorous method in controversy—His attitude toward that of the Revolution—General view of his writings on the subject.

V.—His chief contributions to the Revolutionary dispute—His "Examination"—"Causes of American discontents"—"On the Rise and Progress of the Differences between Great Britain and her American Colonies"—"Dialogue between Britain, France, Spain, Holland, Saxony, and America"—"A Catechism relative to the English Debt"—His emblematic picture of Britannia dismembered.

VI.—His special use of satire in the form of ludicrous analogue—Burlesque of extravagant stories told in England respecting the colonies—"Rules for Reducing a Great Empire to a Small One"—"An Edict by the King of Prussia"—Great effects of the latter both in England and in America—His satire on the Anglo-German traffic in troops for America.

VII.—The history of the Revolution as composed of Franklin's passing comments on its successive stages—A continuous reading of all his Revolutionary writings, needful for an adequate impression of their worth or charm.

I.

ONE peculiarity attaching to Franklin's part in the American Revolution arises from the fact that nearly the whole of that Revolution took place in his absence. In November, 1764, he went to England as the agent of Pennsylvania, charged with the duty of protesting against the passage of the Stamp Act; and in England he remained for nearly eleven years. Returning to America in May, 1775, he remained here only until October, 1776, when, "at the age of seventy-two or seventy-four, and at the risk of his head," as Horace Walpole wrote, he "bravely embarked on board an American frigate"[1] as commissioner to the court of France. In France he then remained until September, 1785. Coming back to America in that year, he died in 1790. Thus, during the twenty years which may be set apart as the period of the American Revolution, Franklin himself was in America only two years and a half.

Nevertheless, it is doubtful if any other brain than his had more to do with the shaping of the thought of the American Revolution, or any other hand a more potent pressure in the ordering of its event. Though separated from his country by the breadth of the Atlantic, never was there a moment during all those years when his country was not conscious of his inseparable and indispensable connection with the development of its destiny. Indeed, in that very spectacle of his personal absence from the scene of great transactions over which he was believed to wield a tremendous control, was something to give an added stimulus to the imaginations of men, and to enhance both in America and in Europe the vast influence which he had in both. From his modest lodgings in London during the first eleven years of the Revolution, from his quiet hotel in a suburb of Paris during the last eight years of it, he seemed to be the arch-magician, who, by his mastery of the secrets of nature, knew how to send abroad over land and sea invisible forces to sway mankind to his will. Under such circumstances, it is easy to perceive how his renown as an electrician threw a weird and an exaggerating light upon his prestige as a statesman and a revolutionist. "Our colonies might be well enough," was a saying among Englishmen in 1774, "were it not for Dr. Franklin, who has, with a brand

---

[1] Cited in his "Benjamin Franklin," 229, by J. T. Morse, Jr. The reader will notice that Franklin's age is slightly overstated by Walpole.

lighted from the clouds, set fire to all America."[1] In 1775, Samuel Johnson depicted Franklin as a "master of mischief" who had taught his countrymen "how to put in motion the engine of political electricity, . . . and to give the great stroke by the name of Boston."[2] Among the innumerable prints of Franklin scattered through France, were many that represented him as an old philosopher serenely seated in his chair, with flashes of lightning playing in the sky above his head, while beneath the portrait was some inscription attributing to him the power to use that lightning as his ally in the liberation of America and of mankind: as, under the drawing by Carmontelle,—

> "On l'a vu désarmer les Tirans et les Dieux :"[3]

or, under the portrait by Cochin,—

> "C'est l'honneur et l'appui du nouvel hémisphère ;
> Les flots de l'Océan s'abaissent à sa voix ;
> Il réprime ou dirige à son gré le tonnerre :
> Qui désarme les dieux, peut-il craindre les rois ?"[4]

It was for a similar use that Turgot produced his incomparable line

> "Eripuit coelo fulmen, septrumque tyrannis."[5]

With the grotesque humor even then characteristic of much popular writing in America, one of our own newspapers sent forth, in 1777, the droll announcement, that Dr. Franklin

---

[1] This is stated by Matthew Robinson, afterward Lord Rokeby, in his pamphlet entitled "Considerations on the Measures . . . with respect to the British Colonies in North America," 61.

[2] "Taxation no Tyranny," 68.

[3] Hale, "Franklin in France," Part i. 84–85.

[4] "The Works of Charles Sumner," viii. 13.

[5] "Œuvres de M. Turgot," ix. 140. A most interesting discussion of the origin and influence of Turgot's line, is given in "The Works of Charles Sumner," viii. 1–38. For its bearing on our relations with France during the American Civil War, Sumner's paper was originally published in November, 1863, in "The Atlantic Monthly," xii. 648–662.

was about "to produce an electrical machine of such wonderful force that, instead of giving a slight stroke to the elbows of fifty or a hundred thousand men who are joined hand in hand, it will give a violent shock even to nature herself, so as to disunite kingdoms, join islands to continents, and render men of the same nation strangers and enemies to each other; and that, by a certain chemical preparation from oil, he will be able to smooth the waves of the sea in one part of the globe, and raise tempests and whirlwinds in another, so as to be universally acknowledged for the greatest physician, politician, mathematician, and philosopher, this day living."[1]

II.

At the time of his voyage to England in 1764—that being his third voyage thither—he was already the most celebrated person that his country had then produced,—a fact sufficiently attested by Hume's salutation of him as "the first philosopher and indeed the first great man of letters" for whom Europe was beholden to America.[2] He was then fifty-eight years of age, and independent in his private circumstances. He had known a long and varied experience in commercial life, in politics, in legislative and administrative work. He had been a successful journalist, under the somewhat petty and clumsy conditions of journalism in those days. He was the projector of many mechanical

[1] "The New Jersey Gazette," for December 31, 1777, given in Frank Moore, "Diary of the American Revolution," i. 504.

[2] "The Complete Works of Benjamin Franklin," Bigelow ed., iii. 190. In the present chapter, my references to Franklin's writings will be mostly to the collection of them just mentioned, but inaccurately entitled "Complete." Even with this collection before him, every scholar will need to make use of the earlier collection by Jared Sparks. Since the death of Sparks, there has been a tendency among us to forget or to undervalue his important and indeed almost herculean labors as a pioneer in American historical scholarship. Happily this tendency, which was too ill-founded to have lasted long, has received a wholesome check through the publication, in 1893, of Professor Herbert B. Adams's careful work on "The Life and Writings of Jared Sparks."

and institutional devices for adding to the welfare and happiness of the human race. He was distinguished beyond all other men of his time in the one branch of science to which the men of his time were looking with the greatest interest. Finally, he was the author of a multitude of writings, covering a wide range of subjects, some of which had already made their way wherever the English language was known, and were read and relished for their shrewdness, their wit, their practical helpfulness, their alliance of prudence with generosity and good humor, their pure, pithy, and sparkling style.

It is a trait of Franklin as a man of letters, that while in his early life he took infinite pains to become a good writer, he did so, apparently, not from mere literary ambition, but chiefly as a means to some immediate practical end—particularly that of getting on in the world.[1] Accordingly, nearly everything he wrote was sent forth alone, and without his name, and was then allowed to shift for itself without any further pains or care on his part. This seeming freedom from solicitude as to the whereabouts or the well-being of his literary children, may be noted in the reply he made, during his second residence in England, to a request from Lord Kames for copies of all his published writings:—" I had daily expectations of procuring some of them from a friend to whom I formerly sent them when I was in America, and postponed writing to you, till I should obtain them; but at length he tells me he cannot find them. Very mortifying this to an author—that his works should so soon be lost! So I can only send you my 'Observations on the Peopling of Countries,' which happens to have been reprinted here; 'The Description of the Pennsylvania Fireplace,' a machine of my contriving; and some little sketches that have been printed in the 'Grand Magazine,' which I should hardly own, did I not know that your friendly partiality would make them seem at least tolerable."[2]

[1] For example, "Franklin's Works," Bigelow ed., i. 46, 47–49, 50–51, 146.

[2] "Franklin's Works," Bigelow ed., iii. 38–39.

The disposition, as shewn in these sentences, humorously to underrate his own performances and by all means to avoid every sort of self-glorification, does not leave him at any time; and whoever, in 1764, desired to know what Franklin had then done in letters, had still to get other testimony than Franklin's. Already, so early as in 1751, and without his knowledge, had been published in London a collection of his scientific writings, entitled " Experiments in Electricity made at Philadelphia "—a little book which was made larger in 1752, and again larger in 1754, and was also many times republished on the continent in Latin, French, German, and Italian. His greatest prolificacy, however, had been in writings of a more general kind, dealing shrewdly and often playfully with traits of human nature, with the vices and foibles of society, with ethical and religious subjects, with all aspects of current politics in America as touching finance, the treatment of Indians, the treatment of negroes, military preparations, forms of government both colonial and intercolonial, and the relations of the colonies to England. Besides innumerable juvenile experiments in prose and verse,—ballads, lampoons, burlesques, paragraphs, disquisitions, epigrams, emblems, proverbs,—the most of which, happily, are lost beyond recovery, —he had published the essays of " The Busy-Body "; several dialogues in the manner of Xenophon, such as " Public Men," and " Concerning Virtue and Pleasure "; the satirical letters of " Celia Single," " Anthony Afterwit," and " Alice Adder-tongue "; " Articles of Belief and Acts of Religion "; " Self-Denial not the Essence of Virtue "; " On True Happiness "; " The Waste of Life "; " A Modest Inquiry into the Nature of a Paper Currency "; " On Government "; " The Importance of Gaining and Preserving the Friendship of the Indians "; " Observations concerning the Increase of Mankind and the Peopling of Countries "; " Plain Truth, or, Serious Considerations on the Present State of the City of Philadelphia and the Province of Pennsylvania "; " Plan of Union for the Colonies ";

and " The Interest of Great Britain Considered with regard to her Colonies and the Acquisition of Canada and Guadaloupe." Finally, no other class of his writings down to that time had appealed to so numerous and so eager a multitude of readers, as those in which he undertook to teach men the art of worldly prosperity, as " Necessary Hints to those that would be Rich," and " The Way to Wealth as Clearly Shown in the Preface of an Old Almanac entitled ' Poor Richard Improved,' " the latter containing the humorous and needle-witted speech of Father Abraham, which, as a recent biographer of Franklin has truly said, " is the most famous piece of literature the colonies produced." [1]

Undoubtedly, his best work in letters was done after the year 1764, and thenceforward down to the very year of his death; for, to a degree not only unusual but almost without parallel in literary history, his mind grew more and more vivacious with his advancing years, his heart more genial, his inventiveness more sprightly, his humor more gay, his style brighter, keener, more deft, more delightful. Yet even in these earlier writings of his, Franklin is always Franklin; and their vast popularity and effectiveness were due to qualities essentially the same as those which marked his later and still better work:—the pure English of the best writers and of the best talkers, simplicity, brevity, lightness of touch, strength without effort, the absence of declamation and of rhetorical parade, melody, point, extraordinary insight into human nature together with a frank identification of himself with its frailties, a singular desire and gift for helping other people to solve their most troublesome problems, and, finally, pervading all, and giving irresistible charm to all, his humor,—a humor which perfectly answers

[1] John Bach McMaster, " Benjamin Franklin as a Man of Letters," 129; wherein is to be found, also, Franklin's account of a witch-trial at Mount Morris,—a specimen of his wit not included in any of Franklin's collected writings. Ibid. 71–74. The most of the productions mentioned by me in the text, have been reprinted within the first three volumes of the Bigelow edition of the Works of Franklin.

to Thackeray's fine definition of it as something made up of "wit and love," the best humor being "that which contains most humanity, that which is flavored throughout with tenderness and kindness."[1] Writing in 1758 to his sister Jane, whom he dearly loved, and who was very devout according to the severe Calvinistic manner of the period, Franklin quotes an acrostic wherein religion is likened to a building, of which faith, hope, and charity are the three stories. "Faith," says he, in commenting upon this bit of imagery, "is then the ground floor, hope is up one pair of stairs. My dear beloved Jenny, don't delight so much to dwell in those lower rooms, but get as fast as you can into the garret, for in truth the best room in the house is charity. For my part, I wish the house was turned upside down—it is so difficult, when one is fat, to go up stairs; and not only so, but I imagine hope and faith may be more firmly built upon charity, than charity upon faith and hope."[2]

Yet no one could read far in Franklin and conclude that his charity was of the soft and eyeless sort. To a writer who enquired by what means he could find out the faults of the girl whom he was courting, and especially whether she had the virtues she seemed to have, Franklin replied,—"Commend her among her female acquaintance."[3] As a maker of epigrams, the man who wrote, "The noblest question in the world is, what good may I do in it," and "Keep your eyes wide open before marriage, half shut afterwards," and "Deny thyself for self's sake," and "He is no clown that drives the plow, but he that does clownish things," and "He that can have patience, can have what he will," also wrote, "Three may keep a secret, if two of them are dead," and "Sal laughs at everything you say; why? because she has fine teeth," and "God heals—the Doctor takes the fee," and "Who has deceived thee so oft, as thyself?" and "Search others for their virtues, thyself for thy vices," and

[1] "Miscellaneous Essays, Sketches, and Reviews," by W. M. Thackeray, 319.

[2] The Works of Franklin, Sparks ed., vii. 184.

[3] The Works of Franklin, Bigelow ed., i. 318.

"The proof of gold is fire; the proof of a woman, gold; the proof of a man, woman."[1]

III.

For the period of the Revolution, the writings of Franklin fall naturally into two principal divisions—first, those connected with the Revolutionary controversy, and, secondly, those almost entirely apart from it.

Among the latter, of course, are to be reckoned his numerous papers on scientific discoveries and mechanical inventions; a considerable number of his personal letters—these being, perhaps, the wisest and wittiest of all his writings; many short sketches, usually playful in tone, often in the form of apologues or parables; finally, the first, and the best, part of his "Autobiography," which, during the hundred years succeeding its first publication in 1791, has probably been the most widely read book of its class in any language, and which, "treated as a piece of writing, and judged as literature . . . must be pronounced," according to a recent critic, "the equal of Robinson Crusoe, one of the few everlasting books in the English language."[2] Here,

[1] These and other examples of Franklin's proverbial philosophy are chiefly gathered from "Poor Richard's Almanac," and with many others are to be found collected in Bigelow's edition of his Works, i. 452–461; in James Parton, "Life and Times of Benjamin Franklin," i. 228–233. For the sources of many of Franklin's proverbs, the reader is also referred to my "History of American Literature during the Colonial Time," ii. 122.

[2] McMaster, "Benjamin Franklin as a Man of Letters," 269. All editions of the "Autobiography" prior to that of John Bigelow, Philadelphia, 1874, are incomplete and corrupt in text. Bigelow's edition is from the original manuscript, and, being supplemented by much other material from Franklin's writings, is entitled "The Life of Benjamin Franklin, Written by Himself": Three volumes, Philadelphia, 1874. For the first time in any collected edition of Franklin's writings, an unmutilated version of the "Autobiography" appeared in 1887 in the first volume of Bigelow's edition of "The Complete Works of Benjamin Franklin," wherein the editor has also given an amusing account of the recovery by him, in Paris and London in 1866 and 1867, of the original manuscript. Many curious details as to the vicissitudes through which this manuscript had gone from the time it left the hand of its author, are given by Bigelow in the

then, as a product of Franklin's general literary activity during the Revolutionary period, is a considerable body of literature not concerned in the strifes of that bitter time, almost faultless in form, and so pervaded by sense, gayety, and kindness, as to be among the most precious and most delightful of the intellectual treasures of mankind.

Among so many pieces of writing, there must be an inequality of merit; and perhaps some of those which have been most frequently quoted and most loudly praised, are not altogether the most deserving of it, such as "The Whistle,"[1] and "An Economical Project,"[2] both of which bear traces of a conscious effort at pleasantry, and of pleasantry, also, which, as Lord Jeffrey said, has in it "something childish."[3] On the other hand, the delicious trifle entitled "The Ephemera: An Emblem of Human Life,"[4] and the "Dialogue between Franklin and the Gout,"[5] are executed, as Lord Jeffrey also declared, "with the lightness and spirit of genuine French compositions"; while "A Parable of Persecution,"[6] and we may add, "A Parable of Brotherly Love,"[7] "A Tale of Poor Jacques Montrésor,"[8] and the latter part of the essay on "The Handsome and Deformed Leg,"[9] have "all the point and facility of the fine pleasantries of Swift and Arbuthnot, with something more of directness and apparent sincerity."[10] It may be doubted, also, whether for spontaneity, grace, and pure frolic, all inspired

---

first volume of his "Life of Benjamin Franklin," where it forms an introductory paper entitled "Historical Sketch of the Fortunes and Misfortunes of the Autograph Manuscript of Franklin's Memoirs of His Own Life."

[1] Works of Franklin, Bigelow ed., vi. 239–242.

[2] Ibid. 277–283.

[3] "Edinburgh Review," viii. 341.

[4] Works of Franklin, Bigelow ed., vi. 237–239.

[5] Ibid. vii. 140–149.

[6] Ibid. v. 372–374.

[7] Ibid. 376–378.

[8] Ibid. v. 261.

[9] Ibid. vi. 253–255.

[10] These words of Lord Jeffrey were applied only to the first of the pieces mentioned in the text. I have used them as justly descriptive of the others also.

and illuminated by that sort of gallantry which can best be described as Parisian, any of his so-called "Bagatelles" is now more charming than the love-challenge of this septuagenarian widower addressed to the brilliant and not immature Madame Helvetius, widow of the famous philosopher whose name she was so proud to bear:—"Mortified at the barbarous resolution pronounced by you so positively yesterday evening, that you would remain single the rest of your life as a compliment to the memory of your husband, I retired to my chamber. Throwing myself upon my bed, I dreamt that I was dead, and was transported to the Elysian Fields. I was asked whether I wished to see any persons in particular; to which I replied that I wished to see the philosophers. 'There are two who live here at hand in this garden; they are good neighbors, and very friendly towards one another.'—'Who are they?'—'Socrates and Helvetius.'—'I esteem them both highly; let me see Helvetius first, because I understand a little French, but not a word of Greek.' I was conducted to him; he received me with much courtesy, having known me, he said, by character, some time past. He asked me a thousand questions relative to the war, the present state of religion, of liberty, of the government in France. 'You do not inquire, then,' I said, 'after your dear friend Madame Helvetius; yet she loves you extremely. I was in her company not more than an hour ago.' 'Ah,' said he, 'you make me recur to my past happiness, which ought to be forgotten in order to be happy here. For many years I could think of nothing but her, though at length I am consoled. I have taken another wife, the most like her that I could find; she is not indeed altogether so handsome, but she has a great fund of wit and good sense, and her whole study is to please me. She is at this moment gone to fetch the best nectar and ambrosia to regale me; stay awhile, and you will see her.' 'I perceive,' said I, 'that your former friend is more faithful to you than you are to her; she has had several good offers, but has refused them all. I will confess to you that I loved her extremely; but she was cruel to me, and rejected me peremptorily for your sake.' 'I pity you, sincerely,' said he, 'for she is an excellent woman, handsome and amiable. But do not the Abbé de la R. . . . . and the Abbé M. . . . . visit her?' 'Certainly they do; not one of your friends has dropped her acquaintance.' 'If you had gained the Abbé M. . . . . with a bribe of good coffee and cream, perhaps you would have succeeded; for he is as deep a reasoner as Duns Scotus or St. Thomas; he arranges and methodizes his arguments in such a manner that they are almost irresistible. Or if by a fine edition of some old classic you had gained the Abbé de la R. . . . . to speak against you, that would have been still better, as I always observed that when he recommended anything to her, she had a great inclination to do directly the contrary.' As he finished these words the new Madame Helvetius entered with the nectar, and I recognized her immediately as my former American friend, Mrs. Franklin! I reclaimed her, but she answered me coldly: 'I was a good wife to you for forty-nine years and four months, nearly half a century; let that content you. I have formed a new connection here, which will last to eternity.'—Indignant at this refusal of my Eurydice, I immediately resolved to quit those ungrateful shades, and return to this good world again, to behold the sun, and you! Here I am; let us avenge ourselves!" [1]

IV.

Of course, of chief importance for the purpose of our present studies, are those writings of Franklin which deal with the controversies of the American Revolution, and which, while they may be called controversial writings, illustrate in a delightful way Franklin's habit of eliminating from all controversy its churlish and merely rasping traits. He has himself told us how he came to acquire his method.

---

[1] Works of Franklin, Bigelow ed., vi. 269–271.

As a somewhat forward lad, he had fallen into a disputatious habit,—" a very bad habit," as he afterwards came to see. " Persons of good sense, I have since observed, seldom fall into it, except lawyers, university men, and men of all sorts that have been bred at Edinburgh."[1] From this disagreeable habit his escape seems to have been due, in the first instance, to his good luck in meeting with a copy of Xenophon's " Memorable Things of Socrates," wherein he found many examples of the Socratic method of conducting a dispute:—" I was charmed with it, adopted it, dropt my abrupt contradiction and positive argumentation, and put on the humble inquirer and doubter." " I continued this method some few years, but gradually left it, retaining only the habit of expressing myself in terms of modest diffidence, never using, when I advanced anything that may possibly be disputed, the words ' certainly,' ' undoubtedly,' or any others that give the air of positiveness to an opinion, but rather say, . . . ' I imagine it to be so,' or, ' it is so, if I am not mistaken.' "[2] Accordingly, in the long and angry disputes of the American Revolution, the part taken in them by Franklin was very much like that which Socrates might have taken had he been born in Boston in the early part of the eighteenth century, had he been for many years a printer and a politician in Philadelphia, and had he filled at London and Paris the diplomatic stations that were filled by Franklin. Indeed, the likeness between Franklin and Socrates was more than superficial; for besides the plebeian origin of both and some trace of plebeian manners which clung to both, and the strain of animal coarseness from which neither was ever entirely purified, they both had an amazing insight into human nature in all its grades and phases, they were both indifferent to literary fame, they were both humorists, they both applied their great intellectual gifts in a disciplinary but genial way to the improvement of their fellow-men, and in dealing controversially with the opinions of others they both understood and practised the

---

[1] Works of Franklin, Bigelow ed., i. 46–47. [2] Ibid. 50–51.

strategy of coolness, playfulness, an unassuming manner, moderation of statement, the logical parallel, and irony.

Being officially employed in Europe during nearly the entire period of the American Revolution, he was everywhere recognized as something far more than the official representative of America. Through his fame in science and letters, through his intimacy with great men, through the picturesqueness and the fascination of his personality, finally, through his journalistic sense in detecting from day to day the set of the winds and tides of public opinion and how to avail himself of both in the interests of his country, he became, in fact, the one conspicuous interpreter to Europe of the grievances and the purposes of America, and the one conspicuous interpreter to America of the attitude of Europe.

In studying the mass of Franklin's literary contributions to the Revolutionary controversy between 1763 and 1783, we shall find much help in noting that his relation to that controversy had two strongly contrasted phases: first, his sincere and most strenuous desire that the dispute should not pass from the stage of words to that of blows, and thence to a struggle for American secession from the empire; and, secondly, after the stage of blows had been reached, his championship of American secession through war as the only safe or honorable course then left to his countrymen. The line of division between these two phases of opinion and action, falls across the spring and early summer of 1775. Prior to that time, all his writings, serious or jocose, are pervaded by the one purpose of convincing the English people that the American policy of their government was an injustice and a blunder, and of convincing the American people that their demand for political rights would certainly be satisfied, if persisted in steadily and without fear, but also without disloyalty and without unseemly violence. Subsequent to that time, having accepted with real sorrow the alternative of war and of war for American secession, all his writings, serious or jocose, are pervaded by the one purpose of making that war a successful one,—a result to which, as a writer, he could best contribute by such appeals to public opinion in America as should nourish and quicken American confidence in their own cause, and by such appeals to public opinion in Europe as should win for that cause its moral and even its physical support. For reasons that must be obvious, his general literary activity was far greater during the first phase of this controversy, than during the second.

V.

Rising above the throng of his writings upon the American question in all its varying issues and aspects, from the beginning to the end, are some eight or ten productions which stand out as most worthy of mention in this place.

The first of these is the celebrated pamphlet entitled "The Examination of Doctor Benjamin Franklin, in the British House of Commons, relative to the Repeal of the American Stamp Act, in 1766."[1] Though a mere report of a certain memorable transaction in parliament, this pamphlet is, in reality, the result of a most consummate piece of political and editorial craftsmanship on the part of Franklin himself—a master without a master in the art of touching the springs of popular conviction and sympathy. First published in London in 1767, it had in England "a great run," as even Franklin permitted himself to acknowledge.[2] Being promptly translated into French, it was also widely circulated upon the continent, and for its pithy, dramatic, and amusing way of putting the American case, it was read by multitudes of people in many countries who thus got their first distinct impression as to the nature of the trouble then brewing in America, and as to the American people themselves—their number, character, resources, dispositions, opinions, purposes. Moreover, if the pamphlet thus gave a great impulse to the American cause in Europe —an impulse which was at once transmitted with tremendous

[1] Works of Franklin, Bigelow ed., iii. 407–450. [2] Ibid. iv. 28.

effect to America, also—not less did it contribute to the reputation and standing of Franklin himself on both sides of the Atlantic; for, by its incidental and modest exhibition of his marvelous presence of mind, under the shower of questions that were rained upon him in the House of Commons, of his unfailing resources both in knowledge and in argument, of his frankness, reasonableness, shrewdness, wit, temper, tact, good humor, it simply extended to the public outside the house the impression he had produced inside it, namely, that thenceforward, upon the American question, this elderly and quiet philosopher was to be reckoned with as a statesman and a diplomatist of the first order. "From this examination of Doctor Franklin," said the "Gentleman's Magazine" for July, 1767, "the reader may form a clearer and more comprehensive idea of the state and disposition of America, and of the expediency or inexpediency of the measure in question, and of the character and conduct of the minister who proposed it, than from all that has been written upon the subject in newspapers and pamphlets, under the titles of essays, letters, speeches, and considerations, from the first moment of its becoming the object of public attention till now." [1]

Early in the year 1768, under the guise of an Englishman having unusual acquaintance with the colonies, he published in the "London Chronicle" a long and sprightly article on the "Causes of American Discontents before 1768." [2] Though greatly mutilated and weakened by the editor of the journal in which it first appeared,—so that, as Franklin complained, with its teeth drawn and its nails pared, it could "neither scratch nor bite," and could only "paw and mumble," [3]—there was enough left of it to shew Franklin's great skill in winning favor for his side of the question by a novel and a half-grumbling presentation of its claims, and even by an ironical disparagement of them.

---

[1] "The Gentleman's Magazine and Historical Chronicle," xxxvii. 368.

[2] Reprinted in the Works of Franklin, Bigelow ed., iv. 97–111.

[3] Ibid. iv. 98 note.

So, too, in 1774, over the signature of "A Londoner," he contributed to the "Public Advertiser" a series of short articles "On the Rise and Progress of the Differences between Great Britain and her American Colonies,"[1] in which, with the frankness of a discontented Englishman, he caustically exposes the dunce-like methods of the ministry in dealing with the American problem, and the stupid pertinacity of those writers for the English press who seemed to think that they were solving that problem by calling the Americans hard names and by propagating all sorts of calumnies against them. "Surely," exclaims the "Londoner" at the close of his last article, "the great commerce of this nation with the Americans is of too much importance to be risked in a quarrel which has no foundation but ministerial pique and obstinacy! . . . Will our reviling them as cheats, hypocrites, scoundrels, traitors, cowards, tyrants, etc., etc., according to the present mode in all our papers, make them more our friends, more fond of our merchandize? Did ever any tradesman succeed, who attempted to drub customers into his shop? And will honest John Bull, the farmer, be long satisfied with servants that before his face attempt to kill his plough-horses?"[2]

Probably no writer ever understood better than he how to make dull subjects lively, and how, by consequence, to attract readers to the consideration of matters in themselves unattractive. As he well knew, the European public, whether upon the continent or in Great Britain, were not likely to give their days and nights to the perusal of long and solemn dissertations on the rights and wrongs of his countrymen in the other hemisphere. Accordingly, such dissertations he never gave them, but, upon occasion, brief and pithy and apparently casual statements of the American case; exposing, also, the weak points of the case against his own, by means of anecdotes, epigrams, jeux-d'esprit; especially contriving to throw the whole argument into some sort of dramatic form,—as in "A Dialogue between Britain,

[1] Works of Franklin, Bigelow ed., v. 323–338. [2] Ibid. 337–338.

France, Spain, Holland, Saxony, and America," [1] or as in "A Catechism relative to the English Debt" [2]; or, again, setting forth in pictorial form some stirring aspect of the dispute, as, in 1774, his famous emblematic drawing to illustrate "the result of England's persistence in her policy towards the colonies," [3] wherein Britannia is represented as a huge desolate female-figure occupying a conspicuous place on the globe, but with all her limbs—that is, her colonies—cut off and lying scattered about—these dismembered limbs being severally labelled Virginia, New England, Pennsylvania, and New York. In this sorry plight, as Franklin says in the "Explanation" accompanying the picture, Britannia lifts "her eyes and mangled stumps to Heaven; her shield, which she is unable to wield, lies useless by her side; her lance has pierced New England; the laurel branch has fallen from the hand of Pennsylvania; the English oak has lost its head, and stands a bare trunk, with a few withered branches; briers and thorns are on the ground beneath it; the British ships have brooms at their topmast heads, denoting their being on sale; and Britannia herself is seen sliding off the world,—no longer able to hold its balance,—her fragments overspread with the label, 'Date obolum Belisario.'" [4]

VI.

It remains to be mentioned that Franklin's favorite weapon in political controversy—a weapon which, perhaps, no other writer in English since Dean Swift has handled with so much cleverness and effect—was that of satire in the form of ludicrous analogue, thereby burlesquing the acts and pretensions of his adversary, and simply overwhelming him with ridicule. His very first dash into the Revolutionary controversy after his arrival in England in 1764, furnishes a case in point; when, in a letter to a newspaper, over the signature of "A Traveler," he chaffs the English

[1] Works of Franklin, Bigelow ed., vi. 118–122. [2] Ibid. 122–124.
[3] Ibid. v. 416–417. [4] Ibid. 416–417.

public about their habit of swallowing preposterous stories concerning the colonies, as then commonly told them in their journals,—himself, however, ironically maintaining the truth of these very stories, and even capping them by others just as true: as the one about the tails of the American sheep being " so laden with wool, that each has a little car or wagon on four little wheels to support and keep it from trailing on the ground "; or, as the one about the inhabitants of Canada " making preparations for a cod and whale fishery this summer in the upper lakes. Ignorant people may object that the upper lakes are fresh, and that cod and whales are salt-water fish; but let them know, sir, that cod, like other fish, when attacked by their enemies, fly into any water where they can be safest; that whales, when they have a mind to eat cod, pursue them wherever they fly, and that the grand leap of the whale in the chase up the Falls of Niagara is esteemed, by all who have seen it, as one of the finest spectacles in nature." [1]

Moreover, with Franklin, as had been the case with Dean Swift before him, this species of satire took a form at once so realistic and so comically apt, as to result in several examples of brilliant literary hoaxing—a result which, in the controversy then going on, was likely to be beneficial to the solemn and self-satisfied British Philistine of the period, since it compelled him for once to do a little thinking, and also to stand off and view his own portrait as it then appeared to other people, and even in spite of himself to laugh at his own portentous and costly stupidity in the management of an empire that seemed already grown too big for him to take proper care of. Of Franklin's work in the vein of literary burlesque, three pieces claim mention for their preëminent wit and point:—first, " Rules for Reducing a Great Empire to a Small One," [2] secondly, " An Edict by the King of Prussia," [3] both printed in the English newspapers in the early autumn of 1773; and, thirdly, a pre-

---

[1] Works of Franklin, Bigelow ed., iii. 378–379. [2] Ibid. v. 233–234.
[3] Ibid. 214–220.

tended letter of instructions "From the Count de Schaumbergh to the Baron Hohendorf commanding the Hessian Troops in America,"[1] this being dated at Rome, 18 February, 1777.

Referring to the first two of these pieces, soon after their publication, Franklin told his son that his object in writing them was to expose the conduct of England toward the colonies, "in a short, comprehensive, and striking view, and stated, therefore, in out-of-the-way forms, as most likely to take the general attention." "In my own mind," he adds, "I preferred the first, as a composition, for the quantity and variety of the matter contained, and a kind of spirited ending of each paragraph. But I find that others here generally prefer the second."[2] Probably, the chief reason for the greater attention paid in England to the second piece is to be found in the more direct and palpable character of its satire, dealing as it did with ideas and even phrases then uncommonly familiar to the English public. It made its appearance in the midst of the busy preparations then in progress for sending out the guileful tea-ships; when, of course, the very air was vibrant with allusions to the almost limitless claims of the mother country upon her American children, to the propriety and beauty of the English laws for controlling the commerce and manufactures of the colonies, and, above all, to the base ingratitude of England's American children in objecting to being taxed at will by their affectionate national parent. Under these circumstances it occurred to Franklin to set forth in some lively way the absurdity of all this; especially, that it was an argument which proved much more than its inventors would care to be responsible for. If, indeed, England had such limitless claims upon the American colonies because she was their

---

[1] Works of Franklin, Bigelow ed., vi. 74-78. This, of course, is the English version of the letter; but it was a part of the jest to assume that the letter was originally written in German or in French—probably in French. The French version is given by M. de Lescure, in his "Correspondance secrète inédite sur Louis XVI.," etc., i. 31-33.

[2] Ibid. 241-242.

mother country, why had not Germany, the mother country of England, the same claims upon her? This idea, accordingly, Franklin worked out in a manner thoroughly Franklinian,—causing to be published, first, in the "Public Advertiser," what purported to be a solemn edict of Frederick the Great,—"Given at Potsdam, this twenty-fifth day of the month of August, one thousand seven hundred and seventy-three, and in the thirty-third year of our reign,"[1]—wherein that monarch, in a tone of command very natural to him, uses the characteristic words of the English acts of parliament regulating the commerce and manufactures of the American colonies, and then proclaims on behalf of Prussia the same regulations over "the island of Great Britain": "And all persons in the said island are hereby cautioned not to oppose in any wise the execution of this our edict, or any part thereof, such opposition being high treason; of which all who are suspected shall be transported in fetters from Britain to Prussia, there to be tried and executed according to the Prussian law."[2]

In England this travesty made a great hit;—all the more so for the reason, as Franklin explained to his son, "that people in reading it were, as the phrase is, 'taken in,' till they had got half through it, and imagined it a real edict, to which mistake, I suppose, the king of Prussia's character contributed."[3] Some of its effects, the author himself had the good luck to witness, and in a way of which he has left an amusing account. Having sent his satire to the newspaper, he immediately went down to the country-seat of his friend, Lord le Despencer, where among other guests happened to be Paul Whitehead, the poet. One morning while most of the company were chatting in the breakfast-parlor, Whitehead "came running in to us out of breath, with the paper in his hand. 'Here!' says he, 'here's news for ye! Here's the king of Prussia claiming a right to this kingdom!' All stared, and I as much as anybody; and he went

[1] Works of Franklin, Bigelow ed., v. 220. [2] Ibid. 219.
[3] Ibid. 243.

on to read it. When he had read two or three paragraphs, a gentleman present said: 'Damn his impudence; I dare say we shall hear by next post, that he is upon his march with one hundred thousand men to back this.' Whitehead, who is very shrewd, soon after began to smoke it, and looking in my face said, 'I 'll be hanged if this is not some of your American jokes upon us.' The reading went on, and ended with abundance of laughing, and a general verdict that it was a fair hit." [1] Indeed, Lord Mansfield, who, of course, was not in that company, called the satire "very able and very artful," and expressed the belief that it "would do mischief by giving here a bad impression of the measures of government, and in the colonies by encouraging them in their contumacy," [2] all of which, certainly, was precisely the effect which it was intended to have.

The last of the three specimens of satire above mentioned, the Count de Schaumbergh's letter of instructions, seems to have been written by Franklin not long after his arrival in France in the latter part of 1776, and was intended to hold up to the execration of the civilized world both parties in the transaction by which the king of England bought of certain petty princes in Germany the troops with which to butcher his late American subjects. In some respects, this is the most powerful of all the satirical writings of Franklin. More, perhaps, than is the case with any other work of his, it displays, with marvelous subtlety and wit, that sort of genius which can reproduce with minute and perfect verisimilitude the psychological processes of some monstrous crime against human nature,—a crime which it thus portrays both to the horror and the derision of mankind. "Since the death of Swift," says John Bigelow in referring to this pretended letter of the Hessian trafficker in the bodies and souls of his subjects, "who, besides Franklin, was sufficiently a master of this kind of satire to have written it?" [3]

---

[1] Works of Franklin, Bigelow ed., v. 243. [2] Ibid. 224.

[3] Works of Franklin, vi. 74 note. M. de Lescure, in giving the French version of this letter, makes no allusion to Franklin, but says, in a foot-note:

VII.

As Franklin was by far the greatest man of letters on the American side of the Revolutionary controversy, so a most luminous and delightful history of the development of thought and emotion during the Revolution might be composed, by merely bringing together detached sayings of Franklin, humorous and serious, just as these fell from his tongue or pen in the successive stages of that long conflict: it would be a trail of light across a sea of storm and gloom.

Nevertheless, not by illustrative fragments of what he wrote or said, any more than by modern descriptions however vivid, can an adequate idea be conveyed of the mass, the force, the variety, the ease, the charm, of his total work as a writer during those twenty tremendous years. Undoubtedly, his vast experience in affairs and the sobriety produced by mere official responsibility, had the effect of clarifying and solidifying his thought, and of giving to the lightest products of his genius a sanity and a sureness of movement which, had he been a man of letters only, they could hardly have had in so high a degree. It is only by a continuous reading of the entire body of Franklin's Revolutionary writings, from grave to gay, from lively to severe, that any one can know how brilliant was his wisdom, or how wise was his brilliance, or how humane and gentle and helpful were both. No one who, by such a reading, procures for himself such a pleasure and such a benefit, will be likely to miss the point of Sydney Smith's playful menace to his daughter,—" I will disinherit you, if you do not admire everything written by Franklin."

" Il est évident, pour quiconque lit cette lettre, qu'elle n'est qu'un jeu d'esprit et de malignité destiné a railler le commerce insouciant et lucratif d'hommes (la traite des soldats) qu'on accusait les princes allemands, surtout de Hanovre et de Hesse, de faire cyniquement avec les puissances belligérantes en quête de mercenaires." " Correspondance secrète,"etc., i. 31.

CHAPTER XXXIX.

THE WRITERS OF HISTORY.

I.—Two expressions of the historic spirit during the Revolution—One resulting in local colonial history—The other resulting in histories of the Revolutionary movement and therefore representing the colonies as moving forward into statehood and a new national life.

II.—Stephen Hopkins as a representative of the historic spirit applied to local themes—His fragment on "The Planting and Growth of Providence," 1762 and 1765—Amos Adams and his "Concise Historical View of the Planting and Progressive Improvement of New England," 1769—Nathan Fiske's "Historical Discourse" for the town of Brookfield, 1775.

III.—Robert Proud, and his "History of Pennsylvania."

IV.—How religious affiliations overleaped colonial barriers and led to more comprehensive historical work—Morgan Edwards and his "Materials towards a History of the American Baptists," 1770—The intelligence and validity of his method as an historian—The scope of his work—Examples of its quality.

V.—Another intercolonial historian is Isaac Backus, preacher and politician—His "History of New England, with Particular Reference to the Denomination Called Baptists," 1777 and 1784—His motive in writing history—His method strictly scientific, notwithstanding his lack of disinterestedness—Value of his work.

VI.—Thomas Hutchinson as an historian dealing with themes both colonial and Revolutionary—The peculiar value of his contributions to American history—His writing of history but the by-play of a busy man of affairs—His ancestry—His career as merchant and politician—His attitude toward the Revolutionary controversy.

VII.—Hutchinson's early passion for the study of history, particularly constitutional history—His preparation for the writing of it—His idea of the importance of primary documents, and his unrivaled collection of them—The publication in 1764 of the first volume of his "History of the Colony of Massachusetts Bay"—His work in writing the second volume interrupted by a Boston mob in August, 1765, looting his house and destroying many of his papers—Fortunate recovery of the manuscript of the second volume—Its publication in 1767—Characteristics of this volume.

VIII.—Hutchinson summoned to England in 1774—His own special purpose in going there—Failure of his efforts to dissuade the government from its impolitic measures towards the colonies—The sorrows of his exile in England —Resumes there his "History," the third volume of which he finishes in 1778—Contains his own version of the Revolution down to the close of his administration as governor of Massachusetts—Its first publication in 1828.

IX.—Traits of Hutchinson as an historian—The distinctive tone of each of his three volumes—His evident truthfulness—His judicial tone—The severest test of his fairness applied in the writing of his third volume—An examination of Palfrey's estimate of him as an historian—The essence of his politics with reference to the Revolutionary dispute—His portrait of Governor Joseph Dudley, as in some respects a portrait of himself.

X.—A pretended historical work by Samuel Peters, "A General History of Connecticut," 1781—The career of Peters—The notoriety acquired by his book—Its grotesque fabrications in the service of calumny—Clearly not intended by himself as a mere historical romance or a satire in the form of burlesque history—Its author's mania for facts which never had an existence.

XI.—The development of the military stage of the Revolution accompanied by a general perception of its historic significance, and of the need of making and preserving records of it—Examples of historical work in its crudest form—Especially the diaries of eye-witnesses of its events—James Thacher's "Military Journal of the American Revolutionary War"—"A Journal of Occurrences," by Major Return Jonathan Meigs—George Rogers Clark's "Campaign in the Illinois"—Tench Tilghman's "Journal," and his "Diary"—"The Journal of Lieutenant William Feltman."

XII.—The beginnings of professed histories of the Revolution—Jonas Clark's "Brief Narrative" of the events of April 19, 1775—David Ramsay as a collector of materials for a history of the Revolution—William Henry Drayton as an historian of the Revolution—A portion of his work burned by order of Congress—His two volumes on the history of the war in the southern colonies.

XIII.—Mercy Warren as an historian of the Revolution—Her great opportunities for knowing the men and events of the period—Her "History of the Rise, Progress, and Termination of the American Revolution"—Its undisguised partisanship—Its literary qualities—Its historical portraits.

XIV.—William Gordon, and his indefatigable efforts to obtain oral and written testimony concerning the Revolution—His evident purpose to be truthful and fair—Fearing American prejudices against an impartial history of the Revolution, he goes to England to publish his work, but encounters there similar prejudices—How his manuscript was tampered with—The great value of his work, even as thus mutilated.

I.

WITHIN the two decades of the American Revolution, are to be found two distinct expressions of the historic spirit among this people. In the first place, from a consciousness of the meaning and worth of the unique social experiments then already made by each of these thirteen little republics, came the impulse which led to the writing of their local history. Afterward, from a similar consciousness of the meaning and worth of the immense events which began to unfold themselves in the collective political and military experience of these thirteen little republics, then rapidly melting together into a larger national life under the fires of a common danger, came the impulse which led to the writing of their general history. It is necessary for us to note the more important documents which still testify to the activity and the vigor of such historic spirit in this land, amid circumstances not at all favorable to its cultivation.

II.

An early and a genuine representative of the historic spirit was Stephen Hopkins, the Rhode Island statesman, who, as early as in October, 1762, while governor of that colony, began to publish in a weekly newspaper the results of his researches into "The Planting and Growth of Providence." After printing, in that year and in 1765, some eight chapters of his intended book, he was obliged by public occupations to break off these congenial labors—to which, indeed, he was never afterward able to return. What he thus wrote is therefore but a fragment, telling the story of Rhode Island only from its origin to the year 1745. Though but a fragment, however, it is quite enough to reveal in its author the best qualities of an historian,—love of truth, fair-mindedness, the power to see the meaning of facts and to set them in order, finally the gift of lucid, neat, and impressive statement.[1]

[1] The publication of Hopkins's fragment began in "The Providence Gazette" for October 20, 1762. Being then suddenly stopped, it did not begin again until January 12, 1765, when the "Gazette" reprinted the portion already published. The publication of the remaining portions of the work, was then kept up in the "Gazette" for January 12, 19; February 2, 9, 16; March 16, 30. The worth of this bit of early American history was fittingly recognized by the

Not unworthy of a passing glance, as embodying in rudimental form the true temper and method of history, is Amos Adams's "Concise Historical View [1] of the Perils, Hardships, Difficulties and Discouragements which have attended the Planting and Progressive Improvement of New England," published in Boston in 1769. The author was minister of the First Church of Roxbury, a graduate of Harvard, an orator of captivating and stimulating gifts, a leader of men, a martyr at last to his uncalculating zeal in the service of the sick and the troubled.[2] That he had the historian's hand and brain is shewn by the cleverness with which, in this little book, he plucks from a vast medley of facts the salient and characteristic ones; by his lucid generalization; by the sobriety of his treatment of the ultimate dispute with the English ministry.[3]

On the last day of the year 1775, in the midst of all the tumult and terror of war, Nathan Fiske, pastor of the Congregational Church in Brookfield, Massachusetts, delivered to his people a calm and carefully wrought "Historical Dis-

---

officers of the Massachusetts Historical Society, who, in 1822, gave a reprint of it in their "Collections," 2 series, ix. 166–203. In 1885, a reprint was given in the "Collections of the Rhode Island Historical Society," vii. 13–65. This version is much to be preferred, as it is annotated with characteristic thoroughness, precision, and good taste by Mr. William Eaton Foster, who, in his well-known monograph on "Stephen Hopkins," Part i. 134–135; Part ii. 161, 165, 167, 191, 200–201, had already called attention to that statesman's fondness and aptitude for historical work.

[1] It is a note of the times that this capital sketch of American colonial history was struck off in the shape of two discourses actually delivered from the pulpit, with political and moral lessons of local application. It was reprinted in London in 1770, with a slight change of title, and with a curtailment of the aforesaid lessons.

[2] A peculiarly life-like portrait of Amos Adams was drawn in miniature by his contemporary and friend, John Eliot, in his "Biographical Dictionary," 4–5.

[3] Being a man of considerable range in action and sympathy, Adams had repeatedly sent to the press his discourses, the best of them, probably, being his sermon, in 1759, "On the Reduction of Quebec"; and his two sermons, in 1767, "On Religious Liberty," published in the year following that of their delivery.

course,"[1] relating to that town: a true example of the historic spirit applied to local experience; a monograph strong in fiber, and having the added charm of its author's sincere, elastic, and clean-cut style. Of course, it was impossible for him at such a time to deal only with their past; and there is even yet something to thrill the heart in the closing paragraphs in which he sets forth the havoc and horror of that year, and compares the barbarity of their own kinsmen —the civilized foe then ready to spring at their throats— with the pitiless ways of that savage and alien enemy against whom they had for so many generations been upon their guard.

III.

A very sombre representative of the historic spirit in America during the period here treated of, was Robert Proud, a Quaker, born in England in 1728, and from 1759 until his death in 1813 a reluctant and an unassimilated denizen of Pennsylvania. A bachelor, a school-master, a recluse, with a cloud of sorrow and of mystery hanging over his life, using Latin with more facility than English, he was wholly out of accord with the hopes, the ambitions, the tendencies of the age and neighborhood upon which his lot was cast. Being opposed to war in general, and to the war of the American Rebellion in particular, he nursed in solitude the bitterness of his spirit, which, indeed, must have grown more bitter from his attempts to utter it in verse like this:

> "For, what man,
> Though of every thing bereft,
> Though no earthly solace left,
> Here with rebel powers would dwell,
> And not shun the state of hell—
> While he can!"[2]

---

[1] Published, Boston, 1776.

[2] "Memoirs of the Hist. Soc. of Pennsylvania," vol. i. ed. of 1864, p. 488. Between pages 486 and 492 are given other examples of this poor man's excruciating struggles with English verse.

Tall, gaunt, of a stern countenance, his beak-like nose overhung by heavy eye-brows, a huge and patriarchal cocked hat predominating over his tremendous gray wig, his right hand grasping a long ivory-headed cane, he was occasionally to be seen striding in melancholy grandeur along the roads or lanes in the neighborhood of Philadelphia—a figure of terrifying picturesqueness—frowning with implacable disapproval upon all the ways and works of the people among whom he was doomed to dwell.[1]

It was in such a mood, it was in the midst of such conditions, that this bilious and sorrowful pedagogue passed the painful years from 1776 to 1780, in writing "The History of Pennsylvania, in North America, from the Original Institution and Settlement of that Province under the first Proprietor and Governor William Penn, in 1681, till after the Year 1742,"[2]—a book of very exact and extremely solidified information, wherein the author quotes long documents, elaborates moral platitudes, and tells the truth—as he sees it—in slow, weighty, and sleep-diffusing sentences.

IV.

A noteworthy example of the true historic spirit then at work among us—at work after the right method even when expressing itself in the crudest form—is to be seen in a book entitled "Materials towards a History of the American Baptists,"—the author being Morgan Edwards, a Welshman, who, after acquiring some distinction as a Baptist preacher in England and in Ireland, settled in Philadelphia in 1761 in order to take charge of a Baptist congregation there.[3]

The work was planned by him on a large scale. It was to

---

[1] The best account of Proud to be met with, is by Charles West Thomson, entitled "Notices of the Life and Character of Robert Proud," and forming pages 417–435 of "Memoirs of the Hist. Soc. of Pennsylvania," vol. i., ed. of 1864.

[2] Published in two volumes, Philadelphia, 1797–1798.

[3] A brief sketch of his singular character and career may be seen in W. B. Sprague, "Annals," etc., vi. 82–85.

include all the American colonies in which the Baptists had made any history,—that is, in which they had ever been; and it was to extend to at least twelve volumes. Only the first two volumes were ever written, and these were published in Philadelphia in 1770. The author had, indeed, gathered together the substance of a third volume; but this, as he informed the public, he could not expect to see printed, "because of an asthma and atrophy, which hurry him out of the world."[1] In spite of this announcement of his speedy exit, the Welsh fire within him seems to have blazed up again, and to have been more than a match even for "an asthma and atrophy"; for, instead of being hurried out of the world in 1770, he held his own in it just twenty-five years longer, dying at his leisure in 1795.

The intelligence and the validity of his method as an historian are well shewn in his own frank avowal that the data for his two volumes were "collected partly from knowledge, partly from church-books, and partly from informations. Collections from the two former may be exact; but those from the other may not be so, because old memories are unsafe records. If any should discover errors and give notice thereof to the editor, he will take the first opportunity to rectify them, and be much obliged to the informers."[2]

The first volume has to do with the Baptists of Pennsylvania, the second with those of New Jersey. In the former colony, they are of five sorts—"First Day Baptists," "Seventh Day Baptists," "Keithians," "Tunckers," and "Mennonites"; in the latter colony they are of only four sorts—"First Day Baptists," "Seventh Day Baptists," "Tunckers," and "Rogerenes." Dealing, then, in its place and order, with each of these subdivisions of his sect, the author proceeds to spread out before us a multitude of local and personal details—the pettiness and aridity of which are in his comment often relieved by some touch of tender wisdom, of shrewd observation, or of satiric humor.

---

[1] "Materials," etc., ii. 151.

[2] "Advertisement," in vol. i. signed by the author.

Thus, of those German Baptists who were called " Tunckers," he says that the name was given to them " in derision "; that it came from the German word " ' tunken,' to put a morsel into sauce," and that it " is as much as to say ' Sops.' " Nevertheless, " as the term signifies Dippers, they may rest content with the nickname, since it is the fate of Baptists in all countries to bear some cross or other." [1]

His account of the Rogerene Baptists, while evidently fair, has an amusing sub-acid flavor. " This distinction of a sect took its rise at New London in Connecticut, about the year 1674," when one John Rogers of that town formed a church of his own, the first members of it being his father, his mother, two of his brothers, and his sister. As to its creed, the chief peculiarities were these four: " All days are alike since the death of Christ "; " No medicines are to be used, nor doctors nor surgeons employed "; " No grace at meals "; " All prayers to be mental and not vocal, except when the spirit of prayer compels to the use of the voice." [2] Having thus founded his church, it was proper that John Rogers should take an early occasion to shew a strong hand as its ruler. Accordingly, his " first act of discipline was the excommunication of his brother Jonathan, for using medicine, and refusing to do things which would bring on him the lash of the civil magistrate." Moreover, " this John Rogers was not only the founder of the sect . . . but the hero of the cause in suffering, and writing, and defying." In fact, the last seems to have been rather his favorite and most shining function. " He had not been long at the head of the cause, before he printed and published " a sort of encyclical, in which he made " an open declaration of war against the great red dragon, and against the beast to which he gives power, and against the false church which rides upon the beast, and against the false prophets who are established by the dragon and the beast, and against the image of the beast." To this he added " a proclamation of deri-

[1] " Materials," etc., i. 64.

[2] Ibid. 147–148.

sion against the sword of the devil's spirit,—which is prisons, stocks, whips, fines, and revilings."[1]

But as even this proclamation failed, in the opinion of the Rogerenes, sufficiently to enliven the situation, they proceeded to more active measures. For example, as it was their duty "to exert themselves" against the idol called the Sabbath, they would on that day "be at work near meeting-houses, and take work into meeting-houses—the women knitting, and the men whittling and making splits for baskets, and every now and then contradicting the preachers. This was seeking persecution; and they had plenty of it, insomuch that the New Englanders left some of them neither liberty, nor property, nor whole skins." While, however, the New Englanders thus made the mistake of taking the Rogerenes seriously, and of gratifying them with the boon of persecution, the people of New Jersey, being either wiser in their generation, or else blessed with a keener perception of the ludicrous aspect of things, quite disconcerted them in the performance of such antics, by a contemptuous gentleness which seemed to announce the Rogerenes as mild lunatics, rather than as heroes or martyrs. "I do not find," says our author, "that the Rogerenes have suffered by fines or corporal punishment in Jersey more than once, and that was for disturbing a Presbyterian congregation at Baskingridge. In other places, they have been taken out of meeting-houses with much pleasantry, and shut up in stables, penfolds, and once in a hog-pen—till worship was over." "Paul speaks of some people 'who pleased not God, and were contrary to all men.' It were uncharitable to apply this to the Rogerenes; but facts, for a course of one hundred and sixteen years, look too much like—'contrary to all men.' And as for the spirit that actuated them, it was as different from the meek and humble spirit of Jesus, as any two things could be. . . . Had the Rogerenes lived in the time of the Cynics, they would have been ranked with them."[2]

---

[1] "Materials," etc., ii. 147–148.

[2] Ibid 149–150.

Finally, as to John Rogers himself, the historian finishes a portrait of him by two strokes of the pen, which almost deserve to be called masterly. The founder of the sect of Rogerenes certainly desired persecution, but not persecution in every possible form: "what troubled John Rogers most was their taking his wife from him, and giving her to a lawyer of the name of Pratt." Nevertheless, even he had his revenge—if not upon the "lawyer of the name of Pratt," at least upon the rest of the world: for "he published a commentary on the Revelation. He that hath patience to read it, let him read it." [1]

V.

A man who lacked many of the literary qualifications for an historian but who yet had the root of the matter in him, was Isaac Backus, a Baptist minister, born in 1724 at Norwich, Connecticut, and both upon his father's side and upon his mother's allied to some of the oldest and most honorable families in New England.[2] He began to preach when he was but twenty-two, and he continued to preach until he was eighty-two; having been, during all those years, tireless in labor, a visitor of the sick and sorrowing, in journeys often, in conflicts many,—above all things, a father of his despised sect, a champion of its civil and religious rights, a dauntless apostle of the doctrine—then almost a paradox among us—of the total separation of church and state. In 1772, elected by the Baptist churches in Massachusetts, he became their "agent," and in their name he went before congresses, conventions, and legislatures, doing much to shape the new laws of that new time into conformity with the majestic principle that, in matters religious, no man may be interfered with by the civil authority.

This man it was who, being preacher, pastor, politician,

---

[1] "Materials," etc., ii. 149.

[2] A brief sketch of him is to be found in Sprague, "Annals," etc., vi. 54–58. The chief authority, however, is "A Memoir of the Life and Times of the Rev. Isaac Backus," by Alvah Hovey.

agitator, became also historian—in the latter capacity illustrating some of the primary virtues appertaining thereto. So effectually did he strive in this task, even amid the distractions of the great war, that he was able to publish, in 1777, the first volume, and, in 1784, the second volume, of his monumental work,—"A History of New England, with particular Reference to the Denomination of Christians called Baptists: containing the first principles and settlements of the Country; the rise and increase of the Baptist churches therein; the introduction of arbitrary power under the cloak of religion; the Christian testimonies of the Baptists and others against the same, with their sufferings under it, from the beginning to the present time."[1]

His call to this great office of historian did not come to him either through literary ambition or even through the antiquarian zest: it came, apparently, through his belief that, ever since the settlement of New England, monstrous crimes against religious liberty had been there perpetrated by the civil and religious leaders of the commonwealth; and that, as the history of the commonwealth had been written chiefly by the very men who had perpetrated these crimes, or by their natural representatives, its history had never been truly or fairly written. "As every one is orthodox to himself, they who have oppressed others have always denied it." "If it should be found that near all the histories of this country which are much known, have been written by persons who thought themselves invested with power to act as lawgivers and judges for their neighbors, under the name either of orthodoxy or of immediate power from heaven, the inference will be strong that our affairs have never been set in so clear a light as they ought to be."[2]

---

[1] The first volume brings the history down to 1690; the second, to 1784. A third volume was published in 1796, continuing the history to that year. An abridgement of the three volumes was published in one volume in 1804, the history being once more brought down to date. Finally, a new edition of the original work, revised by David Weston, was published in two volumes, in 1871.

[2] "A History of New England," i. Pref.

Therefore, to set "our affairs" in a clearer light—in other words, with respect to the history of New England, to drag to the surface a series of tremendous facts which have hitherto been thrust below and kept out of sight—such is the principal purpose of this historian. He accuses his predecessors of being partisan; and if, in the opposite direction, he is equally partisan, he would perhaps insist that it was his duty to be so, in order to redress the long-disturbed balance of historic testimony. "Only the author must say, that he has acted under a full belief that with what measure we mete, it shall be measured to us again; so that we cannot injure others in any case, without therein wronging our own souls."[1]

At any rate, he is not to be turned aside from his stern task of exposing evil-doers, merely because those evil-doers happen to be dead and to be venerated. "The greatest objection that I have heard against this design is, that we ought not to rake up the ashes of our good fathers, nor to rehearse those old controversies, which will tend to increase our present difficulties. But what is meant by this objection? To reveal secrets, or to repeat matters that have been well settled between persons or parties, is forbidden, and its effects are very pernicious; but what is that to a history of public facts, and an examination of the principles and conduct both of oppressors and of the oppressed?"[2]

Being upon our guard, then, against this writer's prepossession, we may note that his method of procedure anticipates every feature of modern historic research: a tireless hunt for the original documents, a tireless study of them, a reference of every problem to them, the use in essential particulars of their very words, finally, a perception of the worthlessness of every historic affirmation that stands without its source definitely given. "Let us," says he, "hear those fathers tell their own story."[3] In order to do this, he makes no difficulty of journeys far and near; of turning

---

[1] "A History of New England," i. Pref. [2] Ibid. [3] Ibid. 1–2.

over patiently the manuscript records of churches, towns, colonies, States; of writing out with his own hand the exact language of the fathers. "Here, therefore," he is able to say, at last, "are a great number of particulars with good vouchers to support them."[1]

The result of all this toil is, indeed, a book without classic symmetry or charm, with no amenities of style, without the calm grandeur of disinterestedness, yet thorough and genuine in all its parts, honest in purpose, every page of it bearing the stamp of "simplicity, perspicuity, integrity, and manliness,"[2] the whole quite needful to be reckoned with by any one who would grasp the significance of the history of New England for its first two centuries.

VI.

Reaching the line which, in these historical essays, divides Colonial themes from those of the Revolution, we confront a writer who, in his capacity as historian, not only towers above all his contemporaries, but deals with themes which are both Colonial and Revolutionary. This writer is the man so famous and so hated in his day as a Loyalist statesman and magistrate, Thomas Hutchinson, the last civilian who served as governor of Massachusetts under appointment of the king.

A recent and a very competent American critic[3] has characterized the three volumes of Thomas Hutchinson's "History of Massachusetts Bay" and the one volume of his "Collection of Original Papers" as "the four most precious books" touching that portion of American history. Indeed, that in these volumes Hutchinson has illustrated the fundamental virtues of an historian, and that he deserves to be ranked as, upon the whole, the ablest historical writer produced in America prior to the nineteenth century, are conclusions as to which there is now substantial agree-

[1] "A History of New England," i. Pref.

[2] Hovey, "A Memoir . . . of Isaac Backus," 32.

[3] William Frederick Poole, in "The Dial," vol. v. number 51.

ment among scholars. James Savage called him "the most diligent and exact of all writers of colonial history, since Winthrop."[1] Charles Francis Adams, the elder, put many eulogies into few words when he described Hutchinson as an historian who "is seldom inaccurate."[2] Charles Deane, who regarded Hutchinson's historical labors as of "the highest value," partly accounted for their worth by the remark, that "Hutchinson's mind was eminently a judicial one," and that "candor, moderation, and a desire for truth, appear to have guided his pen."[3] William Frederick Poole, after pointing out that Hutchinson "had opportunities of access to original papers such as no person now possesses," declared that he had also made an adequate use of his unrivaled opportunities:—"He had the tastes, the capacity for close application and research, the judicial understanding, and the freedom from prejudice and partisanship, which characterize the genuine historian. His style, if not always elegant, is clear and simple, and singularly free from that sensational and rhetorical method of statement which is the bane of much of the historical writing of the present day."[4] It is far from being a reason for abating anything from the glory due to such achievements in historical literature, that they were but the recreation and by-play of a most laborious man-of-affairs, who, as politician, legislator, and magistrate, was from manhood to old age in the thick of nearly all important business pertaining to the interests of his country; who, prior to 1765, was incomparably the most popular and the most influential statesman in New England; and who, from the year of the Stamp Act until that of his own death in London fifteen years afterward, was the most powerful American statesman in the ranks of the Loyalist party.

In writing the early history of Massachusetts, Thomas

---

[1] John Winthrop, "The History of New England," with Notes by James Savage, i. 296, note.

[2] "The Works of John Adams," i. 103.

[3] "Mass. Hist. Soc. Proc.," iii. 147.

[4] "The N. E. Hist. and Gen. Register," xxiv. 381–382.

Hutchinson was in effect writing the history of his own ancestors, some of whom had been eminent, some of whom had been notorious, in the colony almost from the year of its foundation. He was born in Boston in 1711. Immediately upon his graduation at Harvard College in 1727, he entered the counting-house of his father, who was a prosperous merchant. Clear-headed, thorough, methodical, indefatigable, he at once developed a high capacity for business, both commercial and political. In 1737, he was chosen a selectman for the town of Boston, and a month or two later, one of its representatives in the colonial legislature. The burning question in politics at that time was public finance, —a subject on which Thomas Hutchinson was, probably, the greatest master produced in America prior to Robert Morris, Pelatiah Webster, and Alexander Hamilton. Thirty-five years before the Declaration of Independence, there was in Massachusetts a large and vociferous party resolved upon various schemes for fiat money and for wild-cat banking. Against all these schemes, this young politician set himself with fearless and most intelligent opposition,—thus shewing at the beginning of his long political career that trait of intellectual and moral independence which he continued to exercise to the very end of it. From the age of twenty-six when he was elected to his first office, until the age of sixty-three when he resigned his last one, he was kept constantly and conspicuously in the public service, either as selectman, member of the house of representatives, speaker of the house, member of the council, commissioner to the general congress at Albany in 1754, commissioner on many negotiations with the Indians, judge of probate, justice of the common-pleas, chief-justice, lieutenant-governor, and finally governor. Before the outbreak of the great controversy between the colonies and the British government, no other man in America had, to so high a degree as Hutchinson, the confidence both of the British government on the one hand, and of his own countrymen on the other. Had his advice been taken in that controversy by either of the two parties who had so greatly confided in him, the war of the Revolution would have been averted.[1] His advice was twofold: first, that the British government should be content with the assertion of the constiutional principle of the supremacy of parliament, and forbear from exercising it in the article of American taxation; and, secondly, that the Americans should forbear from denying the constitutional principle of the supremacy of parliament, in view of the assurance that, upon their doing so, that principle should never be exercised in any form of colonial taxation. To these two ideas of public policy and of public righteousness, Thomas Hutchinson, as is now known, remained faithful unto death,—in his fidelity to them sacrificing, on the one hand, popularity, home, fortune, and the privilege of burial by the side of his loved ones, and, on the other hand, some portion even of his personal favor with the king. Thus, in his championship of a noble, even if baffled, scheme for the liberty and unity of the English-speaking race, this statesman of Massachusetts takes his stand, in the history of the American Revolution, by the side of Joseph Galloway of Pennsylvania, as a typical American Loyalist.

VII.

While the writing of history was for Hutchinson but the recreation and by-play of a life immersed in outward busi-

---

[1] It may help the modern reader to some appreciation of the pre-Revolutionary standing of Thomas Hutchinson to read an entry made by John Adams in his diary for March 17, 1766—the very month of the repeal of the Stamp Act—wherein, with his usual orotundity of statement, he mentions the trophies of this New England Miltiades by which the ambitious young lawyer could not sleep: "Has not his merit been sounded very high, by his countrymen, for twenty years? Have not his countrymen loved, admired, revered, rewarded, nay, almost adored him? Have not ninety-nine in a hundred of them really thought him the greatest and best man in America? . . . Nay, have not the affection and admiration of his countrymen arisen so high as often to style him the greatest and best man in the world?" "The Works of John Adams," ii. 189-190. Six years afterward, John Adams wrote in his diary that he and his kinsman, Samuel Adams, had always "concurred in sentiment that the liberties of this country had more to fear from one man, the present Governor Hutchin-

ness, the study of history seems to have been a passion with him almost from his childhood. Speaking of himself in the third person, he once wrote in his diary:—" History was his favorite study; and when a boy, before he went to college, he chose rather to spend an evening in reading Morton's 'New England Memorial,' Church's 'History of the Indian War,' Dr. Mather's 'Lives of the New England Governors,' etc., than to be at play with boys in the street. And he had made some advances in the English History. The tragical account of King Charles's sufferings and death happening to fall into his hands, tho' it produced tears, he went through it with eagerness; and Baker's 'Chronicle,' and Fox's 'Martyrology,' being among his father's books, afforded him much entertainment."[1] Among the papers left by Hutchinson at his death, was found this additional note of self-description:—" In the course of my education, I found no part of science a more pleasing study than history, and no part of the history of any country more useful than that of its government and laws. The history of Great Britain and of its dominions was of all others the most delightful to me; and a thorough knowledge of the nature and constitution of the supreme and of the subordinate governments thereof I considered as what would be peculiarly beneficial to me in the line of life upon which I was entering; and the public employments to which I was early called, and sustained for near thirty years together, gave me many advantages for the acquisition of this knowledge."[2] It should be added that, even then, Hutchinson had the scientific idea of the importance of primary documents. Through his great eminence in the community, and through his ceaseless zeal in the collection of such documents, he was enabled in

---

son, than from any other man, nay, than from all other men in the world. This sentiment was founded in their knowledge of his character, his unbounded ambition, and his unbounded popularity." Ibid. 295.

[1] "The Diary and Letters of His Excelleney Thomas Hutchinson, Esq." Edited by his great-grandson, Peter Orlando Hutchinson, i. 47.

[2] Cited by Charles Deane in his admirable paper on "Hutchinson's Historical Publications." "Mass. Hist. Soc. Proc.," iii. 147.

the course of many years to bring together a multitude of manuscript materials of priceless value touching the history of New England.

With such materials at his command, and using with diligence those fragments of time which his unflagging energy enabled him to pluck from business and from sleep, he was ready, in July, 1764, amid the first mutterings of that political storm which was to play havoc with these peaceful studies and to shatter the hopes of his life-time, to send to the printer, in Boston, the first volume of "The History of the Colony of Massachusetts Bay, from the First Settlement thereof in 1628, until . . . 1691."[1]

The great place in public life then held by the author of this book, the fulness of his learning, his ability, the fairness of his method in dealing with the subject, finally, the incomparable interest which that subject had for the people to whom it was addressed, all combined, even amid the ferocities and clamors of politics, to give to its publication very considerable eclat. In spite of the distractions of that angry and perilous period, the author at once set to work upon his second volume, which was to carry the history of Massachusetts down to the year 1750. In this noble task he had proceeded for a considerable time, and had brought the story as far on as to the year 1730, "when," as he afterward wrote, "a misfortune befell me which had like to have rendered my past labor of no effect and to have prevented me from proceeding any farther."[2] This misfortune, of course, was the riotous attack upon his house in Boston by a mob maddened by rum and by the false charge that Hutchinson had been in favor of the passage of the Stamp Act.

---

[1] By an advertisement in the Boston "Evening Post," it appears to have been issued December 17, 1764. In the following year, it was reprinted in London, and that reprint was called "The Second Edition." By a typographical error, the final character in the intended date upon the title-page was left off, and thus the second edition purports to have been published in MDCCLX, four years before the first edition. My references are to this second edition.

[2] Part of the Preface to the second volume of his "History."

It was on the evening of Monday, the twenty-sixth of August, 1765, that the Lieutenant-Governor, according to a narrative written by some friend five days afterward, received warning, while he was at supper in his own house with his motherless children, "that the mob was coming to him. He immediately sent away his children, and determined to stay in the house himself; but, happily, his eldest daughter returned, and declared she would not stir from the house unless he went with her: by which means she got him away, which was undoubtedly the occasion of saving his life. For, as the mob had got into the house, with a most irresistible fury, they immediately looked about for him, to murder him, and even made diligent enquiry whither he was gone. They went to work with a rage scarce to be exemplified by the most savage people. Every thing moveable was destroyed in the most minute manner, except such things of value as were worth carrying off,—among which were near one thousand pounds sterling in specie, besides a great quantity of family plate, and so forth." "As for the house, which, from its structure and inside finishing, seemed to be from a design of Inigo Jones, or his successor, it appears that they were a long while resolved to level it to the ground. They worked three hours at the cupola before they could get it down, and they uncovered part of the roof; but I suppose that the thickness of the walls, which were of very fine brick-work adorned with Ionic pilasters worked into the wall, prevented their completing their purpose, though they worked at it till day-light. The next day, the streets were found scattered with money, plate, gold rings, and so forth, which had been dropt in carrying off." "But the loss to be most lamented is, that there was in one room, kept for that purpose, a large and valuable collection of manuscripts and original papers, which he had been gathering all his life-time, and to which all persons who had been in possession of valuable papers of a public kind, had been contributing, as to a public museum. As these related to the history and policy of the country, from the time of its settlement to the present, and was the only collection of its kind, the loss to the public is great and irretrievable,—as it is to himself the loss of the papers of a family which had made a figure in this province for a hundred and thirty years."[1]

Among the treasures which thus lay scattered abroad in the wet and filthy streets for several hours of that night of barbarity, was his unfinished manuscript for the second volume of his History of Massachusetts; and though for several days afterward the historian quite despaired of recovering it, yet, through the help of his friend and neighbor, the Reverend Andrew Eliot, all but eight or ten sheets were rescued from destruction. Bespattered with rain and mud, stamped and torn by the hoofs of horses and of men, much of this recovered manuscript proved to be so far legible that it could be transcribed by the author, who was also able to supply the rest.[2] Accordingly, resuming his work, and carrying forward the story to the year 1750, he published his second volume in the early summer of the year 1767,—not far from the very day on which parliament, by the passage of the Townsend Act, perpetrated the ineffable folly of plunging the empire into such tumults as led to its disruption.[3]

---

[1] These paragraphs are from a letter, probably by Governor Bernard, and dated August 31, 1765. It was printed, without signature, in the Appendix to the celebrated English pamphlet entitled "The Conduct of the Late Administration Examined." London: 1767, pages xlii–xlviii.

[2] The first sheets of this first draught of Hutchinson's second volume, which thus survived that horrid night, and which still bear the stains and bruises of the outrage put upon them, are now preserved in the library of the State of Massachusetts. Hutchinson himself had told us, in the Preface to that volume, that the copy sent to the press was a transcript made by himself from this first draught; but it remained for William Frederick Poole to make the interesting and valuable discovery that the copy from which the book was printed is not so good as that original draught: "Incidents and opinions contained in the earlier draught are changed, abridged, and sometimes omitted, in the later draught. In matters of fact, the earlier draught is often more precise and accurate than the printed text." "The N. E. Hist. and Gen. Reg.," xxiv. 381.

[3] "The Evening Post," of Boston, for July 13, 1767, advertises Hutchinson's second volume as "just published."

Notwithstanding the lurid and bitter incidents amid which it was written, the second volume of Hutchinson's History of Massachusetts, like the first one, has the tone of moderation and of equanimity suggestive of a philosopher abstracted from outward cares, and devoted to the disinterested discovery and exposition of the truth. Only in the Preface is there any allusion to the indignity from the fatal effects of which the historian and his History had so narrowly escaped. After narrating concisely the events which led to the temporary loss of his own manuscript, and to the permanent loss of other documents still more valuable, he contents himself with a single sentence of austere and not unrighteous indignation:—"I pray God to forgive the actors in, and advisers to, this most savage and inhuman injury; and I hope their posterity will read with pleasure and profit what has so narrowly escaped the outrage of their ancestors."

VIII.

From the time of the publication of the second installment of his work, sixty-one years were to elapse before the public should receive ocular evidence that the author had had the fortitude, amid the calamities which overwhelmed his later years, to go on with his historical labors, and to complete a third and final volume, telling the story of Massachusetts from the year 1750 until the year 1774—the year in which he laid down his office as governor, and departed for England.

He was summoned thither at his own desire, in order to report in person to the king and ministry the condition of affairs in America, and especially in his own province. Moreover, if we may accept the solemn and pathetic declarations now to be found scattered through the letters and diaries which he wrote in England, a nearer and a dearer purpose prompted him to ask permission to go there: it was that he might, by direct personal appeal, dissuade the government from persisting in its impolitic measures toward the colonies, and might thus avert from his country the ineffable calamity of a fratricidal war—the nearness of which he could not fail to see.[1]

Of course, his mission to England was a failure. The quarrel had already gone too far; already upon both sides blood had become too hot; and, before very long, both at the levees of the king and at the audiences of the ministers, the somewhat dreary and monitory tales of this fumbling New England courtier fell upon impatient ears, until, indeed, they were quenched in the ultimate disaster of a royal snub.[2] In the meantime, no slight, no misfortune, could quench his love for his country, his longing to save it from misery, his longing to return to it and to lay his body where was buried that of the wife of his youth. " I am not able

[1] For his opposition to the parliamentary taxation of the colonies, and for his efforts to secure some mitigation of the Boston port bill and, in other ways, to soften ministerial measures and to prevent a resort to hostilities, the reader may find it of interest to turn to the following pages of the first volume of his "Diary and Letters":—70, 188, 189, 197, 203, 214, 217, 219, 220, 233, 261, 285–286, 375, 381, 500.

[2] Some sorrowful hints of all this are given by Hutchinson himself in his "Diary," as where he mentions, in a bewildered sort of way, the first time that the king passed him at a levee without speaking to him or looking at him. John Adams, who so roundly hated Hutchinson, and who, in 1785, went to London as American minister, seems to have used some of the leisure which the disdain of that court conferred upon him, in gathering up items of gossip touching the humiliations of Hutchinson's last years. "Fled in his old age," writes John Adams, of the last royal governor of Massachusetts, "from the detestation of a country where he had been beloved, esteemed, and admired, and applauded with exaggeration—in short, where he had been everything from his infancy—to a country where he was nothing; pinched by a pension, which, though ample in Boston, would barely keep a house in London; throwing round his baleful eyes on the exiled companions of his folly; hearing daily of the slaughter of his countrymen and conflagration of their cities; abhorred by the greatest men and soundest part of the nation, and neglected, if not despised by the rest, hardened as had been my heart against him, I assure you I was melted at the accounts I heard of his condition. Lord Townsend told me that he put an end to his own life. Though I did not believe this, I know he was ridiculed by the courtiers. They laughed at his manners at the levee, at his perpetual quotation of his brother Foster, searching his pockets for letters to read to the king, and the king turning away from him with his head up, etc." "Works," x. 261–262.

to subdue a natural attachment to the very soil and air, as well as to the people, of New England."[1] "The prospect is so gloomy that I am sometimes tempted to endeavor to forget that I am an American, and to turn my views to a provision for what remains of life in England; but the passion for my native country returns."[2] "People in high and low life agree in advising me to settle in England; but I cannot give up the hopes of laying my bones in New England, and hitherto I consider myself as only upon an excursion from home."[3] "For myself, I have been offered the fulfillment of every promise or assurance given me before I left America; but I had no aim at honors or titles, and would now be content to give up all claim to them, and to all emoluments whatsoever, and to spend the remainder of life in obscurity, if upon those terms I could purchase the peace and prosperity of my country."[4] "I assure you I had rather die in a little country farm house in New England, than in the best nobleman's seat in Old England."[5] "New England is wrote upon my heart in as strong characters as Calais was upon Queen Mary's."[6]

Borne down with sorrow, amazed and horror-stricken at the fury of the storm that was overturning his most prudent calculations, and was sweeping him and his party from all their moorings out into an unknown sea, and, for them and for all men, was changing the very face of the world, he found some solace in resuming in England the historical task which he had left unfinished. In his diary for the twenty-second of October, 1778, its completion is recorded in this modest note:—"I finished the revisal of my History, to the end of my Administration, and laid it by."[7] Laid by certainly it was, so far as concerned men's knowledge or their charitable speeches, if not to foreign nations, at least to the next ages; and not until the year 1828, was it permitted to come forth to the light of day, and then, largely, through the magnanimous intervention of a group of noble-minded American

[1] "Diary and Letters," of Hutchinson, i. 128. [2] Ibid. 215.
[3] Ibid. 231. [4] Ibid. 263. [5] Ibid. 356. [6] Ibid. 283. [7] Ibid. ii. 218.

scholars in the very city which, in his later life-time, would not have permitted his return to it.[1]

IX.

A great historian, Hutchinson certainly was not, and, under the most favorable outward conditions, could not have been. He had the fundamental virtues of a great historian —love of truth, love of justice, diligence, the ability to master details and to narrate them with accuracy. Even in the exercise of these fundamental virtues, however, no historian in Hutchinson's circumstances could fail to be hampered by the enormous preoccupations of official business, or to have his judgment warped and colored by the prepossessions of his own political career. While Hutchinson was, indeed, a miracle of industry, it was only a small part of his industry that he was free to devote to historical research. However sincere may have been his purpose to tell the truth and to be fair to all, the literary product of such research was inevitably weakened, as can now be abundantly shewn, by many serious oversights and by many glaring misrepresentations, apparently through his failure to make a thorough use of important sources of information then accessible to him, such as colonial pamphlets, colonial newspapers, the manuscripts of his own ancestors and of the Mathers, and especially the general court records of the province in which he played so great a part. As to the rarer intellectual and spiritual endowments of a great historian,—breadth of vision, breadth of sympathy, the historic imagination, and the power of style,—these Hutchinson

[1] The third volume of Hutchinson's History, preserved, indeed, but for a time almost forgotten, by his descendants in England, was issued in London, in 1828, by John Murray, who was induced to undertake so unpromising an enterprise by the liberality of the president of the Massachusetts Historical Society, the president of Harvard College, the governor of Massachusetts, and Mr. James Savage. It was chiefly through the historical zeal and the persistence of the gentleman last named, that success was given to the long negotiations with the English Hutchinsons and their London publisher. The story of this is briefly told by Charles Deane in "Mass. Hist. Soc. Proc.," iii. 144–147.

almost entirely lacked. That he had not the gift of historical divination, the vision and the faculty divine to see the inward meaning of men and of events, and to express that meaning in gracious, noble, and fascinating speech—Hutchinson was himself partly conscious. "I am sensible," he says, with his usual modesty, respecting the first volume of his History, "that whoever appears in print should be able to dispose his matter in such order, and clothe it with such style and language, as shall not only inform but delight the reader. Therefore, I would willingly have delivered over everything I have collected to a person of genius for such a work. But seeing no prospect of its being done by any other, I engaged in it myself, being very loth that what had cost me some pains to bring together, should be again scattered and utterly lost." [1]

His first volume seems to have been written under a consciousness that his subject was provincial, and even of a local interest altogether circumscribed. In the second volume, one perceives a more cheery and confident tone, due, probably, to the prompt recognition which his labors had then received not only in Massachusetts but in England. In the third volume, are to be observed signs of increasing ease in composition, a more flowing and copious style, not a few felicities of expression.

That, in all these volumes, he intended to tell the truth, and to practice fairness, is also plain: to say that he did not entirely succeed, is to say that he was human. His purpose to be fair in his handling of all controversies of which he had to take account, is well stated by himself with reference to a single one of them:—"I am apprehensive some of my readers will be apt to doubt the impartiality of the relation. . . . I am not sensible of having omitted any material fact, nor have I designedly given a varnish to the actions of one party, or high coloring to those of the other. . . . I profess to give a true relation of facts. I see no difference between publishing false facts for truths, and omitting any

---

[1] Preface to the first volume.

which are material for the forming a just conception of the rest."[1] A striking instance of his judicial tone is to be noted in the story, given by him in his first volume, of the career of his ancestress, Mistress Anne Hutchinson. Indeed, many of the first readers of that volume thought that, in many particulars, he had carried his impartiality too far: they accused him of coldness of heart in giving so hard, dry, and unfeeling a narrative of the Indian wars,—especially of the sufferings of his own countrymen, even of his own kindred, at the hands of the savages.[2] In his second volume, the whole of which was written after the beginning of his own unpopularity, and a part of it even after the looting and demolition of his house, there is a tinge of still deeper political conservatism, and of a sad, if not cynical, conviction that in New England a public servant might have to choose between popularity and fidelity to his own sense of right.[3] Of course, the supreme test of historical fairness was reached when he came to the writing of his third volume,—which was, in fact, the history not only of his contemporaries but of himself, and of himself in deep and angry disagreement with many of them. It is much to his praise to say that, throughout this third volume, the prevailing tone is calm, moderate, just, with only occasional efforts at pleading his own cause, with only occasional flickers of personal or political enmity. Unquestionably, in his descriptions of such antagonists of his as Hancock, Bowdoin, Cushing, the Adamses, the Otises, he does make statements which imply in them weaknesses and faults—in some instances, faults of a very serious nature. Even in these instances, the historian's censures of them may perhaps be called gentle, even sweet, by comparison with the unrestrained and blasting censures of him, which, as he well knew, several of these men were accustomed publicly to ex-

[1] "History," etc., ii. 288.

[2] It will be remembered that Anne Hutchinson and many of her family were cruelly massacred by the Indians.

[3] For example, volume ii. 196, 226, 231.

press. Moreover, with the exception of the charge of pecuniary dishonor against Samuel Adams—wherein the historian put upon record what he and many of his contemporaries believed to be true—it is not now entirely clear that his estimates of his principal antagonists differ very much from the estimates of them now held by disinterested students of that age.

A profound writer upon the history of New England[1] has expressed the opinion that, as an historian, Hutchinson was unfitted for the work he undertook, either because he had no heart, or because he had no heart for his country,—being out of sympathy with the strongest and best currents of the life of its people. That Hutchinson had a heart—a tender and a true one—and that he had a heart even for his own country, has now been placed beyond doubt by the publication of his private papers. Moreover, in culture, in opinion, in religious faith, in conduct, he was himself a representative New England Puritan. Furthermore, there was no element of civic greatness or felicity which he did not covet for his countrymen, and strive to procure. Even with their fundamental conception as to the proper form for their own political rights, he was in accord,—declaring that our ancestors "left their native country with the strongest assurances that they and their posterity should enjoy the privileges of free natural-born English subjects," and praying that those privileges might "be preserved inviolate to the latest posterity."[2] Even in their magnificent dream of a great American empire, he shared,—giving it as one reason, in fact, for preserving the records of "the rise and progress of the several colonies," that those colonies were destined, "in a few generations," to have great historic importance by becoming constituent parts of "a mighty empire."[3] The issue upon which, at last, this most popular of New England men broke with many of his contempo-

---

[1] J. G. Palfrey, in "3 Mass. Hist. Soc. Proc.", ix. 173–174.

[2] Hutchinson, "History," etc., i. Preface iv.

[3] Hutchinson, "Original Papers," etc., Preface i.

raries, and fell out of line with what finally proved to be the course of events, was an issue touching the method of realizing this magnificent dream. Hutchinson believed that it could be realized, and that it ought to be realized, by the process of a natural and legal development, in full peace and amity with the mother land—in short, by evolution. They believed, on the other hand, that such process would be either too doubtful or too slow; that their magnificent dream could best be realized by a sudden attack upon their constitutional environment, by a swift and violent rupture of legal and traditionary ties—in short, by revolution. Accordingly, it is only in the third volume of his History that Hutchinson can truly be said to be out of sympathy with the dominating currents of the life of his countrymen. Nevertheless, for that period also, what he thus wrote, even if it breathes the tone of a baffled and an alienated man, is of high value as the testimony of one who took a great part in the events which he endeavors to narrate.

No one should approach the reading of Hutchinson's "History of Massachusetts Bay" with the expectation of finding in it either brilliant writing or an entertaining story. From beginning to end, there are few passages that can be called even salient—but almost everywhere an even flow of statesmanlike narrative; severe in form; rather dull, probably, to all who have not the preparation of a previous interest in the matters discussed; but always pertinent, vigorous, and full of pith. Notwithstanding Hutchinson's modest opinion of his own ability in the drawing of historical portraits, it is probable that in such portraits of distinguished characters, both among his contemporaries and among his predecessors, the general reader will be likely to find himself the most interested. One of these portraits is that of Joseph Dudley, governor of Massachusetts, by royal appointment, from 1702 to 1715. Perhaps Hutchinson may have wrought at this sketch with especial care, as being conscious that in the character and in the earlier career of Governor Dudley were some features of resemblance to his own, even as he may also have believed that the later triumphs of his predecessor in office, were but a prophecy of those that then awaited him:—" No New England man had passed through more scenes of busy life than Mr. Dudley. His friends intended otherwise. He was educated for the ministry, and if various dignities had been known in the New England churches, possibly he had lived and died a clergyman; but without this, nothing could be more dissonant from his genius. He soon turned his thoughts to civil affairs; was first a deputy or representative of the town of Roxbury; then an assistant; then agent for the colony in England, where he laid a foundation for a commission, soon after, appointing him president of the council of Massachusetts Bay only, but, under Andros, for all New England. Upon the Revolution, for a short time, he was sunk in disgrace, but soon emerged. He appeared, first, in the character of chief justice at New York; then, returning to England, became lieutenant-governor of the Isle of Wight and member of parliament for Newtown, both which places he willingly resigned for the chief command in his own country. Ambition was the ruling passion; and perhaps, like Cæsar, he had rather be the first man in New England than the second in Old. Few men have been pursued by their enemies with greater virulence, and few have been supported by their friends with greater zeal. . . . Some of his good qualities were so conspicuous, that his enemies could not avoid acknowledging them. He applied himself with the greatest diligence to the business of his station. The affairs of the war and other parts of his administration were conducted with good judgment. In economy he excelled, both in public and private life. He supported the dignity of a governor without the reproach of parsimony, and yet, from the moderate emoluments of his post, made an addition to his paternal estate. The visible increase of his substance made some incredible reports of gross bribery and corruption to be very easily believed; but, in times when party spirit prevails, what will not a governor's enemies believe, however injurious and absurd? . . . His cringing to Randolph, when in his heart he despised him, was a spot in his character; and his secret insinuations, to the disadvantage of his country, was a greater,—both being for the sake of recommending himself to court favor. I think it is no more than justice to his character to allow, that he had as many virtues as can consist with so great a thirst for honor and power."[1]

---

[1] Hutchinson, "History of Massachusetts Bay," ii. 213–214. Besides the two editions already mentioned of the first two volumes of this work, there was published in 1795 a third edition, "With Additional Notes and Corrections," the first volume having been printed at Salem and the second at Boston. The mechanical execution of this edition is inferior; while the notes are few and meagre, and the so-called corrections unimportant. For this edition of the first two volumes, and for the only edition of the third volume, was issued in New York, in 1879, an "Index to Persons and Places mentioned in Hutchinson's Massachusetts . . . made by J. Wingate Thornton, Historiographer, and somewhat corrected by Charles L. Woodward, Book Peddler." For other writings of Hutchinson, should be mentioned a pamphlet on the paper-money dispute, published in 1736 ("Diary and Letters," i. 53), and now unknown; "The Case of the Provinces of Massachusetts Bay and New York, respecting the Boundary Line between the two Provinces," Boston, 1764—probably the same production as that mentioned by William Allen ("Am. Biog. Dict.," 462) as "a brief state of the claim of the colonies, etc."; "The Letters of Governor Hutchinson," written in 1768 and 1769 to his friend Thomas Whately, M.P., and surreptitiously procured by Franklin, and printed in Boston in 1773 and in London in 1774; many of Hutchinson's official speeches and other papers as lieutenant-governor and as governor of Massachusetts, republished in the collection of state-papers edited by Alden Bradford, Boston, 1818; many letters of his printed in "Massachusetts Archives," xxvi.; finally "Strictures upon the Declaration of the Congress at Philadelphia: In a Letter to a Noble Lord, etc." London, 1776. There are also many important manuscript letters, and other unpublished papers of Hutchinson, to be found in the library of the State of Massachusetts, and in the library of the Massachusetts Historical Society. Since this chapter was written, Professor James Kendall Hosmer has published an extended biography of Hutchinson, based upon a direct study of all the materials left by Hutchinson, and furnishing an example of historic fair-mindedness in the treatment of a subject hitherto commonly swamped in mere partisanship. Whoever would have before him all that can now be urged against Hutchinson, both as an historian and as a statesman, by a scholar minutely acquainted with the sources of Massachusetts history, may be fully gratified by reading the trenchant criticism on Dr. Hosmer's book, by Abner C. Goodell, Jr., in "The American Historical Review," for October, 1896, pp. 163–170.

X.

Somewhere in the debatable land between history, fiction, and burlesque, there wanders a notorious book, first published anonymously in London in 1781, and entitled "A General History of Connecticut, from its first Settlement under George Fenwick, Esq. to its latest Period of Amity with Great Britain; including a Description of the Country, and many curious and interesting Anecdotes. To which is added an Appendix, wherein new and the true Sources of the present Rebellion in America are pointed out, together with the particular Part taken in it by the People of Connecticut in its Promotion. By a Gentleman of the Province." [1]

Though the authorship of this book was never acknowledged by the man who wrote it, there is no doubt that it was the work of Samuel Peters, an Anglican clergyman and a Loyalist, a man of commanding personal presence, uncommon intellectual resources, powerful will, and ill-balanced character. He was born in Hebron, Connecticut, in 1735; was graduated at Yale College in 1757; and having soon after received ordination in England, he became minister of the Episcopal parish in his native town, in which capacity he there remained from about the year 1760 until 1774. That he labored all his life under a certain perturbation of those faculties which are meant to confer upon a man good sense, is partly shewn by the fact, mentioned by his own nephew, that this missionary of a Church planted among a people already prejudiced against it, " aped the style of an English nobleman, built his house in a forest, kept his coach,

[1] Second edition, London: 1782. Of the first London edition an American reprint was issued in New Haven in 1829,—an ill-looking book, on flimsy paper, with eight melancholy "engravings" on wood. A second American reprint of the first London edition was published in excellent form in New York, in 1877, edited by Samuel Jarvis McCormick, a great-grandson of Samuel Peters. A list of Peters's numerous published writings is given by Franklin Bowditch Dexter, in his "Yale Biographies," ii., 485-487,—a work of great learning, precision, and fairness, which has appeared since my account of Peters was written.

and looked with some degree of scorn upon republicans."[1] Very naturally, he opposed with frank and bitter aggressiveness the Revolutionary politics then rampant among his neighbors; and having in 1774 drawn upon himself the painful attentions of the "Sons of Liberty," he fled in great wrath from the town and the colony. For a few weeks thereafter, he found refuge in Boston, whence he sailed for England in October, 1774. There he abode until his return to America in 1805. During the five or six years immediately following his arrival in England, he seems to have had congenial employment in composing his "General History of Connecticut," as a means apparently of wreaking an undying vengeance upon the sober little commonwealth in which he was born and from which he had been thus ignominiously cast out. The result of this long labor of hate, was a production, calling itself historical, which was characterized by a contemporary English journal[2] as having "so many marks of party spleen and idle credulity" as to be "altogether unworthy of the public attention."

In spite, however, of such censure both then and since then, this alleged "History" has had, now for more than a hundred years, not only a vast amount of public attention, but very considerable success in a form that seems to have been dear to its author's heart—that of spreading through the English-speaking world a multitude of ludicrous impressions to the dishonor of the people of whom it treats. It cannot be denied that for such a service, it was most admirably framed; since its grotesque fabrications in disparagement of a community of Puritan dissenters seem to have proved a convenient quarry for ready-made calumnies upon that sort of people there and elsewhere, and even, in the opinion of some on-lookers, to have supplied "many respectable and reverend authors with facilities for breaking the

---

[1] John S. Peters, sometime governor of Connecticut, in Sprague, "Annals," etc., v. 194.

[2] "The Monthly Review," cited in J. H. Trumbull, "The True Blue Laws," etc., 33–34.

ninth commandment without incurring personal responsibility."[1]

Respecting this singular book, it is perhaps possible to suggest but one theory which can relieve its author of a certain term of reproach never justly applied to an honest man. Did he not write his so-called "History" in a spirit of mere irony and burlesque? Have we not here another of those cases of literary misinterpretation, wherein what was meant for jest has been taken in earnest? A glance through the preface, still more, a glance through the text, should be enough to disperse such a supposition. After even so slight an inspection, probably no disinterested and competent critic can doubt that Peters intended his narrative to be accepted by the world as authentic history. But authentic history it is not. What then? For a political satire, one can feel respect—a respect even proportioned to the keenness and fierceness of its wit. An historical romance, also, however grotesque, however incredible, one may be able to read with some amusement, and at any rate without necessary moral disapproval. But a narrative obviously intended to be taken by its readers as a truthful and faithful record of facts, which yet is saturated by exaggerations and perversions of those facts, is interfused and overlaid by fictions, —many of them, likewise, of a nature to bring contempt and obloquy upon the people thus dealt with,—this is such a monstrosity in literature as literature has no place nor name for.

There once lived in Connecticut another professed historian of that commonwealth—but a man of extreme truthfulness and precision of statement—Benjamin Trumbull[2] by name, born in the same town with Samuel Peters, and in the same year, a fellow-student, likewise, with Peters in the same college, and his acquaintance and correspondent

[1] J. Hammond Trumbull, "The True Blue Laws," etc., 34, where may be seen some evidence in justification of the above remark.

[2] Author of "A Complete History of Connecticut, Civil and Ecclesiastical," etc. Two volumes. New Haven: 1818.

during a long life. A few words of quiet testimony once uttered by Trumbull may help us to assign Samuel Peters and his book to the category to which they both belong: "Of all men with whom I have ever been acquainted, I have thought Dr. Peters the least to be depended upon as to any matter of fact."[1] Moreover, much of what otherwise remains to us in the form of book,[2] or letter, or anecdote, either from Peters or about him, has the effect of adding strength to the conclusion that he was himself a victim of his own almost unrivaled gift for confounding the things he had actually known, with the things he had merely imagined. His appears to have been one of those exceedingly creative minds, which are unable to give an account of the simplest facts, without adding to them great and perhaps unconscious embellishments of fancy. Indeed, his capacity for such embellishments may be said to have had a brilliance that was even hectic and morbid. For an ordinary person afflicted in this way, there exists among healthy people of the Anglo-Saxon race a single descriptive word which has the merit of cogent brevity and explicitness. Probably, however, for an extraordinary person, like Samuel Peters, some may think it needful to resort to a more erudite and a more courteous description. Certainly, as a narrator of facts, he seems to have had so marvelous an alacrity for those which never had any existence, as to have won for himself the honor of being described not as a liar, but as a victim of that magnificent ailment now known as pseudomania.[3]

---

[1] Transposed from the form of sentence as given by J. Hammond Trumbull, in "The Rev. Samuel Peters, His Defenders and Apologists," 26.

[2] For example, his "History of the Rev. Hugh Peters, A.M.," New York, 1807,—a work wholly without historical character: loose and reckless in assertion, violent in temper, flabby in style, the product of a mind which one instinctively feels to have been not careful for precision, not orderly and well-poised, not thoroughly sane.

[3] The reader who may care to examine all that can be said, in full detail, upon both sides of the controversy respecting Samuel Peters, is referred, first of all, to the book itself, Peters's "General History of Connecticut"; then to

XI.

So soon as the Revolutionary conflict had reached its military stage, there began to be manifest among us a consciousness of its unusual significance, and the need of making and keeping records of it. We may not entirely disregard the tokens of this historic purpose even in a form so humble and so crude as that of diaries and other off-hand records of passing events. Especially noteworthy are some of the military journals which have survived from those times.

James Thacher, who, at the outbreak of hostilities, was a student of medicine at Barnstable, Massachusetts, entered the medical service of the army on the fifteenth of July, 1775, and continued in that service until the first of January, 1783,—accompanying the army upon nearly all of its most celebrated movements, and making the acquaintance of nearly all of its most celebrated men. Some sort of journal of this very interesting life of his, he seems to have kept; and had he chosen, at any time afterward, to publish

---

"The True Blue Laws of Connecticut and New Haven," etc., by J. Hammond Trumbull, Hartford, 1876; to "The Churchman" for March 24, 1877, containing an article on "Virginia and Civil Liberty," by Thomas W. Coit; to "The Churchman" for May 26, and June 2, 1877, containing articles on "Dr. Samuel Peters," by his great-grandson, Samuel Jarvis Mc Cormick; to "The Churchman" for August 11, and September 1, 1877, containing articles in review of Trumbull's book on "The True Blue Laws of Connecticut and New Haven," etc.; to the reprint of Peters's "General History of Connecticut," edited, with additions to the Appendix, etc., by Samuel Jarvis Mc Cormick, New York, 1877; and to J. Hammond Trumbull's rejoinder to these criticisms, entitled "The Rev. Samuel Peters, His Defenders and Apologists," Hartford, 1877. Upon the whole, the most dispassionate and the fairest account of Peters, and also the saddest one, is the straightforward documentary sketch written by his kinsman, the late Governor John S. Peters, of Hebron, Connecticut, to be found in Sprague, "Annals," etc., v. 191–200. The judgment respecting Peters, which I have expressed above, is based almost entirely upon a study of the evidence furnished by that sketch and by the printed writings of Peters. To this judgment I have come reluctantly, after three deliberate sieges of investigation separated from one another by intervals of several years, and in spite of my private sympathy with the ecclesiastical position of the man himself, of my appreciation of his many kindly and attractive qualities, and of my desire to discharge a judicial duty without giving pain to living persons, particularly, as in the present case, to living persons of the highest worth.

that journal just as it stood, in all its primitive crudity, with every break, blunder, pen-slip, raggedness of phrase, and other ear-mark of the original situation sticking to it and authenticating it, its value to all readers could not have been small. Unfortunately, however, he was not content with so humble a ministration to the cravings of posterity for Revolutionary memories. He was a facile and a somewhat effusive writer; and in preparing for the press his memoranda, which he published in 1823 under the title of "A Military Journal during the American Revolutionary War," he seems to have recomposed and expanded the original record, to have removed from it every trace of brevity, haste, perturbation, surprise, or uncertainty, to have diluted and rounded out all his rough jottings into flowing and conventional literary periods, and to have intermingled with his original materials a mass of later information, inference, reminiscence, or rhapsody,—leaving the reader in total darkness as to what portion of the journal was written during the Revolutionary War, and what forty years afterward, and, as a consequence, robbing his book of much of the charm and of the trustworthiness which would have attached to the sort of work which it professes to be—but is not.

A valid specimen of the military diary is "A Journal of Occurrences"[1] as kept by Major Return Jonathan Meigs of Connecticut, an officer in the heroic little army which marched in 1775, under the command of Benedict Arnold, through the wilderness of Maine for the invasion of Canada. Without the waste of a word, without a boast or a whine, it gives the essential facts appertaining to that most gritty, painful, and disastrous job,—the stark details of labor, suffering, courage, cowardice, in the long march, the arrival upon the river bank opposite Quebec, the crossing, the ascent to the Heights of Abraham, the attack, the failure.

---

[1] I found at the library of Harvard College a very old copy of this "Journal," printed without place or date of publication. It is said to have first appeared in the "American Remembrancer" in 1776. It was republished in New York in 1876, with an introduction and notes by Charles Ira Bushnell.

An able soldier's story of an able soldier's great achievement under conditions of the utmost hardship and hazard, is the sketch of his "Campaign in the Illinois in 1778–1779,"[1] by George Rogers Clark: a bit of writing, this, by a swordman's pen amusingly authenticated in its disdain of such rubbish as orthography and syntax; a straight-forward narrative full of action, magnanimous emotion, and graphic power, and of imperishable interest, likewise, as a record of the way in which the young republic got its foot well planted on the broad lands of the northwest, holding it there thenceforward as against all comers, whether Spaniard, Frenchman, or Briton.

Without being spoiled by any effort at elaborateness, yet shewing the facility and neatness of a practised writer, is the "Journal of Tench Tilghman," while acting as secretary to the commissioners appointed by Congress to treat with the Six Nations at German Flats, in the summer of 1775; also, his "Diary of the Siege of Yorktown."[2]

Another genuine example of the military diary is "The Journal of Lieutenant William Feltman,"[3] from May, 1781, to April, 1782, embracing memoranda relating to the siege of Yorktown and the Southern Campaign.

XII.

A notable example of genuine work in the writing of some portion of the history of the Revolution, by a contemporary witness of its scenes, was occasioned by the first return of the anniversary of the slaughter at Lexington, namely, "A Brief Narrative of the Principal Transactions of That Day," —a clear, vivid, thrilling story as told by Jonas Clark, and by him added to a sermon[4] which he preached in Lexington Church on the nineteenth of April, 1776.

---

[1] Published as "Number Three," in the "Ohio Valley Historical Series," Cincinnati: 1869.

[2] This "Diary" with the earlier "Journal" was first published in the Appendix to "Memoir of Tench Tilghman," Albany, 1876.

[3] First published, Philadelphia, 1853.

[4] Published in Boston, 1777; republished in the same place, in folio, with

David Ramsay, of Charleston, South Carolina, an eminent actor in the Revolution, began to qualify himself to be its historian by collecting documentary materials therefor, which, however, he appears not to have put to any literary use until after the close of this period.

A fellow-townsman of Ramsay's, William Henry Drayton, a member of the Continental Congress from South Carolina, had, also, formed the project of writing the history of the American Revolution. Upon his death at Philadelphia in September, 1779, there was found among his papers in that city a number of manuscripts shewing that he had already made considerable progress in the work. On the ground, however, that these manuscripts contained important secrets of state, they were at once destroyed. Luckily, Drayton had left at home two volumes written prior to his residence in Philadelphia, and embodying a narrative of events in the southern colonies, between the latter part of 1773 and the latter part of 1776. These volumes, having thus escaped the doom which had befallen his papers in Philadelphia, were subsequently used by his son, John Drayton, as the basis for a work published in Charleston in 1821, entitled "Memoirs of the American Revolution." [1]

XIII.

Another contemporary of the American Revolution who had a keen perception of its value as a subject for historical treatment, was Mercy Warren, a woman distinguished in those times by the vigor of her intelligence, her wide reading, her wit, her social charm, her high-spirited bearing amid the agitations and dangers upon which her life was cast. She was born in Barnstable, Massachusetts, in 1728. Being the daughter of James Otis, colonial jurist and poli-

---

illustrations, in 1875, in connection with the centennial commemoration of that epoch-making event. A delightful sketch of Jonas Clark, written by William Ware, is in Sprague, "Annals," etc., i. 514–519.

[1] The name of the younger Drayton alone is allowed to appear on the title-page—a manifestation of almost incredible vanity and selfishness on his part.

tician, sister of James Otis, Revolutionary orator, and wife of James Warren, able and trusted leader in the most aggressive measures of the Revolution, it may be said of her that, from childhood to old age, she had been accustomed to see at her own fireside the boldest, the most accomplished, the most sagacious of the political and military chieftains of America, to hear their talk, and to participate in it. She was admired and confided in by John Adams, Washington, Jefferson; with these and other men eminent in the affairs of her country, both at home and abroad, she long corresponded on terms of confidence; and as she was "stimulated to observation by a mind that had not yielded to the assertion, that all political attentions lay out of the road of female life,"[1] she became an expert in the public transactions of the world in her day, and a penetrating judge of the characters of the men who had a principal share in them.

Upon the development of the American Revolution, she resolved, since she could not be an actor in it, that she would be a delineator of it: "At a period when every manly arm was occupied, and every trait of talent or activity engaged, either in the cabinet or the field, . . . I have been induced to improve the leisure Providence had lent, to record as they passed, in the following pages, the new and unexperienced events exhibited in a land previously blessed with peace, liberty, simplicity, and virtue."[2]

The result was a "History of the Rise, Progress and Termination of the American Revolution, Interspersed with Biographical, Political and Moral Reflections,"—a work which, although not published until the year 1805, seems to have been composed, in large part, almost contemporaneously[3] with the events of which it speaks.

Even a casual glance is enough to discover to us that this is a history of the great Anglo-American Controversy from

---

[1] Mercy Warren, "History," etc., i, Pref. iv. [2] Ibid. Pref. iii.

[3] Fairly to be inferred from sentences in the first three pages of the Preface.

the particular point of view of the Otises, the Warrens, and the Adamses of New England. Here is no pretense to historic disinterestedness, to judicial coolness or judicial breadth. Here from beginning to end, is a frank, strong, well-spiced story of a renowned race-quarrel, by one who had a passionate share in every stage of it, and who had an honest abhorrence for those—especially among her own countrymen—who took the side opposite to her own. These people are "the malignant party"[1]; to describe their ablest leader is "to exhibit the deformed features" of the human species[2]; to name him is to name "a notorious parricide."[3] Of course, with this tone of undisguised partisanship ringing through the book, no reader of it can ever be off his guard. Indeed, one comes rather to enjoy the naïveté, the verve, the piquant flavor of this heroic vindictiveness, as an amusing survival of a dispute so long dead,—as a note of authenticity, likewise, in a document which sprang from the very froth and ferment of those high rages of which it gives the outward manifestation.

The literary form of the work is not to be despised. Its chief faults are diffuseness, the swamping of narrative in disquisition, the solemn announcement of ethical and political truisms. Upon the whole, however, as a history of the American Revolution, it is a life-like and a powerful delineation of a great period, and by a writer who had, and who used, extraordinary opportunities for knowing its origin, its growth, its vicissitudes, its ablest men, its most prominent events, its most secret passages. Doubtless, those parts of the book to which the modern reader is most likely to turn, are its portraits of the men prominent in the Revolution on either side—more particularly of the men toward whom Mercy Warren was unable to exhibit that twice-blest quality somewhat ironically announced in her baptismal name. Not a few of these character-sketches have a neatness in disapproval and a discriminating acridity of touch, which must have been keenly enjoyed by almost all persons

[1] "History," i. 60. [2] Ibid. 78. [3] Ibid. 123.

—excepting the subjects of them. Governor Francis Bernard, for example, " was by education strongly impressed with high ideas of canon and feudal law, and fond of a system of government that had been long obsolete in England, and had never had an existence in America."[1] Thomas Hutchinson " was dark, intriguing, insinuating, haughty and ambitious ; while the extreme of avarice marked each feature of his character. His abilities were little above the line of mediocrity; yet by dint of industry, exact temperance, and indefatigable labor, he became master of the accomplishments necessary to acquire popular fame. Though bred a merchant, he had looked into the origin and the principles of the British constitution, and made himself acquainted with the several forms of government established in the colonies; he had acquired some knowledge of the common law of England, diligently studied the intricacies of Machiavelian policy, and never failed to recommend the Italian master as a model to his adherents."[2] As to General Gage, " it was indeed unfortunate for him, that he had been appointed to the command of an army and the government of a province, without the talents that qualified for the times. He was naturally a man of a humane disposition, nor had his courage ever been impeached; but he had not the intrigue of the statesman to balance the parties, nor the sagacity necessary to defeat their designs; nor was he possessed of that soldierly promptitude that leaves no interval between the determination and execution of his projects."[3] General Charles Lee " was plain in his person even to ugliness, and careless in his manners to a degree of rudeness. He possessed a bold genius and an unconquerable spirit: his voice was rough, his garb ordinary, his deportment morose. . . . He cherished the American cause from motives of resentment, and a predilection in favor of freedom, more than from a just sense of the rights of mankind. Without religion or country, principle or attachment, gold was his deity, and liberty the idol of his fancy: he hoarded the

---

[1] " History," etc., i. 42. [2] Ibid. 79. [3] Ibid. 241.

former without taste for its enjoyment, and worshipped the latter as the patroness of licentiousness rather than the protectress of virtue. He affected to despise the opinion of the world, yet was fond of applause. Ambitious of fame, without the dignity to support it, he emulated the heroes of antiquity in the field, while in private life he sunk to the vulgarity of the clown." [1]

XIV.

From the year of the Declaration of Independence onward to the close of the Revolution, probably no other man in America was more eager and more indefatigable in the effort to obtain materials—oral, written, and printed—touching the history of that great movement than was William Gordon, an adoptive American, who, born in England in 1740, came to this country in 1770, drawn hither by his sympathy with the American cause, and who from 1772 to 1786 was pastor of the Third Congregational Church in Roxbury, Massachusetts. A blunt, restless, headstrong person, quite unhampered by shyness or reticence, "somewhat vain, and not accurate nor judicious, very zealous in the cause, and a well-meaning man, but incautious," [2] he plunged at once and with great ardor into the politics of his newly-chosen country; and at the end of four years, being "struck with the importance of the scenes that were opening upon the world," [3] he formed the resolution to record them worthily, for the benefit of mankind. In order to qualify himself for this large task, he made his purpose widely known; traveled up and down the land in pursuit of knowledge under difficulties; became a familiar figure in council, congress, and camp; ransacked manuscript records [4];

---

[1] "History," etc., i. 292.

[2] J. Adams, "Works," ii. 424.

[3] W. Gordon, "History," etc., i. Pref.

[4] Thus, in order to make himself acquainted with the antecedent history of the country, he even read "near thirty folio manuscript volumes" of the records of Massachusetts Bay. So, also, he had from Congress the extraordinary favor of being allowed to inspect "such of their records as could with propriety be submitted to the perusal of a private person." "History," etc., Pref.

begged or borrowed letters, memoranda, and all sorts of confidential documents; compared notes with other laborers in the same field [1]; and hobnobbing with leading statesmen and generals,[2] set their talk a flowing in the channel of those events of which they knew best the inward meaning, and even got from them careful written statements of fact, as well as the privilege of looking into their own "papers both of a public and private nature."

As a collector of materials for history, therefore, Gordon seems to have had the true method. Had he the true method, also, as a writer of history? It was his purpose, certainly, that the very truth about the American Revolution should be told, even at the risk of giving mortal offense to any person or party concerned in it. "I shall endeavor," he wrote in 1782, "that what I write shall be not only the truth, but the truth truly represented; for you may tell the truth so as to make a lie of it in the apprehensions of him who reads or hears the tale." [3]

It is probable that in the actual composition of his work, he did not go very far until, near the close of the Revolution, its historic character had been placed beyond doubt or reversal. At any rate, not until the spring of 1786 was he quite ready to send the book to press.[4] For the purpose

[1] For example, with David Ramsay of South Carolina, who permitted him to see the materials for his "History of the War in Carolina." "History," etc., Pref.

[2] He derived much information from Washington, Gates, Greene, Lincoln aud Otho Williams. He became so intimate with Gates that he sometimes addressed him as "My dear Horatio." In the voluminous papers of Gates, still unpublished, but in the good keeping of the New York Historical Society, I noted many proofs of Gordon's tact and diligence in drawing from that officer his knowledge of Revolutionary events: *e. g.*, one letter in 1780; three in 1781; three in 1782; and two in 1783.

[3] MS. letter to General Gates, 16 October, 1782, in the "Gates Papers."

[4] I regard Gordon's book as belonging only in part to the period treated of by me in the present work: it was prepared during the Revolution; it was chiefly written and published after the Revolution. This is why I here speak of it at all, and also why I do not speak of it at greater length—at a length, indeed, somewhat more commensurate with its real importance as a history of our Revolution by a contemporary observer.

of doing so, he deemed it prudent to go back to England, where, indeed, he had long before resolved to spend the remainder of his life. So early as the year 1782, he had explained all this to General Gates, in a letter which is full of significance as affecting both the attitude of the American people at that time toward the history of their Revolution, and also the intended frankness of his own narrative in blurting out a good deal of truth about it that would be disagreeable to them: "The eastern country is so altered in its manners, and through the contagions of the times the face of affairs is so changed, that I mean after the war to return to London, where my nearest and dearest friends reside. . . . Should Great Britain mend its constitution by the shock it has received, and the dangerous fever, in which it has been, prove the occasion of its working off its bad humors, life, liberty, property, and character will be safer there than on this side the Atlantic; and an historian may use the impartial pen there with less danger than here. The credit of the country and of individuals who now occupy eminences will be most horribly affected by an impartial history." [1]

Soon after his arrival in England, however, Gordon made the discovery—which seems to have surprised him—that objections to an impartial history of the American Revolution were not confined to the western side of the Atlantic. If he had left America in order to escape from one set of prejudices, he had come to England only to dash his head and his heart against another set, equally bitter, equally unrelenting. His old friend, John Adams, then in London as American envoy near the Court of St. James, gave long afterward, in a letter to Elbridge Gerry, some account of poor Gordon's new embarrassment: "It is with grief that I record a fact, which I ought to record, relative to Gordon's history. His object was profit. He was told that his book would not sell, if printed according to his manuscript. . . . He was told, besides, that the style was so bold

[1] MS. letter to Gates, 16 October, 1782, in the "Gates Papers."

that it would damn the work, and that many things were so favorable to America and others so disgraceful to Britons that neither would be borne. Accordingly, the style and spirit was altered and accommodated more to the British taste and feelings."[1] In one particular, at least, this testimony of John Adams seems to have been unfair to Gordon. Of course, Gordon hoped to get some profit from the sale of his book—in the preparation of which he had made a great outlay, not only in time, but in money also. His possible failure to obtain such profit, however, was not the most serious consequence with which he was threatened, should he dare to publish his book just as he had written it; for, having submitted the manuscript to an English friend, competent to advise in such a matter, he was assured that, besides being, as the English would think, "too favorable to the Americans," it was full of what the English law would regard as libels,—"libels against some of the most respectable characters in the British army and navy; and that if he possessed a fortune equal to the Duke of Bedford's, he would not be able to pay the damages that might be recovered against him—as the truth would not be allowed to be produced in evidence."[2]

For us, of course, it is now easy to see precisely what, under such circumstances, Gordon should have done: he should have deposited his manuscript in some safe custody—there to remain until, in a later age and long after he himself should have left the world, the English-speaking peoples on both sides of the Atlantic might have so far cooled from the anger generated by their Great Dispute as to be willing to read an impartial account of it. To such a sacrifice of immediate reputation, and especially of immediate fortune, Gordon had not the strength to submit. Accordingly, either by his own hand or by the hand of another,

---

[1] In J. T. Austin, "The Life of Elbridge Gerry," Part i., 520.

[2] "Recollections of a Bostonian," a series of letters published in "The Boston Centinel," in 1821–1822, and reprinted in Niles, "Prin. and Acts of the Rev.," 479–486. The passage quoted by me is on page 483.

his book underwent serious mutilation: its form was entirely recast; a multitude of expressions were toned down; many details of fact were modified; entire passages of the narrative, amounting to an hundred pages at the least, were stricken out altogether.[1]

All this, certainly, is most lamentable; and the discovery, if such a thing were possible, of the unmutilated manuscript of Gordon's "History of the Rise, Progress, and Establishment of the Independence of the United States of America," would now be an event of capital interest to all students of modern history.[2] The book, as we have it, though written by a man who strove hard to be accurate, is defaced by many errors both of fact and of opinion; and yet with all its faults of whatever kind, and even in competition with the subsequent historical labors of more than a century, this account of the American Revolution holds its ground as one of the best yet produced by any one upon that vast uprising of human nature. It can hardly be possible for any reader of Gordon's book, to resist the impression that he was an honest man, and meant to be a truthful and a fair historian.

---

[1] The chief evidence touching the mutilation of Gordon's "History" may be found in Austin, "The Life of Elbridge Gerry," Part i. 520; in Niles, "Prin. and Acts of the Rev.," 482–483; and in "The Hist. Mag.," vi. 82.

[2] "The History of the Rise, Progress, and Establishment of the Independence of the United States of America: Including an Account of the late War, and of the Thirteen Colonies from their Origin to that Period," by William Gordon, D.D., was "printed for the author" in London in 1788, "and sold by Charles Dilly, in the Poultry, and James Buckland, in Pater-Noster Row." It consisted of four dignified volumes, in large type and of good paper. In 1789, there appeared at New York the first American edition, wherein, by help of small type and thin paper, the work was reduced to three volumes, of mean and impoverished aspect. The English edition, besides being the better to look at, is also of the purer text. I cannot doubt that the private papers of Gordon are worth searching for in England. A fairly-good life of him is still lacking. The brief sketch in the "Dictionary of National Biography" has a full supply of those amusing errors of detail which occur in so many of its articles on Anglo-American subjects. The amplest account of Gordon which I have met with, is by James Spear Loring, in "The Historical Magazine," vi. 41–49; 78–83. This, however, besides being disorderly and garrulous, is in other respects unsatisfactory.

Everywhere, also, in its incidental strokes of information, in a thousand casual hints and glances of meaning, one perceives the immense advantage he derived from his intimate communication with the great civilians and soldiers who conducted the Revolution from its beginning to its end. It is true that his brief residence in the country which he made his own with so much ardor, rendered it impossible for him to see the real relation of some events, to understand the true character of some persons; but even that disadvantage had its compensation in his freedom from local and hereditary bias, in the unhackneyed freshness of his judgment, in a sort of aloofness of vision which gave something of the just perspective and of the impartiality that are conferred by actual distance in space or in time. Finally, the fact speaks well for this history of the American Revolution that, at the time of its publication, it dissatisfied both sides in the controversy —a valid token that it was not the product of servility to either side.

BIBLIOGRAPHY.

The following is intended to be a complete list of the printed materials—books, pamphlets, broadsides, and periodical publications—cited in the present work on "The Literary History of the American Revolution." Each document is mentioned in alphabetical order, either according to its author's name, or, where that is unknown, according to the first word in its title, excluding the definite and indefinite articles. In the case of extremely long titles, I have sometimes given only their primary and more distinguishing portions. Moreover, in the footnotes throughout the book, I have sought to save room by giving, in many instances, only an abridged form of the titles therein cited, doing so, however, in such a way as to enable the reader, by turning to the following list, to find the exact title referred to, as well as the particular edition used by me.

It will be readily understood that the materials included in this list form but a fraction of those actually examined by me in the course of my researches among the writings which have survived to us from our Revolutionary period. Perhaps I ought to add that these researches, when not satisfied within my own library or within that of Cornell University, have laid upon me the pleasant necessity, during the past twenty years, of paying visits not only to the British Museum and to the Public Record Office in London, but to the chief historical libraries in the older portions of our republic—particularly to those of Richmond, Washington, Baltimore, Philadelphia, New York, Brooklyn, New Haven, Providence, Worcester, Cambridge, and Boston.

ADAIR, JAMES, The History of the American Indians; particularly those Nations adjoining to the Mississippi, East and West Florida, Georgia, South and North Carolina, and Virginia.
London: 1775.

ADAMS, ABIGAIL, Correspondence of Miss Adams, Daughter of John Adams, second President of the United States. Edited by her Daughter. Two volumes.
New York and London: vol. i. 1841; vol. ii. 1842.
[See Smith, Abigail Adams.]

ADAMS, AMOS, A Concise, Historical View of the Perils, Hardships, Difficulties, and Discouragements which have attended the Planting and Progressive Improvement of New England.
Boston : 1769.

ADAMS, CHARLES FRANCIS, editor. See the Works of John Adams.

ADAMS, CHARLES FRANCIS, editor. See Letters of John Adams.

ADAMS, CHARLES FRANCIS, editor. See Letters of Mrs. Adams, the Wife of John Adams.

ADAMS, HERBERT BAXTER, The Life and Writings of Jared Sparks, Comprising Selections from his Journals and Correspondence. Two volumes.
Boston : 1893.

ADAMS, JOHN, Letters of, Addressed to His Wife. Edited by His Grandson, Charles Francis Adams. Two volumes.
Boston : 1841.

ADAMS, JOHN, The Works of. With a Life of the Author. Notes and Illustrations by Charles Francis Adams. Ten volumes.
Boston : 1856.

ADAMS, JOHN, Novanglus : or, A History of the Dispute with America, from its Origin in 1754 to the Present Time. Written in 1774.
[See The Works of John Adams, iv. 3–177].

ADAMS, JOHN. See Novanglus and Massachusettensis.

ADAMS, MRS., The Wife of John Adams, Letters of. With an Introductory Memoir by her Grandson, Charles Francis Adams. Two volumes.
Boston : 1841.

ADAMS, SAMUEL, The True Sentiments of America : Contained in a Collection of Letters sent from the House of Representatives of the Province of Massachusetts Bay to Several Persons of high Rank in this Kingdom ; together with certain Papers relating to a supposed Libel on the Governor of that Province, and a Dissertation on the Canon and Feudal Law.
London : 1768.
[There has been much debate over the authorship of the documents here collected ; but it is now well ascertained that the most of them were by Samuel Adams. Of course, the "Dissertation" was by John Adams.]

ADAMS, ZABDIEL, Massachussetts Election Sermon, May 29, 1782.
Boston : 1782.

ALEXANDER, SAMUEL DAVIES, Princeton College During the Eighteenth Century.
New York : n. d.
[The entry of copyright is of the year 1872.]

ALLEN, ETHAN, A Vindication of the Opposition of the Inhabitants of Vermont to the Government of New York.
" Printed by Alden Spooner, 1779, Printer to the State of Vermont."

ALLEN, ETHAN, Reason the Only Oracle of Man: or, A Compenduous System of Natural Religion. Alternately adorned with Confutations of a Variety of Doctrines incompatible with it; Deduced from the most exalted Ideas which we are able to form of the Divine and Human Characters, and from the Universe in General.
Bennington: 1784.

ALLEN, ETHAN, A Narrative of Colonel Ethan Allen's Captivity. Written by Himself. Burlington: 1846.
[This edition is inaccurately styled "fourth edition." It also leaves off the voluminous title given to the book by the author himself.]

ALLEN, WILLIAM, The American Biographical Dictionary: Containing an Account of the Lives, Characters, and Writings of the most eminent Persons deceased in North America, from its first Settlement.
Third Edition. Boston: 1857.

ALMON, J., Prior Documents.
London: 1777.
[The above is the convenient running-title of a book which has a different title on the title-page, as follows: A Collection of Interesting Authentic Papers, relative to the Dispute between Great Britain and America, shewing the Causes and Progress of that Misunderstanding, from 1764 to 1775.]

ALMON, J., The Remembrancer, or Impartial Repository of Public Events. For the Year 1776.
Three parts. London: 1776.

ALMON, J., The Remembrancer, or, Impartial Repository of Public Events for the Year 1778 and beginning of 1779. Volumes vii. and viii.
London: 1779.

AMERICAN Archives: Fourth Series. Containing a Documentary History of the English Colonies in North America, From the King's Message to Parliament, of March 7, 1774, to the Declaration of Independence by the United States. Edited by Peter Force. Six volumes.
Washington: 1837–1846.

AMERICAN Archives: Fifth Series. Containing a Documentary History of the United States of America, From the Declaration of Independence, July 4, 1776, to the Definitive Treaty with Great Britain, September 3, 1783. By Peter Force. Three volumes.
Washington: 1848–1853.
[The Fifth Series is unfinished.]

AMERICAN Chronicles of the Times (The), The First Book of. [Colophon.]
Philadelphia: 1774–1775.
[This edition, which I found in the Library Company of Philadelphia, is in six Chapters forming together 70 pp. The imprint is at the end of each Chapter. The first Chapter was issued in October, 1774, the last in February, 1775. In the library of the Mass. Hist. Soc. is an edition printed by D. Kneeland, Boston; containing but five Chapters without paging, the imprint at the end of the third Chapter giving the date as 1775. In the library of the late Mr. C. Fiske Harris of Providence, was an edition printed in Boston, by John Boyle, 1775, likewise having only five Chapters, and without paging. I am led to suspect that the work was written not far from Philadelphia; in short that it was one of the innumerable anonymous literary hoaxes of Francis Hopkinson.]

AMERICAN Gazette (The). No. ii.
London: 1768.

AMERICAN History, Magazine of. Volume viii.
New York: 1882.

AMERICAN Liberty Song (The).
In broadside. n. p: n. d.
[The copy used by me is in the library of the Pa. Hist. Soc.]

AMERICAN Museum (The): or, Repository of Ancient and Modern Fugitive Pieces, etc., Prose and Poetical. Eleven volumes.
Philadelphia: 1787–1792.

AMERICAN Philosophical Society, Transactions of. Volume iv.
Philadelphia: 1799.

ANDREWS, JAMES DEWITT, editor. See The Works of James Wilson, edition of 1896.

ANDREWS, JOHN, Esq., of Boston, Letters of, 1772–1776. Compiled and edited from the original MSS., with an Introduction, by Winthrop Sargent.
Cambridge: 1866.
[Reprinted from the "Proceedings of the Mass. Hist. Soc."]

ANDROS, THOMAS, The Old Jersey Captive: or, A Narrative of the Captivity of Thomas Andros (now Pastor of the Church in Berkeley) on board the Old Jersey Prison Ship at New York, 1781. In a Series of Letters to a Friend, suited to inspire Faith and Confidence in a Particular Divine Providence.
Boston: 1833.

ARBUTHNOT, JOHN, The History of John Bull.
London, Paris, New York, and Melbourne: 1889.
[This is one of the volumes in Cassell's National Library.]

ARNOLD, MATTHEW, On the Study of Celtic Literature.
London : 1863.

ATLANTIC Monthly (The). A Magazine of Literature, Art, and Politics.
Volume xii. Boston : 1863.
Volume liv. Boston : 1884.

AUSTIN, JAMES TRECOTHIC, The Life of Elbridge Gerry, With Contemporary Letters.
Part i. To the Close of the American Revolution. Boston : 1828.
Part ii. From the Close of the American Revolution. Boston : 1829.

BACKUS, ISAAC, A History of New England, With particular Reference to the Denomination of Christians called Baptists. . . . Collected from most authentic Records and Writings, both Ancient and Modern.
Volume i. Boston 1777.
Volume ii. Providence : 1784, [with the following title] A Church History of New England. Extending from 1690, to 1784. Including a concise View of the American War, and of the Conduct of the Baptists therein, with the present State of their Churches.
Volume iii. Boston : 1796, [with the following title] A Church History of New England. Extending from 1783 to 1796. Containing an Account of the Religious Affairs of the Country, and of the Oppressions therein on Religious Accounts, with a particular History of the Baptist Churches in the Five States of New England.

BACKUS, ISAAC, An Abridgment of the Church History of New England, from 1602 to 1804. Containing a View of their Principles and Practice, Declensions and Revivals, Oppression and Liberty. With a concise Account of the Baptists in the Southern Parts of America. And a Chronological Table of the Whole.
Boston : 1804.
[This Abridgment was re-printed in volume i. of "The Baptist Library," pages 89–181.
Prattsville : 1843.]

BACKUS, ISAAC, A History of New England, With Particular Reference to the Denomination of Christians called Baptists. Second Edition, with Notes by David Weston. Two volumes.
Newton : 1871.

BALCH, THOMAS, editor. See The Examination of Joseph Galloway.

BALDWIN, EBENEZER, Annals of Yale College to 1831.
New Haven : 1831.

BALLADS and Poems relating to the Burgoyne Campaign, Annotated by William Leete Stone.
Albany : 1893.

[This collection forms No. 20 of Munsell's Historical Series. It includes, besides the contemporary verses on Burgoyne, many modern commemorations in verse of the various transactions connected with his campaign. Indeed, most of the materials in this book are modern ; and the annotations are by a writer who has long been a specialist in that particular topic of our history.]

BANCROFT, EDWARD, An Essay on the Natural History of Guiana in South America. Containing a description of many curious productions in the animal and vegetable systems of that country, together with an account of the religion, manners, and customs of several tribes of its Indian inhabitants ; interspersed with a variety of literary and medical observations, in several letters from a gentleman of the medical faculty, during his residence in that country.
London : 1769.

BANCROFT, EDWARD, Remarks on the Review of the Controversy between Great Britain and her Colonies.
London : 1769. Re-printed New London : 1771.

BANCROFT, EDWARD, The History of Charles Wentworth, Esq. In a Series of Letters. Interspersed with a Variety of Important Reflections, calculated to improve Morality, and promote the Economy of Human Life. Three volumes.
London : 1770.
[I am indebted to the American Antiquarian Society for the loan of these extremely rare volumes.]

BANCROFT, EDWARD, A Narrative of the Objects and Proceedings of Silas Deane as Commissioner of the United Colonies to France : made to the British Government in 1776. Edited by Paul Leicester Ford.
Brooklyn : 1892.

BANCROFT, GEORGE, History of the United States. Ten volumes.
Boston : 1869–1874.

BANCROFT, GEORGE, History of the United States of America. The Author's Last Revision. Six volumes.
New York : 1891.

BARTON, ANDREW, Disappointment : or, The Force of Credulity. A New American Comic Opera, of Two Acts.
New York : 1767.

BARTON, BENJAMIN SMITH, New Views of the Origin of the Tribes of America.
Philadelphia : 1797.

BATTLE OF BROOKLYN (The :) A Farce of Two Acts. As it was performed on Long Island on Tuesday, the 27th Day of August, 1776, by the Representatives of the Tyrants of America assembled at Philadelphia.
New York : 1776.

BEARDSLEY, EBEN EDWARDS, Life and Times of William Samuel Johnson. Second Edition, revised and enlarged.
Boston: 1886.
[The first edition was published in 1876.]

BEARDSLEY, EBEN EDWARDS, Life and Correspondence of the Right Reverend Samuel Seabury, D.D. Second edition.
Boston: 1881.

BEATTY, CHARLES, The Journal of a Two Months' Tour with a View of Promoting Religion among the Frontier Inhabitants of Pennsylvania.
London: 1768.

BELKNAP, JEREMY, D.D., The Historian of New Hampshire, Life of; with Selections from his Correspondence and Other Writings. Selected and Arranged by his Grand-Daughter.
New York: 1847.

BELLAMY, JOSEPH, The Works of, With a Memoir of His Life and Character. Two volumes.
Boston: 1853.

BIGELOW, JOHN, editor. See The Life of Benjamin Franklin, Written by Himself.

BIGELOW, JOHN, editor. See The Complete Works of Benjamin Franklin.

BLACKWOOD'S Edinburgh Magazine. Volume xli. December—June, 1837.
Edinburgh and London: 1837.
Volume lii. July—December, 1842.
Edinburgh and London: 1842.

BLAND, RICHARD, A Fragment on the Pistole Fee, claimed by the Governor of Virginia, 1753. Edited by William Chauncey Ford.
Brooklyn: 1891.

BLAND, RICHARD, A Letter to the Clergy of Virginia.
Williamsburgh: 1760.

BLAND, RICHARD, An Enquiry into the Rights of the British Colonies; Intended as an Answer to "The Regulations lately made concerning the Colonies, and the Taxes imposed upon them considered." In a Letter addressed to the Author of that Pamphlet.
London: 1769.

BLEECKER, ANN ELIZA, The Posthumous Works of, in Prose and Verse. To which is added a Collection of Essays, Prose and Poetical, by Margaretta V. Faugeres.
New York: 1793.

BLOCKHEADS (The): or, the Affrightened Officers. A Farce.
Boston: 1776.
[This has been attributed to Mercy Warren.]

BLOCKHEADS (THE), or, Fortunate Contractor. An Opera in Two Acts, as it was performed at New York. The Music entirely new, composed by several of the most eminent Masters in Europe. Printed at New York. London Re-Printed for G. Kearsley, 1782.

BOLTON, ROBERT, Jr., History of the Protestant Episcopal Church in the County of Westchester, from its Foundation, A.D., 1693, to A.D., 1853, New York: 1855.

BOSTON CHRONICLE, (THE) for 1769, and 1770.

BOSWELL, JAMES, Life of Johnson. Edited by George Birkbeck Hill. Six volumes.
Oxford: 1887.

BOUCHER, JONATHAN, A View of the Causes and Consequences of the American Revolution; in Thirteen Discourses, preached in North America between the Years 1763 and 1775, with an Historical Preface.
London: 1797.

BOUCHER, JONATHAN, Glossary of Archaic and Provincial Words. Parts i. and ii.
London: 1832–1833.
[The work was thus left unfinished. No more has since been published.]

BRACKENRIDGE, HENRY MARIE, Biographical Notice of Hugh Henry Brackenridge. Appendix to the latter's Modern Chivalry.
Philadelphia: 1846.

BRACKENRIDGE, HUGH HENRY, The Battle of Bunker's Hill. A Dramatic Piece, Of Five Acts, In Heroic Measure. By a Gentleman of Maryland.
Philadelphia: 1876.

BRACKENRIDGE, HUGH HENRY, The Death of General Montgomery at the Siege of Quebec. A Tragedy.
Philadelphia: 1777.

BRACKENRIDGE, HUGH MONTGOMERY, Six Political Discourses Founded on the Scripture.
Lancaster: n. d.
[Hildeburn gives it as 1778. This is the same as Hugh Henry Brackenridge.]

BRACKENRIDGE, HUGH HENRY, Modern Chivalry.
Philadelphia: 1846.
[This edition contains only the first volume of the work; has a preface and

a biographical notice of the author, by his son, Henry Marie Brackenridge; and illustrations by Darley. The first volume was originally published in 1796; the work was made complete in two volumes in 1804-1807; was republished with final corrections and additions by the author in 1819,—the place of publication in each case being Pittsburgh.]

BRADFORD, ALDEN, Memoir of the Life and Writings of Rev. Jonathan Mayhew, D.D.
Boston: 1838.

BRECK, SAMUEL, Recollections of, With Passages from His Note-Books (1771-1862.) Edited by H. E. Scudder.
Philadelphia: 1877.

BRITISH POETRY, The Family Library of. Edited by James T. Fields and Edwin P. Whipple.
Boston: 1880.

BRYANT, WILLIAM CULLEN, and SYDNEY HOWARD GAY, A Popular History of the United States. Four volumes.
New York: 1876-1881.

BUCKLE, HENRY THOMAS, History of Civilization in England. Volume i. Second edition.
London: 1858.

BULLOCK, CHARLES JESSE, The Finances of the United States from 1775 to to 1789, With Especial Reference to the Budget.
Madison: 1895.
[Bulletin of the University of Wisconsin, Economics, Political Science, and History Series, volume i., number 2.]

BURGESS, JOHN W., Political Science and Comparative Constitutional Law.
Volume i. Sovereignty and Liberty.
Volume ii. Government.
Boston and London: 1891.

BURKE, EDMUND, The Works of. Twelve volumes.
Boston: 1871. Fourth edition.

BURTON, WILLIAM EVANS, The Cyclopædia of Wit and Humor. Two volumes.
New York: 1858.

CALHOUN, JOHN CALDWELL, The Works of. Edited by Richard K. Crallé. Six volumes.
Volume i. Charleston: 1851.
Volumes ii.-vi. New York: 1855.

CAMPBELL, CHARLES, History of the Colony and Ancient Dominion of Virginia.
Philadelphia: 1860.

CAMPBELL, THOMAS, The Complete Poetical Works of. With a Memoir of his Life, and an Essay on his Genius and Writings.
New York : 1850.

CARPENTER, STEPHEN CULLEN, Memoirs of Thomas Jefferson. Two volumes.
New York : 1809.

CARVER, JONATHAN, Travels through the Interior Parts of North America, in the Years 1766, 1767, and 1768.
London : 1778.

CARVER, JONATHAN, The New Universal Traveller ; containing a full and distinct Account of all the Empires, Kingdoms, and States in the Known World.
London : 1779.
[It is said that Carver was not the compiler of this book, and that he was paid for the use of his name upon the title-page.]

CARVER, JONATHAN, A Treatise on the Culture of the Tobacco Plant ; With the Manner in which it is usually cured. Adapted to Northern Climates, and designed for the Use of the Landholders of Great Britain and Ireland.
Dublin : 1779.
[The only copy known to me is in the library of Mr. John Nicholas Brown, of Providence.]

CARVER, JONATHAN, Travels through the Interior Parts of North America, in the Years 1766, 1767, and 1768. Third edition, with an Account of the Author.
London : 1781.

CARVER, JONATHAN, Abridgment of his Travels in "A New and Complete Collection," etc., by John Hamilton Moore.

CARVER Centenary (The).
St. Paul : 1867.

CARVER, JONATHAN, A Short History and Description of Fort Niagara, with an Account of its Importance to Great Britain. Written by an English Prisoner, 1758. Signed J. C——r.
Reprinted from The Royal Magazine, for September, 1759, and edited by Paul Leicester Ford.
Brooklyn : 1890,

CELEBRATED Speech of a Celebrated Commoner (The).
London : 1766.

CHANNING, WILLIAM ELLERY, The Works of. Six volumes. Nineteenth complete edition.
Boston : 1869.

CHASTELLUX, M. LE MARQUIS DE, Voyages de, dans l'Amérique Septentrionale, dans les années 1780, 1781, and 1782.
Seconde Édition. A Paris : 1788.
[Two volumes.]

CHAUNCY, CHARLES, A Discourse on the Good News from a Far Country. Delivered July Twenty-fourth, a Day of Thanksgiving to Almighty God . . . on Occasion of the Repeal of the Stamp Act.
Boston : 1766.

CHAUNCY, CHARLES, Trust in God, the Duty of a People in a Day of Trouble. A Sermon preached May 30, 1770.
Boston : 1770.

CHAUNCY, CHARLES, A Letter to a Friend, giving a concise but just Representation of the Hardships and Sufferings the Town of Boston is exposed to, and must undergo, in consequence of the late Act of the British Parliament.
Boston : 1774.

CHAUNCY, CHARLES, The Accursed Thing must be taken away from among the People, if they would reasonably hope to stand before their Enemies. A Sermon preached at the Thursday-Lecture in Boston, September 3, 1778.
Boston : 1778.

CHAUNCY, CHARLES, Salvation of All Men, illustrated and vindicated as a Scripture-Doctrine, in numerous Extracts from a Variety of pious and learned Men who have purposely writ upon the Subject. . . . By One who wishes well to all Mankind.
Boston : 1782.

CHAUNCY, CHARLES, Divine Glory brought to View, in the Final Salvation of All Men. A Letter to the Friend of Truth, by One who wishes well to all Mankind.
Boston : 1783.

CHAUNCY, CHARLES, The Mystery Hid from Ages and Generations, made manifest by the Gospel-Revelation : or, the Salvation of All Men the Grand Thing aimed at in the Scheme of God.
London : 1784.

CHEETHAM, JAMES, The Life of Thomas Paine.
New York : 1809.

CHURCH, BENJAMIN, The Times, a Poem by an American.
Boston : 1765.

CHURCH, BENJAMIN, Elegy on the Death of the Reverend Jonathan Mayhew, D.D., who departed this Life, July 9th, Anno Domini, 1766.
Boston : n. d.

CHURCH, BENJAMIN, An Address to a Provincial Bashaw. O Shame! where is thy Blush? By a Son of Liberty. Printed in the Tyrannic Administration of St. Francisco, 1769. n. p.
[The Provincial Bashaw, of course, is Governor Francis Bernard.]

CHURCH, BENJAMIN, An Elegy to the Memory of . . . the Rev. George Whitefield.
Boston: 1770.

CHURCHMAN (The). An Illustrated Weekly News-Magazine.
New York. Founded in 1845.

CLARK, GEORGE ROGERS, Sketch of His Campaign in the Illinois in 1778–9, With an Introduction by Hon. Henry Pirtle of Louisville, and an Appendix containing the Public and Private Instructions to Col. Clark; and Major Bowman's Journal of the Taking of Post St. Vincents.
Cincinnati: 1869.
[Ohio Valley Historical Series. Number three.]

CLARK, JONAS, A Sermon, preached at Lexington, April 19, 1776: . . . To which is added a Brief Narrative of the principal Transactions of That Day.
Boston: 1777.
[This "Brief Narrative" was reprinted in folio, and illustrated, Boston: 1875.]

CLARKE, JOHN, Sermon at the Interment of Rev. Dr. Samuel Cooper.
Boston: 1784.

CLARKE, JOHN, A Discourse delivered at the First Church in Boston, February 15, 1787, at the Interment of the Rev. Charles Chauncy, etc.
Boston: 1787.

COLLECTION of Scarce and Valuable Tracts (A). . . . Revised, Augmented, and Arranged by Walter Scott. Thirteen volumes.
London: 1809–1815,
[This collection is somewhat improperly lettered on the back as "Lord Somers's Tracts."]

COLUMBIAN Muse (The). A Selection of American Poetry, from Various Authors of Established Reputation.
New York: 1794.

CONDUCT of the Late Administration Examined (The). With an Appendix, containing Original and Authentic Documents.
London: 1767.
[This celebrated pamphlet was probably by Charles Lloyd. The Appendix, which contains fifty-four pages, has the letters, probably written by Governor Bernard and others, giving an account of the disturbances in Boston in the summer and autumn of 1765.]

CONNECTICUT Academy of Arts and Sciences, Memoirs of. Vol. i., part iv.
New Haven: 1816.

CONNECTICUT Journal and New Haven Post-Boy (The), for 1770, and for 1773.

CONSIDERATIONS upon the Rights of the Colonists to the Privileges of British Subjects, Introduced by a Brief Review of the Rise and Progress of English Liberty, and Concluded with some Remarks upon our present Alarming Situation.
New York: 1766.

CONTROVERSY between Great Britain and her Colonies Reviewed (The).
Boston: 1769.
[Probably by William Knox.]

CONWAY, MONCURE DANIEL, The Life of Thomas Paine. With a History of his literary, political, and religious Career in America, France, and England. Two volumes.
New York: 1892.

CONWAY, MONCURE DANIEL, editor. See The Writings of Thomas Paine.

COOKE, JOHN ESTEN, The Virginia Comedians; or, Old Days in the Old Dominion. Two volumes.
New York: 1883.
[The first edition was published in same place, 1854.]

COOMBE, THOMAS, The Harmony between the Old and New Testaments Respecting the Messiah.
Philadelphia: 1774.

COOMBE, THOMAS, Edwin, or, The Emigrant: an Eclogue, to which are added Three Other Poetical Sketches.
Philadelphia: 1775.

COOMBE, THOMAS, The Peasant of Auburn, or, The Emigrant. A Poem.
Philadelphia: n. d.
[The two foregoing titles stand for the same poem.]

COOPER, MYLES, The American Querist: or, Some Questions Proposed Relative to the present Disputes between Great Britain and her American Colonies. By a North American: n. p. 1774.

COOPER, MYLES, A Friendly Address to all Reasonable Americans, On the Subject of Our Political Confusions: in which the necessary Consequences of violently opposing the King's Troops, and of a general Non-Importation, are fairly stated.
New York: 1774.

COOPER, MYLES, A Sermon . . . at Oxford, December 13, 1776.
Oxford: 1777.

COOPER, SAMUEL, The Crisis.
Boston: 1754.

CORRESPONDENCE of the American Revolution, edited by Jared Sparks. Four volumes.
Boston: 1853.

COWPER, WILLIAM, The Works of, Comprising his Poems, Correspondence, and Translations, with a Life of the Author by the Editor, Robert Southey. Eight volumes.
London: 1854.

CRALLÉ, RICHARD K., editor. See the Works of John Caldwell Calhoun.

CREASY, SIR EDWARD, The Imperial and Colonial Constitutions of the Britannic Empire, excluding Indian Institutions.
London: 1872.

CREVECŒUR, J. HECTOR ST. JOHN DE, Letters from an American Farmer: Describing certain Provincial Situations, Manners, and Customs, not generally known; and conveying some Idea of the late and present interior Circumstances of the British Colonies in North America. Written for the Information of a Friend in England, by J. Hector St. John, a Farmer in Pennsylvania. A new Edition, with an accurate Index.
London: 1783.

CREVECŒUR, J. HECTOR ST. JOHN DE, Lettres d'un cultivateur américain, écrites a W. S. Écuyer, Depuis l'année 1770, jusqu' à 1781. Traduites de l'Anglois par. . . .
Paris: 1784.
[Not having at hand the French copy which I have used, I borrow this title from Sabin, "Dictionary," etc., v. 76. My impression is that this is by no means the first French edition.]

CREVECŒUR, J. HECTOR ST. JOHN DE, Briefe eines Amerikanischen Landmanns an den Ritter W. S.., in den Jahren 1770 bis 1781. Aus dem Englischen ins Französische . . . und jetzt aus dem Französichen übersetzt und mit einigen Anmerkungen begleitet von Johann August Ephraim Götze. Drei Bänder.
Leipzig: 1788.

CREVECŒUR, J. HECTOR ST. JOHN DE, Voyage Dans la Haute Pensylvanie Et Dans L'État De New York, Par un Membre adoptif de la Nation Onéida. Traduit et publié par l'auteur des Lettres d'un Cultivateur Américain. Trois tomes.
Paris: 1801.

CRISIS, (The), or, a Full Defence of the Colonies.
London: 1766.
[Written, as by an Englishman, before the repeal of the Stamp Act. Argues against England's right to tax unrepresented colonies.]

CURTIS, GEORGE TICKNOR, Constitutional History of the United States from their Declaration of Independence to the Close of their Civil War. In two volumes. Volume i.
New York : 1889.
[The author died without having published the second volume, which was issued in 1896.]

CURWEN, SAMUEL, (Journal and Letters of the Late), Judge of Admiralty, etc., an American Refugee in England, from 1775 to 1784, comprising Remarks on the prominent men and measures of that period. To which are added biographical notices of many American Loyalists and other eminent persons. By George Atkinson Ward.
New York and Boston : 1842.

CUSHING, WILLIAM, Anonyms : A Dictionary of Revealed Authorship.
Cambridge : 1890.

DEANE, SILAS, Paris Papers ; or, Mr. Silas Deane's late Intercepted Letters, to His Brothers and Other Intimate Friends in America.
New York : n. d.

DEANE Papers (The) : Collections of the New York Historical Society, for the Years 1886, 1887, and 1888.

DEAS, ANNE IZARD, editor. See Correspondence of Mr. Ralph Izard.

DELANCEY, EDWARD FLOYD, Philip Freneau the Huguenot Patriot-Poet of the Revolution, and his Poetry : n. p.
[Reprinted from the Proceedings of the Huguenot Society of America, ii., No. 2, 1891.]

DELAPLAINE, JOSEPH, Delaplaine's Repository of the Lives and Portraits of Distinguished American Characters.
[Vol. i., in two parts, of which the first appeared in 1815–1816, and the second in 1817. Of vol. ii. only the first part ever appeared, and that in 1818. The place of publication was Phila.]

DEMOGEOT, J., Histoire de la Littérature Française.
Paris : 1860.

DETAIL and Conduct of the American War, under Generals Gage, Howe, and Burgoyne, and Vice Admiral Lord Howe : With a very full and correct State of the Whole of the Evidence, as given before a Committee of the House of Commons : and the celebrated Fugitive Pieces which are said to have given Rise to that celebrated Enquiry. The Whole Exhibiting a circumstantial, connected, and complete History of the real Causes, Rise, Progress, and Present State of the American Rebellion. Third Edition.
London : 1780.
[The first and second editions of this work were under a different title, beginning with the words, "A View of the Evidence," etc.]

DEXTER, HENRY MARTYN, The Congregationalism of the Last Three Hundred Years, as seen in its Literature.
New York: 1880.

DIAL (The). A Monthly Journal of Current Literature. Volumes i–xxi.
Chicago: 1879–1896.
[This journal has been edited from its foundation by Mr. Francis F. Browne.]

DICKINSON, JOHN, A Reply to a Piece called the Speech of Joseph Galloway, Esq.
London: 1765,

DICKINSON, JOHN, The Late Regulations respecting the British Colonies on the Continent of America, Considered in a Letter from a Gentleman in Philadelphia to his Friend in London.
Philadelphia: n.d.
[This pamphlet, at first published anonymously, was reprinted in the Wilmington edition of Dickinson's "Political Writings," i. 45–90, where the date 1765 is given to it.]

DICKINSON, JOHN, Lettres d'un Fermier de Pensylvanie aux habitans de L'Amerique Septentrionale. Traduites de l'Anglois.
Amsterdam: 1769.

DICKINSON, JOHN, The Political Writings of. Two volumes.
Wilmington: 1801.

DICKINSON, JOHN, The Writings of. Edited by Paul Leicester Ford. Volume i.
Philadelphia: 1895.
[The work, still in process of publication, is to appear in three volumes, of which the first two are devoted to the Political Writings, and the third to the Correspondence.]

DICTIONARY of National Biography. Edited by Leslie Stephen and Sidney Lee. Volume xxii.
London: 1890.

DISCOURSE (A) delivered at Providence . . . upon the 25th Day of July, 1768, at the Dedication of the Tree of Liberty.
Providence: 1768.

DOANE, GEORGE WASHINGTON, editor. See The Remains of Charles Henry Wharton.

DODGE, JOHN, A Narrative of the Capture and Treatment of John Dodge, by the English at Detroit. Written by Himself.
Philadelphia: 1779.

DRAKE, FRANCIS SAMUEL, Dictionary of American Biography, Including Men of the Time.
Boston: 1872.

DRAYTON, JOHN, Memoirs of the American Revolution, From its Commencement to the Year 1776 inclusive, as relating to the State of South Carolina, and occasionally referring to the States of North Carolina and Georgia. Two volumes.
Charleston : 1821.

DRAYTON, WILLIAM HENRY, Letter from Freeman of South Carolina to the Deputies of North America, assembled in the High Court of Congress.
Charleston : 1774.

DUANE, WILLIAM, editor. See Diary of Christopher Marshall.

DUCHÉ, JACOB, Observations on a Variety of Subjects, Literary, Moral and Religious ; in a Series of Original Letters, written by a Gentleman of Foreign Extraction, who resided some Time in Philadelphia.
Philadelphia : 1774.
[This book is commonly called Caspipina's Letters, from the assumed name of their author, Tamoc Caspipina.]

DUCHÉ, JACOB The Duty of Standing Fast in our Spiritual and Temporal Liberties. A Sermon, in Christ Church, Philadelphia, 7 July, 1775, before the First Battalion, etc.
Philadelphia : 1775.
[This sermon was published in London the same year.]

DUCHÉ, JACOB, The American Vine. A Sermon preached before Congress, 20 July, 1775.
Philadelphia : 1775.

DUCHÉ, JACOB, Briefe, welche Beobachtungen über verschiedene Gegenstande der Literatur, Religion, und Moral enthalten, nebst dem Leben des Herren Penn. Aus dem Englischen.
Leipzig : 1778.

DUCHÉ, JACOB, Discourses on Various Subjects. Two volumes. Third edition.
London : 1790.
[The first edition was published in 1779.]

DUCHÉ, JACOB, The Duché Letter to General Washington : n.p. n.d.
[This is a pamphlet of 8 pp., which was printed from a copy among the Duché MSS. offered for sale in Philadelphia in 1893.]

DUFFIELD, GEORGE, A Sermon Preached in the Third Presbyterian Church in the City of Philadelphia on Thursday, December 11, 1783.
Philadelphia : 1784.

DULANY, DANIEL, Considerations on the Propriety of imposing Taxes in the British Colonies, for the Purpose of raising a Revenue by Act of Parliament. Second edition.
London : 1766.

DUYCKINCK, EVERT AUGUSTUS, AND GEORGE LONG, Cyclopædia of American Literature; embracing Personal and Critical Notices of Authors, and Selections from their Writings. From the earliest Period to the Present Day; with Portraits, Autographs, and other Illustrations. Two volumes.
New York: 1855.

DUYCKINCK, EVERT AUGUSTUS AND GEORGE LONG, Cyclopædia of American Literature, etc. Edited by Michael Laird Simons. Two volumes.
Philadelphia: n.d.
[The copyright of this revised edition is dated 1875.]

DUYCKINCK, EVERT AUGUSTUS, editor. See Philip Freneau, Poems relating to the American Revolution.

EDINBURGH Review, or, Critical Journal (The).
Volume viii. Edinburgh: 1806.
Volume lxxxi. Edinburgh: 1845.

EDWARDS, MORGAN, Materials towards a History of the American Baptists. In Twelve Volumes.
Volumes i. and ii. Philadelphia: 1770.
[The publication was never carried beyond the first two volumes.]

ELIOT, JOHN, A Biographical Dictionary, Containing a Brief Account of the First Settlers, and Other Eminent Characters among the Magistrates, Ministers, Literary and Worthy Men, in New England.
Boston: 1809.

ELLIS, GEORGE EDWARD, Half-Century of the Unitarian Controversy.
Boston: 1857.

EMERY, SAMUEL HOPKINS, The Ministry of Taunton. Two volumes.
Boston: 1853.

EMMONS, NATHANIEL, The Works of, edited by Jacob Ide. Six volumes.
Boston: 1842.

ENCYCLOPÆDIA Britannica (The). Ninth edition. Twenty-four volumes.
Edinburgh: 1875–1888.

EVANGELISCH- lutherisches Gesangbuch der Hannoverschen Landeskirche.
Hannover: 1888,

EVANS, ISRAEL, A Discourse at Easton, to the Members of the Western Army on their Return from the Expedition against the Five Nations.
Philadelphia: 1779.

EVANS, NATHANIEL, Poems on Several Occasions, With Some Other Compositions.
Philadelphia: 1772.

EVEREST, CHARLES WILLIAM, The Poets of Connecticut; With Biographical Sketches.
Hartford: 1844.

FALL of British Tyranny (The): or, American Liberty Triumphant. The First Campaign. A Tragi-Comedy of Five Acts, as lately planned at the Royal Theatrum Pandemonium at St. James'. The Principal Place of Action in America. Published according to Act of Parliament.
Philadelphia: 1776.

FAMILIAR Letters of John Adams and His Wife Abigail Adams, During the Revolution. With a Memoir of Mrs. Adams, By Charles Francis Adams.
New York: 1876.

FEDERAL and State Constitutions (The), Colonial Charters, and Other Organic Laws of the United States. Compiled under an Order of the United States Senate by Ben. Perley Poore, Clerk of Printing Records. Second edition. Two Parts.
Washington: 1878.

FELLOWS, JOHN, The Veil Removed; Or Reflections on David Humphreys' Essay on the Life of Israel Putnam.
New York: 1843.

FEW Political Reflections (A) submitted to the Consideration of the British Colonies, by a Citizen of Philadelphia.
Philadelphia: 1774.
[This pamphlet was attributed by the late Lloyd Smith to Richard Wells.]

FIELDS, JAMES T., editor. See British Poetry, The Family Library of.

FISKE, JOHN, Editor (with JAMES GRANT WILSON) of Appletons' Cyclopædia of American Biography. Six volumes.
New York: 1887–1889.

FISKE, JOHN, The American Revolution. Two volumes. Third edition.
Boston: 1891.

FISKE, NATHAN, An Historical Discourse Concerning the Settlement of Brookfield, and its Distresses during the Indian Wars.
Boston: 1776.

FISKE, NATHAN, An Oration Delivered at Brookfield, November 14, 1781, in Celebration of the Capture of Lord Cornwallis and his whole Army.
Boston: n. d.

FISKE, NATHAN, The Moral Monitor; or, A Collection of Essays on Various Subjects. Two volumes.
Worcester: 1801.

FITCH, THOMAS, Reasons why the British Colonies in America should not be charged with Internal Taxes by Authority of Parliament, Humbly Offered for Consideration, In Behalf of the Colony of Connecticut.
New Haven: 1764.

FORCE, PETER, editor. See American Archives, Fourth Series, and Fifth Series.

FORD, PAUL LEICESTER, Bibliotheca Chaunciana. A List of the Writings of Charles Chauncy. Elzevir Club Series. No. 6.
Brooklyn: 1884.
[Ten copies printed. My copy is number nine.]

FORD, PAUL LEICESTER, Bibliotheca Hamiltoniana. A List of Books written by or relating to Alexander Hamilton.
New York: 1886.

FORD, PAUL LEICESTER, Check-List of American Magazines Printed in the Eighteenth Century.
Brooklyn: 1889.

FORD, PAUL LEICESTER, Some Notes towards an Essay on the Beginnings of American Dramatic Literature, 1606–1789.
[Of this monograph 25 copies were printed as "Manuscript for suggestion and revision," 1893; for one of which I am indebted to the courtesy of the author.]

FORD, PAUL LEICESTER, editor. See The Writings of John Dickinson. New edition.

FORD, PAUL LEICESTER, editor. See the Writings of Thomas Jefferson.

FORD, PAUL LEICESTER, editor. See A Narrative, etc., of Edward Bancroft.

FORD, PAUL LEICESTER, editor. See Jonathan Carver, A Short History and Description of Fort Niagara.

FORD, PAUL LEICESTER, editor. See Isaac Wilkins, My Services and Losses, etc.

FORD, WORTHINGTON CHAUNCEY, editor. See the Writings of George Washington.

FORD, WORTHINGTON CHAUNCEY, editor. See the Washington-Duché Letters.

FORD, WORTHINGTON CHAUNCEY, editor. See Letters of William Lee.

FOSTER, WILLIAM EATON, Stephen Hopkins, A Rhode Island Statesman. A Study in the Political History of the Eighteenth Century. Two parts.
Providence: 1884.
[This book is No. 19, in Rhode Island Historical Tracts.]

FOUR Dissertations on the Reciprocal Advantages of a Perpetual Union between Great Britain and her American Colonies.
London : 1766.

FOWLER, WILLIAM CHAUNCEY, Memorials of the Chaunceys, including President Chauncy, his Ancestors and Descendants.
Boston : 1858.

FOX, CHARLES JAMES, Memorials and Correspondence of. Edited by Lord John Russell. Three volumes.
London : 1853–1854.

FRANKLIN, BENJAMIN, The Works of. Edited by Jared Sparks. Ten volumes.
Boston : 1847.

FRANKLIN, BENJAMIN, The Life of, Written by Himself. Now first Edited from Original Manuscripts and from His Printed Correspondence and other Writings. Three volumes.
Philadelphia : 1874.

FRANKLIN, BENJAMIN, The Complete Works of. Compiled and Edited by John Bigelow. Ten volumes.
New York : 1887–1888.

FRANKLIN, WILLIAM TEMPLE, Memoirs of the Life and Writings of Benjamin Franklin. First edition, Three volumes.
London : 1818.

FRENEAU, PHILIP, The Poems of. Written chiefly during the Late War.
Philadelphia : 1786.
[This is the first collected edition of Freneau's poems ; and the only copy I have ever seen, is now the property of the Massachusetts Historical Society. My references are to the reprint of this edition, mentioned in the next title.]

FRENEAU, PHILIP, Poems on Various Subjects, but Chiefly Illustrative of the Events and Actors in the American War of Independence. By Philip Freneau. Reprinted from the Rare Edition printed at Philadelphia in 1786. With a Preface.
London : 1861.
[This is the outside title, but within is reproduced the old title, which I have used in my citations.]

FRENEAU, MR. PHILIP, Miscellaneous Works of, Containing his Essays and Additional Poems.
Philadelphia : 1788.
[The only copy ever seen by me is in the library of the Massachusetts Historical Society.]

FRENEAU, PHILIP, Poems on Several Occasions: Poems Written between the Years 1768 and 1794, By Philip Freneau of New Jersey. A new edition, revised and corrected by the author, including a considerable number of pieces never before published.
Monmouth, N. J. Printed at the Press of the Author at Mount Pleasant, near Middletown-Point: M,DCC,XCV, and of American Independence, XIX.

FRENEAU, PHILIP, Poems Written and Published during the American Revolutionary War, and now Republished from the Original Manuscripts; Interspersed with Translations from the Ancients, and Other Pieces not heretofore in Print. Third edition. Two volumes.
Philadelphia: 1809.

FRENEAU, PHILIP, Poems relating to the American Revolution. With an Introductory Memoir and Notes by Evert A. Duyckinck.
New York: 1865.

FROTHINGHAM, RICHARD, The Rise of the Republic of the United States.
Boston: 1872.

GALLOWAY, JOSEPH, The Speech of Joseph Galloway, Esq., One of the Members for Philadelphia County, in Answer to the Speech of John Dickinson, Esq.; delivered in the House of Assembly, of the Province of Pennsylvania, May 24, 1764, on Occasion of a Petition drawn up by Order, and then under the Consideration of the House, praying his majesty for a Royal, in lieu of a Proprietary, Government.
Philadelphia: 1764.

GALLOWAY, JOSEPH, Die Rede Herrn Joseph Galloways, eines der Mitglieder des Hauses für Philadelphia County, zur Beantwortung der Rede welche Hr. John Dickinson, u.s.w. Aus dem Englischen übersetzt. Philadelphia, gedruckt und zu finden bey Henrich Miller, in der Zweiten-strasse: n.d.

GALLOWAY, JOSEPH. To the Public. Folio. One leaf. Philadelphia, September 29, 1764.

GALLOWAY, JOSEPH. Advertisement. To the Public. Folio. One leaf. Philadelphia, December 20, 1765.

GALLOWAY, JOSEPH, A Candid Examination of the Mutual Claims of Great Britain and the Colonies. With a Plan of Accommodation on Constitutional Principles.
New York: 1775.

GALLOWAY, JOSEPH, A Reply to an Address to the Author of a Pamphlet entitled A Candid Examination, etc., by the Author of the Candid Examination.
New York: 1775.

GALLOWAY, JOSEPH, Letters to a Nobleman on the Conduct of the War in the Middle Colonies.
London : 1779.

GALLOWAY, JOSEPH, A Letter to the Right Hon. Lord Viscount H-e, On his Naval Conduct of the American War.
London : 1779.

GALLOWAY, JOSEPH, Observations upon the Conduct of S-r W-m H-e at the White Plains, as related in the Gazette of Dec. the 30th, 1776.
London : 1779.

GALLOWAY, JOSEPH, The Examination of Joseph Galloway, Esq., late Speaker of the House of Assembly of Pennsylvania, Before the House of Commons, in a Committee on the American Papers. With explanatory Notes.
London : 1779.

GALLOWAY, JOSEPH. A Reply to the Observations of Lieut. Gen. Sir William Howe, on a Pamphlet entitled Letters to a Nobleman, in which his Misrepresentations are detected, and those Letters are supported by a Variety of new Matter and Argument. . . . By the Author of Letters to a Nobleman.
London : 1780.

GALLOWAY, JOSEPH. An Account of the Conduct of the War in the Middle Colonies. Extracted from a late Author. Second edition.
London : 1780.

GALLOWAY, JOSEPH, Historical and Political Reflections on the Rise and Progress of the American Rebellion.
London : 1780.

GALLOWAY, JOSEPH, Plain Truth ; or, A Letter to the Author of Dispassionate Thoughts on the American War.
London : 1780.

GALLOWAY, JOSEPH, Cool Thoughts on the Consequences to Great Britain of American Independence ; on the Expense of Great Britain in the Settlement and Defense of the American Colonies ; on the Value and Importance of the American Colonies and the West Indies to the British Empire.
London : 1780.

GALLOWAY, JOSEPH, A Letter from Cicero to the Right Hon. Lord Viscount H-e : Occasioned by his late Speech in the H-e of C-ns.
London : 1781.

GALLOWAY, JOSEPH, Letters from Cicero to Catiline the Second. With Corrections and Explanatory Notes.
London : 1781.

GALLOWAY, JOSEPH, Fabricius ; or, Letters to the People of Great Britain, on the Absurdity and Mischiefs of Defensive Operations Only in the American War, and on the Causes of the Failure in the Southern Operations.
London : 1782.

GALLOWAY, JOSEPH, Political Reflections on the Late Colonial Governments, in which their original Constitutional Defects are pointed out, and shewn to have naturally produced the Rebellion which has unfortunately terminated in the Dismemberment of the British Empire. By an American.
London : 1783.

GALLOWAY, JOSEPH, Observations on the Fifth Article of the Treaty with America, and on the Necessity of appointing a Judicial Enquiry into the Merits and Losses of the American Loyalists.
London : 1783.

GALLOWAY, JOSEPH, The Claim of the American Loyalists Reviewed and Maintained upon incontrovertible Principles of Law and Justice.
London : 1788.

GALLOWAY, JOSEPH, The Examination of Joseph Galloway, Esq., by a Committee of the House of Commons. Edited by Thomas Balch.
Philadelphia : 1855.

GAY, EBENEZER, Two Discourses in Boston, July 27, 1766, on the Decease of Rev. Jonathan Mayhew.
Boston : 1766.

GAY, SYDNEY HOWARD, editor, in association with WILLIAM CULLEN BRYANT, in the preparation of A Popular History of the United States.

GENTLEMAN'S Magazine and Historical Chronicle (The).
Volume xxxvii. London : 1767.
Volume xlvi. London : 1776.

GILMAN, CAROLINE HOWARD, editor. See Letters of Eliza Wilkinson.

GOEDEKE, KARL, editor. See Schillers sämtliche Werke.

GOLDSMITH, OLIVER, The works of. Edited by Peter Cunningham. Four volumes.
London : 1854.

GOODRICH, SAMUEL GRISWOLD, Recollections of a Lifetime. Two volumes.
New York : 1857.

GORDON, WILLIAM, The Separation of the Jewish Tribes, after the death of Solomon, accounted for, and applied to the present day, In a sermon preached before the General Court, on Friday, July the 4th, 1777, being the anniversary of the Declaration of Independence.
Boston : 1777.

GORDON, WILLIAM, The History of the Rise, Progress, and Establishment of the Independence of the United States of America: Including an Account of the late War, and of the Thirteen Colonies from their Origin to that Period. Four volumes.
London: 1788.
[The running title through the book is The History of the American Revolution.]

GORDON, WILLIAM, History of the Rise, Progress, and Establishment of the Independence of the United States of America, including an Account of the late Civil War. Three volumes.
New York: 1789.

GOSSE, EDMUND, Questions at Issue.
New York: 1893.

GRANT, ANNE, Memoirs of an American Lady; With Sketchs of Manners and Scenes in America, as they Existed before the Revolution. With a Memoir of Mrs. Grant, by James Grant Wilson.
Albany: 1876.

GRAYDON, ALEXANDER, Memoirs of His Own Time. With Reminiscences of the Men and Events of the Revolution. Edited by John Stockton Littell.
Philadelphia: 1846.

GREEN, JACOB, A Vision of Hell, and a Discovery of some of the Consultations and Devices there in the Year 1767. By Theodorus Van Shermain.
n.p. n.d.

GREEN, JOHN RICHARD, A Short History of the English People.
New York: 1883.

GREENE, GEORGE WASHINGTON, The Life of Nathaniel Greene. Three volumes.
New York: 1871.

GRISWOLD, RUFUS W., The Poets and Poetry of America. Fourth edition.
Philadelphia: 1843.

HALE, EDWARD EVERETT, and EDWARD EVERETT, Jr., Franklin in France. From Original Documents, most of which are now published for the First Time. Part i., Boston: 1887; Part, ii., Boston: 1888.

HAMILTON, ALEXANDER, A Full Vindication of the Measures of the Congress, from the Calumnies of their Enemies; in Answer to a Letter under the signature of A. W. Farmer. Whereby his Sophistry is exposed, his Cavils confuted, and his Wit ridiculed.
New York: 1774.

HAMILTON, ALEXANDER, The Farmer Refuted: or, A more impartial and comprehensive View of the Dispute between Great Britain and the Colonies: intended as a further Vindication of the Congress, in Answer to a Letter from A. W. Farmer, entitled a View of the Controversy, etc.
New York: 1775.

HAMILTON, ALEXANDER, The Works of. Edited by Henry Cabot Lodge. Nine volumes.
New York: 1885–1886.

HANSARD, T. C., The Parliamentary History of England. Volumes xv., xvi., and xvii.
London: 1812.

HART, OLIVER, Dancing Exploded.
Charleston: 1778.

HARVARD University. Library Bulletin. June, 1878—October, 1882.
Cambridge: 1882.

HARVARD University, Library of. Bibliographical Contributions. Edited by Justin Winsor, Librarian. No. 8. Calendar of the Arthur Lee Manuscripts.
Cambridge: 1882.

HAWKS, FRANCIS LISTER, Contributions to the Ecclesiastical History of the United States. Volume ii. A Narrative of Events connected with the Rise and Progress of the Protestant Episcopal Church in Maryland.
New York: 1839.

HENRY, WILLIAM WIRT, Patrick Henry: Life, Correspondence and Speeches. Three volumes.
New York: 1891.

HILDEBURN, CHARLES RICHÉ, A Century of Printing. The Issues of the Press in Pennsylvania 1685–1784. Two volumes.
Philadelphia: 1885–1886.

HILDEBURN, CHARLES RICHÉ, Sketches of Printers and Printing in Colonial New York.
New York: 1895.

HILDEBURN, CHARLES RICHÉ, Francis Hopkinson, in Pennsylvania Magazine of History and Biography, ii., 314–324.

HILDRETH, RICHARD, The History of the United States of America. Six volumes.
New York: 1871.

HILL, GEORGE BIRKBECK, editor. See James Boswell, Life of Johnson.

HILL, GEORGE BIRKBECK, editor. See Letters of Samuel Johnson.

HILLS, GEORGE MORGAN, History of the Church in Burlington, New Jersey; Comprising the Facts and Incidents of Nearly Two Hundred Years, from Original Contemporaneous Sources.
Trenton: 1876.

HISTORICAL Account of Bouquet's Expedition against the Ohio Indians, in 1764. With Preface by Francis Parkman, . . . and a Translation of Dumas' Biographical Sketch of General Bouquet.
Cincinnati: 1868.
[Part of Ohio Valley Historical Series. See also, William Smith, An Historical Account, etc.]

HISTORICAL Magazine (The), and Notes and Queries concerning the Antiquities, History, and Biography of America. Volume vi.
New York: 1862.

HOLMES, ABIEL, The Life of Ezra Stiles.
Boston: 1798.

HOLMES, ABIEL, The Annals of America from the Discovery by Columbus in the Year 1492 to the Year 1826. Second edition. Two volumes.
Cambridge: 1829.

HOPKINS, SAMUEL, The Works of, With a Memoir of His Life and Character. Three volumes.
Boston: 1854.

HOPKINS, STEPHEN, An Historical Account of the Planting and Growth of Providence.
First published in The Providence Gazette in 1762 and 1765.
[Reprinted in Collections of the Massachusetts Historical Society, 2 series, ix. 166–203. Boston: 1822.
Reprinted in Collections of the Rhode Island Historical Society, vii. 13–65. Providence: 1885.
The value of the last reprint is greatly enhanced by the annotations of Mr. William Eaton Foster.]

HOPKINS, STEPHEN, The Rights of Colonies Examined. Published by Authority.
Providence: 1765.
[No copy of the original edition is known to be in existence.]

HOPKINSON, FRANCIS, On the Reciprocal Advantages of a Perpetual Union between Great Britain and her American Colonies. The last of Four Dissertations on that subject, written for John Sargent's Medal in 1766.
London: n. d..
[A re-print of the first edition, published in Philadelphia, 1766.]

HOPKINSON, FRANCIS, The Miscellaneous Essays and Occassional Writings of. Three volumes.
Philadelphia : 1792.
[The latter half of the third volume contains, in separate paging, 1–204, Hopkinson's Poems on Several Subjects.]

HOPKINSON, FRANCIS, The Old Farm and the New Farm : A Political Allegory. With an introduction and historical notes by Benson J. Lossing. Second edition.
New York : 1864.

HOSMER, JAMES KENDALL, Samuel Adams.
Boston : 1885.
[In the American Statesmen Series.]

HOSMER, JAMES KENDALL, The Life of Thomas Hutchinson, Royal Governor of the Province of Massachusetts Bay.
Boston : 1896.

HOUGH, FRANKLIN BENJAMIN, editor. See Journal of the Siege of Detroit by Robert Rogers.

HOVEY, ALVAH, A Memoir of the Life and Times of the Rev. Isaac Backus.
Boston : 1859.

HOWARD, MARTIN, A letter from a Gentleman at Halifax, to his Friend in Rhode Island, containing Remarks upon a Pamphlet entitled The Rights of Colonies examined.
Newport : 1765.

HOWARD, MARTIN, A Defense of the Letter from a Gentleman at Halifax, to His Friend in Rhode Island.
Newport : 1765.

HOWELL, REDNAP, A Fan for Fanning and a Touchstone to Trycn. By Regulus.
Boston : 1771.
[I saw a copy of this rare pamphlet in the Lenox Library. It is also reprinted in the North Carolina Magazine, for February and March, 1859.]

HOWELLS, WILLIAM DEAN, A Traveler from Altruria.
New York : 1894.

HUMPHREYS, DAVID, The Miscellaneous Works of.
New York : 1790.

HUTCHINSON, PETER ORLANDO, editor. See The Diary and Letters of Thomas Hutchinson.

HUTCHINSON, THOMAS, The Case of the Provinces of Massachusetts Bay and New York, respecting the Boundary Line between the two Provinces.
Boston : 1764.

HUTCHINSON, THOMAS, The History of the Colony of Massachusetts Bay, from the first Settlement thereof in 1628, until its Incorporation with the Colony of Plymouth, Province of Maine, etc., by the Charter of King William and Queen Mary, in 1691. Volume i. Second edition.
London: M DCC LX.
[The first edition was published in Boston, 1764. This second edition was published in London in 1765, but by an error the final letter V. in the intended date was left off. This mistake has led to many errors in subsequent writers alluding to this book.]

HUTCHINSON, THOMAS, The History of the Province of Massachusetts Bay, from the Charter of King William and Queen Mary, until the Year 1750. Volume ii. Second edition.
London: 1768.
[The first edition of this volume was published in Boston in 1767. An edition of this and the first volume, "with additional Notes and Corrections," was published in Boston in 1795.]

HUTCHINSON, THOMAS, A Collection of Original Papers relative to the History of the Colony of Massachusetts Bay.
Boston: 1769.

HUTCHINSON, Governor, and Lieut. Governor OLIVER, etc., The Letters of. Printed at Boston. And Remarks thereon. With the Assembly's Address, and the Proceedings of the Lords Committee of Council, Together with the Substance of Mr. Wedderburn's Speech relating to those Letters. And the Report of the Lords Committee to His Majesty in Council. Second edition.
London: 1774.

HUTCHINSON, THOMAS, Strictures upon the Declaration of the Congress at Philadelphia: In a Letter to a Noble Lord, etc.
London: 1776.

HUTCHINSON, THOMAS, The History of the Province of Massachusetts Bay, from the Year 1750, until June, 1774. Volume iii.
London: 1828.

HUTCHINSON'S Massachusetts (Last Edition of Volumes i. and ii., Boston, 1795, and only Edition of Volume iii., London, 1828). Index of Persons and Places Mentioned in. Made by J. Wingate Thornton, Historiographer, and somewhat corrected by Charles L. Woodward, Book Peddler.
New York: 1879.

HUTCHINSON, THOMAS, Esq., B.A. (Harvard), LL.D. (Oxon.), The Diary and Letters of His Excellency, Captain-General and Governor-in-Chief of His Late Majesty's Province of Massachusetts Bay, in North America; With an Account of his Administration when he was Member and Speaker of the House of Representatives, and his Government of the Colony during the

difficult Period that preceded the War of Independence. Compiled from the Original Documents still remaining in the Possession of his Descendants, by Peter Orlando Hutchinson. one of his Great-Grandsons.
Volume i., Boston : 1884.
Volume ii., Boston : 1886,

INGERSOLL, JARED, Mr. Ingersoll's Letters relating to the Stamp Act.
New Haven : 1766.

INGLIS, CHARLES, The True Interest of America Impartially Stated, in Certain Strictures on a Pamphlet intitled Common Sense. By an American. Second edition.
Philadelphia : 1776.

INGLIS, CHARLES, Letters of Papinian, in which the Conduct, Present State, and Prospects of the American Congress are examined.
London : 1779.
[This is a reprint of a New York edition.]

IZARD, Mr. RALPH, of South Carolina, Correspondence of, From the Year 1774 to 1804. With a Short Memoir. Volume i.
New York : 1844.
[This work was edited by Izard's daughter, Anne Izard Deas, whose name appears, not on the title-page, but beneath the preface, called "Advertisement." No publication has been made of the subsequent volumes called for by the plan above indicated.]

JAY, JOHN, The Correspondence and Public Papers of. Edited by Henry P. Johnston. Four volumes.
New York : 1890–1893.

JEFFERSON, THOMAS, The Writings of. Edited by H. A. Washington. Nine volumes.
New York : 1853–1854.

JEFFERSON, THOMAS, The Writings of. Collected and edited by Paul Leicester Ford. Volumes i. to viii.
New York : 1892–1897.
[The publication of this work is still in progress.]

JENYNS, SOAME, The Works of. Edited by Charles Nelson Cole. Four volumes.
London : 1790.

JENYNS, SOAME, The Objections to the Taxation of Our American Colonies by the Legislature of Great Britain, Briefly Considered. Second edition.
London : 1765.

JOHNSON, SAMUEL, A Dictionary of the English Language. Two volumes.
London : 1755.

Johnson, Samuel, Taxation no Tyranny: An Answer to the Resolutions and Address of the American Congress. The Third Edition.
London: 1775.

Johnson, Samuel, Letters of. Collected and Edited by George Birkbeck Hill. Two volumes.
New York: 1891.

Johnston, Henry P., Yale and Her Honor-Roll in the American Revolution, 1775–1783.
New York: 1888.

Johnston, Henry P., editor. See The Correspondence and Public Papers of John Jay.

Journals of the American Congress: From 1774 to 1788. Four volumes.
Washington: 1823.

Junius: Including Letters by the Same Writer under Other Signatures; to which are added His Confidential Correspondence with Mr. Wilkes, and His Private Letters to Mr. H. S. Woodfall. A New and Enlarged Edition. With New Evidence as to the Authorship, and an Analysis by the Late Sir Harris Nicholas, G. C. M. G. By John Wade. Two volumes.
London: 1890.

Juvenalis, D. Junii, Saturæ. Erklärt von Andreas Weidner, Direktor des Gymnasiums zu Dortmund. Zweite umgearbeitete Auflage.
Leipzig: 1889.

Kennet, White, An Historical Register and Chronicle of English Affairs before and after the Restoration of King Charles II.
London: 1744.

Kettell, Samuel, Specimens of American Poetry, with Critical and Biographical Notices. Three volumes.
Boston: 1829.

Kingsley, James Luce, Life of Ezra Stiles.
New York: 1855.
[This is part of volume xvi., of Sparks's Library of American Biography.]

Kingsley, William Lathrop, editor. See Yale College.

Knowles, James, editor. See The Nineteenth Century.

Lamb, Charles, The Works of. Four volumes.
Boston: 1862.

Langdon, Samuel, A Sermon before the Congress . . . at Watertown, May 31, 1775.
Watertown: 1775.

LARGE Additions to Common Sense.
Philadelphia : 1776.
[A miscellany of writings by various authors,—Candidus, Demopilus, Sincerus, an English American, and others,—all bearing on the political situation. It was sold as a separate pamphlet at half price to the purchasers of the first two editions of "Common Sense"; and it was annexed to the third edition, published by Robert Bell.]

LATROBE, JOHN HAZLEHURST BONEVAL, Biographical Sketch of Daniel Dulany.
Philadelphia : 1876.
[In the Pennsylvania Magazine of History and Biography, iii. 1–10.]

LAURENS, HENRY, A Narrative of the Capture of Henry Laurens, of His Imprisonment in the Tower of London, etc., 1780, 1781, 1782.
Charleston : 1857.
[This forms part of volume i. of Collections of the South Carolina Historical Society,—the text extending from page 18 to page 68, and the appendix from page 69 to page 83.]

LAURENS, HENRY, of South Carolina, Correspondence of. Edited by Frank Moore.
New York : 1861.
[This is the first volume of "Materials for History," etc., and the only one which has ever appeared.]

LAURENS, HENRY, A Protest against Slavery.
New York : 1861.
[This is a reprint of Laurens's letter of August 14, 1776.]

LAURENS, JOHN, Army Correspondence of, in the Years 1777–8. With a Memoir by William Gilmore Simms.
New York : 1867.

LECKY, WILLIAM EDWARD HARTPOLE, A History of England in the Eighteenth Century. New edition. Seven volumes.
London : 1892.

LEE, ARTHUR, The Monitor.
London : 1768.
[First published in Virginia, and reprinted in the American Gazette, No. 2, 189–218.]

LEE, ARTHUR, The Political Detection; or, The Treachery and Tyranny of Administration, both at Home and Abroad, displayed in a Series of Letters, signed Junius Americanus.
London : 1770.

LEE, ARTHUR, An Appeal to the Justice and Interests of the People of Great Britain, in the present Disputes with America. By an Old Member of Parliament.
London : 1774.

LEE, ARTHUR, Manuscripts in the Library of Harvard University. Bibliographical Contributions, edited by Justin Winsor.
Cambridge: 1882.
[See, also, the Harvard Bulletin, from June, 1878, to October, 1882.]

LEE, CHARLES, Strictures on a Pamphlet entitled A Friendly Address to all Reasonable Americans on the Subject of Our Political Confusions, addressed to the People of America.
Boston: 1775.

LEE, CHARLES, Esquire, Memoirs of the Life of the Late, . . . Second in Command in the Service of the United States of America during the Revolution: To which are added His Political and Military Essays, also, Letters to and from many distinguished Characters both in Europe and America.
London: 1792.

LEE, RICHARD HENRY, Life of Arthur Lee, LL.D. . . . With his political and literary Correspondence and his Papers on diplomatic and political Subjects and the Affairs of the United States during the same Period. Two volumes.
Boston: 1829.

LEE, SIDNEY, editor. See Dictionary of National Biography.

LEE, WILLIAM, Letters of. Collected and Edited by Worthington Chauncey Ford. Three Volumes.
Brooklyn: 1891.

LEONARD, DANIEL, Massachusettensis: or, a Series of Letters, containing a faithful State of many important and striking Facts which laid the Foundation of the present Troubles in the Province of the Massachusetts-Bay; interspersed with Animadversions and Reflections, originally addressed to the People of that Province, and worthy the Consideration of the true Patriots of this Country. By a Person of Honor upon the Spot.
London: 1776.

LEONARD, DANIEL. See Novanglus and Massachusettensis.

LESCURE, M. DE, Correspondance secrète inédite sur Louis XVI., Marie-Antoinette, la Cour et Ville, de 1777 a 1792. Publiée d'après les Manuscrits de la Bibliothèque Impériale de Saint-Pétersbourg, avec une Préface, des Notes, et un Index Alphabetique.
Paris: 1866.
[Two volumes.]

LETTER (A) from a Virginian to the Members of the Congress to be Held at Philadelphia, on the First of September, 1774.
Boston: 1774.
[In the absence of other testimony, I am inclined, from the evidence of thought and style, to attribute this pamphlet to Jonathan Boucher.]

LETTERS to the Ministry, from Governor Bernard, General Gage, and Commodore Hood.
London: n. d.
[This is a reprint of the edition published in Boston in 1769.]

LIBERTY, a Poem, Lately Found in a Bundle of Papers said to be Written by a Hermit in New Jersey.
Philadelphia: 1769.

LIBRARY (The) of American Biography. Edited by Jared Sparks. Twenty-four volumes.
Boston: 1845–1847.
[First series, in ten volumes: second series in fourteen volumes.]

LIND, JOHN, An Answer to the Declaration of the American Congress.
London: 1776.

LIPPINCOTT'S Monthly Magazine. A Popular Journal of General Literature, Science, and Politics. Volume xliii.
Philadelphia: 1889.

LITTELL, JOHN STOCKTON, editor. See Alexander Graydon, Memoirs of His Own Time.

LODGE, HENRY CABOT, Alexander Hamilton.
Boston: 1882.

LODGE, HENRY CABOT, editor. See The Works of Alexander Hamilton.

LOSSING, BENSON J., editor of reprint of Trumbull's M'Fingal.
New York: 1857.
[The copy used by me, is of the year 1864.]

LOYALIST (The) Poetry of the Revolution.
Philadelphia: 1857.
[This book was admirably edited by Winthrop Sargent, who, not placing his name upon the title-page, avowed his connection with the work by subscribing to the Preface the initial letters of his name.]

LOYAL (The) Verses of Joseph Stansbury and Doctor Jonathan Odell, relating to the American Revolution. Now first edited by Winthrop Sargent.
Albany: 1860.

McCORMICK, SAMUEL JARVIS, editor. See Samuel Peters, A General History of Connecticut. American edition of 1877.

McMAHON, JOHN VAN LEAR, An Historical View of the Government of Maryland from its Colonization to the Present Day. Vol. i.
Baltimore: 1831.
[No subsequent volume ever appeared.]

McMASTER, JOHN BACH, Benjamin Franklin as a Man of Letters.
Boston: 1895.

MADISON, JAMES, Letters and Other Writings of. Four volumes.
Philadelphia: 1867.

MAGAZINE (The) of American History.
Volume viii. New York: 1882.
Volume x. New York: 1883.

MARSHALL, CHRISTOPHER, Extracts from the Diary of, Kept in Philadelphia and Lancaster, during the American Revolution, 1774–1781. Edited by William Duane.
Albany: 1877.

MASSACHUSETTS (The) Historical Society, Collections of. 2 Series. Volume ix.
Boston: 1822.

MASSACHUSETTS (The) Historical Society. Proceedings. Vol. vi.
Boston: 1863.

MATERIALS for History Printed from Original Manuscripts. With Notes and Illustrations. By Frank Moore.
New York: Printed for the Zenger Club: 1861.
[Only one volume, that containing the Correspondence of Henry Laurens, has ever appeared.]

MAY, Sir THOMAS ERSKINE, The Constitutional History of England, 1760–1860. Two volumes.
London: 1861.
[Third edition, with a new supplementary chapter, in three volumes, London, 1871.]

MAYHEW, JONATHAN, Seven Sermons . . . Preached as a Lecture in the West Meeting House . . . Begun the first Thursday in June, and ended the last Thursday in August, 1748.
Boston: 1749.

MAYHEW, JONATHAN, A Discourse concerning Unlimited Submission and Non-Resistance to the Higher Powers, with some Reflections on the Resistance made to King Charles the First, and on the Anniversary of his Death,—in which the mysterious Doctrine of that Prince's Saintship and Martyrdom is unriddled.
Boston: 1750.

MAYHEW, JONATHAN, Sermon on the Death of Frederick, Prince of Wales.
Boston: 1751.

MAYHEW, JONATHAN, Massachusetts Election Sermon for May 29, 1754.
Boston: 1754.
[The titles of this and the previous article are not here given with exactness.]

MAYHEW, JONATHAN, Two Sermons . . . in Boston . . . November 23, 1755, occasioned by the Earthquakes . . . on the Tuesday Morning and Saturday Evening preceding.
Boston: 1755.

MAYHEW, JONATHAN, A Discourse . . . occasioned by the Earthquakes in November, 1755; delivered December 18 following.
Boston: 1755.

MAYHEW, JONATHAN, Sermons upon the following Subjects, etc. . . .
Boston: 1755.
[A very copious title-page, whereon are spread out the subjects of the fourteen sermons contained in the book. My copy is the London re-print of the year 1756.]

MAYHEW, JONATHAN, Two Discourses delivered November 23, 1758; being . . . a Day of Public Thanksgiving, relating more especially to the Success of His Majesty's Arms and those of the King of Prussia the last year.
Boston: n. d.
[These discourses contain stirring tributes to the genius and heroism of Frederick, and to the politico-religious significance of his victories.]

MAYHEW, JONATHAN, Two Discourses, delivered October 25, 1759, being . . . a Day of Public Thanksgiving for the Success of His Majesty's Arms, more particularly in the Reduction of Quebec.
Boston: 1759.

MAYHEW, JONATHAN, A Sermon occasioned by the Great Fire in Boston, . . . March 20, 1760.
Boston: 1760.

MAYHEW, JONATHAN, Two Discourses, delivered October 9, 1760, being . . . a Day of Public Thanksgiving for the Success of His Majesty's Arms, more especially in the entire Reduction of Canada.
Boston: 1760.

MAYHEW, JONATHAN, A Discourse occasioned by the Death of the Hon. Stephen Sewall, Esq., Chief-Justice of the Superior Court of Judicature, etc.
Boston: 1760.

MAYHEW, JONATHAN, Practical Discourses, delivered on Occasion of the Earthquakes in November, 1755.
Boston: 1760.
[This is the date of their first publication.]

MAYHEW, JONATHAN, A Discourse occasioned by the Death of King George II. and the happy Accession of His Majesty King George III., . . . delivered January 4, 1761.
Boston: 1761.

MAYHEW, JONATHAN, Striving to Enter in at the Strait Gate, Explained and Inculcated, . . . in Two Sermons.
Boston: 1761.

MAYHEW, JONATHAN, Two Sermons on the Nature, Extent and Perfection of the Divine Goodness.
Boston: 1763.

MAYHEW, JONATHAN, Christian Sobriety, being Eight Sermons on Titus ii., 6, preached with a special View to the Benefit of the Young Men, etc.
Boston: 1763.

MAYHEW, JONATHAN, Observations on the Charter and Conduct of the Society for the Propagation of the Gospel in Foreign Parts.
Boston: 1763.

MAYHEW, JONATHAN, Answer to a Candid Examination in Defence of the Charter of the Society for the Propagation of the Gospel.
Boston: 1764.

MAYHEW, JONATHAN, Remarks on an anonymous Tract, entitled An Answer to Dr. Mayhew's Observations, etc.
Boston: 1764.

MAYHEW, JONATHAN, A Letter of Reproof to Mr. John Cleaveland of Ipswich, occasioned by a Defamatory Libel published under his Name, etc.
Boston: 1764.

MAYHEW, JONATHAN, Popish Idolatry. A Discourse at the Dudleian Lecture, May 8, 1765.
Boston: 1765.

MAYHEW, JONATHAN, The Snare Broken. A Thanksgiving Discourse, preached at the Desire of the West Church in Boston, N. E., Friday, May 23, 1766, occasioned by the Repeal of the Stamp Act.
Boston: 1766.

MEIGS, JOSIAH, An Oration pronounced before a Public Assembly in New Haven, on the Fifth Day of November, 1781, at the Celebration of the Glorious Victory over . . . Cornwallis at Yorktown.
New Haven: 1782.

MEIGS, RETURN JONATHAN, A Journal of Occurrences which happened within the Circle of Observation in the Detachment commanded by Colonel Benedictine Arnold, consisting of Two Battalions which were detached from the Army at Cambridge in the year 1775: n. p.; n. d.

MILTON, JOHN, The Prose Works of. With a Preface, Preliminary Remarks, and Notes, by J. A. St. John. Five volumes.
London: n. d.

MINER, CHARLES, History of Wyoming, In a Series of Letters to His Son, William T. Miner.
Philadelphia: 1845.

MONTHLY Anthology (The); or Magazine of Polite Literature. Ten volumes.
Boston: 1803–1811.

MONTHLY Review (The); or, Literary Journal: By Several Hands. Volume xxxix.
London: 1768.

MOORE, FRANK, Songs and Ballads of the American Revolution.
New York: 1856.

MOORE, FRANK, Diary of the American Revolution. From Newspapers and Original Documents. Two volumes.
New York and London: 1859–1860.

MOORE FRANK, Illustrated Ballad History of the American Revolution. 1765–1783.
New York: 1876.
[This work was to be published by subscription and in "Parts" of about sixty pages each. With the issue of Part vi., the work was discontinued. No formal narrative is attempted; but the selections from contemporary writings, in prose and verse, are "collected and arranged in a somewhat confused order, with annotations.]

MOORE, FRANK, editor. See Materials for History.

MOORE FRANK, editor. See Correspondence of Henry Laurens.

MOORE, GEORGE HENRY, John Dickinson, the Author of the Declaration on taking up Arms in 1775. With a Fac-simile of the Original Draft.
New York: 1890.

MOORE, JOHN HAMILTON, A New and Complete Collection of Voyages and Travels.
London: n. d.
[Contains an abridgement of Jonathan Carver's Travels.]

MORLEY, JOHN, Edmund Burke: A Historical Study.
London: 1867.

MORSE, JOHN TORREY, Jr., The Life of Alexander Hamilton. Two volumes.
Boston: 1876.

MORSE, JOHN TORREY, Jr., Thomas Jefferson.
Boston: 1883.

MORSE, JOHN TORREY, Jr., Benjamin Franklin.
Boston: 1889.

MOTLEY Assembly (The): a Farce, Published for the Entertainment of the Curious.
Boston: 1779.

NATIONAL (The) Portrait Gallery of Distinguished Americans. Conducted by James B. Longacre, and James Herring. Second volume.
Philadelphia, New York, and London: 1835.

NEILL, EDWARD DUFFIELD, Reverend Jacob Duché, the First Chaplain of Congress.
[See Pennsylvania Magazine of History and Biography, ii. 58–73.]

NEW (The) London Gazette, from September 6, 1765, to November 1, 1765.
[Manuscript copies of five essays therein by Stephen Johnson, made under the direction of Professor E. E. Salisbury of Yale College, and placed at my disposal by his courtesy.]

NILES, H., Principles and Acts of the Revolution in America.
Baltimore: 1822.

NINETEENTH Century (The). A Monthly Review. Edited by James Knowles. Number 131, January, 1888.
London: 1888.

NOTES and Queries: A Medium of Intercommunication for Literary Men, General Readers, etc. Ninety-two volumes.
London: 1849–1895.

NOVANGLUS and Massachusettensis; or, Political Essays, published in the Years 1774 and 1775, on the principal points of Controversy between Great Britain and her Colonies. The former by John Adams, late President of the United States; the latter by Jonathan Sewall, then King's Attorney General of the Province of Massachusetts Bay. To which are added a number of Letters lately written by President Adams to the Honorable William Tudor, some of which were never before published.
Boston: 1819.
[This book was published under the auspices of John Adams. The positive announcement, made upon the title page, that Sewall was the author of "Massachusettensis," is repeated in the Preface, written by John Adams, who there gives a sketch of the man whom he says he "knew" from the first to be the writer with whom he had held controversy. Two years afterward, he learned that for nearly fifty years he had been attributing these letters to the wrong man, and that they were in reality the work of Daniel Leonard. Apparently as a compliment to President Adams, an absurd arrangement is given to the two sets of letters: those of Novanglus are placed before the letters of Massachusettensis, which preceded them in time, and to which they are a reply. Accordingly, he who reads the book intelligently, is obliged to read it backwards.]

OBSERVATIONS on the Reconciliation of Great Britain and the Colonies. . . . By a Friend of American Liberty.
Philadelphia: 1776.
[According to Sabin, Mr. Franklin Burdge attributes this pamphlet to Jacob Green. This opinion cannot be adopted, if we accept the testimony of Green's son, President Ashbel Green, who states that Green was one of the early advocates of Independence. This pamphlet deprecates a resort to Independence.]

OCCUM, SAMSON, A Sermon Preached at the Execution of Moses Paul, an Indian.
Salem: 1773.

OPPRESSION, a Poem by an American. With Notes by a North Briton.
Boston: 1765.
[This is a reprint of the original edition as published in London.]

ORATIONS Delivered at the Request of the Inhabitants of the Town of Boston, to commemorate the Evening of the Fifth of March, 1770, When a number of Citizens were killed by a Party of British Troops, in a Time of Peace.
Boston: n. d.
[The Preface is dated Boston, January, 1785.]

OSGOOD, DAVID, A Sermon on Thanksgiving Day, December 11, 1783.
Boston: 1784.

OTHER Side of the Question (The); or, A Defence of the Liberties of North America. In Answer to a late "Friendly Address to all Reasonable Americans on the Subject of our Political Confusions." By a Citizen.
New York: 1774.
[The copy used by me belonged to George Bancroft, and is now in the Lenox Library.]

OTIS, JAMES, The Rudiments of Latin Prosody; With a Dissertation on Letters and the Principles of Harmony in Poetic and Prosaic Composition. Collected from Some of the best Writers.
Boston: 1760.

OTIS, JAMES, A Vindication of the Conduct of the House of Representatives of the Province of the Massachusetts Bay, more particularly in the last Session of the General Assembly.
Boston: 1762.

OTIS, JAMES, The Rights of the British Colonies Asserted and Proved. Second edition.
London: n. d.

OTIS, JAMES, A Vindication of the British Colonies, against the Aspersions of the Halifax Gentleman, in his Letter to a Rhode Island Friend.
London: 1769.
[My references are to this copy, in the library of Cornell University; which, however, I compared with the original Boston edition, as loaned me by the librarian of Harvard College.]

OTIS, JAMES, Brief Remarks on the Defence of the Halifax Libel on the British-American Colonies.
Boston: 1765.

OTIS, JAMES, Considerations on behalf of the Colonists, In a Letter to a Noble Lord. Second edition.
London: 1765.

PAINE, THOMAS, A Dialogue between the Ghost of General Montgomery, just arrived from the Elysian Fields, and an American Delegate, in a Wood near Philadelphia.
Philadelphia: 1776.
New York: Privately Reprinted. 1865.
[On page 36 of the second volume of the present work, I refer to the above tract as "confidently attributed to Paine," and at the same time I call attention to certain literary qualities in it which seem to suggest that it was from some other writer. I have since recalled the fact that soon after the publication of the "Dialogue," Paine himself publicly denied that he was its author.]

PAINE, THOMAS, The Political Writings of. Two volumes.
Boston: 1870.

PAINE, THOMAS, The Writings of. Collected and Edited by Moncure Daniel Conway. Four volumes.
New York: 1894–1896.
[This collection may fairly be regarded as the final edition of the writings of Paine. Those of his writings which were produced before the close of the period embraced in my work, occupy the first volume and the first 131 pages of the second volume of Conway's edition. As my own chapters on Paine were written long before the publication of the latter, my references, unless otherwise stated, are to the Boston edition of Paine, 1870.]

PARKMAN, FRANCIS, The Conspiracy of Pontiac, and the Indian War after the Conquest of Canada. Ninth edition, revised with Additions. Two volumes.
Boston: 1880.

PARTON, JAMES, The Life and Times of Benjamin Franklin. Two volumes.
Boston: 1892.

PATER, WALTER H., Studies in the History of the Renaissance.
London: 1873.

PATRIOT (The) Preachers of the American Revolution. With Biographical Sketches. 1766–1783.
n. p.: 1860.
[The entry for copyright is in the Southern District of New York.]

PENNSYLVANIA (The) Magazine of History and Biography.
Volume ii. Philadelphia: 1878.
Volume iii. Philadelphia: 1879.

PENNSYLVANIA, Memoirs of the Historical Society of. Volume i. Being a republication, edited by Edward Armstrong.
Philadelphia: 1864.

PERRY, THOMAS SERGEANT, Life and Letters of Francis Lieber.
Boston: 1882.

PETERS, SAMUEL, A General History of Connecticut, From its First Settlement under George Fenwick, Esq., to its Latest Period of Amity with Great Britain; Including a Description of the Country, and many curious and interesting Anecdotes. To which is added an Appendix, wherein new and the true Sources of the present Rebellion in America are pointed out, together with the particular Part taken by the People of Connecticut in its Promotion. By a Gentleman of the Province. Second edition.
London: 1782.
[The first edition appeared in London, in 1781.]

PETERS, SAMUEL, A General History of Connecticut, etc.
Reprint of the first London edition, New Haven: 1829.

PETERS, SAMUEL, A General History of Connecticut, etc.
Reprint of the first London edition, with addition to the appendix, notes, and extracts from letters, verifying many important statements made by the author, by Samuel Jarvis McCormick.
New York: 1877.

PETERS, SAMUEL, A History of the Reverend Hugh Peters, A.M.
New York: 1807.

PICKERING, OCTAVIUS, The Life of Timothy Pickering. Volume i.
Boston: 1867.
[Upon the author's death, the work, left by him unfinished, was completed, in three additional volumes, by Charles Wentworth Upham.]

PITT, WILLIAM, Earl of Chatham, Correspondence of. Ed. by William Stanhope Taylor, Esq., and Captain John Henry Pringle. Four volumes.
London: 1838–1840.

PLAIN Truth, Addressed to the Inhabitants of America; Containing Remarks on a late Pamphlet entitled Common Sense . . . Written by Candidus.
Philadelphia: 1776.

POORE, BEN. PERLEY, Editor. See the Federal and State Constitutions.

POPE, ALEXANDER, The Works of, In Nine Volumes, Complete, With his Last Corrections, Additions and Improvements, . . . together with the Commentary and Notes of Mr. Warburton.
London: 1753.

PORTER, ELIPHALET, A Sermon at the First Religious Society, Roxbury, on Thanksgiving Day, December 11, 1783.
Boston : 1784.

POWER and Grandeur (The) of Great Britain founded on the Liberty of the Colonies ; and the Mischiefs attending the Taxing them by Act of Parliament Demonstrated.
New York : 1768.

PRINGLE, JOHN HENRY, editor, See William Pitt, Earl of Chatham, Correspondence of.

PRIOR Documents. See J. Almon.

PRIOR, Sir JAMES, Life of Edmond Malone.
London : 1860.

PROUD, ROBERT, The History of Pennsylvania, in North America, From the original Institution and Settlement of that Province, under the first Proprietor and Governor William Penn, in 1681, till after the Year 1742. Two volumes.
Philadelphia : 1797–1798.

QUINCY, ELIZA SUSAN, editor. See Josiah Quincy, Memoir of the Life of Josiah Quincy, Junior.

QUINCY'S Massachusetts Reports. Reports of Cases argued and adjudged in the Superior Court of Judicature of the Province of Massachusetts Bay, Between 1761 and 1772. By Josiah Quincy, Junior. . . . Edited by his great-grandson, Samuel M. Quincy. With an Appendix upon the Writs of Assistance.
Boston : 1865.
[This Appendix is an important contribution to the history of the subject, and is by Mr. Justice Gray, of the Supreme Court of the United States.]

QUINCY, JOSIAH, Junior, Observations on the Act of Parliament Commonly Called the Boston Port-Bill ; with Thoughts on Civil Society and Standing Armies.
Boston : 1774.

QUINCY, JOSIAH, Memoir of the Life of Josiah Quincy, Junior, of Massachusetts Bay : 1744–1775. Third Edition. Edited by Eliza Susan Quincy.
Boston : 1875.

RANDALL, HENRY STEPHENS, The Life of Thomas Jefferson. Three volumes.
New York : 1858.

REED, WILLIAM BRADFORD, Life and Correspondence of Joseph Reed. Two volumes.
Philadelphia : 1847.

REGULATIONS (The) lately made concerning the Colonies, and the Taxes imposed upon them, considered.
London: 1765.
[In his own copy of this important pamphlet, Jared Sparks wrote: "By Geo. Grenville. Some say by Mr. Campbell, one of the agents for Georgia, but without proof." Whether actually written by Grenville or not, it undoubtedly was written under his eye, and may be taken as representing him.]

RESIGNATION. In Two Parts, and A Postscript to Mrs. B.
London. Philadelphia re-printed: 1764.
[The "Postscript," at least, was probably by Elizabeth Fergusson; and "Mrs. B." is believed to have been Mrs. Boudinot.]

RHODE ISLAND Historical Society (The), Collections of. Volume vii.
Providence: 1885.

ROBINSON, HENRY CRABB, Diary, Reminiscences, and Correspondence of. Selected and edited by Thomas Sadler. Two volumes. Third edition.
London and New York: 1872.

ROBINSON, MATTHEW, (afterward Lord Rokeby), Considerations on the Measures Carrying on with respect to the British Colonies in North America.
Boston: 1774.
[Originally printed in London.]

RODGERS, JOHN, The Divine Goodness Displayed in the American Revolution; A Sermon Preached in New York, December 11, 1783.
New York: 1783
[Reprinted in Patriot Preachers of the Am. Rev., 312–343.]

RODGERS, JOHN, Sermon at Princeton, May 6th, 1795, occasioned by the death of Rev. John Witherspoon.
New York: 1795.

ROGERS, Major ROBERT, Journals of: Containing an Account of the several Excursions he made under the Generals who commanded upon the Continent of North America during the late War.
London: 1765.
[A very corrupt edition of this work, under the title of "Reminiscences of the French War," etc., was published at Concord, New Hampshire, in 1831.]

ROGERS, ROBERT, A Concise Account of North America: Containing a Description of the several British Colonies on that Continent, including the Islands of New Foundland, Cape Briton, etc.
London: 1765.

ROGERS, ROBERT, Ponteach : or the Savages of America. A Tragedy.
London : 1766.
[I first saw a copy of this very rare book in the library of Mr. John Nicholas Brown, Providence, R. I., and subsequently used the copy in the Fiske Harris Collection now belonging to the library of Brown University. That it was written by Rogers, either wholly or in part, is a matter of inference.]

ROGERS, ROBERT, Journal of the Siege of Detroit. Edited by Franklin B. Hough.
Albany : 1860.
[This forms part of No. iv. of Munsell's Historical Series.]

RUSSELL, Lord JOHN, editor. See Memorials and Correspondence of Charles James Fox.

SABIN, JOSEPH, A Dictionary of Books relating to America, From its Discovery to the Present Time. Nineteen volumes, together with a part of volume xx.
New York : 1868–1892.

SABINE, LORENZO, Biographical Sketches of Loyalists of the American Revolution, with an Historical Essay. Two volumes.
Boston : 1864.

SADLER, THOMAS, editor. See Diary, etc., of Henry Crabb Robinson.

ST. JOHN, JAMES AUGUSTUS, editor. See The Prose Works of John Milton.

SALMON, THOMAS, A New Geographical and Historical Grammar. Eleventh edition.
London : 1769.

SAMPSON, EZRA, Sermon at Roxbury Camp, before Colonel Cotton's Regiment, July 20, 1775.
Watertown : 1775.

SANDERSON, JOHN, Biography of the Signers of the Declaration of Independence. Nine volumes.
Philadelphia : 1823–1827.

SANFORD, ENOCH, History of the Town of Berkley, Mass.
New York : 1872.

SARGENT, WINTHROP, editor. See the Loyal Verses of Stansbury and Odell.

SARGENT, WINTHROP, editor. See The Loyalist Poetry of the Revolution.

SARGENT, WINTHROP, editor. See Letters of John Andrews.

SAVAGE, JAMES, editor. See The History of New England, by John Winthrop.

SCHARF, JOHN THOMAS, History of Maryland, From the Earliest Period to the Present Day. Three volumes.
Baltimore : 1879.

SCHILLER, The Poems and Ballads of. Translated by Sir Edward Bulwer Lytton, Bart. Tauchnitz edition.
Leipzig: 1844.

SCHILLER, The Poems and Ballads of. Translated by Sir Edward Bulwer Lytton, Bart. From the Last London Edition.
New York: 1866.

SCHILLERS sämtliche Werke in fünfzehn Bänden. Mit Einleitungen von Karl Goedeke.
Stuttgart.
[These volumes, which are without date, are a part of the Cotta'sche Bibliothek der Weltlitteratur.]

SCOTT, SIR WALTER, editor. See a Collection of Scarce and Valuable Tracts.

SCOTT, SIR WALTER, The Poetical Works of, with a Memoir of the Author. Nine volumes.
Boston: 1857.

SCOTT, SIR WALTER, The Journal of: From the Original Manuscript at Abbotsford. Two volumes.
New York: 1890.

SCUDDER, HORACE ELISHA, editor. See Recollections of Samuel Breck.

SEABURY, SAMUEL, Free Thoughts on the Proceedings of the Continental Congress, held at Philadelphia September 5, 1774: wherein their Errors are exhibited, their Reasonings confuted, and the fatal Tendency of their Non-Importation, Non-Exportation, and Non-Consumption Measures are laid open to the plainest Understandings; and the only Means pointed out for preserving and securing our present happy Constitution. . . . By a Farmer.
n. p. 1774.

SEABURY, SAMUEL, The Congress Canvassed; or, An Examination into the Conduct of the Delegates, at their Grand Convention held in Philadelphia, September 1, 1774. Addressed to the Merchants of New York. By A. W. Farmer, Author of Free Thoughts, etc.
n. p.: 1774.

SEABURY, SAMUEL, A View of the Controversy between Great Britain and her Colonies: Including a Mode of determining their present Disputes, finally and effectually, and of preventing all future Contentions. In a Letter to the Author of A Full Vindication of the Measures of the Congress from the Calumnies of their Enemies. By A. W. Farmer, Author of Free Thoughts, etc.
New York: 1774.

SEABURY, SAMUEL, An Alarm to the Legislature of the Province of New York, occasioned by the present Political Disturbances in North America: Addressed to the Honorable Representatives in General Assembly Convened.
New York: 1775.

SEABURY, SAMUEL, The Republican Dissected, or, The Anatomy of an American Whig, By A. W. Farmer.
New York: 1775.
[Advertised in Rivington's New York Gazetteer for April 20, 1775, as "speedily to be published." I have found no evidence that it ever saw the light.]

SECRET Journals of the Acts and Proceedings of Congress, From the First Meeting thereof to the Dissolution of the Confederation, by the Adoption of the Constitution of the United States. Four volumes.
Boston: 1821.

SEDGWICK, THEODORE, Jun., A Memoir of the Life of William Livingston.
New York: 1833.

SEWALL, JONATHAN. See Novanglus and Massachusettensis.

SEWALL, JONATHAN, The Americans Roused, in a Cure for the Spleen; or, Amusement for a Winter's Evening: Being the Substance of a Conversation on the Times, over a Friendly Tankard and Pipe.
New England: Printed.
New York, Re-printed, by James Harrington: n. d.

SIMMS, WILLIAM GILMORE, editor. See Army Correspondence of John Laurens.

SIMONS, MICHAEL LAIRD, editor. See Duyckinck, Cyclopædia of American Literature, revised edition.

SLOANE, WILLIAM MILLIGAN, The French War and the Revolution.
New York: 1893.

SMITH, GOLDWIN, The United States. An Outline of Political History 1492–1871.
New York: 1893.

SMITH, HORACE WEMYSS, Life and Correspondence of the Reverend William Smith, D.D. Two volumes.
Philadelphia: 1880.

SMITH, SYDNEY, The Works of. Fourth edition. Three volumes.
London: 1848.

SMITH, WILLIAM, An Historical Account of the Expedition against the Ohio Indians in the Year 1764, under the Command of Henry Bouquet, Esquire, Colonel of Foot, and now Brigadier General in America.
Cincinnati: 1868.
[This is a reprint of the London edition of 1766, under the modern title of "Historical Account of Bouquet's Expedition against the Ohio Indians in 1764," and forming one of the "Ohio Valley Historical Series."]

SMITH, WILLIAM, D.D., Late Provost of the College and Academy of Philadelphia, The Works of. Two volumes.
Philadelphia: 1803.

SMYTH, ALBERT H., The Philadelphia Magazines and their Contributors 1741–1850.
Philadelphia: 1892.

SOUTH CAROLINA Historical Society, Collections of. Volume i.
Charleston: 1857.

SOUTHEY, ROBERT. See the Works of William Cowper.

SPARKS, JARED, editor. See the Writings of George Washington.

SPARKS, JARED, editor. See the Works of Benjamin Franklin.

SPARKS, JARED, editor. See the Library of American Biography.

SPARKS, JARED, editor. See Correspondence of the American Revolution.

SPRAGUE, WILLIAM B., Life of Timothy Dwight, in Sparks's Library of American Biography, xiv. 223–364.

SPRAGUE, WILLIAM B., Annals of the American Pulpit; or Commemorative Notices of Distinguished American Clergymen of Various Denominations, From the early Settlement of the Country to the Year 1855. With Historical Introductions. Nine volumes.
New York: 1859–1869.

STATUTES (The) at Large. Vol. ix.
London: 1765.

STEDMAN, EDMUND CLARENCE, Poets of America.
Boston and New York: 1885.

STEPHEN, LESLIE, History of English Thought in the Eighteenth Century. Two volumes. Second edition.
London: 1881.

STEPHEN, LESLIE, editor. See Dictionary of National Biography.

STILES, EZRA, Oratio Funebris pro Exequiis Jonathan Law.
Novi Londini: 1751.

STILES, EZRA, In Gratulatione Nobilissimi et amplissimi Viri B. Franklini . . . Oratio quam ad illum in Aula Acad. Yal. Nov. Angl. habuit Ezra Stiles, Nonis Februarii, MDCCLV.
[Printed in W. T. Franklin's Memoirs . . . of Benjamin Franklin, i. 443–447.]

STILES, EZRA, A Discourse on the Christian Union: the Substance of which was delivered before the Reverend Convention of the Congregational Clergy in the Colony of Rhode Island, assembled at Bristol, April 23, 1760.
Boston: 1761.

STILES, EZRA. A Discourse on Saving Knowledge: Delivered at the Installment of the Reverend Samuel Hopkins, A.M., into the Pastoral Charge of the First Congregational Church in Newport, Rhode Island, Wednesday, April 11, 1770.
Newport: 1770.

STILES, EZRA, Oratio Inauguralis habita in Sacello Colegii Yalensis.
Hartfordiæ: M.DCC.LXXVIII.

STILES, EZRA, The United States elevated to Glory and Honor. A Sermon preached before His Excellency, Jonathan Trumbull, Esq., LL.D., Governor of and Commander in Chief, and the Honorable the General Assembly, of the State of Connecticut, convened at Hartford, at the anniversary election, May 8th, 1783.
New Haven: 1783.

STILES, EZRA, A Funeral Sermon, delivered . . . at the Interment of the Reverend Mr. Chauncey Whittelsey.
New Haven: 1787.

STILES, EZRA, A History of Three of the Judges of King Charles I. Major General Whalley, Major General Goffe, and Colonel Dixwell.
Hartford: 1794.
[The larger portion of Stiles's writings have never been printed. Many of his manuscripts are in the possession of Yale University, and consist of about fifty volumes, besides many papers not bound.]

STILLÉ, CHARLES JANEWAY, A Memoir of the Reverend William Smith, D.D., Provost of the College Academy and Charitablė School of Philadelphia.
Philadelphia: 1869.

STILLÉ, CHARLES JANEWAY, The Life and Times of John Dickinson. 1732–1808.
Philadelphia: 1891.

STONE, WILLIAM LEETE, editor. See Ballads and Poems relating to the Burgoyne Campaign.

STORK, WILLIAM, A Description of East-Florida; With a Journal Kept by John Bartram of Philadelphia . . . upon a Journey from St. Augustine up the River St. John's. Third edition.
London: 1769.

SUMNER, CHARLES, The Works of. Fifteen volumes.
Boston: 1870–1883.

TAYLOR, WILLIAM STANHOPE. See William Pitt, Earl of Chatham, Correspondence of.

THACHER, JAMES, A Military Journal during the American Revolutionary War, from 1775 to 1783. With an Appendix, containing Biographical Sketches of several General officers. Second edition.
Boston: 1827.
[A later edition, with expanded title, was published in Hartford, in 1862.]

THACHER, JAMES, American Medical Biography: or, Memoirs of Eminent Physicians who have flourished in America. To which is prefixed a Succinct History of Medical Science in the United States from the First Settlement of the Country. Two volumes.
Boston: 1828.

THACHER, OXENBRIDGE, Considerations on Lowering the Value of Gold Coins Within the Province of Massachusetts Bay.
Boston: 1761.

THACHER, OXENBRIDGE. The Sentiments of a British American.
Boston: 1764.

THACKERAY, WILLIAM MAKEPEACE, The Four Georges.
London: 1869.

THACKERAY, WILLIAM MAKEPEACE, Miscellaneous Essays, Sketches and Reviews.
London: 1886.

THOMAS, ISAIAH, The History of Printing in America. Two volumes.
Albany: 1874.

THOMSON, JAMES, Complete Works of. With Life, Critical Dissertation, and Explanatory Notes, by the Rev. George Gilfillan.
New York: 1854.

THORNTON, JOHN WINGATE, The Pulpit of the American Revolution: or, the Political Sermons of the Period of 1776. With a Historical Introduction Notes, and Illustrations.
Boston: 1860.

TICKNOR, GEORGE, Life, Letters and Journals of. Two volumes.
Boston: 1876.
[This work was in part prepared by George S. Hillard.]

TILGHMAN, TENCH, Memoir of . . . Together with an Appendix containing Journals and Letters, Hitherto Unpublished.
Albany: 1876.

TRUE (The) Sentiments of America: Contained in a Collection of Letters sent from the House of Representatives of the Province of Massachusetts Bay to Several Persons of high Rank in this Kingdom: together with certain Papers relating to a supposed Libel on the Governor of that Province, and a Dissertation on the Canon and the Feudal Law.
London: 1768.

TRUMBULL, BENJAMIN, A Complete History of Connecticut, Civil and Ecclesiastical. From the Emigration of its first Planters from England in the Year 1630, to the Year, 1764, and to the Close of the Indian Wars. Two volumes.
New Haven: 1818.

TRUMBULL, JAMES HAMMOND, The Origin of M'Fingal.
Morrisania: 1868.
[First published in The Historical Magazine, for Jan., 1868.]

TRUMBULL, JAMES HAMMOND. The True-Blue Laws of Connecticut and New Haven and the False Blue-Laws invented by the Rev. Samuel Peters. To which are added Specimens of the Laws and Judicial Proceedings of other Colonies, and some Blue-Laws of England in the Reign of James I.
Hartford : 1876.

TRUMBULL, JAMES HAMMOND, The Rev. Samuel Peters, His Defenders and Apologists With a Reply to The Churchman's Review, etc.
Hartford : 1877.
[Reprinted from The Hartford Daily Courant.]

TRUMBULL, JOHN, An Essay on the Use and Advantages of the Fine Arts, Delivered at the Public Commencement in New Haven, September 12th, 1770.
New Haven : n. d.

TRUMBULL, JOHN, M'Fingal : A Modern Epic Poem. Canto First, or The Town Meeting.
Philadelphia : 1775.
[Not published till Jan., 1776. Author's name not given. The copy used by me is the London reprint of 1776.]

TRUMBULL, JOHN, M'Fingal : A Modern Epic Poem, In Four Cantos.
Hartford : 1782.
[For M'Fingal in its completed form, this is the editio princeps. I have used the reprint of it, edited, with introduction and notes by Benson J. Lossing, New York : 1864.]

TRUMBULL, JOHN, The Poetical Works of.
Hartford : 1820.

TUCKER, GEORGE, Life of Thomas Jefferson, with Parts of his Correspondence before unpublished.
Philadelphia : 1837.

TUDOR, WILLIAM, The Life of James Otis.
Boston : 1823.

TURGOT, M DÉ, Ministre d'État, Œuvres, Précédées et accompagnées de Mémoires et de Notes sur sa Vie, son Administration, et ses Ouvrages. Tome neuvième.
Paris : 1810.

UPHAM, CHARLES WENTWORTH, The Life of Timothy Pickering. Volumes ii., iii., and iv.
Boston : 1873.
[The first volume was written by Octavius Pickering.]

VERSES on Doctor Mayhew's Book of Observations, etc. By a Gentleman of Rhode Island.
Providence : 1763.
[By E. F. Slafter, the authorship of this bunch of doggerel is attributed to one John Alpin.]

VILLEMAIN, ABEL FRANÇOIS, Cours de Littérature Française : Tableau de la Littérature au XVIIIe Siècle. Nouvelle édition.
Paris : 1868.
[The portion of this work devoted to the eighteenth century is in four volumes.]

WADE, JOHN, editor. See Junius.

WARBURTON, WILLIAM, editor. See the Works of Alexander Pope.

WARD, GEORGE ATKINSON, editor. See Journal and Letters of the Late Samuel Curwen.

WARREN, MERCY, The Adulateur. A Tragedy as it is now Acted in Upper Servia.
Boston : 1773.

WARREN, MERCY, The Group, As lately Acted and to be Re-Acted to the Wonder of all Superior Intelligences, nigh Headquarters at Amboyne.
Boston : 1775.

WARREN, MERCY, Poems Dramatic and Miscellaneous.
Boston : 1790.

WARREN, MERCY, History of the Rise, Progress and Termination of the American Revolution. Interspersed with Biographical, Political and Moral Reflections. Three volumes.
Boston : 1805.

WASHINGTON-DUCHÉ Letters (The). Now printed for the first time from the original manuscripts, with an introductory note by Worthington Chauncey Ford.
Brooklyn : 1890.
[Privately printed.]

WASHINGTON, GEORGE, The Writings of, edited by Jared Sparks. Twelve volumes.
Boston and New York : 1834–1847.

WASHINGTON, GEORGE, The Writings of, edited by Worthington Chauncey Ford. Fourteen volumes.
New York and London : 1889–1893.

WASHINGTON, HENRY AUGUSTINE, editor. See the Writings of Thomas Jefferson.

WEBSTER, PELATIAH, Political Essays on the Nature and Operation of Money, Public Finances, and Other Subjects : Published during the American War, and continued up to the present Year, 1791.
Philadelphia : 1791.

WELLS, KATE GANNETT, An Old New England Divine, in The Atlantic Monthly, for August, 1884, pp. 247–257.

WELLS, WILLIAM VINCENT, The Life and Public Services of Samuel Adams, Being a Narrative of his Acts and Opinions, and of his Agency in producing and forwarding the American Revolution. With Extracts from his Correspondence, State Papers, and Political Essays. Three volumes.
Boston : 1865.

WEST Church (The) and its Ministers.
Boston : 1856.

WESTON, DAVID, editor. See Isaac Backus, A History of New England, etc.

WHARTON, CHARLES HENRY, The Remains of. With a Memoir of his Life, by George Washington Doane, D.D., Bishop of the Diocese of New Jersey. Two volumes.
Philadelphia : 1834.

WHARTON, CHARLES HENRY, A Poetical Epistle to George Washington, Esquire, Commander-in-Chief of the Armies of the United States of America.
Boston : 1881.
[This edition was printed from the original manuscript, and is the one from which I have made my citations.]

WHAT Think Ye of the Congress Now? or, An Enquiry how far the Americans are bound to abide by, and execute, the Decisions of the late Congress.
New York : 1775.

WHEATLEY, PHILLIS, Poems on Various Subjects Religious and Moral.
London : 1773.

WHEATLEY, PHILLIS, Liberty and Peace, a Poem by Phillis Peters.
Boston : 1784.
[Phillis Wheatley was then Mrs. Peters.]

WHEATLEY, PHILLIS, The Negro-Slave Poet of Boston, Letters of. Edited by Charles Deane. Privately printed.
Boston : 1864.

WHIPPLE, EDWIN P., editor. See British Poetry, the Family Library of.

WHITAKER, NATHANIEL, An Antidote against Toryism, or, the Curse of Meroz.
Newburyport : 1777.

WHITAKER, NATHANIEL, The Reward of Toryism.
Newburyport : 1783.

WHITTIER, JOHN GREENLEAF, editor. See The Journal of John Woolman.

WILKINS, ISAAC, My Services and Losses in Aid of the King's Cause during the American Revolution. Edited by Paul Leicester Ford.
Brooklyn : 1890.

WILKINSON, ELIZA, Letters of, during the invasion and possession of Charleston, S. C. by the British in the Revolutionary War. Arranged from the original manuscripts by Caroline Gilman.
New York: 1839.

WILSON, BIRD, Memoir of the Life of the Right Reverend William White, D.D., Bishop of the Protestant Episcopal Church in the State of Pennsylvania.
Philadelphia: 1839.

WILSON, JAMES, Considerations on the Nature and Extent of the Legislative Authority of the British Parliament.
Philadelphia: 1774.
[Also to be found in the Philadelphia edition of the Works of Wilson, iii. 199–246.]

WILSON, JAMES, The Works of. Published under the Direction of Bird Wilson. Three volumes.
Philadelphia: 1804.

WILSON, JAMES, The Works of, Associate Justice of the Supreme Court of the United States, and Professor of Law in the College of Philadelphia; being his Public Discourses upon Jurisprudence and the Political Science, including Lectures as Professor of Law, 1790–1792. Edited by James de Witt Andrews. Two volumes.
Chicago: 1896.

WILSON, JAMES GRANT, editor (with JOHN FISKE) of Appletons' Cyclopædia of American Biography. Six volumes.
New York: 1887–1889.

WINSOR, JUSTIN, editor. See Library of Harvard University. Bibliographical Contributions. No. 8.

WINSOR, JUSTIN, Narrative and Critical History of America. Eight Volumes.
Boston: n. d.

WINTHROP, JOHN, The History of New England from 1630 to 1649. From his Original Manuscripts. With Notes . . . by James Savage.
Volume i., Boston: 1825.
Volume ii., Boston: 1826.

WITHERSPOON, JOHN, The Works of, . . . Containing Essays, Sermons, etc. . . . together with his Lectures on Moral Philosophy, Eloquence and Divinity, his Speeches in the American Congress, and many other valuable Pieces, never before published in this Country. Nine volumes.
Edinburgh: 1804–1805.

WOOD'S New England's Prospect.
Boston: 1865.
[Published by the Prince Society.]

WOOLMAN, JOHN, Considerations on the True Harmony of Mankind and How it is to be Maintained.
Philadelphia: 1770.

WOOLMAN, JOHN, The Works of. In Two Parts.
Philadelphia: 1774.

WOOLMAN, JOHN, A Journal of the Life, Gospel Labors, and Christian Experiences of, . . To which are added his Works, containing his last Epistle and other Writings.
Dublin: 1794.

WOOLMAN, JOHN, The Journal of. With an Introduction by John Greenleaf Whittier.
Boston: 1873.
[With his true perception of intellectual and spiritual values, Whittier wisely places in the Appendix Woolman's essay—"A Word of Remembrance and Caution to the Rich."]

YALE College. A Sketch of its History, With Notices of its Several Departments, Instructors, and Benefactors, Together with Some Account of Student Life and Amusements. By Various Authors. Edited by Wm. Lathrop Kingsley. Two volumes.
New York: 1879.

ZUBLY, JOHN JOACHIM, The Stamp Act Repealed. . . . A Sermon preached at Savannah, June 25, 1766.
Georgia printed. South Carolina reprinted, Charleston: 1766.

ZUBLY, JOHN JOACHIM, An Humble Enquiry into the Nature of the Dependency of the American Colonies upon the Parliament of Great Britain, and the right of Parliament to lay Taxes on the said Colonies. By a Freeholder of South Carolina.
n. p. 1769.

ZUBLY, JOHN JOACHIM, The Law of Liberty: a Sermon on American Affairs, preached at the opening of the Provincial Congress of Georgia.
Philadelphia: 1775.
[The best part of this publication is the address of dedication to the Earl of Dartmouth.]

INDEX.

BY MORTIMER A. FEDERSPIEL, PH.D., LL.B., LATE FELLOW IN AMERICAN HISTORY, CORNELL UNIVERSITY.

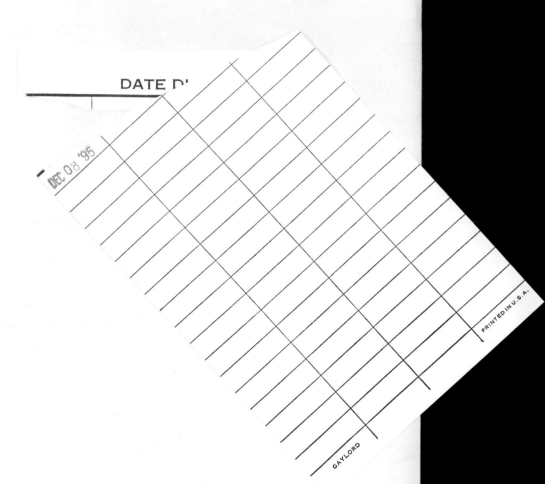